Contents

Communication Practices and Democratic Society

Edited by Lee Artz

KENDALL/HUNT PUBLISHING COMPANY
4050 Westmark Drive   Dubuque, Iowa 52002

Cover art by Marques.

Introduction:
Communication and Democracy

Communication includes a multitude of verbal and non-verbal practices which allow us to exchange, share, and construct meaningful messages for organizing, explaining, and experiencing our individual and collective lives. Practices are those ways in which we customarily, habitually, and repeatedly behave or act. Thus, communication practices refer to those common human interactions by which we perform or carry out the discovery, creation, and sharing of information, understanding, knowledge, beliefs, and even values. The process of communication is also manifold: one part of communication includes information gathered from observing and interacting with our surroundings; another part gives meaning and value to those informational reports and observations, usually through conversation among participants. These two sides of the process—the informational and the rhetorical—mutually construct communication. Significantly, the communication process can unfold in a variety of ways and through a variety of means which may affect both the accumulation of information and the construction of meaning. Dominant communication practices in any society, depend on its social and technological development, and its most prevalent social relations. This collection of readings seeks to improve our understanding of the character and consequence of dominant communication practices by introducing those practices within their social, cultural, and historical contexts.

Throughout history, new communication practices based on technological advances have often supplanted previous practices, changing human interaction in dramatic and often unexpected ways. The development of the printing press, for example, not only reduced the necessity for and authority of scribes and priests who previously controlled privileged religious texts, it also permitted widespread distribution of political texts, encouraged literacy, exposed accepted knowledge and beliefs to more public debate, and inadvertently aided the Protestant reformation. Similar dramatic change has accompanied the development of other communication practices driven by expanding media technology, such as the mass-circulation newspaper, telegraph, telephone, radio, television, and personal computers.

Today, we live in a mass society, a mass-mediated society, an "information" age. Information is available quickly, easily, and in great quantities. Often, information confronts us whether we want it or not. We now have access to more information than any one individual could want, use, or even process in a lifetime. Why do we have so much information? What is it? Do we need it? Who produces it? Why? What difference does it make to our comprehension whether we hear, read, or watch various messages?

Drawn from a variety of disciplines and perspectives, the essays assembled here address these questions and others concerning communication form, practice, and consequence. In addition to considering how a communication modality (oral, literate, audio, televisual) might affect our understanding of various messages, selected readings also express a critical concern for the connections between communication practices, democracy, and community. Many communication texts, especially those concerned with media practices, often concentrate on technology and how it expands consumer access to information. An emphasis on the power and influence of technology, however, tends to overlook possible alternative and more democratic communication practices.

Focusing on communication practices and democratic society, this text takes a different approach. Promises about the information superhighway with its pleasures and riches for all are viewed with some skepticism. Judging from previous communication upheavals (such as those surrounding the rise of literacy, the penny press, or electronic broadcasting, for instance), new communication practices do not benefit everyone equally. In fact, as the readings suggest, the impulse for research, development, and promotion of particular media technologies most often corresponds to the communication needs of some political, social, or economic elite. Of course, communication technologies and practices are always subject to ongoing conflicts, negotiations, and contestations within and between societies, but the outcome depends more on the social relations of force than on the inherent nature of any particular technology. A less deterministic view conceives of communication practice as simultaneously a social product, social tool, and social process.

Every dominant communication practice arises as the resulting *product* of habitual social interaction. Groups of humans have always collectively interacted with nature to sustain life. In the process, human interaction also produced communication—language, speech, and non-verbal systems. Even in our contemporary "information" society, we continue to produce and reproduce our way of life by exploiting nature in complex and often convoluted ways. We likewise produce communication practices which roughly correspond to how we construct our physical and social existence. For example, a list of derogatory English words for female, African-American, or Asian will be considerably longer than a list of derogatory English words for male, white, or British. The words we know individually have been collectively produced over time in and by societies which have had European white males in positions of power. Few derogatory words have been produced for the British because as a people they have seldom been in negative social positions. On the other hand, historically, the physical conditions of women, African-Americans, and other non-Europeans in the United States and Western Europe has always been inferior and often deplorable. The practice of insult, like all communication practice, is a social product.

Communication is also a social *tool*. When Humpty Dumpty tells Alice in Wonderland, "A word means just what I choose it to mean—neither more nor less," he was indicating the use of words as tools for constructing his world. Alice replies, "the question is whether you can make words mean so many different things." No, says Humpty, the question is "which is to be master—that's all." In other words, who gets to use the tools and for what purpose? Those who decide how words will be used have tremendous social power. Naming objects, persons, and relations may identify them, but it also expresses the social values, perspectives, and expectations of those who have the power to identify.

In the *Language of Oppression*, Haig Bosmajian writes, "The power which comes from names and naming is related directly to the power to define others—individuals, races, sexes, ethnic groups. Our identities, who and what we are, how others see us, are greatly affected by the names we are called and the words with which we are labelled . . . names, words, and language can be and are used to inspire us, to motivate us to humane acts, to liberate us, they can also be used to dehumanize human beings and to 'justify' their suppression and even their extermination" (5-6). In short, words are tools for defining and marking who will be accepted and included in social groups, in society.

But how can communication practice be both a product and a tool? Communication can simultaneously be both because communication is fundamentally a dialectical and contradictory social process. Communication is a dynamic, contradictory, unstable practice which is constantly being reconstructed even as it reconstructs social understandings. As societies change, communication changes and as communication changes, societies change. Certainly, communication shapes our perception of the world, yet we alter our perceptions and our communication to achieve our own ends. Competing social groups can use communication as a catalyst for social change or a bulwark for the status quo. In other words, we may create our own worlds, but we do so under conditions not of our own making. We work with the language, knowledge, values we receive and alter the language, knowledge, and values based on our experiences and goals. The production and use of words, language, and images are created from the past, employed and contested in the present, and will likely be discarded in the future—all in the *process* of developing and changing our social relationships.

Some of the readings included in this text draw attention to how patterns of thought and cultural norms are the product of changing communication forms and practices (Havelock, Ong, Kellner, Williams, e.g.). Others address how more symmetrical and interactive communication practices might serve as tools for developing citizen participation and democratic life (Peters, Villanueva, Artz, e.g.). As a collection, these readings underscore how much communication is a social process, stressing that each new communication practice has developed in response to specific needs of existing social institutions and emerging technological capabilities. The readings also address the interlocking questions of communication, knowledge, community, and democratic life.

The first section introduces the theme of "Communication Practices and Democratic Society." The following section highlights these issues by considering the communication of contemporary cultural practices. Subsequent readings follow the development of communication practices chronologically from orality through literacy, print, radio, and television. While many of the readings on specific media raise questions of democracy and participation, the closing chapters take up more directly the issues of power, control, and citizen access to the production of communication. Throughout, each section is preceded by a brief introductory commentary.

REFERENCES

Bosmajian, Haig A. *The Language of Oppression*. New York: University Press of America, 1983.

PART I | Media, Knowledge, and Society

We often hear politicians and media pundits decry the decline in contemporary civic values. Of course, previous societies and cultures had similar concerns about the breakdown in social values and individual behavior, but modern mass society appears to raise such problems to a dramatic new level.

Accepted assumptions about right and wrong, individual rights and social responsibilities, respect and authority, and the common ground for social discourse all seem to be washed away in a flood of media images: "shock-jock" radio dee-jays; openly sexual suggestiveness in music, movies, and advertisements; news reports of gang warfare, police brutality, gated communities, target markets, and recurring personal and political scandals by authorities in government, church, and business. Perhaps low participation in the political process can best be explained by disgust and avoidance, rather than apathy.

Increasingly, the atomized consumer-citizen relies on the latest technology—CD player, car phone, modem, beeper, satellite dish tv—to avoid the larger unpleasantness or to meet some highly individualized need. But if we sit alone in our living rooms viewing our widescreen HDTV, send out Internet messages over our portable PC modem, and shut out the world with our own digital-quality cd headphones, what happens to human interaction? What happens to our sense of community? When and where do "target audiences" participate in decisions about their world?

In the first reading, John Peters turns to educator and philosopher John Dewey to answer these questions. As Peters relates Dewey, the problems of society are problems of self, communication, community life, and democracy. According to Dewey, communication develops as a set of interactive practices within a community which make possible knowledge, art, science, and other human creations. The potential of each individual depends on which communication practices a community uses to discover, create and exchange knowledge and resources.

To maximize individual self-realization, a community needs to create the widest possible exchange of experience, knowledge, and benefit for each and all. In other words, Dewey's "Great Community" depends on *shared, interactive,* and *participatory* communication. In short, communication within a democratic community cannot be a private affair, but must be a public, participatory practice.

Democratic communication faces some severe obstacles according to Ben Bagdikian, the former Dean of Journalism at the University of California. What happens to a democracy (and knowledge!) if information communicated lacks citizen contribution and is privately produced by a handful of experts? If knowledge and understanding arise from the communication of shared experiences, then restricting participation in the construction of communication about the world necessarily weakens the knowledge and information produced. Control of informa-

1

tion by a few experts, however well-meaning and well-informed, undermines democratic communication, the production of knowledge, and the validity of decisions made based on such knowledge. Consider a classroom of students looking out the window. Each student honestly and accurately describes what can be seen from his or her seat. Yet, however accurate, individual reports are inadequate, partial, and incomplete explanations of the world outside. Similarly, news and information about the world from a handful of news sources, filtered by a handful of media companies, however accurate, provides at best a partial, incomplete, and distorted explanation of events.

In the United States, most citizens gather news about the world through the mass media, primarily newspapers and television, but as Bagdikian explains, the mass media have become monopolized by about two dozen corporations dedicated to profits rather than news. Because the windows to the world of the news media exclude one-third to one-half of the population, Bagdikian sees a conflict between the interests of advertisers and the media monopoly and the social needs of an informed public in a mass, democratic society.

Edmund Carpenter directs our attention to the technology through which communication practices in mass society have developed. Carpenter foreshadows some of the readings to come by considering the characteristics of different communication media, noting that each medium has its own "grammar" or language. Readings in Section Three by Walter Ong and Eric Havelock delve further into the characteristics of orality and literacy, but here Carpenter notes that changes in the primary mode of communication from oral to written, then print, sound, and audiovisual also affected the mode of thinking. Writing encouraged analytical, linear thinking; television disrupts time and place promoting uncertainty and imagination.

Carpenter's work may be somewhat dated (1960), but he illustrates well how various media not only stimulate different responses but rely upon different human senses and sensibilities. Carpenter represents a still prevalent belief in the powerful influence of technology on communication and society. A protege of technological determinist Marshall McLuhan, the author of *The Medium is the Message*, Carpenter challenges concerns about mass media interference with democracy. For Carpenter, "the mass media *are* democracy."

As a whole this section identifies a complex but important issue for our society—the role of mass media communication practices in building a "Great Community" of democratic communicators.

1 | Dewey, Democracy, and Communication
John Durham Peters

. . .

The Place of Communication in Dewey's Thought

Dewey sketches a complex vision of social life that links together an understanding of the self, communication, community life, and democracy. He has a theory of mass communication (though he did not call it that) prior to the appearance of the mass media as we know them. Further, his theory is inseparable from larger concerns for social, political, and moral order: what Dewey called "democracy." I will briefly examine each aspect of Dewey's vision of social life and communication, showing how Dewey's thinking transcends older divisions such as self/society, reason/desire, symbol/reality, all of which inform classic liberal thinking about mind and society (Unger, 1975).

The Self

Dewey's notions of the self owe much to William James's destruction of the idea of an essential self, spiritual or transcendental in nature, in *The Principles of Psychology* (1890, Ch. 10). James saw the self as a multifarious collection of experiences, possessions, roles, projects, and passions, unified biologically. James, like Dewey after him, celebrates rather than laments the disappearance of the essential self. For James and Dewey the plurality of the self is a liberation, not a scandal. It liberates from the stultifying metaphysical crutches invented to assure the self a solid existence, and allows people to go about the business of forming selves from the materials of their experience.

Since the self does not stand remote from but is constituted by its experiences, no ritual separation into sacred reason and profane desire is possible. As James said, sense and intellect, reason and desire "are wrapped and rolled together as a gunshot in the mountains is wrapt and rolled in fold on fold of echo and reverberative clamor." In pragmatist thinking, the contest of reason and desire was a pseudoproblem, a consequence of a faulty picture of human nature, and a natural consequence of the myth of the autonomous, rational self. (The harmony of reason and desire, self and society, is worked out most fully in Cooley, 1902/1983).

Dewey's moral and political theory is based on this Jamesian conception of the self, mixed with a faith that the vocation of humanity is self-realization. For Dewey (1898:205), self-realization or growth was "the most general category of moral life," the keystone in the arch of virtues. One of Dewey's most distinctive projects was the attempt to combine the German idealist notion of each person developing his or her powers in an unfolding process of *Bildung* (formation, education) with the pragmatist denial of any fixed human essence. For Dewey, if the self exists prior to its "realization," self-realization is a mere unfolding of an innate telos already existing *in potentia*. If the self exists apart from its realization, then self-realization is a process of acquisition—mere abstract consumption. Dewey rejects both conceptions (which might be called the Aristotelian and possessive individualist theories, respectively) of the self. Instead, "the self has no existence excepting in terms of what it has to do, and what it has to do is a function of the whole situation . . . the self *is* the realization and the realization *is* the self" (1898:206; emphasis in original). He leaves no room for souls or spirits: the self is nothing other than the form it takes, and those forms are "a function of the whole situation," that is, dependent on the whole social and moral order at a given point in time. Self-realization occurs through the works of one's hands and the words of one's mouth, but opportunities to work and to speak depend on the rest of the social order.

Community

From there, Dewey proposes a conception of community. This is a vision of multitudinous, diverse social life which offers a limitless variety of paths to self-realization. Only in the company of others is genuine self-realization possible at all. A society of one would have none of the treasures invented by the collective historical genius of the race—intellectual, material, practical, medicinal, culinary, technical, whatever—through which to grow. "Liberty," Dewey (1927:150) said, "is that secure release and fulfillment of personal potentialities which takes place only in rich and manifold association with others" (cf. Cooley, 1902, Ch. 12). Modern society (despite tendencies to abstraction and distance) increases the accessibility of different contributions to human life and opens many avenues for self-creation. The particular conditions people find themselves in are not strangle-holds on freedom but the necessities for a rich, full, concretely universal self. "There is no self until you ask what the self is called to do in relation to other people" (Dewey, 1898:207). Dewey "held that self-realization and the good of the community were the same end viewed from two different perspective . . . The good of each was the good of all, and the good of all was the good of each" (Westbrook, 1980:39).

Democracy

This form of social life, the abundant community, is precisely what Dewey meant by *democracy*. Dewey held that democracy was more than a form of government. He was an insistent defender of the belief that democracy is a whole way of life, a form of social organization in which all can realize their personalities in full. In a famous statement (Dewey, 1927:148): "Regarded as an idea, democracy is not an alternative to other principles of associated life. It is the idea of community life itself." Though his philosophical opinions went through a striking metamorphosis as Dewey matured, this theme ran throughout his career, from his youthful idealism to his mature instrumentalism (Westbrook, 1980:37). In an early essay, "The Ethics of Democracy" (1888/1969), he argued, "To say that democracy is only a form of government is like saying that home is a more or less geometrical arrangement of bricks and mortar; that the church is a building with pews, pulpit, and spire. It is true; they certainly are so much. But it is false; they are so infinitely more" (p. 240). Democracy is not captured in its mere material forms. Rather, it "is a form of moral and spiritual association. . . . It is the form of society in which every man [or woman] has a chance and knows that he [she] has it—and we may add, a chance to which no possible limits can be put, a chance which is truly infinite, the chance to become a person. . . . It means that in every individual there lives an infinite and universal possibility; that of being a king and priest. . . . democracy is an ethical idea, the idea of a personality, with truly infinite capacities, incorporate with every man [woman]. Democracy and the one, the ultimate, ethical ideal of humanity are to my mind synonyms" (p. 240, 244, 248). Dewey attacked a "numerical" conception of democracy, which he said makes "mince-meat" out of the social organism. For him American democracy was not only a particular passing experiment, but a (yet incomplete) attempt to create the universal and necessary social context for the fulfillment of human nature.

Democracy for Dewey is hence simply the universal end-point to which any attempt to build a social order based on the full realization of human potential will arrive. In a rich, harmonious community, the potentials of the individual and of the species converge. Classically, only God was thought to embody in a single personality all the potentials of the species; now, democracy offers the chance to each person, as Dewey said, to be a king and priest. Like Mill (1859/1967) and Whitman (1897) before him, Dewey saw the specific grace of democracy and the sign of its success in the personalities it produced, or rather, the personalities that created themselves under its care.

Communication

For Dewey communication was not the problem of putting private minds *en rapport* one with another. It is not the intimate communion of individual minds as classically formulated by liberal thinkers such as Locke. Rather, communication is the problem of getting people to be full, participating members in the public life of a community. Without this common partaking, then society is a mere symbiosis, not a democratic, human association. As Dewey said (1915:87) democracy is "primarily a mode of associated living, of conjoint communicated experience." Democracy is a structure of possible experiences. What then is his conception of experience?

Dewey's notion of communication is based on the striking claim that experience is public, not private. Sidney Hook notes (1968:219) that many have misunderstood Dewey by taking *experience* to mean "first-person, incommunicable, unsharable subjectivity." Dewey himself argued (1916:3-8) that experience is a sum of structures in the world as they are focused in consciousness. Experience is a set of practices of action and appreciation found in a community. It is the repertoire of stories that can be told and situations in which they can be told. The mature Dewey was not an idealist who grounded the objectivity of meaning in cosmic Mind or Self; his social philosophy was precisely the attempt to see experience as objective and supraindividual without falling back on transcendental modes of argument. A democratic community is one that possesses a collection of human artifacts and practices available for the self-realization of members of a community. For Dewey (as for Peirce before him, and Heidegger, Wittgenstein, and their followers after him) the flow (or what Peirce called the "metaboly") of meaning took place *outside* the individual mind. Dewey *materialized* language and culture and *externalized* meaning and experience. He treated experience as part of the furniture of social life, not a mental event or construct. For Dewey, the individual's autonomy was not threatened by the exteriority of meaning, but empowered to become fully human through absorbing the aesthetic and practical productions of the human family.

Dewey's notion of communication is closely related to this notion of "intelligence," which resides in "the improvement of the methods and conditions of debate, discussion and persuasion" (Dewey, 1927:208). It consists of practices of speech, thought, and action and is similar to James's (1907:166) notion of common sense—the habits of thought handed down through myriad generations and preserved in language. Intelligence for Dewey is quintessential public: it is the objective stock of possibilities of reasoning and discourse available in a community. Each creative or self-creative act is indebted to previous labors and laborers: a poet to those who developed language and poetic forms; a musician to those who developed instruments; an athlete to the many who have refined the practices of games and institutions of sport; and analogously, a self to those who invented ways of being human. "The things in civilization we most prize are not of ourselves. They exist by grace of the doings and sufferings of the continuous human community of which we are a link" (Dewey, 1934:87). Civilization, therefore, is the residue of the intelligence created by a myriad of actors and deposited in social institutions, law, religion, art, language, technique, etc. The difference between the savage and the civilized, for instance, is the store of intelligence available to the latter. Communication is the practice of getting people collectively to partake of this treasure trove of public experience. Culture, while objective, is also diverse; hence it is not tyrannically constraining but objectively various. Communication for Dewey is thus not the process to which minds come into contact, one with another; it is a matter of discursive practices and communities—of cultural *forms* and *forums*.

Communication was the answer to the problems of American democracy Dewey gave in his foremost work on political theory, *The Public and its Problems* (1927). In it, he argued that the public realm had gone into "eclipse": "Till the Great Society is converted into a Great Community, the Public will remain in eclipse. Communication alone can create a Great Community. Our Babel is not one of tongues but of the signs and symbols without which shared experience is impossible" (p. 142). The "public" for Dewey in a way is a language factory. Its task was to invent forms of discourse needed for the exigencies of social life. By so doing, the collective level of "intelligence" would be raised without improving "original endowments one whit": a "mechanic can discourse of ohms and amperes as Sir Isaac Newton could not in his day" (p. 210). His most concrete proposal of the book was a massive reinvention of discursive possibilities—specifically, the mobilization of scientists and artists to invent new signs, symbols, and forms and discourse that would prove useful for altering the way things are and for expressing the deep meanings of everyday experiences. "The function of art has always been to break through the crust of conventionalized and routine consciousness. Common things, a flower, a gleam of moonlight, the song of a bird, not things rare and remote, are means with which the deeper levels of life are touched so that they spring up as desire and thought. This process is art" (pp. 183-4).

However, such improvement of the general discursive and aesthetic life could not proceed, according to Dewey, without a revival of the local, face-to-face community: "There is no limit to the liberal expansion and confirmation of limited personal intellectual endowment which may proceed from the flow of social intelligence when that circulates by word of mouth from one to another in the communications of the local community" (Dewey, 1927:219). Dewey thus conceived communication to be the solution to the crisis of democracy. Communication for him combined objective, supraindividual cultural forms (the "intelligence" that results from scientific inquiry and artistic creation) and social forums ("local communal life") in which these forms become the common property of all.

In sum, Dewey proposed a new liberalism. It was based on the individual to the extent that the unfolding of personal powers was its cornerstone. But it added a distinctive belief in the objectivity or publicness of experience, with a whole array of corrosive arguments against classic liberal notions of the individual self as a reasoning island that must fight off social attachments from without and the blind and hungry gnawings of desire from within. Human liberation was not freeing the individual from all constraint, but growth in a social world with other people. He advocated what MacPherson (1973) calls "developmental liberty"—freedom *to* develop rather than freedom *from* impediment. Further, if reality is made and remade by human labor, then politics will be less about how to interpret reality than how to create it (Carey, 1982). Democracy then is the collective determination of reality. Dewey agreed with James that the disappearance of the notion of "the Truth, conceived as the one answer, determinate and complete, to the one fixed enigma which the world is believed to propound" (James, 1907:157) was a call to creative truth-making rather than a cause for mourning. The impossibility of ever settling a question by reference to "the facts" only served to reorient human disputes more fruitfully: away from the dead-end belief that there is a final answer "out there" toward the establishment of productive ways of collectively determining and producing reality—Dewey's "methods and conditions of debate, discussion, and persuasion."

In what follows, I want to argue that Dewey's conception of communication and social order is superior to the liberal notions that preceded it and followed it as well. While all liberalisms are clearly based on some kind of privilege to speech as key to political and social order, Dewey's liberalism takes human minds, communities, and selves to be created out of the practice of speech, rather than preexisting it. Hence speech and communication cease to be an eternal problem of bridging the poles of self and other, individual and community, private and public (Unger, 1975)....

REFERENCES

Carey, James W. (1982). "The mass media and critical theory: An American View," in M. Burgoon (ed.) *Communication Yearbook 6*. Beverly Hills: Sage, pp. 18-33.

Carey, James W. (1985). "Overcoming resistance to cultural studies," in Michael Gurevitch and Mark R. Levy (eds.) *Mass Communication Review Yearbook 5*, Beverly Hills: Sage, pp. 23-36.

Cooley, Charles Horton (1983). *Human Nature and the Social Order*, New Brunswick, N.J.: Transaction Books. First published 1902.

Dewey, John (1969). "The ethics of democracy." *The Early Works of John Dewey, 1882-98*, Vol. 1. Carbondale, Illinois: Southern Illinois University Press, pp. 227-49.

Dewey, John (1915). *Democracy and Education: An Introduction to the Philosophy of Education*. New York: MacMillan.

Dewey, John (1916). "Introduction." *Essays in Experimental Logic*, Chicago: University of Chicago Press, pp. 1-74.

Dewey, John (1927). *The Public and Its Problems*. New York: Henry Holt.

Dewey, John (1934). *A Common Faith*. New Haven: Yale University Press.

Hook, Sidney (1969). "John Dewey and the crisis of American liberalism, " *Antioch Review*, pp. 218-32.

James, William (1890). *The Principles of Psychology*. New York: Henry Holt.

James, William (1974). *Pragmatism: A New Name for Some Old Ways of Thinking*. New York: Meridan. First published 1907.

MacPherson, C. B. (1973). "Berlin's division of liberty," *Democratic Theory: Essays in Retrieval*. Oxford: Claredon Press, pp. 95-119.

Unger, Roberto Mangabeira (1975). *Knowledge and Politics*. New York: Free Press.

Westbrook, Robert Brett (1980). *John Dewey and American Democracy*. Ph.D. Diss., Stanford University.

Whitman, Walt (1897). *Democratic Vistas*, in *Complete Prose Works*. Philadelphia: David McKay.

2 | Media and Democracy
Ben Bagdikian

* * *

Americans, like most people, get images of the world from their newspapers, magazines, radio, television, books, and movies. The mass media become the authority at any given moment for what is true and what is false, what is reality and what is fantasy, what is important and what is trivial. There is no greater force in shaping the public mind; even brute force triumphs only by creating an accepting attitude toward the brutes.

Authorities have always recognized that to control the public they must control information. The initial possessor of news and ideas has political power—the power to disclose or conceal, to announce some parts and not others, to hold back until opportunistic moments, to predetermine the interpretation of what is revealed. Leaders of democracies no less than medicine men, shamans, kings, and dictators are jealous of their power over ideas, as eager to control information as they are to control armies.

Controlled information has a morbid history. It is not morbid solely because it violates the ideology of democracy, though it does that. It is morbid because it is usually wrong. Unchallenged information is inherently flawed information. If it is in error to begin with, it is not open to correction. If it is correct at the time, it will soon be obsolete. If it changes without uninhibited response from the real world, it becomes detached from the real world. For a realistic picture of society there is no such thing as a central authority.

But the righteousness of power is irresistible. Every authority figure in the Western world once knew for certain that the world was flat and silenced anyone who pointed out the error. The authorities knew the earth was the center of the universe and constructed illfated philosophies based on the illusion. When the bubonic plague decimated the population of Europe, the authorities burned not guilty rats but guiltless "witches." For two thousand years the best doctors treated fevers by draining the patients' blood and kindly killed more human beings than the most murderous cannon.

The authorities were wrong. Their errors created intellectual sterility and immeasurable human misery. But they were not wrong because they were always unintelligent or evil. They were wrong and they remained wrong because their information, which they sincerely believed, was not effectively challenged by open and competitive ideas.

The Age of Enlightenment created a new kind of society. It rejected dictators and kings. It celebrated democracy and individual freedom. It acknowledged that the democratic consent of the governed is meaningless unless the consent is informed consent. Controlled information has survived in the twentieth century's grim parade of dictatorships, but these dictatorships have been the enemies of democracy and they have ultimately failed. The first amendment of the most sacred document in the quintessential democracy of the Enlightenment, the United States, guarantees freedom of expression. Diversity of expression was assumed to be the natural state of enduring liberty.

Modern technology and American economics have quietly created a new kind of central authority over information—the national and multinational corporation. By the 1980s, the majority of all major American media—newspapers, magazines, radio, television, books, and movies—were controlled by fifty giant corporations. These corporations were interlocked in common financial interest with other massive industries and with a few dominant international banks.

There are other media voices outside the control of the dominant fifty corporations. Most are small and localized, and many still disappear as they are acquired by the giants. The small voices, as always, are important, a saving remnant of diversity. But their diminutive sounds tend to be drowned by the controlled thunder of half the media power of a great society.

The United States has an impressive array of mass communications. There are 1,700 daily newspapers, 11,000 magazines, 9,000 radio and 1,000 television stations, 2,500 book publishers, and 7 movie studios. If each of these were operated by a different owner there would be 25,000 individual media voices in the country. Such a large number would almost guarantee a full spectrum of political and social ideas distributed to the population. It would limit the concentration of power since each owner would share influence over the national mind with 24,999 other owners. The division of the market into so many companies would mean firms would be smaller, which would make it easier for newcomers to enter the scene with new ideas.

But there are not 25,000 different owners. Today fifty corporations own most of the output of daily newspapers and most of the sales and audience in magazines, broadcasting, books, and movies. The fifty men and women who head these corporations would fit in a large room. They constitute a new Private Ministry of Information and Culture.

Modern technology and social organization have intensified the problems of centralized control of information. In an earlier age citizen talked to citizen about public policies that affected them. Each community could gather in a hall or church to decide its own fate. Deciding its fate was real because in older, agricultural societies each community came close to self-sufficiency and remote events had marginal meaning. That method of politics disappeared long ago. In place of the small towns are huge urban complexes where no citizen can know most other members of the community. No town hall or church could possibly hold all the voters. Each citizen's fate is shaped by powerful forces in distant places. The individual now depends on great machines of information and imagery that inform and instruct. The modern systems of news, information, and popular culture are not marginal artifacts of technology. They shape the consensus of society.

It is a truism among political scientists that while it is not possible for the media to tell the population what to think, they do tell the public what to think about. What is reported enters the public agenda. What is not reported may not be lost forever, but it may be lost at a time when it is most needed. More than any other single private source and often more than any governmental source, the fifty dominant media corporations can set the national agenda....

For the first time in the history of American journalism, news and public information have been integrated formally into the highest levels of financial and nonjournalistic corporate control. Conflicts of interest between the public's need for information and corporate desires for "positive" information have vastly increased.

This book describes two alarming developments in the mass media in the last twenty-five years. One is the impact of concentrated control of our media by the fifty corporations. The other development is the subtle but profound impact of mass advertising on the form and content of the advertising-subsidized media—newspapers, magazines, and broadcasting.

The last twenty-five years have not seen unrelieved degradation of the media. Much has improved. Journalism has experienced growth in its social perceptions, fresh creativity in drama and art, and ingenious applications of communication techniques, sometimes for social good. But these improvements have been paralleled and often overwhelmed by the effects of the control of large corporations.

The fifty corporations in control of most of our media differ in policies and practices. Their subsidiaries' products vary in quality, some excellent, many mediocre, some wretched. The corporations are led by men and women who differ in personality and values. In the massive output of the fifty corporations there is a wide variety of kinds of stories, ideas, and entertainments, including information that sometimes is critical of giant corporations.

The problem is not one of universal evil among the corporations or their leaders. Nor is it a general practice of constant suppression and close monitoring of the content of their media companies. There is, in the output of the dominant fifty, a rich mixture of news and ideas. But there are also limits, limits that do not exist in most other democratic countries with private enterprise media. The limits are felt on open discussion of the system that supports giantism in corporate life and of other values that have been enshrined under the inaccurate label "free enterprise."

Many of the corporations claim to permit great freedom to the journalists, producers, and writers they employ. Some do grant great freedom. But when their most sensitive economic interests are at stake, the parent corporations seldom refrain from using their power over public information.

Media power is political power. The formal American political system is designed as though in response to Lord Acton's aphorism that power corrupts and absolute power corrupts absolutely. Media power is no exception. When fifty men and women, chiefs of their corporations, control more than half the information and ideas that reach 220 million Americans, it is time for Americans to examine the institutions from which they receive their daily picture of the world.

3 | Media Languages
Edmund Carpenter

English is a mass medium. All languages are mass media. The new mass media—film, radio, TV—are new languages, their grammars as yet unknown. Each codifies reality differently; each conceals a unique metaphysics. Linguists tell us it's possible to say anything in any language if you use enough words or images, but there's rarely time; the natural course is for a culture to exploit its media biases.

Writing, for example, didn't record oral language; it was a new language, which the spoken word came to imitate. Writing encouraged an analytical mode of thinking with emphasis upon lineality. Oral languages tended to be polysynthetic, composed of great, tight conglomerates, like twisted knots, within which images were juxtaposed, inseparably fused; written communications consisted of little words chronologically ordered. Subject became distinct from verb, adjective from noun, thus separating actor from action, essence from form. Where preliterate man imposed form diffidently, temporarily—for such transitory forms lived but temporarily on the tip of his tongue, in the living situation—the printed word was inflexible, permanent, in touch with eternity: it embalmed truth for posterity.

This embalming process froze language, eliminated the art of ambiguity, made puns "the lowest form of wit," destroyed word linkages. The word became a static symbol, applicable to and separate from that which it symbolized. It now belonged to the objective world; it could be seen. Now came the distinction between being and meaning, the dispute as to whether the Eucharist *was* or only *signified* the body of the Sacrifice. The word became a neutral symbol, no longer an inextricable part of a creative process.

Gutenberg completed the process. The manuscript page with pictures, colors, correlation between symbol and space, gave way to uniform type, the black-and-white page, read silently, alone. The format of the book favored lineal expression, for the argument ran like a thread from cover to cover: subject to verb to object, sentence to sentence, paragraph to paragraph, chapter to chapter, carefully structured from beginning to end, with value embedded in the climax. This was not true of great poetry and drama, which retained multiperspective, but it was true of most books, particularly texts, histories, autobiographies, novels. Events were arranged chronologically and hence, it was assumed, causally; relationship, not being, was valued. The author became an *authority*, his data were serious, that is, *serially* organized. Such data, if sequentially ordered and printed, conveyed value and truth; arranged any other way, they were suspect.

The newspaper format brought an end to book culture. It offers short, discrete articles that give important facts first and then taper off to incidental details, which may be, and often are, eliminated by the make-up man. The fact that reporters cannot control the length of their articles means that, in writing them, emphasis can't be placed on structure, at least in the traditional linear sense, with climax or conclusion at the end. Everything has to be captured in the headline; from there it goes down the pyramid to incidentals. In fact there is often more in the headline than in the article; occasionally, no article at all accompanies the banner headline.

The position and size of articles on the front page are determined by interest and importance, not content. Unrelated reports from Moscow, Sarawak, London, and Ittipik are juxtaposed; time and space, as separate concepts, are destroyed and the *here and* now presented as a single Gestalt. Subway readers consume everything on the front page, then turn to page 2 to read....

Books and movies only pretend uncertainty, but live TV retains this vital aspect of life. Seen on TV, the fire in the 1952 Democratic Convention threatened briefly to become a conflagration; seen on newsreel, it was history, without potentiality.

The absence of uncertainty is no handicap to other media, if they are properly used, for their biases are different. Thus it's clear from the beginning that Hamlet is a doomed man, but, far from detracting in interest, this heightens the sense of tragedy.

Now, one of the results of the time-space duality that developed in Western culture, principally from the Renaissance on, was a separation within the arts. Music, which created symbols in time, and graphic art, which created symbols in space, became separate pursuits, and men gifted in one rarely pursued the other. Dance and ritual, which inherently combined them, fell in popularity. Only in drama did they remain united.

It is significant that of the four new media, the three most recent are dramatic media, particularly TV, which combines language, music, art, dance, They don't, however, exercise the same freedom with time that the stage dares practice. An intricate plot, employing flash backs, multiple time perspectives and overlays, intelligible on the stage, would mystify on the screen. The audience has no time to think back, to establish relations between early hints and subsequent discoveries. The picture passes before the eyes too quickly; there are no intervals in which to take stock of what has happened and make conjectures of what is going to happen. The observer is in a more passive state, less interested in subtleties. Both TV and film are nearer to narrative and depend much more upon the episodic. An intricate time construction can be done in film but in fact rarely is. The soliloquies of *Richard III* belong on the stage; the film audience was unprepared for them. On stage Ophelia's death was described by three separate groups: one bears the announcement and watches the reactions simultaneously. On film the camera flatly shows her drowned where "a willow lies aslant a brook."

Media differences such as these mean that it's not simply a question of communicating a single idea in different ways but that a given idea or insight belongs, primarily, though not exclusively, to one medium, and can be gained or communicated best through that medium.

Thus the book was ideally suited for discussing evolution and progress. Both belonged, almost exclusively, to book culture. Like a book, the idea of progress was an abstracting, organizing principle for the interpretation and comprehension of the incredibly complicated record of human experience. The sequence of events was believed to have a direction, to follow a given course along an axis of time; it was held that civilization, like the reader's eye (in J.B.

Bury's words), "has moved, is moving, and will move in a desirable direction. Knowledge will advance, and with that advance, reason and decency must increasingly prevail among men." Here we see the three main elements of book lineality: the line, the point moving along that line, and its movement toward a desirable goal.

The Western conception of a definite moment in the present, of the present as a definite moment or a definite point, so important in book-dominated languages, is absent, to my knowledge, in oral languages. Absent as well, in oral societies, are such animating and controlling ideas as Western individualism, and three-dimensional perspective, both related to this conception of the definite moment, and both nourished, probably bred, by book culture.

Each medium selects its ideas. TV is a tiny box into which people are crowded and must live; film gives us the wide world. With its huge screen, film is perfectly suited for social drama, Civil War panoramas, the sea, land erosion, Cecil B. DeMille spectaculars. In contrast, the TV screen has room for two, at the most three, faces, comfortably. TV is closer to stage, yet different....

Current confusion over the respective roles of the new media comes largely from a misconception of their function. They are art-forms, not substitutes for human contact. Insofar as they attempt to usurp speech and personal, living relations, they harm. This, of course, has long been one of the problems of book culture, at least during the time of its monopoly of Western middle-class thought. But this was never a legitimate function of books, nor of any other medium. Whenever a medium goes claim jumping, trying to work areas where it is ill-suited, conflicts occur with other media, or, more accurately, between the vested interests controlling each. But, when media simply exploit their own formats, they become complementary and cross-fertile.

Some people who have no one around talk to cats, and you can hear their voices in the next room, and they sound silly, because the cat won't answer, but that suffices to maintain the illusion that their world is made up of living people, while it is not. Mechanized mass media reverse this: now mechanical cats talk to humans. There's no genuine feedback.

This charge is often leveled by academicians at the new media, but it holds equally for print. The open-mouthed, glaze-eyed TV spectator is merely the successor of the passive, silent, lonely reader whose head moved back and forth like a shuttlecock.

When we read, another person thinks for us; we merely repeat his mental process. The greater part of the work of thought is done for us. This is why it relieves us to take up a book after being occupied by our own thoughts. In reading, the mind is only the playground for another's ideas. People who spend most of their lives in reading often lose the capacity for thinking, just as those who always ride forget how to walk. Some people read themselves stupid. Chaplin did a wonderful take-off of this in *City Lights*, when be stood up on a chair to eat the endless confetti that he mistook for spaghetti.

Eliot remarks: "It is often those writers whom we are lucky enough to know whose books we can ignore; and the better we know them personally, the less need we may feel to read what they write."

Frank O'Connor highlights a basic distinction between oral and written traditions: "By the hokies, there was a man in this place one time by name of Ned Sullivan, and he had a queer thing happen to him late one night and he coming up the Valley Road from Durlas.' This is how a folk story begins, or should begin.... Yet that is how no printed short story should begin, because such a story seems tame when you remove it from its warm nest by the cottage fire, from the sense of an audience with its interjections, and the feeling of terror at what may lurk in the darkness outside."

Face-to-face discourse is not as selective, abstract, nor explicit as any mechanical medium; it probably comes closer to communicating an unabridged situation than any of them, and, insofar as it exploits the give-take of dynamic relationship, it's clearly the most indispensably human one....

...Thus there were, in the CBC studios, four controlled groups who simultaneously received a single lecture and then immediately wrote an identical examination to test both understanding and retention of content. Later the experiment was repeated, using three similar groups; this time the same lecture was (1) delivered in a classroom, (2) presented as a film (using the kinescope) in a small theatre, and (3) again read in print. The actual mechanics of the experiment were relatively simple, but the problem of writing the script for the lecture led to a consideration of the resources and limitations of the dramatic forms involved

It immediately became apparent that no matter how the script was written and the show produced, it would be slanted in various ways for and against each of the media involved; no show could be produced that did not contain these biases, and the only real common denominator was the simultaneity of presentation. For each communication channel codifies reality differently and thus influences, to a surprising degree, the content of the message communicated. A medium is not simply an envelope that carries any letter; it is itself a major part of that message. We therefore decided not to exploit the full resources of any one medium, but to try to chart a middle-of-the-road course between all of them.

The lecture that was finally produced dealt with linguistic codifications of reality and metaphysical concepts underlying grammatical systems. It was chosen because it concerned a field in which few students could be expected to have prior knowledge; moreover, it offered opportunities for the use of gesture. The cameras moved throughout the lecture, and took close-ups where relevant. No other visual aids were used, nor were shots taken of the audience while the lecture was in progress. Instead, the cameras simply focused on the speaker for 27 minutes.

The first difference we found between a classroom and a TV lecture was the brevity of the latter. The classroom lecture, if not ideally, at least in practice, sets a slower pace. It's verbose, repetitive. It allows for greater elaboration and permits the lecturer to take up several *related* points. TV, however, is stripped right down; there's less time for qualifications or alternative interpretations and only time enough for *one* point. (Into 27 minutes we put the meat of a two-hour classroom lecture.) The ideal TV speaker states his point and then brings out different facets of it by a variety of illustrations. But the classroom lecturer is less subtle and, to the agony of the better students, repeats and repeats his identical points in the hope, perhaps, that ultimately no student will miss them, or perhaps simply because he is dull. Teachers have had captive audiences for so long that few are equipped to compete for attention via the new media.

The next major difference noted was the abstracting role of each medium, beginning with print. Edmund M. Morgan, Harvard Law Professor, writes:

One who forms his opinion from the reading of any record alone is prone to err, because the printed page fails to produce the impression or convey the idea which the spoken word produced or conveyed. The writer has read charges to the jury which he had previously heard delivered, and has been amazed to see an oral deliverance which indicated a strong bias appear on the printed page as an ideally impartial exposition. He has seen an appellate court solemnly declare the testimony of a witness to be especially clear and convincing which the trial judge had orally characterized as the most abject perjury.[1]

Selectivity of print and radio are perhaps obvious enough, but we are less conscious of it in TV, partly because we have already been conditioned to it by the shorthand of film....

As in a movie theatre, only the screen is illuminated, and, on it, only points of immediate relevance are portrayed; everything else is eliminated. This explicitness makes TV not only personal but forceful. That's why stage hands in a TV studio watch the show over floor monitors, rather than watch the actual performance before their eyes.

The script of the lecture, timed for radio, proved too long for TV. Visual aids and gestures on TV not only allow the elimination of certain words, but require a unique script. The ideal radio delivery stresses pitch and intonation to make up for the absence of the visual. That flat, broken speech in "sidewalk interviews" is the speech of a person untrained in radio delivery.

The results of the examination showed that TV had won, followed by lecture, film, radio, and finally print. Eight months later the test was readministered to the bulk of the students who had taken it the first time. Again it was found that there were significant differences between the groups exposed to different media, and these differences were the same as those on the first test, save for the studio group, an uncertain group because of the chaos of the lecture conditions, which had moved from last to second place. Finally, two years later, the experiment was repeated, with major modifications, using students at Ryerson Institute. Marshall McLuhan reports:

In this repeat performance, pains were taken to allow each medium full play of its possibilities with reference to the subject, just as in the earlier experiment each medium was neutralized as much as possible. Only the mimeograph form remained the same in each experiment. Here we added a printed form in which an imaginative typographical layout was followed. The lecturer used the blackboard and permitted discussion. Radio and TV employed dramatization, sound effects and graphics. In the examination, radio easily topped TV. Yet, as in the first experiment, both radio and TV manifested a decisive advantage over the lecture and written forms. As a conveyor both of ideas and information, TV was, in this second experiment, apparently enfeebled by the deployment of its dramatic resources, whereas radio benefited from such lavishness. "Technology is explicitness," writes Lyman Bryson. Are both radio and TV more explicit than writing or lecture? Would a greater explicitness, if inherent in these media, account for the ease with which they top other modes of performances?[2]

Announcement of the results of the first experiment evoked considerable interest. Advertising agencies circulated the results with the comment that here, at last, was scientific proof of the superiority of TV. This was unfortunate and missed the main point, for the results didn't indicate the superiority of one medium over others. They merely directed attention toward differences between them, differences so great as to be of kind rather than degree. Some CBC officials were furious, not because TV won, but because print lost.

The problem has been falsely seen as democracy vs. the mass media. But the mass media *are* democracy. The book itself was the first mechanical mass medium. What is really being asked, of course, is: can books' monopoly of knowledge survive the challenge of the new languages?

The answer is: no. What should be asked is: what can print do better than any other medium and is that worth doing?

NOTES

[1] G. Louis Joughin and Edmund M. Morgan, *The Legacy of Sacco and Vanzetti, New* York, Harcourt, Brace & Co., 1948, p. 34.

[2] From a personal communication to the author.

PART II | Communication in Everyday Life

7 A. M. (or later?). The alarm clock sounds (digital or analog?). Music rolls out of the radio (country, jazz, E-Z rock?). You rise from bed (in the dorm? your apartment? your parent's house?). You shower (and put on make-up? shave?). You dress (heels, sneakers? Nike or Reebok?) You take breakfast (cornflakes? toaster waffles?), coffee (Colombian or Nigerian?), juice (Florida or Brazil?) and milk (with or without BgH?). 8 A. M. You leave (for school or work by bus, train, car, or bike—mountain or racing?).

Within the first hour of every day, we participate in hundreds of communication practices, most of them unconsciously, most of them reflecting or shaping who we are and how we will interact with others. Mundane, ritualistic, often unintended, the communication practice of everyday surrounds us much like water surrounds fish. It's just there, we need it, we live in it, we seldom notice it. When we do notice, we read great meaning into simple practices. The music, the make-up, the means of transportation communicate our "identity" to others. It lets them know if we should be considered trendy, hip, young, aware of social values—or not. The readings in this section raise questions about the seemingly simple practices of everyday life. In the first article, cultural studies scholar Susan Willis looks at the taken-for-granted activities of domestic labor and proposes that folding clothes communicates social worth—non-paid homemakers are seen as non-productive, their work invisible; paid laundry services are seen as productive, albeit unenviable. Although domestic labor creates and sustains wage laborers, the social value communicated by and about domestic labor depends on larger social relations, including relations between men and women. Technology made domestic labor more visible in the 40s, 50s, and 60s but only because the home became a site for selling consumer goods to women.

Here, Willis introduces the complex concept of *commodity*—an item made primarily for sale—which defines our consumer society. The amount of commodities produced marks the wealth of a nation; the amount of commodities possessed marks the wealth of an individual. More importantly, commodities are produced by humans in unique social relations which organize the production and distribution of goods and services according to their market value. One consequence has been the devaluation of human relations and their social worth.

For example, historically, women in the male gaze have often been objects; women have even shopped for commodities (hair color, lipstick, eye shadow, clothing) to become better commodities themselves. Under these conditions, how are women valued? Even with women entering the workforce and management positions, what is their "worth" in a commodity-driven society? Not too long ago, the Enjoli woman could earn the "bacon," cook it up in a pan, and still never let her husband forget he was a man!

Willis asks if such images are changing? After all, we now have stay-at-home "Mr. Moms," dads like Bill Cosby and those on "Full House" and "Parenthood" and single, professional career women like Murphy Brown. To Willis, changing gender roles, even "femininizing masculinity," simply means that formerly "female" tasks are now permissible in the context of purchasing commodities. We have more male shoppers, but domestic labor is still devalued because it does not appear on the market.

Willis pursues this topic by looking at the relationship between domestic labor and child's play. As technological innovation diminished household chores in the 50s and increased leisure time, it also increased playtime and created a mass market for toys. Willis notes that stoves (and other toys) are commodity "toys" only because the user doesn't actually have to cook (or work). She also seeks a connection between adult roles and children's play. If women perform most domestic labor and girls play with toy stoves does an interlocking code system link adult labor with child's play, communicating meaning about gender and social roles? After all, we have separate colors for boys and girls. Toy stores have separate aisles. Perhaps family practices, school activities, and media images communicate separate aisles for boys' and girls' social development? Lydia Sargent's list of toys and the article from *Child* magazine suggest as much.

Certainly, playing with toys is an important communication practice. Social scientist Laurel Walum has demonstrated that toys are "a particularly cogent source for learning about cultural values" (46). Studies have shown the importance of communication in play. Indeed, more than half of play is spent in establishing roles. Toys help children define social relationships—who will be in charge? Who will be the care-giver? How will they resolve disputes? What has value and why? Moreover, children learn the importance of consumption through toys. Willis argues that as a child's desire for a toy is realized in purchase, they experience "the transition to adolescence as an act of consumption" (32).

In the second selection, propaganda critics James Combs and Dan Nimmo discuss how some toys become cultural "icons"—representations of important social values and perspectives. Barbie, for example, is much more than a doll. She represents and teaches the norms of accepted (or desired) female beauty and behavior. Shouldn't all young girls look and act like a doll? Shouldn't their daily lives be consumed with dressing, dating, relationships and the consumption of fashion? Of course, in advertisements and play, Barbie communicates other messages. As Dr. Barbie or Astronaut Barbie, the doll expresses a certain feminist competence and potential. But with her impossible female form and expensive evening gown in hand, Barbie doesn't let go of the importance of youth, body shape, and fashion. Moreover, Barbie may be an icon of "feminine," but she doesn't stand alone (or just next to Ken!). Barbie joins an endless and pervasive conversation about femininity that is communicated through other toys, fashion magazines, talk shows, soap operas, Saturday morning cartoons, sit-coms, wedding announcements, and the English language.

Combs and Nimmo place Barbie in a contemporary "ideo-culture" which permits the propagation of dominant messages. Certainly, our media-dominated culture (often disguised as "entertainment") surrounds and penetrates our existence. Try to find a time or location without commercial interruption. However, just because Combs and Nimmo create a world submerged in propaganda, we don't have to go there with them. We should be able to distinguish between intentional propaganda and manipulation from the simply non-reflective communication practices of an advertising-driven mass media. Later readings by Williams and Kellner should illuminate social communication more fully. Likewise, Combs and Nimmo come up short on the importance of participation in democratic communication. "Talking back" to the mass media does not fulfill the need for citizen deliberation, conversation, and decision-making in a "Great Community." Nonetheless, this contribution identifies how habitual practices of everyday life—infused with economic and political interests—help shape our beliefs and behavior.

Can anything be more habitual, more necessary to human life than eating? Everyone needs to eat and drink. The "need" for burgers and beer must be created, however. The success of McDonald's illustrates how one of the most natural human practices can become a golden opportunity to sell hamburgers. George Ritzer presents McDonald's as a symbol for our mass production-for-profit society. In this reading on McDonald's, we see how much common everyday practices can express and create social knowledge.

Most Americans know the objects and identities of the quick-food industry: McDonald's, Taco Bell, Wendy's, Dunkin' Donuts, Subway. We also recognize other national "quick" service chains: Jiffy Lube, LensCrafters, USA Today, NutriSystem, and KOA campgrounds, for example. All of these enterprises thrive on efficiency, calculability, predictability, and control—characteristics Ritzer calls "McDonaldization." Ritzer balances the benefits of clean, affordable, convenient, and accessible services for millions with the attendant increased consumption, uncreative sameness, and institutionalization of formerly participatory human interactions. At McDonald's, dining (an historically social experience) becomes an instance of speed and efficiency. The consumer may be treated cordially, but without any real personal contact. The communication between diner and server is impersonal as is much of the communication between co-workers. And what happens to the family meal?

McDonald's and our fast-serve society seems natural, but not necessarily influential. Yet, "McDonaldization" and its replication by other service industries fosters impersonal, individualized consumption at the expense of shared, community exchanges and activities. The "need for speed" expresses a need for immediate gratification, consumption over satisfaction. Ritzer wonders why society must move so fast? Who feels good after eating fast food? Speed increases consumption, sales, and profits, but relying on "McServices" for human needs places commodity over community.

Ritzer's comments on the irrationality of cultural production driven by speed, efficiency, and profit have broad implications for the uses of developing communication technology. How will millions of individual consumers surfing 500 channels on Rupert Murdoch's Sky TV participate in policy-making and community-building activities? Do we want McNews and Information? Do we really want drive-thru communication practices?

While not tied to Dewey's thesis on communication and democracy, these readings illustrate the centrality of his concerns to our understanding of contemporary social life. Casting citizens as consumers, ignoring or avoiding citizen rights as producers, and reducing social needs to those of speedy consumption creates communication practices unfavorable to democratic reflection and participation, undermining human creativity in the process.

Perhaps one question is how do we develop the needs which various fast-service outlets meet? Who benefits from messages like the designer jeans ad that says simply: "Look. Want. Have . . . ?" Does such communication meet the need for clothing? If Combs and Nimmo are right that needs must be cultivated, tended, and propagated, then consumer-driven, ad-driven needs are not so "natural" but arise from our culture. Indeed, meeting the needs of the consumer (whether quickly and conveniently, or not) superficially addresses a more significant need for knowledge construction, democratic decision-making, and community building.

REFERENCES

Walum, Laurel. *The Dynamics of Sex and Gender: A Sociological Perspective*. Chicago: Rand McNally, 1977.

Willis, Susan. *A Primer for Daily Life*. New York: Routledge, 1990.

4 | Playing House: Domestic Labor as Culture

Susan Willis

"You be baby, I be mommy"

Charlotte, age 2

When a housewife takes her family's clothes off the line or out of the dryer, sorts them, and leaves them in neat little piles for the rest of the family members to put away, she performs one of the repetitive daily tasks that defines domestic labor as the creation of use value. The distinction between the home as the site for the creation of use value and the workplace where exchange values are produced is one of the points Sally Alexander developed in her study of women's work in the nineteenth century. As she put it, capitalism intervened into a pre-existing sexual division of labor to exacerbate the subordination of homeplace and wife:

> *By distinguishing between production for use and production for exchange, and by progressively subordinating the former to the latter, by confining production of use to the private world of the home and female labor, and production for exchange increasingly to the workshop outside the home, and male labor, capitalism ensured the economic dependence of women upon their husbands or fathers for a substantial part of their lives.*

(Alexander, 1976: 77)

Today a housewife's labor is very rarely seen as productive. She seldom actually makes her family's clothes; rather, she daily replenishes their use. As with the maintenance of clothing, all the tasks performed in the home ensure that those family members who work outside the home for pay will go out of the door in the morning capable of making commodities for exchange; and hence, actively contributing to the creation of surplus value. This is the economics of production under capitalism, Currently, there is some debate as to whether or not work performed by women in the home contributes to the production of surplus value. It might be argued that women's labor in the home produces a value-creating commodity: labor power. Or it might be said that the housewife indirectly enhances her husband's time spent producing surplus value. The Women's Studies Group at the University of Birmingham, states its position this way: domestic labor as "The production of use values under non-wage relations of

---

From *Primer for Daily Life* by Susan Willis. Reprinted by permission of Routledge.

production, within the capitalist mode of production [does not] contribute directly to the creation of surplus value" (Women's Studies Group, 1978).

As I see it, no matter how we construe the economics of domestic labor, our culture as a lived experience defines a dramatic split between home and workplace. This separation is so much a part of the ideology of late twentieth-century capitalism that the piece-work produced by many women in their homes (including after-hours typing and garment assembly) is as invisible as domestic labor itself. Such labor does not disrupt the notion of the home as a privatized world. The housewife's labor and the use value she creates are culturally perceived as "outside" the labor process and are, therefore, rendered all but invisible. All those neat little piles of clothes stacked end to end could stretch from Maine to California and still the society as a whole would not see in them the production of use. Indeed, women artists have mounted exhibitions that highlight the repetitive nature of the work of reproducing daily life. One such is a series of photographs assembled by the southern California artist Elenore Antin. These show great quantities of boots and shoes that Antin put in long lines and photographed in such a way as to show the shoes rounding corners, disappearing over hills, or entering buildings. Where women on welfare are apt to interpret the lines of shoes as representing the experience of waiting on line for social services, women in the middle classes are more apt to interpret the shoe series as an expression of commodity seriality and the repetitious nature of daily tasks.

Much recent attention has focused on gender roles. Certainly the number of major research projects funded by the Rockefeller Foundation has stimulated inquiry into how gender is related to the socially ascribed roles for men and women. In terms of domestic labor, the common line of reasoning has been to denounce the polarization of gender roles in the home and urge that men assume responsibility for many household tasks as a way of combating male domination. So, then, what if the woman's husband did all the washing, drying, and sorting of the family clothes? Would this change the nature of the work? Or even the way in which it is perceived? Marxist feminists generally maintain that patriarchy pre-dates capitalism and that capitalist economic structures have simply incorporated male domination into them. Following this line of argument, we might say that men's performance of household labor undermines patriarchal notions about gender, but it does not affect the economic subordination of domestic labor to wage labor.

A different approach to women's oppression in the home is to focus on the privatization of domestic work and the isolation of the housewife. In simple and grim terms, the housewife is "Isolated, the only adult in a private house" (Women's Studies Group, 1978: 36). Yet, she is the only one, who will meet her children's needs and demands. Both Janice Radway (1984) and Tania Modleski (1982), in their studies of women's popular fiction, point to the oppressive nature of living solely for another's needs in their explanations of why women "escape" into romance. Isolated, but not alone; giving care, but never replenished, the woman experiences the home as a prison house which is both physically and emotionally draining. Within this characterization of domestic labor, one corrective strategy might be to recreate the extended family and to apportion household chores more evenly between all household members. So, then, what if the woman's children performed all the tasks required to maintain the family's clothes? Would this render use value socially appreciable?

I would argue that only the failure to create use value can be made visible. Say the housewife left all the clothes in the dryer for a week—just let them pile up until nobody had anything to wear. The absence of replenished use value would be remarked upon, whereas its creation is simply taken for granted.

Why is this so? The answer is that what counts in capitalism is exchange value. This is a wage labor society. If you do not work for a wage, you are not felt to be a worker. This is a commodified society. If your activities do not include making, selling, or buying commodities, your endeavors are not seen as making a contribution. The question I will pose from a number of perspectives throughout this chapter is how we might begin to restore the importance of use value in a society where everything is measured against exchange. What is more, I want to ask if we can imagine use value itself as something that is not already overshadowed by its relationship to exchange value. Even as we recognize that housework constitutes the creation of use values, we must not assume that our experience of use value under capitalism is any less fetishized than our experience of commodities. We tend to associate commodity fetishism only with the production of exchange values. In contrast, use value is felt to be pure and autonomous, something that harks back to precapitalist societies where use and the circulation of useful objects was a cementing bond between people. This notion of use value does not pertain today. Those piles of laundered clothes awaiting the children who will put them away in drawers and closets are little different from the cans of peas on the supermarket shelf. Both exemplify the erasure of the labor and social relations that go into their production. It is striking how commodity capitalism, then, finds ways to re-introduce the presence of lost labor. For instance, there is now a new line of products marketed to render use value perceptible. These are the "fresh scents" and static-free sheets that the housewife can buy in order to put appreciable traces of her care and labor into her laundry. This is a commodity culture's response to the absolute impossibility of demonstrating the social nature of use value. Can we confront the tremendous influence of the commodity form in our daily lives by struggling to recognize the social value of use in domestic labor? Can we imagine what the piles of clothes would look like to a society that had not invented the commodity form? Such a stretch of the imagination may well be possible only in feminist science fiction. Short of exercising the imagination to such an extent, and in the real world of opposition politics, some Marxist feminists have promoted wages for housework as a means of eliminating women's oppression: "Pay women—not the military" (Brown, 1983:23). This would be tantamount to changing the larger economy. If women are subordinated because domestic labor is invisible, then wages for housework creates parity with labor done outside the home for pay. Selma James advances the argument to suggest that wages for housework would also amend women's inferior position in workplace jobs: "The subordination to the wage of the man in the home and the subordinating nature of [domestic] labor weakens the woman wherever else she is working" (James, 1975:18). Wages for housework represents the most highly developed position one can take while in a capitalist economy and struggling toward a Marxian economy. It is guided by the cold, hard line of economic reasoning. It fully abandons the possibility of redeeming the social significance of use value and affirms exchange value as the basis for struggle and the measure for all value....

...I want to assess what seems to be a positive change in gender roles in the light of John Fiske's analysis of *Miami Vice* (Fiske, 1987). Fiske points to a "feminization of masculinity" that we might be tempted to apply to the influx of men into the kitchen and the number of young boys learning to appreciate cooking with the Fisher-Price kitchen. In developing his analysis Fiske draws on the commonly accepted fact of capitalist economics that women are primarily defined as consumers. This is a line of reasoning that many feminists have taken up. For instance, in her book on the department store, entitled *Just Looking*, Rachel Bowlby shows how the construction of femininity is very much like shopping. A women is being looked at (consumed by the male gaze) while looking at and consuming commodities for sale. A women's sense of self is of a self being consumed while she is herself consuming (Bowlby, 1985: 32). What Fiske goes on to show is that *Miami Vice* puts its macho masculine figures, Crockett and Tubbs, in the position traditionally defined as feminine. We viewers consume them with our eyes while they are shown to be unabashed consumers of luxury commodities, such as cologne, gold chains, and platinum cigarette cases and lighters. While Fiske applauds *Miami Vice* for the way it feminizes its male heroes, I think we might step back from both the TV program and the Fisher-Price kitchen unit and question whether what is going on is the feminization of masculinity or the commodification of both men and women. It may well be that capitalism, having exploited the women's market, is now reaching out to make men equal to women as consumers. It is true that many more men now participate in shopping as a leisure-time activity (particularly in shopping malls) than would ever have dreamed of doing so in the past. Gender roles are changing, but so too are the economics of commodity capitalism.

Let's Play House

...I [have] developed the point that when children play they put use value into their commodities: that is, toys. Commodities are the hollowed-out representations of the social relations that go into their production but which are erased under capitalist production. In play, children use their toys to create a context for the recovery of these social relationships. When they play with super hero action figures, little boys decide between themselves what roles they will enact and how they will relate to each other. Good guy, bad guy, sorcerer, or super-brute— the toy figure is a pretext for defining a complicated system of social relationships between the players. Children are not aware of the social relations that are erased in the production of their plastic superhero figures, thus rendering each an example of commodity fetishism; but their play demonstrates that they are truly aware of the social relationships that constitute use. Much of children's play involves discussion and dispute over social relationships.

"You be baby, I be mommy": this is how my own daughter, Charlotte, initiates every game of "house." She does not say, "Let's play house." After all, the house is only the context for the definition of roles. What she is in effect saying is "Let's play role reversal."

The amazing fact about children's domestic role-playing games is that more than 50 percent of the game is spent simply deciding the roles each child will assume. I once observed a group of boys attempting to play a game of "house." They had decided on a father, a couple of brothers, and a son. The game fell apart when they tried to make one of the boys "servant." Clearly, someone had to do the work, and clearly father, brothers, and son had better things to do. With no girls to play mother and no thoughts of gender crossing, the game ended for want of a "servant." (Although it could well have continued if the boys had considered the male technological solution and made one of the family members into a robot.) The process of role debating and role assigning took about half an hour. Although the game never really started, the entire time was devoted to a form of play, as the father, brothers, son, and unassigned others were all in the process of working out their roles and testing their relationships.

In her comprehensive study of the bases for women's oppression, Michele Barrett makes an important distinction between the "ideology of the family" and the "household" (Barrett, 1980).

The ideology of the family is the place where patriarchy and capitalism coincide to ensure the oppression of women. Where patriarchy would see women solely as procreators of the species, capitalism inferiorizes women by making social reproduction secondary to the economics of production. The family binds women's nurturing functions to the status of economic marginality. In contrast, I propose that Barrett's notion of household suggests a possible site for imagining social relationships that include family, but transcend its ideology. As Barrett defines it the household is the organizational center for all the material factors that enter into domestic labor. I want to take Barrett's objective conceptualization of household one step further and make it the basis for beginning to think of how we might transform daily-life social relationships. Such a conceptualization of household requires that we actively engage in questioning people's roles and relationships. It is not enough that the patriarch washes the dishes. What the examples drawn from children's play demonstrate is that the roles are of less importance than the process of deciding the roles, and the relationships between people are of less consequence than the efforts made to change the relationships. My intent is not to prioritize childhood, but to suggest that because children in our society have largely been freed from work into play, they are in situations where their efforts are spent experimenting with social relationships, testing the limits, redefining themselves and their friends. When Charlotte begins the game, "You be baby, I be mommy," she puts herself in a situation where she experiments with the complicated combination of authority and nurturing: "Now baby, eat your dinner," "Now baby, don't cry," "Now baby, go to sleep." Do we adults use our households as contexts for actively creating, exploring, reversing social relationships? Or do we spend each day reenacting gender and role assumptions? Charlotte's play does both.

It recreates all the traditional gender categories; but, by the very nature of play, it sets these at a distance where they become objects to ponder, to subvert or teasingly support, to experience with enjoyment or anger.

The concept of household holds forth extremely important possibilities of reconceptualizing familial relationships—but the forces of patriarchy and capitalism are exceedingly resourceful in their efforts to contain new directions in our thinking about society as well as social change itself. I want to give two examples from contemporary mass culture that demonstrate the containment of all the hopeful possibilities that the conceptualization of household holds forth. The first of these is the TV series *Full House*. This is an extremely interesting exercise in patriarchy 1980s-style. The show features a widowed father of three young girls and the father's two single male room-mates, who, in the show's kinship system, become known as "uncles." *Full House* makes every episode topical. Domestic chores and gender are at issue on a weekly basis: "It's your turn to change the diapers / pack the school lunches / do the shopping." One can see the men sorting and stacking those neat little piles of freshly washed clothes. However, the possibility of overturning male dominance is absolutely denied by the obvious reassertion of patriarchy that puts three adult men in charge of three female children. To be a woman is to be a child; adulthood is manhood. A woman's only operative power is, thus, the old standby: coyness and subversion. "Here, Uncle Jesse, will you remove my stinger?" This is what one of the little girls says as she pokes her bee-costumed butt into her father's room-mate's face. "Uncle" Jesse, of course, rolls his eyes and the show ends with a bit of canned laughter. What is interesting about *Full House* is its wide appeal to children of varying ages. I have observed children from 3 years old to 16, contentedly wrapped up in the TV dilemmas of fatherhood. Everyone knows authority is at stake just as everyone knows authority will not be truly undermined. In the patriarchal approach to toilet training, the "Dads" simply tell the toddler that since she can now walk, she will have to walk to the potty like the rest of them. The show puts men in nurturing positions only to represent authority and redefine patriarchal sexual relationships.

The power of patriarchy to reaffirm itself in situations where men assume the caring roles traditionally ascribed to women has led me to question one of my long-held political convictions. Like many women, I was heartened to see post-1960s work crews composed of men and women: there are women construction workers, town maintenance workers, telephone line "persons." Yet, like many women, I was dismayed by how little challenged gender has been by women's access to many traditional male roles. It occurred to me that the real socially transformative struggle might not be for women to achieve muscle producing jobs, or even the headships of corporations, but for men to struggle in masses to be nurses, teachers, dietitians, recreation directors, social workers—all the low-paying, socially sustaining jobs that are inevitably associated with women's caring roles in the home and reserved for women in the workforce (Barrett, 1980: 157). *Full House* suggests that in a society where social reproduction is undervalued, men in caregiving roles will not transform the economics of capitalism, but they will provide a means for the reaffirmation of patriarchy.

The other example of how commodity capitalism contains the notion of household and prevents its becoming the site for transformational thinking about gender is apparent in the new *HG* magazine, formally known as the sedate and stuffy *House and Garden*. The magazine's new pages feature intimate peeks into tastefully stunning decor. These are the furnishing, accessories, arrangements, color, fabrics, and the decorators who put them all together to define and promote the new yuppie society. Whatever changes might be happening at large in terms of gender and class (and in terms of the abandonment of the older *House and Garden* clientele in favor of the new *HG* readership) are not at question because the magazine's photo-layout presents the illusion that social relationships are analogous to spatial relationships. The erasure of the social is achieved in a more complete fashion than it was in the nineteenth-century doll's house where one still had a sense of social hierarchy represented in the upstairs, downstairs, and attic arrangements of household tasks and occupants. The new *HG* represents the containment of the potentially transformative notion of household, because everything in it is not shown in dynamic relationship, but is instead presented as a commodity. Everything is photographed, flattened, packaged, and made to took as accessible as the magazine's advertisements for cars, clothes, and cologne. The new *HG* demonstrates how commodity capitalism denies the possibility of depicting social activity and relationships by absorbing active social process into the decorative and spatial.

The change from *House and Garden* to the logo-inspired *HG* summons up a particularly important association with the professional men's fashion magazine, *GQ*. The suggestion is that the transition from the specifically feminine connotations of house and garden to the monogrammatic shorthand of *HG* indicates that many men are now assuming domestic tasks previously deemed fitting only for women. I tend to see the new *HG* in the light of the criticism I brought to bear on previous examples of the "feminization of masculinity." If the new *HG* suggests that the upkeep of domestic and garden space is now an acceptable endeavor for men, it does so under the sign of the logo and in relation to the optimal commodification of horticultural and domestic activities, products, and the settings that these produce.

We may well condemn the way in which male domination has largely confined women to labor in the home and in the garden while excluding many from employment in the workplace. Nevertheless, women in different regions, at different points in time, and in different economic situations have found ways to make their homes and gardens into the visible custodians of their labor. In supplanting the more womanly and out-of-date *House and Garden,* the new HG does more than sweep away the privileged middle-class connotations the magazine once had. It effectively buries all past periods when women's work in the house and garden was valued because it was recognized as integral to the wellbeing of the society as a whole. In our enthusiasm for the unisex, uniclass *HG,* we ought not to forget the example of seventeenth-century New England. This was a time when house and garden truly traced the limits of a woman's world. Behind the closed doors and straight wooden house-fronts that typify colonial New England architecture, women performed their indoor housekeeping tasks. Such labor was largely invisible. But every indoor task had its visible referent in the seventeenth-century dooryard garden. Here in the space between door and street, women cultivated herbs: the sage and comfrey, and countless others needed to preserve and flavor food, cure the sick, dye fabrics, and aromatize household interiors. The dooryard garden was a growing testament to the multiplicity of women's productive roles. They nursed and healed the sick, they clothed and fed their families, they decorated their homes, and they were artists who created in the landscaping code of the time a personal aesthetic out of crushed oyster-shell walkways, raised beds, and plant arrangements.

The seventeenth-century New England dooryard garden poses a challenge to us living in the last decade of the twentieth century. Can we today imagine the productive unit of household and dooryard garden as anything but confining? Can we step back from our centuries' long struggle to expand the terrain of women's labor, not to recreate the seventeenth century, but to grasp how such a productive unit affirmed the social value of women's domestic labor? Can we use the example of the dooryard garden to re-educate ourselves in order to make fresh assessments of domestic labor today? If commodity capitalism turns the products of domestic labor into fetishized objects, the dooryard garden turns living objects into the concrete manifestations of social value.

By focusing on domestic labor from a number of cultural perspectives, we can begin to imagine possible utopian household alternatives that would inhibit the influences of patriarchy and commodity capitalism. Such a project is not new to women's thinking, and writing. As Jane Tompkins demonstrates in her astutely political reading of *Uncle Tom's Cabin,* Harriet Beecher Stowe quickened her reader's imagination with a view into a wholly transformed nation that would be centered, not in government or capitalist economics, but in the Quaker settlement kitchen. This is the kitchen of Rachel Halliday, where "the preparation of breakfast exemplifies the way people will work in the ideal society; there will be no competition, no exploitation, no commands" (Tompkins, 1985: 143) In such a world, the elimination of patriarchy could not be more explicit. As Tompkins points out, "Stowe reconceives the role of men in human history: while Negroes, children, mothers, and grandmothers do the world's primary work, men [are portrayed grooming] themselves contentedly in a corner" (Tompkins, 1985: 146).

Similar images of radically transformed domestic space occur throughout contemporary black women's writing. When Toni Morrison takes us as readers into Pilate's house in *Song of Solomon,* she puts us at the center of a communal social space where women participate equally in domestic tasks without the need for authority: where economic independence does not promote a desire for profit; and where a simple task, like boiling an egg, can be infinitely pleasurable. I have argued that the "three-woman households" that occur throughout Morrison's writing enable the author to reconceptualize social and sexual relationships along utopian lines (Willis, 1987b). These involve heterosexual relationships that are not oppresive, and relationships between women across generations that do not obtain in male-dominated nuclear families.

Culture is a battleground, where for centuries the impulse to transform domestic labor—and with it, society as a whole—collides with the containing and oppresive forces of patriarchy and capitalism. The challenge is to recognize utopian moments in culture and use these as a basis for criticizing instances where patriarchy is not condemned, but reasserted; and where social relationships are not redeemed but converted into fetishized objects.

REFERENCES

Alexander, Sally (1976) "Women's work in nineteenth century London: a study of the years 1820–50," in Juliet Mitchell and Ann Oakley (eds) *The Rights and Wrongs of Women*, Harmondsworth: Penguin.

Barrett, Michele (1980) *Women's Oppresion Today: Problems in Marxist Feminist Analysis*, London: Verso.

Bowlby, Rachel (1985) *Just Looking*, London: Methuen.

Brown, Wilmette (1983) *Black Women and the Peace Movement*, London: International Women's Day Convention.

Fiske, John (1987) "Miami vice, Miami pleasure," *Cultural Studies* I: 113–19.

James, Selma (1975) *Sex, Race, and Class*, London: Falling Wall Press.

Modleski, Tania (1982) *Loving with a Vengeance*, New York: Methuen.

Radway, Janice (1984) *Reading the Romance*, Chapel Hill: University of North Carolina Press.

Tompkins, Jane (1985) *Sensational Designs: The Cultural Work of American Fiction 1790–1860*, Oxford: Oxford University Press.

Willis, Susan (1987b) *Specifying: Black Women Writing the American Experience*, Madison: University of Wisconsin Press.

Women's Studies Group, Centre for Contemporary Cultural Studies, University of Birmingham (1978) *Women Take Issue*, London: Hutchinson.

5 | Boys Have Better Toys

Lydia Sargent

For all you gals out there that are worried about the lack of traditional values in today's U.S. of A, take heart. There is a new Barbie on the market: Coca Cola Barbie. More accurately, Soda Fountain Sweetheart Barbie. This is the premier doll in the "nostalgic Coca Cola Fashion Series," a series that "lovingly brings back the magic era of 1907, when the Coca Cola lady was the world's most glamorous advertising symbol." (Before gals had any rights whatsoever—and a beautiful time it was.) By the way, Coke and Barbie (and Wal-Mart) are now available in Indonesia, thereby enabling these two American traditions to help civilize those backward, often violent, Indonesians. Barbie as spokesdoll is an exciting development and one we hope to see more of. We'd like to see Hershey's Barbie, Lemon Pledge Barbie, Pizza Hut Barbie, perhaps even Playtex Tampon Barbie and Pepcid AC Barbie, among other exciting combos.

The news about Coca Cola Barbie reminded the Satire gals that the holidays are approaching—a time when gals can be gals, i.e., bake, shop, wrap, and decorate. Commiefemlesbos have, of course, taken over the toy industry, making it very difficult for normal folks to buy guns and other toys of destruction for boys and soft fragile pink things for girl-gals. This year, one of the Satire gals was getting gift ideas from her grandson when he intoned, "You know, boys are better than girls."

"Really?" our grandma-gal chirped, hardly daring to hope. "Why is that?"

Her grandson answered confidently, even boastfully, "Because boys have better toys."

Gals, I can't tell you how happy this interchange made us. Finally, a generation that understands what traditional values are all about: i.e., males as superior beings by virtue of their possessions; females as Barbie holding a 1907 glass of Coke. One trip to the toy store confirmed that boys are indeed exciting, adventurous, exploring, challenging, rugged individuals with a penchant for violence and murder (fine old American traditions, for sure), while girls are not.

As a public service, we are providing you with the perfect gift list for kids this holiday season.

For Boys Ages 3 and Up:

- Cooltools Race Car with screwdriver, gas can, tool box, and tire jack.

From "Hotel Satire: Boys Have Better Toys" in Z *Magazine*, November 1996, pp. 59–60. Reprinted by permission.

- All-In-One Workshop with pliers, handsaw, wrench, 4 nuts and bolts, pounding surface, and screw holes.
- Great Adventures Pirate Ship complete with flip-out cannon, built-in jail, movable telescope, and removable dinghy that fires a grappling hook. Plus a plank for enemies to walk. Plus a Pirate Island with haunting skull shape and boulder-launching palm trees to ward off angry hordes.
- Lego Mystic Mountain Time Lab with flying time boat, flaming time chair, traveling jet house, spinning hypnodisk, skeleton guard, adjustable telescope, and wacky robot.
- Lego Explorien Starship with folding wings, tilting compartments, decoding equipment, communications satellite, side wing detachable rockets, telescopic laser cannon, and ground vehicle with magnetic arm and claw.
- Kawasaki Ninja ATV from Power Wheels with realistic roar, power lock electric brakes, sturdy oversized tires, and rear mudflaps for a rugged ride.
- Alien Slime Lab, a 19-piece set where you can study samples of Red Planet Alien Skin, and test for conductivity, acidity, DNA potential, iron, and more.
- Radio-controlled Rebound 4x4, a cool all-wheel drive flip vehicle with super-fast 360 degree spins and deep-grooved, dirt-kicking, semi-pneumatic tires for off-pavement, ground-lovin' tread. This vehicle not only meets obstacles, it eats them up!
- Star Wars Action Fleet and Figure Set from the Rebel Alliance and Galactic Empire, including Hans Solo armed with assault rifle and blaster, Chewbacca with bow caster and heavy blaster rifle, plus Y-wing Star-fighter, TIE Intercepter, SLAVE 1, and Jawa Sand-crawler.
- Spiderman Action Figure Villain Set includes Rhino, Stealth Venom, Octo-Spidey, and Carnage Unleashed!
- Dragon Flyz Raptor with flapping aero wings and crushing claw action.
- Goosebumps Terror in the Graveyard Game, an eerie board game where you're trapped among the undead. Goosebumps Fright Pen records up to 12 seconds of sound on the built-in memory including: evil laugh, slurp, growl, eerie moan, scream, and ghostly gasp.
- Radio-Controlled Dagger Racer, a jet turbo dragster with race track realism, stunt shifter to show off rubber-ripping skills, burn out straight-aways, and all-out wheelies.
- X-Men Weapon X-Lab with super strong adamantium skeleton and claws to boost mutant abilities. Feed adamantium ooze into Logan, pump ooze into Wolverine, and more.
- SONY 32-Bit Playstation plus Toshinden Game CD with real-time, 360 degree visuals, 16 megabits of RAM and 8 megabits of V-Ram, button guides, ergonomically designed game controller and video adapter. Games include Beyond the Beyond, Project Horned owl, Crash Bandicoot, 2 Xtreme, Tekken 2, Wipeout XL, Project Overkill, Destruction Derby 2, NFL Gameday, Twisted Metal, Ridge Racer Revolution, Resident Evil, Street Fighter Alpha 2, Samurai Showdown 3, Jumping Flash 2, and Contra/Legacy of War.

For Girls Ages 3 and Up:

- Baby Born. She moves, cries real tears, drinks from her bottle, eats her own special food, wets and uses her own potty! Soft, pliable, she comes with terrycloth outfit, diaper, pacifier, bottle, baby dish, feeding spoon, seven food packets, potty, and baby care and instruction book. Available as Caucasian or African American.

- Take Care of Me Twins. Baby Bubbles and Burps gurgles as bubbles form on her mouth. Wipe her mouth and she burps and gets the hiccups. Baby Sniffles and Sneezes has a runny nose that needs wiping.
- Leslie Doll. She dribbles, she poops, she cries. She also comes with a hanky.
- Adrienne Doll. Her pout is amazingly lifelike and she has real human hair.
- Asian Baby has her own birth certificate!
- Baby Doll Bath Trolley where cleanliness is next to dolliness. Includes a wind-up working faucet, electronic music, basin rubber ducky, towel, brush, sponge, and baby powder dispenser.
- Melanie's Mall is a center for more than just shopping. Take the escalator to Beauty World, then head to the food court, or head out through the revolving door!
- Dream Dress Up Vanity with 3 sections for making dressing up an obsession. Accessories include makeup case, plastic perfume bottle and atomizer, comb, brush, hand mirror, blush, plastic lipstick, and portable phone for fashion emergencies.
- Fingernail Fun Salon Set has 4 fab ways to snazz up your nails: fakes, glitter, rub-on stickers, and 10 press-on color-change nails.
- My Complete Laundry Center features a front-loading washer, ironing board and iron, 6 hangers, 8 clothes pins, detergent, and fabric softener.
- Kitchenette. It's a real kitchen with two burner ranges, sink, coffee maker, cordless phone, clock, and storage cabinets.
- Easy-Bake Mix 'n' Make Center where you can prepare cool drinks and desserts with a measuring cup, cutting board, 4 ice-pop molds, a bowl, spatula, spoon and recipe cards. Plus pudding mixes!
- JoolKitz is a jewelry kit complete with bracelets, earrings, anklets, beads, earring wires, necklace clasps.
- Pretty Miss Motorized 4-Wheeler with painted-on confetti, ribbons, and a bow in front to make the road a prettier place!
- Tandem Doll Stroller with reclining seat, swivel wheels, shopping basket, sun canopy, and wind guard. Hot pink polyester.
- Beautiful Princess Jewelry Set with 21 pieces including a tiara and a scepter, as well as a heart shaped pink vanity case, a second tiara, 2 necklaces, play lipstick, and mirror.
- Supermarket Check-Out with electronic scanner that beeps, a play credit card, and pretend food.
- Dress And Dream Sit & Style Salon complete with sink, spray nozzle, pivoting trays, pretend scissors, shampoo bottle, pretend hair extensions, comb, barrette, and shatter resistant mirror.
- Girl Talk Dateline Game which combines a girls two favorite pastimes: boys and talking on the telephone.
- Mall Madness, the game where an electronic voice lets you know where to find the best buys, then you insert a credit card and make a purchase. Made of pink plastic.

- Career for Girls Game, with careers like fashion designer, school teacher, and rock star. It's updated from the 1950s.
- Slumber Party, a game where each player tries to get rid of her plastic rollers by doing stupid stunts.
- Summer Sophisticate Barbie in tailored slim, fitted, silk-look dress with pink bolero jacket in 1950s style. Accessories include: a pink hat with floral trim, pink purse with strap, sunglasses, hatbox, imitation pearl earrings, necklace, and ring. Also available: Shopping Chic Barbie, Jewel Princess Barbie, Bob Mackie Moon Goddess Barbie, Shopping Fun Barbie and Kelly, Pet Doctor Barbie, Empress Sissy Barbie, and CD-ROM Barbie with on screen fashion design, as well as Barbie Trinket Box, Barbie Fashion Watch, Barbie Radio Controlled Eddie Bauer Ford Explorer with removable seats and BBQ grill, Barbie Umbrella, Barbie Charm Bracelet, Barbie Denim Jacket, Barbie Backpack, Barbie Prom Game, Barbie Slumber Bag, Barbie Camera, Barbie Phone, Barbie Answering Machine, Barbie Roller Skates, Barbie Talking Pager and, of course, Coca Cola Barbie, as mentioned earlier.

So, this November, forget voting. Stop worrying about the direction this country is headed. Be part of the traditional values explosion at your local toy store.

Bring back 1907 when boys were boys and girls were baking, shopping, primping, and happily taking care of burping, pouting, wetting, crying, dribbling, pooping Coca Cola-pushing baby dolls.

6 | Is Your Child Developing a Healthy Sexual Identity?
Ava L. Siegler, Ph.D.

It's a boy! It's a girl! From the moment of a baby's birth, our thoughts and feelings are strongly influenced by the child's gender, a biological given. But the development of a child's sexual identity is a much more complicated process. As parents, we are constantly encouraging boys to be boys and girls to be girls, in all kinds of subtle (and not so subtle!) ways. Even though we may want to offer our children more gender-free opportunities, we still support a great many gender-based distinctions. How many girls, for instance, are given baseballs or tool sets for their birthdays—despite the fact that we'd like them to be able to play baseball or build a cabinet? And how many boys receive dolls or a sewing kit—despite the fact that we want boys to know how to nurture a baby and sew on a button?

> *Your feelings and expectations play a significant role in how comfortable your child is with his budding sexuality.*

We also become anxious when a child does not seem to be taking clear steps toward developing an *expected* sexual identity. Early signs of femininity in boys (playing with girls' toys or wanting to dress in girls' clothes) are particularly alarming. While girls who identify with a boy's world are often called tomboys and are accepted and admired, a boy who identifies with a girl's world is usually called a sissy and is excluded and demeaned. Since boys and girls learn what it means to become a man or a woman through almost 20 years of childhood and adolescence, we want to be sure we're giving our children the right signals all along. Is it all right to let a little boy pretend to be a mommy and dress up in jewelry? Wear nail polish? Play house? Is it okay to let a little girl wear pants all the time? Cut her hair like a boy's? Use a boy's nickname? It can be hard to know when our kids are on the right track and when we need to help them find direction.

Parents often split along gender lines in our responses to our child's social and sexual conflicts. A father might be more worried about protecting his son's masculine identity, while a mother may be more understanding of her son's wish to play at being both sexes. How do you know whether your child is only playing—or whether his wishes are "for real" and indicate a developmental crisis in sexual identity that needs attention?

Reprinted by permission of the author.

WILL MY CHILD BE GAY?

Answers to common concerns about kids and homosexuality

"I'm a single mom, and my son doesn't see his father much. I'm worried that he'll grow up gay because he won't have a role model."

HELPING A BOY BECOME A MAN has as much to do with female confirmation as it does with male identification. Your son can make use of many male models around him to help him mature (his grandpa, an uncle, a neighbor, a teacher, etc.).

"My husband is pretty hard on our son but very easy on our daughter. Someone told me that having a tough father can make you grow up to be homosexual."

IT'S NOT BEING TOUGH THAT'S THE PROBLEM, it's your husband's preference for your daughter. He's giving your son the message that girls get love and attention while boys get discipline and punishment. Make your husband aware of the signal he is sending.

"Our 4-year-old son has curly blond hair that I like to keep long because he looks so beautiful. Whenever strangers see him, they assume that he's a girl. could that cause him to have a sexual identity problem?"

IT'S YOUR ATTITUDE that will cause your son trouble if you continue to focus on his beauty. Strangers already misjudge his sex; cut his hair, and admire him as a boy!

Most of us are very confused about the sources of homosexual identity. Is it an inborn tendency? Is it learned behavior? It's important to realize that homosexuality is a complicated developmental outcome that probably reflects a long series of biological, psychological, and even accidental events. Playing at being the opposite sex, and particularly playing at being the opposite-sex parent, is a normal part of every child's growth and reflects his or her wish to identify with both parents. This kind of play is a rehearsal for adult life; your child is trying out both parental roles. A little boy doesn't become gay because his mom lets him dress up occasionally in her clothes, nor does a young girl become a lesbian because she wants to wear her dad's jacket.

But by the time a boy is 4 or 5 years old, a persistent wish to identify with girls along with a sustained tendency *not* to associate with boys can indicate that he is struggling with his masculine identity. Remember, the key is that this must be an exclusive and obsessive preoccupation. Often, a child's inability to construct a male or a female identity has nothing to do with homosexuality (which isn't crystallized until adolescence, when mature sexuality becomes possible). It's much more likely to mask a child's generalized fears about growing up, his anxiety about competing with his peers, or his worries about the pressures of becoming a man. The stereotypical expectations of male behavior (the rough-and-tumble of athletics, the pushing, the competition, the suppression of feelings) can seem scary to a little boy and make him want to stay a baby—or be a girl, so he can feel more protected.

A reluctance (or refusal) to determine one's sexual identity can also reflect a child's conclusion that one sex or another is favored in his family or possesses more advantages in his world. Or it can be indicative of a child's wish to fulfill (or to rebel against) a parent's sexual expectations.

What Should I Ask Myself?

Before you can address conflicts about masculinity in your child, you need to address them in yourself. Do you feel that boys are rough and crude? Have you had abusive physical or sexual experiences with men? Did your mother dominate your family, undermining your father's masculinity, and are you identifying with her and unwittingly undermining your son's manhood? Be careful you're not giving your little boy the message that it's better or safer to be a girl, or that you're not holding out gender-based expectations that your son feels unable to meet (being tough, fearless, athletic).

Little girls can also be in conflict about their sexual identity. Before you can help your daughter to feel good about herself, you'll need to figure out how you feel about being female. Were boys more valued in your family? Did you envy all of the things that boys did and feel that girls got gypped? You may be unwittingly teaching your daughter to believe that women are less fun, less important, and less interesting.

What Should I Tell My Child?

To reassure a boy who may be at odds with his developing masculinity, address his underlying fears: "It's hard to play with rough boys. It can get scary and make you wish you were still little." Distinguish between play and reality, and permit play: "It's fun to pretend to be a mommy, and I have old hats you can use when you want to play daddy." Give him opportunities to identify with a male role model. Praise him and confirm his sense of self as a boy. Most of all, let him know you like and admire men.

To help your daughter, empathize with her desires while making it clear that she is—and always will be—female, but that it's up to her what kind of girl to be. She may need to mourn the loss of her male fantasies, but your understanding will help her take pride in herself. Your delight in your own gender will assist her in feeling good about being female.

As parents, you want to let your kids express conflicts, but you don't want them to follow a misguided path. Your history, feelings, and expectations play a significant role in your child's sexual identity. If you are honest with yourself, you'll help your children feel comfortable with who and what they are.

7 | Santa, Ken, and Barbie
James Combs and Dan Nimmo

We are living in the age of the "new propaganda," and this book will show you how and why. Propaganda is pervasive in everyday life, something we are all familiar with and learn from. Because of its centrality to our lives, propaganda now constitutes a major form of social power with which we should be familiar. Keep in mind as you read this book that propaganda has consequences. It affects your life and society in a variety of ways you may not be aware of. This book should make you aware of the presence and power of propaganda. Let us begin by discussing some ways in which we can feel the presence of propaganda in our lives....

Christmas, we are told, comes but once a year. Pay attention to another common utterance about Christmas and you learn that it seems to start earlier every year. So perhaps "once a year" will soon be "all year." Be that as it may, Halloween with its ghosts and goblins no sooner ends than myriad signs of Christmas appear. Up go festive Christmas decorations in stores; newspapers, magazines, and television carry stories about the "upcoming season," then fill pages and time with Christmas advertising; soon there are parades, toy drives, charity drives, and other rituals and routines of Christmas; children 6 to 60 are inundated with TV reruns of shows with holiday themes, from "Charlie Brown's Christmas" to multiple versions of Charles Dicken's *A Christmas Carol*; and radio stations and shopping mall sound systems echo the refrains of Christmas songs, hymns, chimes, and carols. What begins in the fall helps create the "Christmas spirit" and culminates in the "Christmas season" amidst feverish rounds of shopping, traveling, visiting, and Yuletide cheer.

Presiding over this lengthy season of joy is a mythical secular deity, Santa Claus. Long since shorn of his religious origins and his punitive functions (such as punishing naughty children by withholding their gifts, a power now even denied the Grinch Who Stole Christmas), Santa Claus is a sanguine and convivial master of ceremonies offering Christmas festivity and cheer. It is correct, of course, that Christmas has long been and remains the religious celebration of the birth of Jesus; millions of Christians across the world exult in the sacred message of the season. (Also, as some skeptics annually remind Christians, the season coincides with the winter solstice celebrated in pagan antiquity). Religious meanings aside for the moment, in our secular

From *The New Propaganda: The Dictatorship of Palaver in Contemporary Politics* by James E. Combs and Dan Nimmo. Copyright © 1993 by Longman Publishing Group. Reprinted by permission of Addison-Wesley Educational Publishers Inc.

society Christmas is the occasion for activities that go beyond the pietistic. For many people, Christmas celebrates an annual ritual of the sale and exchange of material goods, not just the voicing and contemplation of sacred messages. In this milieu Santa Claus is, in the words of one observer, a "symbolic representation of materialism"—a godly if hedonistic figure urging people to join in the festive season through consumption. The message ol' Saint Nick offers to children of all ages is that the acquisition of material items is good, that at an early age they should learn how to buy and know what to consume, for the world is indeed a place of boundless abundance and unlimited consumer choice. Santa, jolly old gent of the holiday season, invites us to join in the Christmas spirit of shopping, giving and getting, and consuming. As an icon of a "consumer culture," Santa Claus is a "uniquely meaningful national hero of American materialism."[1] Kris Kringle is know by many names, but his message has long since ceased to be one of forgiveness and good cheer; rather, he is an *icon of propaganda*, a figure who represents the Christmas spirit that vested interests wish to propagate, and in which many people want to find justification for their seasonal enjoyments. Santa Claus persists as a familiar icon of Christmas not only because children want a gift-god and parents find it all charming; he endures because he is a useful symbol central to the organized propaganda effort that characterizes the holiday season.

By the end of the holidays, with the passing of Christmas Day, then New Year's Day, countless messages of the season have crossed our vision, pierced our ears, invaded our consciousness. They are messages direct and indirect, overt and covert, blatant and subtle. Individually and in combination they have provoked thought and acts—of "what to do about Christmas." And they have done more. Business analysts, ever watchful of signs of bolstered or waning "consumer confidence"—a vital element in sustaining a growing economy—read the figures on Christmas sales. Market analysts, ever watchful of signs betokening new trends in consumer spending—a vital element in charting profit and loss—study how well new products (or time-worn products given new appeal) have attracted fickle buyers. A product that becomes a Christmas fad, say the Cabbage Patch doll, can generate fortunes; a product that bombs, say a microwave version of the pop-up toaster, can be a marketing disaster. So crucial to the health of the American and world economies is the Christmas season, there is little surprise that considerable effort and expense enters into promoting the key Yuletide message: CONSUME!

What brings us this message of sanctifying consumption? Propaganda promotes the message—in slogans and jingles, splashy and colorful TV commercials, upbeat music, smiling pitchmen and -women, striking images and haunting phrases, and promises of fulfillment and happiness. And Santa Claus is an icon of propaganda: a mythical authority urging that we have a right, even a duty, to indulge at Christmastime. Christmas in the modern world has been transformed into an occasion of economic importance. Because of that importance, propaganda has become the dominant form of public economic discourse during the lengthy holiday period, the social language of communication that expedites the desired consumer behavior. That behavior is desired not only by economic interests who wish to hype Christmas sales but also by many people who have a "consuming interest" in enjoying the holiday season and respond to propaganda that suggests how they might do so. Propaganda involves both economic interests and ordinary people in a process of social learning, with both parties to the communicative transaction attempting to learn how to shape behavior at Christmastime, and indeed the year round....

Yuletime propaganda certainly surrounds us, so much that, like a muted but steady sensation of pain or pleasure, we get used to it. We think it has disappeared, but it hasn't. Consider the shopping mall, certainly a consumer's paradise offering the implicit message Shop 'Till You Drop. Suppose it is Christmas and there wanders through the mall a shopper consumed by, and bent on consuming, the spirit of the season. It is time to purchase a gift for that delightful three-year-old niece. Yelping windup puppies, a stuffed camel, a portly clown—all invite the shopper to enter a toy store. The choices are seemingly endless: war toys from assault rifles to tanks and fighter planes; board and computerized games from the perennial favorite Monopoly to Talking Baseball; and dolls, dolls, dolls, even Flo-Jo attired in a colorful running outfit. Our mall shopper pauses, surveys the multitude of goodies, then fixes a gaze on one doll in particular. It is Barbie, one of the veritable superstars of the toy industry. Certainly as deserving of an honored niche in any Toy Hall of Fame as Mickey Mouse, and more so than Snoopy (or certainly Spuds McKenzie!). Let us ponder Barbie for a moment for she (it?) has something to tell us about propaganda.

The Barbie doll is over 30 years old but shows no signs of advancing age. Over 500 million Barbies have been sold by Mattel, a toy manufacturer that claims to control 98 percent of the market for fashion dolls designed for small girls aged three to eight. Barbie is indeed fashionable. Seventy fashion designers, including Bill Blass and Christian Dior, have contributed to Barbie's wardrobe. The Barbie playset incorporates new accessories, friends, and activities each year. There are books on Barbie, a Barbie Fan Club, even a Barbie Hall of Fame. Fans can tour facilities highlighting scenes from the Barbie doll's growth, growing wardrobe, and shifting lifestyle. The Barbie name appears in a wide variety of TV ads—Barbie as rock star, Barbie in her new Ferrari, Barbie handing out with the gang at the beach or soda shoppe along with Ken, Skipper, Miko, and Teresa. Barbie opened the 1990s by joining the military—as an army captain in a deep blue evening dress with gold braid, as an air force pilot wearing a leather flight jacket, and as chief petty officer in the navy donning a "Cracker Jack" white uniform with bell-bottoms, navy blue scarf, and V-neck shirt with service ribbons. (Barbie's uniforms were designed to meet Pentagon requirements. Even her hair was shortened to meet military regulations!)

In a toy and game industry that involves many billions in retail sales annually, Barbie is a major creative and marketing success. Not bad for a doll. But is Barbie only a doll? Hardly. As parents know and child psychologists have discovered, toys are often more than toys. Children learn lessons from their toys. This is what bothers critics of the toy industry who fear that playing with toy assault rifles and zapping video fighter planes teaches instant violence as a pleasurable exercise. But what can be learned from Barbie? Does this popular doll transmit a message other than immediate play, a message of propaganda?

Like jolly ol' Saint Nick, Barbie is a cultural icon. The roll represents something more than a plaything or diversion; combined in Barbie's face, figure, and lifestyle are a host of ideas (call them symbols) about how young girls should look, act, and be. Barbie teaches young girls what growing up in American society is all about. Barbie and her boyfriend Ken teach youngsters of both sexes norms of beauty and behavior. In fact, Barbie and Ken represent a version of the American Dream—that youthful beauty never fades, nor should it be allowed to do so. The youthful accessories (wigs, makeup), furnishings, household surroundings, and costumes constitute lifestyles provided by Mattel, suggesting an endless variety of ways to keep Ken and Barbie young, vibrant, and alive! Eternal youth and beauty is to be had through the pursuit of high consumption leisure.

Did anyone, the designers and manufacturers of Barbie, for instance, *intend* to communicate a message of eternal youth through their creation? Probably not. At least, and as yet, there is no evidence of a small group of designers concocting a scheme to teach millions of girls and boys that youth is a privileged state to be preserved forever through expensive fun. No, if intentions alone are at issue, then Barbie's creators succeeded beyond their wildest expectations ($450 million in 1988 sales alone) in achieving a marketing breakthrough. Nor is it likely that those who buy Barbie dolls—parents and relatives—intend through their gifts to communicate a conscious message about eternal youth. Rather they make the purchase out of love, or to please the child, or to provide the same toys "the other kids have." In any case, the motives of both manufacturer and purchaser are likely limited to immediate monetary interests, without a clear agenda of sweeping cultural indoctrination.[2]

Yet, the Barbie Message is there: somehow children should look like, act like, and be like what Ken and Barbie "mean" in youthful imagination. Other questions: Is that the message the kid-consumers of Barbie and Ken receive? Are they recipients of a subtle message that nobody really intended but that nevertheless is there? The answer to those questions is not easily obtained. But since social observers frequently remind us of the numerous consequences that popular icons such as Ken and Barbie can have in a culture, perhaps we should not so quickly and simply take for granted the idea that our doll friends are dolls and nothing more. Consider a few other factors. The Barbie doll is the consequence of an elaborate advertising effort by Mattel designed to promote the doll and all paraphernalia that accompanies her (including Ken). Here the intended message is clear—to boost Barbie sales. As a by-product of the promotional campaign comes a second possibility about the Barbie Message, one not so obvious. Not only was Barbie sold by means of propaganda (advertising), as is any other commercial product; social observers have argued that *Barbie herself* (the doll and all she has come to represent) is implicit propaganda, a message instructing little girls in what they should want to be as they grow up. And what is that Barbie Message? Some critics see in Barbie a uniform and sinister cultural standard—a "role model" for young girls. That standard is impossible to achieve, for very few young girls will grow up flawlessly beautiful and blond. Cultural critics deem the message demeaning to women, for it implies Barbie is subservient to men in the sense of women's defining themselves by how attractive they are to equally handsome members of the opposite sex—the "well-attired and full-bodied sex object." For example, the original feminine ideal implicit in Barbie was that of cheerleader, majorette, and beauty queen, female roles involving male adoration of feminine beauty and athleticism. The Barbie Message, according to critics, is that Barbie is the lovely but dumb consumer whose major interests in life are to look pretty and to shop in order to do so (an all-consuming interest in twin senses).

By contrast, conservative critics of the Barbie phenomenon see something else in the Barbie Message. In this view, Barbie represents dangerous sensuality, a being committed to hedonism and the worship of the body beautiful to be admired and touched by men (many *Playboy* centerfolds bear a striking resemblance to the tall, willowy, blond doll). But here too, ironically, may also be confirmation of feminist ideal: namely female *independence*. Barbie now has her own substantial careers; her own credit cards; equality with males (Barbie the astronaut, the air force pilot, etc.); and achievement (one advertising slogan for Barbie is, We Girls Can Do Anything). Perhaps somewhere between these two versions of the Barbie Message is the one alluded to earlier, that is, the Barbie who never ages, endures misfortune or illness, bears children, or cries.

Whether the Barbie Message be youth, feminism, or antifeminism, it certainly does not seem at first glance to be particularly important or consequential. Yet according to some psychologists and physicians, Barbie may indeed be injurious to health. Such critics trace the fear that some young women have of growing fat in part to the value placed on looking Barbie-like. That fear may contribute to dangerous dieting, bulimia, and anorexia. Research indicates that elementary school children regard obesity as worse than a handicapping or disabling condition; that desperate and unhealthy attempts to stay thin are prevalent among girls (and some boys) even in the lower grades; and that, as measured by public opinion polls, "getting fat" is a greater fear among adolescents than nuclear war, economic depression, and parental disapproval.[3]

It is easy to overstate the extent to which Barbie might affect such anxieties in young people. The Barbie Message is not the only carrier of the ideal of beauty as shapely thinness. Quickie diets, diet products, exercise programs, and so on, constitute an ever-growing slimness industry that surely predates Ken and Barbie (witness silent movie stars Douglas Fairbanks and Lillian Gish as svelte, thin role models). Nor do Ken and Barbie alone represent the ideal of ageless youth, that is, young is good, old is bad. Youth-restoring products (facial and body balms for women, hair restorers for men), health spas, and cosmetic surgery profit from a dream promoted long before and independently of Barbie's enduring youthful beauty. (And, it should be noted, there are alternative messages: a firm named High Self-Esteem Toys, Inc., marketed what they called the Happy to Be Me doll, a less beautiful and more ordinary-looking female icon who was not thin, sexy, or rich.) For the moment, however, the Barbie image dominates, in some measure because the Barbie Message was propagated through multiple sources over a long period of time, using endless and pervasive repetition of the message to reinforce that dominance. Barbie's appeal may have been latent in American popular culture, but the manufacturer did not leave that appeal to chance.

The lesson of this extended discussion of Santa Claus and Barbie is that propaganda is not always direct, not always apparent, nor confined to what we might offhand think of as propaganda. When we see a political campaign ad or a prepared statement by a public relations spokesperson or a promotional event staged to hype a new movie, we assume that such communications are propaganda. One can often trace the specific intentions of the sources of these messages, figure that the message itself was structured to maximize its effect and calculate its appeal. But as we have seen with Santa Claus and Barbie, propaganda is not always such a clear-cut thing to identify, if for no other reason than that it is such an integral part of our everyday lives. In the final analysis, we ourselves are the carriers, the propagators, of propaganda. Propaganda works because it has become integrated into our habits of communication, habits that we value and respond to because they promise desirable consequences for our lives. In a larger sense, propaganda has become a form of communication that is inextricably interwoven into the process of social communication in modern society, the persistent ways in which we structure and practice communications in order to perpetuate or change social forms, including structures of power and prestige as well as our common practices. When we go to the mall before Christmas and buy a Barbie doll, or wear a Hard Rock Cafe T-shirt, or put a political bumper sticker on our car, or any of innumerable daily actions, we have become part of the process of *social propagandizing*. Even though we all would like to believe that we are immune to the appeals and practices of propaganda, the very ubiquity and success of propaganda suggests that we are not. It may be the case that we are a part of the propaganda process without being aware of it and all that it entails. This may be a large burden to put upon Barbie and Santa Claus, not to mention ourselves; nevertheless, in order to understand propaganda we have to grasp the fact that it is not exotic or remote but is a part of the way of life of modern society....

...Although the new propaganda pervades and envelopes our social world so that it seems to be the communication environment rather than a portion of it, recall that we said earlier that propaganda is not *everything*. To set the new propaganda off from other means of communicating, let us consider various ways we talk with one another. Note that we say "with" one another, not "to" one another. For talk, be it informal chattering, a formal speech, or even mass communication such as a TV ad or movie preview, involves an exchange, that is, some degree of reciprocity. In conversation or oratory, a person talks, others listen, and, even as listeners, talk back by being attentive or inattentive. Gestures, nods, frowns, smiles, and other nonverbal means "talk" as well as do comments, questions, and oral expressions. Barbie and Ken advertised on television to an unseen audience of millions yield a delayed response—in the form of sales or nonsales—that is the transuasional two-way street of the Barbie Message. Similarly, a president of the United States addresses the nation on television; citizens talk back via public opinion polls, letters of opposition or support, discussion or nondiscussion of the speech, indeed even by not watching and by ignoring a president trying hard to be taken seriously. We "talk" to each other both intimately and remotely, and get and give "feedback" to the eternal conversation we as social beings are engaged in all our lives.

In what ways, then, do we talk with one another? Political scientist David V. J. Bell has noted that potentially all talk affects others; when it does, he writes, it by definition has political overtones and, thereby, is political talk. Bell describes three forms of political talk.[4] One is *power talk*, but it is more aptly labeled *force talk*. Here an individual, group, organization, or other "talker" wants another to do or not to do something. The message, according to Bell, is phrased as "If you do X, I will do Y." Implied in the utterance is that the *I* has the resources to promise or threaten the *you* into compliance. In short, one person can force another to comply. "Memorize my lectures and talk (write) them back to me on the exam and I will give you an A in the course; fail to do so and you get an F." "Obey the law or go to jail" carries a more obvious political sanction.

Sometimes people have such complete faith in a talker that promises or threats are unnecessary. "Do X" or "Don't do X" are sufficient statements. Such *authority talk* derives from an unquestioned devotion to authority. Consider the French emperor Napoleon or Nazi Germany's Adolf Hitler at the zenith of their respective regimes. So devoted were many of their followers that any wish from either was a literal command to the populace. Or think back to our old Christmas friend, Santa Claus, during an earlier era when children regarded him as an omniscient, omnipresent observer of their behavior. The words of a popular Christmas ditty spoke the message of authority talk: "Better not cry, better not pout" for "he's making a list and checking it twice, going to find out who's naughty and nice." Beware; "Santa Claus is coming to town."

Napoleon and Hitler are dead, and Santa all jolly and forgiving, not stern. But we still encounter a great deal of authority talk. A reputation for expertise and popularity derived from it—acquired in, say, movies, professional sports, or rock music—provides authority to speak on other matters, including political matters. Athletes, TV weathercasters, movie stars, and other celebrities attempt to associate their popular authority ("This is good because you all know me and can believe me that it is") with not only products and services, but also causes, cultural events, and political candidates. Indeed, Ronald Reagan began as a movie star, who then utilized his considerable celebrity to endorse products (General Electric) and then candidates (Barry Goldwater), paving the way for his successful effort to become a political authority himself, as candidate, governor of California, and president.

As the above examples indicate, force and authority talk can be enlisted to propagate ideas and actions. Still, the talk emphasized in propaganda is usually neither that of force nor authority per se, but rather *influence talk*—David Bell's third form. "If you do X, *you* will [get, have, feel, experience, gain, etc.] Y" is the message of influence. Unlike force talk where the *I* has the capacity to reward or punish, in influence talk the *you* can supply Y but the *I* cannot. "Memorize my lectures or fail" is at best a hollow choice; "don't cry, don't pout" leaves no choice for the youngster's childlike faith in Santa's omnipotence. "*If* you memorize," "*if* you behave," "*if* you vote for me," then you will get an A, Christmas gifts, or a reduction in income taxes, leaves it up to *you* without force or command. Rather than suasive force or suasive authority, the suasion of influence emphasizes that you can choose good things for yourself if you will only make the right choice. Rather than the voice of force that propagates the message "Do as I say or else," or the voice of authority that says "Do as I say because I'm to be believed and obeyed," the voice of influence says "If you choose to do as I say, your choice will be a wise one that will pay off for you." Traditionally, propaganda talk can involve all three messages. A military ruler can use the mass media to help enforce martial law by communicating to people that if they oppose such rule they will be shot. A retired politician may go on the air in days before an election to endorse a candidate, attempting to associate his past authority with the new aspirant to office. But a moment's reflection also makes clear that *in the new propaganda, influence talk has gained a new primacy.*

As *primarily* influence talk, the new propaganda brings both *I* and *you*, both the seed and the culture, into prominent roles in propagating ideas and actions. In horticulture neither seed nor culture alone is sufficient. Seed and culture, mutually reinforcing growth, become one. In influence talk *I* and *you* become one, that is, *we*. In this respect influence talk incorporates precisely the type of persuasion (explicit shaping of beliefs) and suasion (implicit suspension of disbelief) we described previously. One writer on propaganda, Paul Kecskemeti, puts it thus:

> In other words, persuasion requires, ideally speaking, complete emotional and affective resonance between the persuader and the audience. As the propagandist develops his master theme. "There are the sources of your deprivations, and here are the means for removing them," he must not encounter any emotional or affective resistance.[5]

And, emphasizing that what we call the *I* and *you* become *we*, he says "the propagandist voices the propagandees' own feelings." For, in language that sets propaganda apart from force/authority talk,

> "Resonance" implies that the recipient does not experience the master theme or propaganda myth as a belief imposed upon him by an outside authority to which he is required or committed to defer. To be persuasive, the propaganda theme has to be perceived as coming from within. The

propagandist's ideal role in relation to the propagandee is that of alter ego, someone giving expression to the recipient's own concerns, tensions, aspirations, and hopes.[6]

What sets the new propaganda off from being *everything*, thus, is that now the dominant form of talk in propagating ideas and actions is influence talk. Influence talk comes in many varieties; one variety is particularly present in the new propaganda. Any form of talk consists of symbols, that is, something—a word, gesture, picture, object, person, and so on—that stands for, or represents, something else. The word *dog* represents a four-footed canine. Ken and Barbie represent dolls, lifestyles, and profits. The ideas, objects, places, or whatever symbols represent can be specific or ambiguous. A dog is a dog, but Barbie's referent is more ambiguous and may be one or all of the three mentioned in the above sentence. Whether the symbols are specific or vague in what they represent, they compose, singularly or in combination, talk, or to use the American vernacular, *palaver*....

Talk itself has contrasting styles. That is, someone may speak to us in terse, clipped, brief utterances. "We have known since man first landed on the moon that it is not made of green cheese." That is a succinct way of saying what could be expressed in along, rambling, qualified, utterance replete with confusing allusions. Talk, influence talk included, thus consists of specific and/or ambiguous symbols couched in succinct and/or confusing styles. Using these contrasts in symbols and styles we can say that propaganda as influence talk comes in four major varieties:

- *Informative:* succinct, specific comments.
- *Evaluative:* extended, perhaps confusing, specific utterances.
- *Expressive:* succinct, but ambiguous statements.
- *Palaver:* extended, often confusing, messages.

"Congressman Clark is 28 years old; the U.S. Constitution sets a minimum age of 35 to be president; the congressman cannot seek the office now." The message is to the point and informative. People may or may not pay attention, so its propagation is not guaranteed. In either event, Clark is ineligible for the presidency at the moment. Clark ages 10 years and a political organization distributes a 30-page document opposing his candidacy for president; it characterizes him as a communist fascist, free-trading protectionist, workaholic malingerer, gay womanizer, ascetic libertine, and on and on. The document is, in this instance, contradictory and, hence, confusing. But even if all the contradictions were removed, its extended account of why one should not support Clark is evaluative. "We are the world, we are the children," sing Clark supporters, expressing in vague, terse lyrics what they are, but informing us little about Clark's qualifications, an example of expressive propaganda. Finally, Clark wins. In his inaugural address—lasting 45 minutes—he rambles on in vague ways that his administration will seek the "New Society: retaining in millions of ways (unspecified) the heritage of the old, the future of the past, and the past of the present!" That is palaver, defined as dictionaries do, as *talk that charms or beguiles.*

Just as propaganda incorporates force and authority talk into an overarching form of influence talk, so does the new propaganda employ informative, evaluative, and expressive messages, but as adjuncts *primarily* of palaver. The palaver emphasis thus joins the characteristics—pervasiveness, intended and unintended consequences, dramas of courtship—that distinguish the new propaganda. One of the first persons to examine propaganda in a scholarly way, Harold Lasswell, writing in 1927 of earlier forms of propaganda, said, "Democracy has proclaimed the dictatorship of palaver, and the technique of dictating to the dictator is named propaganda."[7] Techniques of new propaganda practice, exalt, and deify palaver while courting, beguiling, and charming people in their everyday lives. Palaver does so with people's willing cooperation, and often at their own instigation. For palaver is the form of talk that engages us in profusions of big talk, circular reasoning, circumlocutions, jawboning and babbling, parleying and cajoling, speaking in riddles, talking our way out of trouble, and so on endlessly. The word *palaver* is apparently derived from the Latin *parabola* (parable, speech, circle), connoting the profusion of talking. In the modern age, palavering is the kind of talk appropriate to the conduct of the new propaganda.

Political, cultural, and commercial palaver thus abound in the world of talk we inhabit. Thus we (the union of *I* and *you*) propagate a daily crop of political spectacles that include dramas of presidential visits to Tokyo, Beijing, Moscow, Warsaw, Paris: of pageants, celebrations, campaign hoopla, the ecstacy of political victory, and the agony of defeat; of officeholders and officeseekers driven from public life because of illicit love affairs, scandals, or gossip; of an inexhaustible supply of congressional hearings full of endless talk and bickering; and of terrorist kidnappings, murder, bombings, accompanied by the profusion of talk about how to deal with terrorists, how to get hostages released, and how to solve the terrorist problem. We are the cultural host of daily talk about school, not to mention talk in school: what's wrong with school, why we need more schooling, the role of school in international competition, whether the German or Japanese schools are better and so on. *We* are the seedbeds for commercial advertising, as witness this ad for the Barbie We Girls Can Do Anything Game:

> *WE GIRLS CAN DO ANYTHING! What will you be when you grow up? That's what young girls learn, playing this fun game. An astronaut, a movie star, a lawyer, a singer or maybe a dancer? Young girls work their way around this board to fulfill their goals and dreams! Join Barbie for lots of imaginative and learning fun. For 2-4 players, ages 5 and up.*[8]

Barbie doll advertising may have originated to sell dolls to little girls; now it sells little girls to the "Anything" of imagination. All in all, in this babble of voices that rains upon us daily is propaganda, which has become the modern form of communication that often emerges from social palaver as the kind of talk that has the most influence, produces the most effect, and has the most social consequences. Talk is cheap, but some talk, especially well-said propaganda, can emerge from the torrent as influential beyond any other way of saying. In that case, such a form of talk becomes a valuable and indispensable part of the ideoculture, defining what we communicate by how we communicate. Propaganda is the palaver of the present that charms and beguiles us more than any other kind of public talk. In such a world, propaganda propagates itself, since it is seen as equal to the task of successful propagation.

In retrospect, this chapter has introduced the interested reader to a diverse crop of ideas about the modern ideoculture of propagation (the process of spreading ideas that may or may not take root), the concomitant practice of propagandizing (the interested activity of propagation), and the form of communication called propaganda (how we most successfully communicate ideas to large groups of people in the modern world). We attempted to avoid confining the process to the putative intentions of the propagator, in part because that tends to restrict propaganda to a rational intender who deceives us into believing his or her palaver. The deception model has its merits, since propaganda is often-times deceptive; but it is inadequate, because of the problems with imputing intention we have pointed out, and also because propaganda is in many cases anything but deceptive. Sometimes propaganda messages are quite straightforward (we sell pork chops at price X), and indeed that is often the best strategy. We have also tried to avoid the information model, the notion—usually put forward by the defenders, and beneficiaries, of propaganda—that it simply provides information to consumers, potential students, voters, and so on, and is a valuable form of social advice and advocacy. This implies that propaganda is either harmless or undeceptive, and we cannot here accept that argument that it has no consequences, positive or negative, nor that it cannot be used by clever propagators to achieve results that are hidden from those "targeted" for a desired effect.

Instead, we have emphasized that the new propaganda is a modern process of learning, involving us in an imaginative activity of social learning that directs and mobilizes our poetic natures and pragmatic interests toward objects in our environment that we learn to desire. A massive propaganda industry has arisen in the modern world to help us in that learning, but in the final analysis propaganda exists, and succeeds, because we are both used to it and find it useful, understand its poetry and find that poetry both enjoyable and instructive. Once we see ourselves as part of the propaganda process, we can then know that our complicit understanding of propaganda has helped make it the most powerful medium of social learning in the modern world. And we are well on the way toward self-knowledge, learning how to make ourselves more autonomous form the influences of such a powerful medium, or at least to understand one of the major communicative forces at work in the modern world.

We noted above that much of propaganda works because it is "communication-pleasure," something that is enjoyable in itself but also speaks to our interests. A TV spot ad, a movie preview, a promotional tape may impress us because it is fun to watch, complemented by the fact that we come to believe that we will get something out of it. It should be noted that propaganda can also involve messages that are "communication-pain." Children subjected to patriotic or religious instruction often find such learning painful. Similarly, much school, military, or commercial propaganda is painful, although sometimes it is effective (making you a better student or soldier, and breaking down "sales resistance" to buying a car or insurance), and sometimes it is ineffective (decades of communist indoctrination that pervaded Eastern European and Soviet society apparently didn't take).[9] But it should also be said that understanding a subject such as propaganda is not all pleasurable. Readers will find some of this book fun and entertaining, and will learn from it. But ultimately coming to understand, and in a sense thereby freeing oneself from, propaganda, involves a modicum of work, self-analysis, and "real-world" application, which is more or less painful. The authors contend that the effort is worth it. Perhaps you cannot escape propaganda, or even make yourself totally immune to it, but at least through effort you can understand what it means to be a part of the propaganda process that characterizes the time and place in which you live, and what it would mean to know enough about propaganda to be freed from it....

NOTES

[1] Russell W. Belk, "A Child's Christmas in America: Santa Claus as Deity, Consumption as Religion," *Journal of American Culture* (forthcoming).

[2] BillyBoy Collection, *Barbie: Her Life and Times with Dolls and Documents from the BillyBoy Collection* (New York: Crown, 1987); Jeanne Marie Laskas, "Our Barbies, Our Selves," *Chicago Tribune Magazine*, May 7, 1989, 37-40, 42; Robert Goldsborough, "Billion-Dollar Barbie the Biggest Hit with Kids," *Advertising Age* 58 (November 8, 1988): 22; *Barbie: The Magazine for Girls*, Winter 1989 (Welsh Publishing).

[3] Robert Goldsborough, "Billion-Dollar barbie the Biggest Hit with Kids," *Advertising Age* 58 (November 8, 1988): 22; Jeanne Marie Laskas, "Our Barbies, Our Selves," *Chicago Tribune Magazine*, May 7, 1989, 37-42; Terrence H. Witkowski, "Advertising Images of Thinness" (Paper presented at the annual conference of the Popular Culture Association, 1985); Linda Lazier-Smith, "Media Images, Advertising, and Ideal Body Shapes; Marketing Eating Disorders" (Paper presented at the annual conference of the Popular Culture Association, 1987).

[4] David V. J. Bell, *Power, Influence, and Authority* (New York: Oxford University Press, 1975).

[5] Paul Kecskemeti, "Propaganda" in Ithiel de Sola Pool, Frederick W. Frey, Wilbur Schramm, Nathan Maccoby, and Edwin B. Parker, eds., *Handbook of Communication* (Chicago: Rand McNally, 1975), p. 864. Compare Kecskemeti's forms of talk with those of David Bell, and with those employed here.

[6] Kecskemeti, "Propaganda," p. 864 (emphasis added).

[7] Harold D. Lasswell, "The Theory of Political Propaganda," *American Political Science Review* 21 (1927): 631.

[8] The ad appears in a mail-order catalog, "Pan-Orama Gifts," (Fall, 1989), p. 33.

[9] William Stephenson, *The Play Theory of Mass Communication* (Chicago: University of Chicago Press, 1967).

8 | McDonaldization

George Ritzer

. . .

McDonald's as "Americana," Sacred "Icon," and at 35,000 Feet

McDonald's as well as its many clones have become ubiquitous and immediately recognizable symbols throughout the United States as well as much of the rest of the world. For example, when plans were afoot to raze Ray Kroc's first McDonald's outlet, hundreds of letters poured into McDonald's headquarters, including the following:

> *Please don't tear it down!... Your company's name is a household word, not only in the United States of America, but all over the world. To destroy this major artifact of contemporary culture would, indeed, destroy part of the faith the people of the world have in your company.*

In the end, the outlet was not torn down, but rather turned into a museum! Said a McDonald's executive, explaining the move, "McDonald's... is really a part of Americana." Similarly, when Pizza Hut opened in Moscow in 1990, a Russian student said, "It's a piece of America."

In fact, McDonald's is such a powerful symbol that we have come to give many businesses nicknames beginning with *Mc* in order to indicate that they follow the McDonald's model. Examples include "*Mc*Dentists" and "*Mc*Doctors" (for drive-in clinics designed to deal quickly and efficiently with minor dental and medical problems), "*Mc*Child" Care Centers (for child care centers like Kinder-Care), "*Mc*Stables" (for the nationwide racehorse training operation of Wayne Lucas), and "*Mc*Paper" (for the newspaper *USA TODAY* and its short news articles often called "News *Mc*Nuggets"). When *USA TODAY* began an aborted television program modeled after the newspaper, some began to call it "News *Mc*Rather."

McDonald's has come to occupy a central place in popular culture. It can be a big event when a new McDonald's opens in a small town. Said one Maryland high school student at such an event, "Nothing this exciting ever happens in Dale City." Newspapers cover fast-food business developments; the opening of the McDonald's in Beijing was big news. McDonald's is spoofed or treated with reverence on television programs and in the movies. A skit on the television show *Saturday Night Live* makes fun of the specialization of such businesses by detailing the trials and tribulations of a franchise that sells nothing but Scotch tape. The movie *Coming to America* casts Eddie Murphy as an African prince whose introduction to America includes a job at "McDowell's," a thinly disguised McDonald's. In *Moscow on the Hudson,* Robin Williams, newly arrived from Russia, obtains a job at McDonald's. H.G. Wells, a central character in the movie *Time After Time,* finds himself transported to the modern world of McDonald's, where he tries to order the tea he was accustomed to drinking in Victorian England. In *Sleeper,* Woody Allen awakens in the future only to encounter a McDonald's. Finally, *Tin Men,* which shows the passage from the era of the Cadillac to that of the Volkswagen, ends with the heroes driving off into a future represented by a huge golden arch looming in the distance.

Many people identify strongly with McDonald's; in fact to some it has become a sacred institution. On the opening of the McDonald's in Moscow, one journalist described it as the "ultimate icon of Americana," while a worker spoke of it "as if it were the Cathedral in Chartres ... a place to experience 'celestial joy.'" Kowinski argues that shopping malls—which we will show to be crucial to McDonaldization—are the modern "cathedrals of consumption" to which we go to practice our "consumer religion." Similarly, a visit to what we shall see is another central element of our McDonaldized society, Walt Disney World, has been described as "the middle-class haj, the compulsory visit to the sunbaked holy city."

McDonald's has achieved its exalted position as a result of the fact that virtually all Americans, and many of those from other countries, have passed through its golden arches, often on innumerable occasions. Furthermore, we have all been bombarded by commercials extolling McDonald's virtues. These commercials have been tailored to different audiences. Some are aimed at young children watching Saturday morning cartoons. Others point toward young adults watching prime-time programs. Still others are oriented toward grandparents who might be coaxed into taking their grandchildren to McDonald's. In addition, McDonald's commercials change as the chain introduces new foods (such as breakfast burritos), creates new contests, and ties its products to things such as new motion pictures. These ever-present commercials, combined with the fact that we cannot drive very far without having a McDonald's pop into view, have served to embed McDonald's deep into our consciousness. In a survey taken in 1986, 96 percent of the schoolchildren polled were able to identify Ronald McDonald, making him second only to Santa Claus in name recognition.

Over the years McDonald's has appealed to us on a variety of different grounds. The restaurants themselves are depicted as spick and span, the food is said to be fresh and nutritious, the employees are shown to be young and eager, the managers appear gentle and caring, and the dining experience itself seems to be fun-filled. We are even led to believe that we contribute, at least indirectly, to charities by supporting the company that supports Ronald McDonald homes for sick children.

McDonald's has continually extended its reach, within American society and beyond. It began as a suburban and medium-sized-town phenomenon, but in recent years it has moved into big cities not only in the United States, but also in many other parts of the world. Fast-food outlets can now be found in New York's Times Square as well as on the Champs Élysées in Paris. They have also now migrated into smaller towns that supposedly could not support such a restaurant. At first, McDonald's and its fastfood clones settled on specific strips of road, such as Route 161 in Columbus, Ohio. Said one local resident, "You want something for the stomach? ... Drive that car down Route 161 and you'll see more eating than you ever saw in your life."

Although such strips continue to flourish, fast-food restaurants are now far more geographically dispersed.

Another significant expansion has occurred more recently as fast-food restaurants have moved onto college campuses, instead of being content, as they have in the past, merely to dominate the strips that surround many campuses. Installed on college campuses with the seeming approval of college administrations, McDonald's is in a position to further influence the lifestyle of the younger generation.

Another, even more recent, incursion has occurred: Fast-food restaurants are taking over the restaurant business on the nation's highways. Now we no longer need to leave the road to dine in our favorite fast-food restaurant. We can stop for fast food and then proceed with our trip, which is likely to end in another community that has about the same density and mix of fast-food restaurants as the locale we left behind. Also in the travel realm, fast-food restaurants are more and more apt to be found in railway stations and airports and even on the tray tables of in-flight meals. The following advertisement appeared on September 17, 1991, in the *Washington Post* (and *The New York Times*): "Where else at 35,000 feet can you get a McDonald's meal like this for your kids? Only on United's Orlando flights." Thus, children can now get McDonald's fare on United Airline's flights to Orlando. How soon before adults can have the same option? How much longer before such meals will be available on all United flights? On all flights everywhere by every carrier?

In other sectors of society, the influence of fast-food restaurants has been more subtle, but no less profound. Few high schools and grade schools have in-house fast-food restaurants, but many have had to alter school cafeteria menus and procedures so that fast food is readily and continually available to children and teenagers. Apples, yogurt, and milk may go straight into the trash can, but hamburgers, fries, and shakes are devoured. Things may be about to change dramatically, however, since Domino's, in conjunction with Marriott, has recently signed an agreement to market Domino's pizza in school cafeterias that are run by Marriott, which presently serves 200 school systems in 20 states and about a 120 million meals a year. The effort to hook schoolchildren on fast food, long a goal of advertisements aimed at this population, reached something of a peak in Illinois where McDonald's outlets operated a program called "A for Cheeseburger." Students who received an A on their report cards were rewarded with a free cheeseburger, thereby linking success in school with McDonald's.

The military has been pressed into offering fast-food menus on its bases and on its ships. Despite the criticisms by physicians and nutritionists, fast-food outlets are increasingly turning up *inside* hospitals. No homes have a McDonald's of their own, but dining within the home has been influenced by the fast-food restaurant. Home-cooked meals often resemble those available in fast-food restaurants. Frozen, microwavable, and preprepared foods, also bearing a striking resemblance to McDonald's meals and increasingly modeled after them, often find their way to the dinner table. Then there is the home delivery of fast foods, especially pizza, as revolutionized by Domino's.

Dunkin' Donuts, "Critter Watch," and "The McDonald's of Sex"

Clearly, McDonald's has not been alone in pressing the fast-food model on American society and the rest of the world. Other fastfood giants, such as Burger King, Wendy's, Hardee's, Arby's, Big-Boy, Dairy Queen, TCBY, Denny's, Sizzler, Kentucky Fried Chicken, Popeye's, Taco Bell,

Chi Chi's, Pizza Hut, Domino's, Long John Silver, Baskin-Robbins, and Dunkin' Donuts, have played a key role, as have the innumerable other businesses built on the principles of the fast-food restaurant.

Even the derivatives of McDonald's are, in turn, having their own influence. For example, the success of *USA TODAY* has led to changes in many newspapers across the nation, for example, shorter stories and color weather maps. As one *USA TODAY* editor put it, "The same newspaper editors who call us McPaper have been stealing our McNuggets." The influence of *USA TODAY* is blatantly manifest in the *Boca Raton News,* a Knight-Ridder newspaper. This newspaper is described as "a sort of smorgasbord of snippets, a newspaper that slices and dices the news into even smaller portions than does *USA TODAY,* spicing it with color graphics and fun facts and cute features like 'Today's Hero' and 'Critter Watch'." As in *USA TODAY,* stories in the *Boca Raton News* usually do not jump from one page to another; they start and finish on the same page. In order to meet this need, long and complex stories often have to be reduced to a few paragraphs. Much of a story's context, and much of what the principals have to say, is severely cut back or omitted entirely. With its emphasis on light and celebrity news, its color maps and graphics, the main function of the newspaper seems to be to entertain.

One issue to be addressed in this book is whether McDonaldization is inexorable and will therefore come to insinuate itself into every aspect of our society and our lives. In the movie *Sleeper,* Woody Allen not only created a futuristic world in which McDonald's was an important and highly visible element, but he also envisioned a society in which even sex underwent the process of McDonaldization. The denizens of his future world were able to enter a machine called an "orgasmatron" that allowed them to experience an orgasm without going through the muss and fuss of sexual intercourse.

In fact, sex, like virtually every other sector of society, has undergone a process of McDonaldization. "Dial-a-porn" allows us to have intimate, sexually explicit, even obscene, conversations with people we have never met and probably never will meet. There is great specialization here, and dialing numbers like 555-FOXX will lead to a very different phone message than dialing 555-SEXY. Escort services advertise a wide range of available sex partners. Highly specialized pornographic movies (heterosexual, homosexual, sex with children, sex with animals) can he seen at urban multiplexes and are available at local video stores for viewing in the comfort of our living rooms. Various technologies (vibrators, as an example) enhance the ability of people to have sex on their own without the bother of having to deal with a human partner. In New York City, an official called a three-story pornographic center "the McDonald's of sex" because of its "cookie-cutter cleanliness and compliance with the law." The McDonaldization of sex suggests that no aspect of our lives is safe from it.

The Dimensions of McDonaldization: From Drive-Throughs to Uncomfortable Seats

Even if some domains are able to resist McDonaldization, this book intends to demonstrate that many other aspects of society are being, or will be, McDonaldized. This raises the issue of why the McDonald's model has proven so irresistible. Four basic and alluring dimensions lie at the heart of the success of the McDonald's model and, more generally, of the process of McDonaldization.

First, McDonald's offers *efficiency*. That is, the McDonald's system offers us the optimum method for getting from one point to another. Most generally, this means that McDonald's proffers the best available means of getting us from a state of being hungry to a state of being full. (Similarly, Woody Allen's orgasmatron offered an efficient method for getting us from quiescence to sexual stimulation to sexual gratification.) Other institutions, fashioned on the McDonald's model, offer us similar efficiency in losing weight, lubricating our cars, filling eyeglass prescriptions, or completing income tax forms. In a fast-paced society in which both parents are likely to work, or where there may be only a single parent, efficiently satisfying the hunger and many other needs of people is very attractive. In a highly mobile society in which people are rushing, usually by car, from one spot to another, the efficiency of a fast-food meal, perhaps without leaving one's car while passing by the drive-through window, often proves impossible to resist. The fast-food model offers us, or at least appears to offer us, an efficient method for satisfying many of our needs.

Second, McDonald's offers us food and service that can be easily *quantified and calculated*. In effect, McDonald's seems to offer us "more bang for the buck." (One of its recent innovations, in response to the growth of other fast-food franchises, is to proffer "value meals" at discounted prices.) We often feel that we are getting a lot of food for a modest amount of money. Quantity has become equivalent to quality; a lot of something means it must be good. As two observers of contemporary American culture put it, "As a culture, we tend to believe deeply that in general 'bigger is better.'" Thus, we order the *Quarter Pounder*, the *Big* Mac, the *large* fries. We can quantify all of these things and feel that we are getting a lot of food, and, in return, we appear to be shelling out only a nominal sum of money. This calculus, of course, ignores an important point: the mushrooming of fast-food outlets, and the spread of the model to many other businesses, indicates that our calculation is illusory and it is the owners who are getting the best of the deal.

There is another kind of calculation involved in the success of McDonald's—a calculation involving time. People often, at least implicitly, calculate how much time it will take them to drive to McDonald's, eat their food, and return home and then compare that interval to the amount of time required to prepare the food at home. They often conclude, rightly or wrongly, that it will take less time to go and eat at the fast-food restaurant than to eat at home. This time calculation is a key factor in the success of Domino's and other home-delivery franchises, because to patronize them people do not even need to leave their homes. To take another notable example, Lens Crafters promises us "Glasses fast, glasses in one hour." Some McDonaldized institutions have come to combine the emphases on time and money. Domino's promises pizza delivery in one-half hour, or the pizza is free. Pizza Hut will serve us a personal pan pizza in five minutes, or it, too, will be free.

Third, McDonald's offers us *predictability*. We know that the Egg McMuffin we eat in New York will be, for all intents and purposes, identical to those we have eaten in Chicago and Los Angeles. We also know that the one we order next week or next year will be identical to the one we eat today. There is great comfort in knowing that McDonald's offers no surprises, that the food we eat at one time or in one place will be identical to the food we eat at another time or in another place. We know that the next Egg McMuffin we eat will not be awful, but we also know that it will not be exceptionally delicious. The success of the McDonald's model indicates that many people have come to prefer a world in which there are no surprises.

Fourth and finally, *control*, especially through the *substitution of nonhuman for human technology*, is exerted over the human beings who enter the world of McDonald's. The humans who work in fast-food restaurants are trained to do a very limited number of things in precisely the way they are told to do them. Managers and inspectors make sure that workers toe the line. The human beings who eat in fast-food restaurants are also controlled, albeit (usually) more subtly and indirectly. Lines, limited menus, few options, and uncomfortable seats all lead diners to do what the management wishes them to do—eat quickly and leave. Further, the drive-through (and in some cases walk-through) window leads diners to first leave and then eat rapidly. This attribute has most recently been extended by the Domino's model, according to which customers are expected to *never* come, yet still eat speedily.

McDonald's also controls people by using nonhuman technology to replace human workers. Human workers, no matter how well they are programmed and controlled, can foul up the operation of the system. A slow or indolent worker can make the preparation and delivery of a Big Mac inefficient. A worker who refuses to follow the rules can leave the pickles or special sauce off a hamburger, thereby making for unpredictability. And a distracted worker can put too few fries in the box, making an order of large fries seem awfully skimpy. For these and other reasons, McDonald's is compelled to steadily replace human beings with nonhuman technologies, such as the soft-drink dispenser that shuts itself off when the glass is full, the french-fry machine that rings when the fries are crisp, the preprogrammed cash register that eliminates the need for the cashier to calculate prices and amounts, and, perhaps at some future time, the robot capable of making hamburgers. (Experimental robots of this type already exist.) All of these technologies permit greater control over the human beings involved in the fast-food restaurant. The result is that McDonald's is able to reassure customers about the nature of the employee to be encountered and the nature of the service to be obtained.

In sum, McDonald's (and the McDonald's model) has succeeded because it offers the consumer efficiency and predictability, and because it seems to offer the diner a lot of food for little money and a slight expenditure of effort. It has also flourished because it has been able to exert greater control through nonhuman technologies over both employees and customers, leading them to behave the way the organization wishes them to. The substitution of nonhuman for human technologies has also allowed the fast-food restaurant to deliver its fare increasingly more efficiently and predictably. Thus, there are good, solid reasons why McDonald's has succeeded so phenomenally and why the process of McDonaldization continues unabated.

A Critique of McDonaldization: The Irrationality of Rationality

There is a downside to all of this. We can think of efficiency, predictability, calculability, and control through nonhuman technology as the basic components of a *rational* system. However, as we shall see in later chapters, rational systems often spawn irrationalities. The downside of McDonaldization will be dealt with most systematically under the heading of the *irrationality of rationality*. Another way of saying this is that rational systems serve to deny human reason; rational systems can be unreasonable.

For example, the fast-food restaurant is often a dehumanizing setting in which to eat or work. People lining up for a burger, or waiting in the drive-through line, often feel as if they are dining on an assembly line, and those who prepare the burgers often appear to be working on a burger assembly line. Assembly lines are hardly human settings in which to eat, and they have been shown to be inhuman settings in which to work. As we will see, dehumanization is only one of many ways in which the highly rationalized fast-food restaurant is extremely irrational.

Of course, the criticisms of the irrationality of the fast-food restaurant will be extended to all facets of our McDonaldizing world. This extension has recently been underscored and legitimated at the opening of Euro DisneyLand outside Paris. A French socialist politician acknowledged the link between Disney and McDonald's as well as their common negative effects when he said that Euro Disney will "bombard France with uprooted creations that are to culture what fast food is to gastronomy."

Such critiques lead to a question: Is the headlong rush toward McDonaldization around the world advantageous or not? There are great gains to be made from McDonaldization, some of which will be discussed below. But there are also great costs and enormous risks, which this book will focus on. Ultimately, we must ask whether the creation of these rationalized systems creates an even greater number of irrationalities. At the minimum, we need to be aware of the costs associated with McDonaldization. McDonald's and other purveyors of the fast-food model spend billions of dollars each year outlining the benefits to be derived from their system. However, the critics of the system have few outlets for their ideas. There are no commercials on Saturday morning between cartoons warning children of the dangers associated with fast-food restaurants. Although few children are likely to read this book, it is aimed, at least in part, at their parents (or parents-to be) in the hope that it will serve as a caution that might be passed on to their children.

A legitimate question may be raised about this analysis: Is this critique of McDonaldization animated by a romanticization of the past and an impossible desire to return to a world that no longer exists? For some critics, this is certainly the case. They remember the time when life was slower, less efficient, had more surprises, when people were freer, and when one was more likely to deal with a human being than a robot or a computer. Although they have a point, these critics have undoubtedly exaggerated the positive aspects of a world before McDonald's, and they have certainly tended to forget the liabilities associated with such a world. More importantly, they do not seem to realize that we are *not* returning to such a world. The increase in the number of people, the acceleration in technological change, the increasing pace of life—all this and more make it impossible to go back to a nonrationalized world, if it ever existed, of home-cooked meals, traditional restaurant dinners, high-quality foods, meals loaded with surprises, and restaurants populated only by workers free to fully express their creativity.

While one basis for a critique of McDonaldization is the past, another is the future. The future in this sense is what people have the potential to be if they are unfettered by the constraints of rational systems. This critique holds that people have the potential to be far more thoughtful, skillful, creative, and well-rounded than they now are, yet they are unable to express this potential because of the constraints of a rationalized world. If the world were less rationalized, or even derationalized, people would be better able to live up to their human potential. This critique is based not on what people were like in the past, but on what they could be like in the future, if only the constraints of McDonaldized systems were eliminated, or at least eased substantially. The criticisms to be put forth in this book are animated by the latter, future-oriented perspective rather than by a romantization of the past and a desire to return to it....

NOTES

The quotations from McDonald's loyalists on page 51 appeared in E.R. Shipp, "The McBurger Stand that Started it All." *The New York Times*, February 27, 1985:3:3, and Pizza Hut's opening in Moscow was covered in "Wedge of Americana: In Moscow, Pizza Hut Opens 2 Restaurants." *Washington Post*, September 12, 1990: B10.

For more about *USA TODAY* (page 51), see Peter Prichard, *The Making of McPaper: The Inside Story of USA Today*. Kansas City: Andrews, McMeel and Parker, 1987; information about the *USA TODAY* television show comes from Richard Zoglin, "Get Ready for McRather." *Time*, April 11, 1988.

The essays in Marshall Fishwick, ed., *Ronald Revisited: the World of Ronald McDonald*. Bowling Green: Bowling Green University Press, 1983, have a great deal more to say about McDonald's central role (page 51, last paragraph). The Maryland high school student quoted in the same paragraph spoke to John F. Harris for his article "McMilestone Restaurant Opens Doors in Dale City." *Washington Post*, April 7, 1988: DI.

The material about McDonald's as icon on page 52 comes from a variety of sources:

Conrad Kottak discusses this idea in "Rituals at McDonald's." In Fishwick, ed., *Ronald Revisited*: 52-8. Bill Keller covers the opening of the Moscow McDonald's in "Of Famous Arches, Beeg Meks and rubles." *The New York Times*, January 28, 1990:1:1,12. William Severini Kowinski elaborates about shopping malls in *The Malling of America: An Inside Look at the Great Consumer Paradise*. New York: William Morrow, 1985: 218. Finally, the quotation about Walt Disney World comes from Bob Garfield, "How I Spent (and Spent and Spent) My Disney Vacation." *Washington Post*, July 7, 1991: B5. See also, Margaret J. King, "Empires of Popular Culture; McDonald's and Disney." In Fishwick, ed., *Ronald Revisited*: 106-19.

Ronald McDonald's name recognition (further down page 52) was reported in Steven Greenhouse, "The Rise and Rise of McDonald's." *The New York Times*, June 8, 1986: 3:1.

For more about new enterprises by McDonald's in small-town USA (page 52), see Laura Shapiro, "Ready for McCatfish?" *Newsweek*, October 15, 1990: 76-7. The quotation about Route 161 comes from N.R. Kleinfeld, "Fast Food's Changing Landscape." *The New York Times*, April 14, 1985: 3: 1, 6.

The material on page 53 about Domino's in the schools comes from Raul Farhi, "Domino's is Going to School." *Washington Post*, September 21, 1990: F3, and "Grade 'A' Burgers." *The New York Times*, April 13, 1986: 12: 15 is the source for the "A for Cheeseburger" program.

On page 54, the quotation about "McNuggets" comes from Prichard, *The Making of McPaper*, 232-3, and the quotation about the *Boca Raton News* comes from Howard Kurtz, "Slicing, Dicing News to Attract the Young" *Washington Post*, January 6, 1991: Al.

Nicholas D. Kristof discussed dial-a-porn (pages 54) in "Court Test is Likely on Dial-a-Porn Service Game." *New York Times*, October 15, 1986: 1: 16. *The New York Times* quoted the city official about the McDonald's of sex in its October 5, 1986, issue, section 3, page 6.

On pages 55–56 the basic components of rationality are drawn from the work of Max Weber, especially *Economy and Society*. Totowa, NJ: Bedminster Press, 1921/1968, as well as that of interpreters of Weber's work such as Stephen Kalberg in his essay, "Max Weber's Types of Rationality: Cornerstones for the Analysis of Rationalization Processes in History." *American Journal of Sociology*, 1980, 85: 1145-79.

On page 57, the criticism of Euro Disney was reported in Alan Riding, "Only the French Elite Scorn Mickey's Debut." *The New York Times*, April 13, 1992: A13.

Among the critics (and their works) mentioned on page 57 are Georg Stauth and Bryan S. Turner, "Nostalgia, Postmodernism and the Critique of Mass Culture." *Theory, Culture and Society*, 5, 1988: 509-26; Bryan S. Turner, "A Note on Nostalgia." *Theory, Culture and Society*, 4, 1987: 147-56.

In the sense described further down page 57, this resembles Marx's critique of capitalism. Marx was not animated by a romanticization of precapitalist society, but rather by the desire to produce a truly human (Communist) society on the base provided by capitalism. Despite this specific affinity to Marxian theory, this book is, as we will see, premised far more on Theories of Max Weber.

PART II | **Exercises**

Complete the following exercises and turn this sheet in to your instructor. Do not sign your name. To prepare for class discussions, reflect on the source and social consequences of the words you listed.

A. In the columns below, list as many synonyms for men and women as you can—including any derogatory or slang terms you may have heard.

Men   Women

B. In the columns below, list as many synonyms as you can for each nationality—including any derogatory or slang terms you may have heard.

British	Polish	Mexican	Chinese

Orality and Literacy

There are over 3500 languages in the world today. Most of them do not have an alphabet. Although cultures of these non-literate languages are often considered "underdeveloped," non-literate cultures can be artistically, philosophically, and socially advanced. Non-literacy is not the same as illiteracy. In fact, all oral cultures (including those in the past) have art, science, and knowledge which organizes and expresses their understanding of the world. The differences then between oral and literate cultures is not only their overall technological development, but also their communicative development. Different communication practices reflect and organize different worlds.

The readings in this section present some of the characteristics of orality and oral cultures. They also indicate some of the changes brought by literacy. Chronologically, orality is the first human communication practice. Moreover, speech is the foundation for all verbal exchanges— be they spoken, printed, or electronically broadcast.

In a sense, oral communication is also the first "technology." The unique physical structure of humans makes possible the creation of sounds—species without the "technology" of larynx and vocal cords cannot create multiple vowel sounds or "talk." By connecting comprehensible, identifiable, and repeatable *sounds* in distinctly identifiable patterns, humans "speak." We create sound-words to represent objects, relations, feelings, and concepts.

Of course, as the "technological" basis for speech, sound only exists as it happens, in action. We can talk fast or we can talk slow. Great tenors of the world can even "hold" a note for many seconds. Yet, for purposes of oral communication, sound cannot be paused or stopped without ceasing to exist. Consequently, because sound is transitory, oral cultures tend to rely on ritual repetition to maintain and reproduce knowledge and meaning.

An important part of ritual communication in oral cultures is non-verbal communication. Communication researchers have identified several non-verbal "systems," including body language (kinesics), distance between speakers (proxemics), physical appearance, touch, voice tone (vocalics), artifacts, and time (chronemics). If one arrives late for an appointment, for instance, time may communicate social position or the lack of commitment to a relationship. The date who arrives in a beat-up Volkswagen communicates through artifact a different message than one who drives up in a shiny BMW. These and other non-verbal systems function much like language in that they have recognizable, shared codes which provide meaning. Non-verbal communication also helps identify social roles, responsibilities, and expectations. And, like languages, they have cultural variations.

Communication theorists Robin Murray and Tom Wengraf (1979) have argued that the history of communication practices and their cultural variations is a process of combining the means of communication with the social relations of communication. Even in pre-literate oral cultures, social relations dramatically affected the use and development of communication. According to Murray and Wengraf, different means of communication allow *more-or-less symmetrical* relations between participants in a communication practice. Of all the modes or forms of communication that we have at our disposal, face-to-face orality is the most inherently symmetrical and democratic—everyone competent in a spoken language has an equal capacity for initiating, responding, avoiding, and participating in oral communication.

However, as Murray and Wengraf argue, the intrinsically symmetrical, democratic nature of speech can be obstructed by other less democratic social practices. We all learn of situations in which we speak only when spoken to: in high school, in court, when stopped by a belligerent cop. In oral cultures power inequities can interfere with the symmetry of orality. During the Middle Ages in Europe, for instance, serfs needed permission to speak to a noble. Given the likely negative consequence, serfs would not usually interrupt a lord or lady or try to determine the topic, content, or duration of the conversation. Murray and Wengraf suggest that if social relations can constrain orality—the most symmetrical mode of communication—then other communication practices are likely subject to similar cultural and social influences. Conversely, if social convention influences symmetry, then perhaps a given communication practice (and its technological prerequisite) may be made more or less symmetrical by adjusting existing social relations. In short, the concept of symmetry in the context of historical conditions presented by Murray and Wengraf may be helpful in understanding the democratic potential of communication practices discussed throughout this book.

In the first reading of this section, Walter Ong, a leading scholar in the study of oral communication, discusses some of the basics of orality. Ong begins with the importance of memory and form. In an oral culture, there is no way to "look up" past events. There are no dictionaries to check the definition of a word. Anything that can or would be known must be recalled from memory. Perhaps because rhythm and formula aid memory, communication in oral cultures tends to be rhythmic, performative, and repetitive in speech and gesture. Ong explains that in oral cultures words acquire meaning through speech, gesture, tone, and "the entire human, existential setting in which the real, spoken word always occurs." Words and meanings may even disappear if they are no longer an important part of the present.

Ong also argues that because oral cultures are dependent on participatory human interaction they tend to be harmonious, holistic, and stable. Ong argues that cultures created and reproduced through oral communication understand the world differently than cultures dependent on literacy or electronic communication. Oral cultures see the world differently because they live in it differently. Understanding in oral cultures tends to be more pragmatic, practical. Knowledge is immediate, concrete.

The invention, introduction, and development of the alphabet disrupts orality, it also upsets the social equilibrium or oral culture. The selection by Eric Havelock, a noted historian of early Western communication, identifies some of the changes in communication and social relations in classical Greece as it passed from orality to literacy. Havelock explains that performance in drama, song, and poetry provided the communicative means for documentation, regulation, and celebration when Greece was an oral culture. Knowledge was available to all, memorized and repeated in poetry and song. Significantly, many of the traditions and practices of orality continued even after the alphabet was invented—early writings were composed according to the rules of poetry, not everyday speech. In his assessment of Greek oral culture, Havelock demonstrates the earlier claim that non-literate cultures are not necessarily undeveloped cultures. Indeed, the dominant mode of communication reflects more the available or chosen means of communication than the creativity of the society and its members.

While communication form does not determine a culture's artistic, intellectual, or social value, it does affect one's knowledge and understanding of the world and thus affects how artistic, intellectual, and social projects are expressed and developed. Orality involves participants in shared, multi-sensory, group interactions. In oral cultures, individuals acquire knowledge through ritual, live performances which stimulate many senses. Literacy, on the other hand, involves individuals in isolated, visual communication experiences. Orality involves community; literates read books alone. While orality communicates through sound, sight, and non-verbal messages, literacy rests on the silent, printed word. In oral cultures one understands the world as it happens, concretely, immediately, in all its simultaneous sensory dimensions. Literacy, on the other hand, encourages abstract, linear thought about the world. A written description necessarily breaks up real world action into sequential narratives—this happened, and this, and that, then this, and so on. We even read left to right, top to bottom, or in some other linear fashion depending on the language of the text. Literacy increases abstraction in thought and language because it can shift time and place. Orality encourages connections with one's immediate existence; written language encourages category and definition of distant things, past things, future things. Later readings explain how other communication forms such as radio or television broadcasting may alter our appreciation and cognitive understanding of the world. The chart presented here illustrates some of the differences between orality and literacy.

SOME GENERAL CHARACTERISTICS OF ORAL AND WRITTEN COMMUNICATION

Orality	Literacy
transitory	permanent
close personal contact	possibility for contact with distant persons
ephemeral, performative	stable
concerned with here and now	increases abstraction, interpretation
democratic, participatory	codifies, regulates social conduct from distance
everyone has access	learned skills follow social divisions
shared ethos, identities	laws, codes established by distant hierarchy
natural, biological human activity	social invention
holistic, multi-sensory	linear, visual
social group, event provides context	text provides context

Poetry in modern Nicaragua provides a contemporary illustration of how orality as a dominant communication practice might function. (Several essays about communication in Nicaragua appear in this text because these offer striking examples of how humans find and mold available communication practices to meet particular social needs.) Poetry has been central to the national political life of Nicaragua. Denied access to any other means of mass communication, illiterate peasants and workers turned to the rural traditions of song and storytelling based on memory and public recitation. For Nicaraguans, poetry was practical because it was accessible and affordable. Poetry filled socio-psychological needs expressing resistance, self-confidence, and national pride. Finally, poetry met the political needs of those struggling for democracy because it circumvented the dictator Somoza's censors and helped organize the dispossessed (largely illiterate) workers and peasants by "broadcasting" a clear political program for democracy.

Performed in churches, neighborhoods, and small town meetings, this poetry functioned as the dominant communication practice for the majority of the nation. Communicated orally and publicly, Nicaraguan poetry and song fulfilled broad communication functions: informing, educating, entertaining, and building community. As in other oral cultures, the content of this communication was drawn from the audience, created by, for, and with the Nicaraguan majority. The "listeners' were none other than the orators and the heroes of the stories told and repeated in rhyme, verse, and song.

Although distant from the typical everyday experience of most North Americans, Nicaraguan poetry appears as a contemporary, participatory communication practice for a mass citizenry—a kind of poetic "Great Community." After Nicaragua's successful (United Nations Award-winning) literacy campaign in 1980, poetry became almost a national pastime, as newly literate citizens tried their hand at *writing* poetry.

REFERENCES

Murray, Robin and Tom Wengraf. "Historic Communication Systems." In *Communication and Class Struggle. Vol 1. Capitalism, Imperialism.* Eds. Armand Mattelart and Seth Siegelaub. New York: International General, 1979: 185-88.

9 | Psychodynamics of Orality
Walter Ong

. . .

Sound exists only when it is going out of existence. It is not simply perishable but essentially evanescent, and it is sensed as evanescent. When I pronounce the word "permanence," by the time I get to the "-nence," the "perma-" is gone, and has to be gone.

There is no way to stop sound and have sound. I can stop a moving picture camera and hold one frame fixed on the screen. If I stop the movement of sound, I have nothing-only silence, no sound at all. All sensation takes place in time, but no other sensory field totally resists a holding action, stabilization, in quite this way. Vision can register motion, but it can also register immobility. Indeed, it favors immobility, for to examine something closely by vision, we prefer to have it quiet. We often reduce motion to a series of still shots the better to see what motion is. There is no equivalent of a still shot for sound. An oscillogram is silent. It lies outside the sound world.

For anyone who has a sense of what words are in a primary oral culture, or a culture not far removed from primary orality, it is not surprising that the Hebrew term *dabar* means "word" and "event." Malinowski (1923, pp. 451, 470–81) has made the point that among "primitive" (oral) peoples generally language is a mode of action and not simply a countersign of thought, though he had trouble explaining what he was getting at since understanding of the psychodynamics of orality was virtually nonexistent in 1923. Neither is it surprising that oral peoples commonly, and probably universally, consider words to have great power. Sound cannot be sounding without the use of power. A hunter can see a buffalo, smell, taste, and touch a buffalo when the buffalo is completely inert, even dead, but if he hears a buffalo, he had better watch out: something is going on. In this sense, all sound, and especially oral utterance, which comes from inside living organisms, is "dynamic."

The fact that oral peoples commonly and in all likelihood universally consider words to have magical potency is clearly tied in, at least unconsciously, with their sense of the word as necessarily spoken, sounded, and hence power-driven. Deeply typographic folk forget to think of words as primarily oral, as events, and hence as necessarily powered: for them, words tend rather to be assimilated to things, "out there" on a flat surface. Such "things" are not so readily associated with magic, for they are not actions, but are in a radical sense dead, though subject to dynamic resurrection (Ong 1977, pp. 230–71).

From *Orality and Literacy* by Walter Ong. Reprinted by permission of Routledge.

Oral peoples commonly think of names (one kind of words) as conveying power over things. Explanations of Adam's naming of the animals in Genesis 2:20 usually call condescending attention to this presumably quaint archaic belief. Such a belief is in fact far less quaint than it seems to unreflective chirographic and typographic folk. First of all, names do give human beings power over what they name: without learning a vast store of names, one is simply powerless to understand, for example, chemistry and to practice chemical engineering. And so with all other intellectual knowledge. Secondly, chirographic and typographic folk tend to think of names as labels, written or printed tags imaginatively affixed to an object named. Oral folk have no sense of a name as a tag, for they have no idea of a name as something that can be seen. Written or printed representations of words can be labels; real, spoken words cannot be.

You Know What You Can Recall: Mnemonics and Formulas

In an oral culture, restriction of words to sound determines not only modes of expression but also thought processes.

You know what you can recall. When we say we know Euclidean geometry, we mean not that we have in mind at the moment every one of its propositions and proofs but rather that we can bring them to mind readily. We can recall them. The theorem "You know what you can recall" applies also to an oral culture. But how do persons in an oral culture recall? The organized knowledge that literates today study so that they "know" it, that is, can recall it, has, with very few if any exceptions, been assembled and made available to them in writing. This is the case not only with Euclidean geometry but also with American Revolutionary history, or even baseball batting averages or traffic regulations.

An oral culture has no texts. How does it get together organized material for recall? This is the same as asking, "What does it or can it know in an organized fashion?"

Suppose a person in an oral culture would undertake to think through a particular complex problem and would finally manage to articulate a solution which itself is relatively complex, consisting, let us say, of a few hundred words. How does he or she retain for later recall the verbalization so painstakingly elaborated? In the total absence of any writing, there is nothing outside the thinker, no text, to enable him or her to produce the same line of thought again or even to verify whether he or she has done so or not. *Aides-mémoire* such as notched sticks or a series of carefully arranged objects will not of themselves retrieve a complicated series of assertions. How, in fact, could a lengthy, analytic solution ever be assembled in the first place? An interlocutor is virtually essential: it is hard to talk to yourself for hours on end. Sustained thought in an oral culture is tied to communication.

But even with a listener to stimulate and ground your thought, the bits and pieces of your thought cannot be preserved in jotted notes. How could you ever call back to mind what you had so laboriously worked out? The only answer is: Think memorable thoughts. In a primary oral culture, to solve effectively the problem of retaining and retrieving carefully articulated thought, you have to do your thinking in mnemonic patterns, shaped for ready oral recurrence. Your thought must come into being in heavily rhythmic, balanced patterns, in repetitions or antitheses, in alliterations and assonances, in epithetic and other formulary expressions, in standard thematic settings (the assembly, the meal, the duel, the hero's "helper," and so on), in proverbs which are constantly heard by everyone so that they come to mind readily and which themselves are patterned for retention and ready recall, or in other mnemonic form. Serious thought is intertwined with memory systems. Mnemonic needs determine even syntax (Havelock 1963, pp. 87–96, 131–2, 294–6).

Protracted orally based thought, even when not in formal verse, tends to be highly rhythmic, for rhythm aids recall, even physiologically. Jousse (1978) has shown the intimate linkage between rhythmic oral patterns, the breathing process, gesture, and the bilateral symmetry of the human body in ancient Aramaic and Hellenic targums, and thus also in ancient Hebrew. Among the ancient Greeks, Hesiod, who was intermediate between oral Homeric Greece and fully developed Greek literacy, delivered quasi-philosophic material in the formulaic verse forms that structured it into the oral culture from which he had emerged (Havelock 1963, pp. 97–8, 294–301).

Formulas help implement rhythmic discourse and also act as mnemonic aids in their own right, as set expressions circulating through the mouths and ears of all. "Red in the morning, the sailor's warning; red in the night, the sailor's delight." "Divide and conquer." "To err is human, to forgive is divine." "Sorrow is better than laughter, because when the face is sad the heart grows wiser" (Ecclesiastes 7:3). "The clinging vine." "The sturdy oak." "Chase off nature and she returns at a gallop." Fixed, often rhythmically balanced, expressions of this sort and of other sorts can be found occasionally in print, indeed can be "looked up" in books of sayings, but in oral cultures they are not occasional. They are incessant. They form the substance of thought itself. Thought in any extended form is impossible without them, for it consists in them.

The more sophisticated orally patterned thought is, the more it is likely to be marked by set expressions skillfully used. This is true of oral cultures generally from those of Homeric Greece to those of the present day across the globe. Havelock's *Preface to Plato* (1963) and fictional works such as Chinua Achebe's novel *No Longer at Ease* (1961), which draws directly on Ibo oral tradition in West Africa, alike provide abundant instances of thought patterns of orally educated characters who move in these oral, mnemonically tooled grooves, as the speakers reflect, with high intelligence and sophistication, on the situations in which they find themselves involved. The law itself in oral cultures is enshrined in formulaic sayings, proverbs, which are not mere jurisprudential decorations, but themselves constitute the law. A judge in an oral culture is often called on to articulate sets of relevant proverbs out of which he can produce equitable decisions in the cases under formal litigation before him (Ong 1978, p. 5).

In an oral culture, to think through something in non-formulaic, non-patterned, non-mnemonic terms, even if it were possible, would be a waste of time, for such thought, once worked through, could never be recovered with any effectiveness, as it could be with the aid of writing. It would not be abiding knowledge but simply a passing thought, however complex. Heavy patterning and communal fixed formulas in oral cultures serve some of the purposes of writing in chirographic cultures, but in doing so they of course determine the kind of thinking that can be done, the way experience is intellectually organized. In an oral culture, experience is intellectualized mnemonically. This is one reason why, for a St. Augustine of Hippo (AD 354–430), as for other savants living in a culture that knew some literacy but still carried an overwhelmingly massive oral residue, memory bulks so large when he treats of the powers of the mind.

Of course, all expression and all thought is to a degree formulaic in the sense that every word and every concept conveyed in a word is a kind of formula, a fixed way of processing the data of experience, determining the way experience and reflection are intellectually organized, and acting as a mnemonic device of sorts. Putting experience into any words (which means transforming it at least a little bit—not the same as falsifying it) can implement its recall. The formulas characterizing orality are more elaborate, however, than are individual words, though some may be relatively simple: the Beowulf-poet's "whale-road" is a formula (metaphorical) for the sea in a sense in which the term "sea" is not.

Further Characteristics of Orally Based Thought and Expression

Awareness of the mnemonic base of the thought and expression in primary oral cultures opens the way to understanding some further characteristics of orally based thought and expression in addition to its formulaic styling. The characteristics treated here are some of those which set off orally based thought and expression from chirographically and typographically based thought and expression, the characteristics, that is, which are most likely to strike those reared in writing and print cultures as surprising. This inventory of characteristics is not presented as exclusive or conclusive but as suggestive, for much more work and reflection is needed to deepen understanding of orally based thought (and thereby understanding of chirographically based, typographically based, and electronically based thought)....

An oral culture may well ask in a riddle why oaks are sturdy, but it does so to assure you that they are, to keep the aggregate intact, not really to question or cast doubt on the attribution. (For examples directly from the oral culture of the Luba in Zaire, see Faik-Nzuji 1970.) Traditional expressions in oral cultures must not be dismantled: it has been hard work getting them together over the generations, and there is nowhere outside the mind to store them. So soldiers are brave and princesses beautiful and oaks sturdy forever. This is not to say that there may not be other epithets for soldiers or princesses or oaks, even contrary epithets, but these are standard, too: the braggart soldier, the unhappy princess, can also be part of the equipment. What obtains for epithets obtains for other formulas. Once a formulary expression has crystallized, it had best be kept intact. Without a writing system, breaking up thought—that is, analysis—is a high-risk procedure. As Lévi-Strauss has well put it in a summary statement "the savage [i.e. oral] mind totalizes" (1966, p. 245).

Redundant or "Copious"

Thought requires some sort of continuity. Writing establishes in the text a "line" of continuity outside the mind. If distraction confuses or obliterates from the mind the context out of which emerges the material I am now reading, the context can be retrieved by glancing back over the text selectively. Backlooping can be entirely occasional, purely *ad hoc*. The mind concentrates its own energies on moving ahead because what it backloops into lies quiescent outside itself, always available piecemeal on the inscribed page. In oral discourse, the situation is different. There is nothing to backloop into outside the mind, for the oral utterance has vanished as soon as it is uttered. Hence the mind must move ahead more slowly, keeping close to the focus of attention much of what it has already dealt with. Redundancy, repetition of the just-said, keeps both speaker and hearer surely on the track.

Since redundancy characterizes oral thought and speech, it is in a profound sense more natural to thought and speech than is sparse linearity. Sparsely linear or analytic thought and speech is an artificial creation, structured by the technology of writing. Eliminating redundancy on a significant scale demands a time-obviating technology, writing, which imposes some kind of strain on the psyche in preventing expression from falling into its more natural patterns. The psyche can manage the strain in part because handwriting is physically such a slow process—typically about one-tenth of the speed of oral speech (Chafe 1982). With writing, the mind is forced into a slowed-down pattern that affords it the opportunity to interfere with and reorganize its more normal, redundant processes.

Redundancy is also favored by the physical conditions of oral expression before a large audience, where redundancy is in fact more marked than in most face-to-face conversation. Not everyone in a large audience understands every word a speaker utters, if only because of acoustical problems. It is advantageous for the speaker to say the same thing, or equivalently the same thing, two or three times. If you miss the "not only..." you can supply it by inference from the "but also...." Until electronic amplification reduced acoustical problems to a minimum, public speakers as late as, for example, William Jennings Bryan (1860-1925) continued the old redundancy in their public addresses and by force of habit let them spill over into their writing. In some kinds of acoustic surrogates for oral verbal communication, redundancy reaches fantastic dimensions, as in African drum talk. It takes on the average around eight times as many words to say something on the drums as in the spoken language (Ong 1977, p. 101).

The public speaker's need to keep going while he is running through his mind what to say next also encouraged redundancy. In oral delivery, though a pause may be effective, hesitation is always disabling. Hence it is better to repeat something, artfully if possible, rather than simply to stop speaking while fishing for the next idea. Oral cultures encourage fluency, fulsomeness, volubility. Rhetoricians were to call this *copia*. They continued to encourage it, by a kind of oversight, when they had modulated rhetoric from an art of public speaking to an art of writing. Early written texts, through the Middle Ages and the Renaissance, are often bloated with "amplification," annoyingly redundant by modern standards. Concern with *copia* remains intense in western culture so long as the culture sustains massive oral residue—which is roughly until the age of Romanticism or even beyond. Thomas Babington Macaulay (1800–59) is one of the many fulsome early Victorians whose pleonastic written compositions still read much as an exuberant, orally composed oration would sound, as do also, very often, the writings of Winston Churchill (1874–1965).

Conservative or Traditionalist

Since in a primary oral culture conceptualized knowledge that is not repeated aloud soon vanishes, oral societies must invest great energy in saying over and over again what has been learned arduously over the ages. This need establishes a highly traditionalist or conservative set of mind that with good reason inhibits intellectual experimentation. Knowledge is hard to come by and precious, and society regards highly those wise old men and women who specialize in conserving it, who know and can tell the stories of the days of old. By storing knowledge outside the mind, writing and, even more, print downgrade the figures of the wise old man and the wise old woman, repeaters of the past, in favor of younger discoverers of something new.

Writing is of course conservative in its own ways. Shortly after it first appeared, it served to freeze legal codes in early Sumeria (Oppenheim 1964, p. 232). But by taking conservative functions on itself, the text frees the mind of conservative tasks, that is, of its memory work, and thus enables the mind to turn itself to new speculation (Havelock 1963, pp. 254–305). Indeed, the residual orality of a given chirographic culture can be calculated to a degree from the mnemonic load it leaves on the mind, that is, from the amount of memorization the culture's educational procedures require (Goody 1968a, pp. 13–14)....

Oral cultures of course have no dictionaries and few semantic discrepancies. The meaning of each word is controlled by what Goody and Watt (1968, p. 29) call "direct semantic ratification," that is, by the real-life situations in which the word is used here and now. The oral mind is uninterested in definitions (Luria 1976, pp. 48–99). Words acquire their meanings only from their always insistent actual habitat, which is not, as in a dictionary, simply other words, but includes also gestures, vocal inflections, facial expression, and the entire human, existential setting in which the real, spoken word always occurs. Word meanings come continuously out of the present, though past meanings of course have shaped the present meaning in many and varied ways, no longer recognized.

It is true that oral art forms, such as epic, retain some words in archaic forms and senses. But they retain such words, too, through current use—not the current use of ordinary village discourse but the current use of ordinary epic poets, who preserve archaic forms in their special vocabulary. These performances are part of ordinary social life and so the archaic forms are current, though limited to poetic activity. Memory of the old meaning of old terms thus has some durability, but not unlimited durability.

When generations pass and the object or institution referred to by the archaic word is no longer part of present, lived experience, though the word has been retained, its meaning is commonly altered or simply vanishes. African talking drums, as used for example among the Lokele in eastern Zaire, speak in elaborate formulas that preserve certain archaic words which the Lokele drummers can vocalize but whose meaning they no longer know (Carrington 1974, pp. 41–2; Ong 1977, pp. 94–5). Whatever these words referred to has dropped out of Lokele daily experience, and the term that remains has become empty. Rhymes and games transmitted orally from one generation of small children to the next even in high-technology culture have similar words which have lost their original referential meanings and are in effect nonsense syllables. Many instances of such survival of empty terms can be found in Opie and Opie (1952), who, as literates, of course manage to recover and report the original meanings of the terms lost to their present oral users....

...Among Luria's findings the following may be noted as of special interest here.

(1) Illiterate (oral) subjects identified geometrical figures by assigning them the names of objects, never abstractly as circles, squares, etc. A circle would be called a plate, sieve, bucket, watch, or moon; a square would be called a mirror, door, house, apricot drying-board. Luria's subjects identified the designs as representations of real things they knew. They never dealt with abstract circles or squares but rather with concrete objects. Teachers' school students on the other hand, moderately literate, identified geometrical figures by categorical geometric names: circles, squares, triangles, and so on (1976, pp. 32-9). They had been trained to give schoolroom answers, not real-life responses.

(2) Subjects were presented with drawings of four objects, three belonging to one category and the fourth to another, and were asked to group together those that were similar or could be placed in one group or designated by one word. One series consisted of drawings of the objects *hammer, saw, log, hatchet*. Illiterate subjects consistently thought of the group not in categorical terms (three tools, the log not a tool) but in terms of practical situations—"situational thinking"—without adverting at all to the classification "tool" as applying to all but the log. If you are a workman with tools and see a log, you think of applying the tool to it, not of keeping

the tool away from what it was made for—in some weird intellectual game. A 25-year-old illiterate peasant: "They're all alike. The saw will saw the log and the hatchet will chop it into small pieces. If one of these has to go, I'd throw out the hatchet. It doesn't do as good a job as a saw (1976, p. 56). Told that the hammer, saw, and hatchet are all tools, he discounts the categorical class and persists in situational thinking: "Yes, but even if we have tools, we still need wood—otherwise we can't build anything" (ibid.). Asked why another person had rejected one item in another series of four that he felt all belonged together, he replied, "Probably that kind of thinking runs in his blood."

By contrast an 18-year-old who had studied at a village school for only two years, not only classified a similar series in categorical terms but insisted on the correctness of the classification under attack (1976, p. 74). A barely literate worker, aged 56, mingled situational grouping and categorical grouping, though the latter predominated. Given the series *axe, hatchet, sickle* to complete from the series *saw, ear of grain, log,* he completed the series with the saw—"They are all farming tools"—but then reconsidered and added about the grain, "You could reap it with the sickle" (1976, p. 72). Abstract classification was not entirely satisfying.

At points in his discussions Luria undertook to teach illiterate subjects some principles of abstract classification. But their grasp was never firm, and when they actually returned to working out a problem for themselves, they would revert to situational rather than categorical thinking (1976, p. 67). They were convinced that thinking other than operational thinking, that is, categorical thinking, was not important, uninteresting, trivializing (1976, pp. 54–5). One recalls Malinowski's account (1923, p. 502) of how "primitives" (oral peoples) have names for the fauna and flora that are useful in their lives but treat other things in the forest as unimportant generalized background: "That is just 'bush'." "Merely a flying animal."

(3) We know that formal logic is the invention of Greek culture after it had interiorized the technology of alphabetic writing, and so made a permanent part of its noetic resources the kind of thinking that alphabetic writing made possible. In the light of this knowledge, Luria's experiments with illiterates' reactions to formally syllogistic and inferential reasoning is particularly revealing. In brief, his illiterate subjects seemed not to operate with formal deductive procedures at all—which is not the same as to say that they could not think or that their thinking was not governed by logic, but only that they would not fit their thinking into pure logical forms, which they seem to have found uninteresting. Why should they be interesting? Syllogisms relate to thought, but in practical matters no one operates in formally stated syllogisms.

Precious metals do not rust. Gold is a precious metal. Does it rust or not? Typical responses to this query included: "Do precious metals rust or not? Does gold rust or not?" (peasant, 18 years of age); "Precious metal rusts. Precious gold rusts" (34-year-old illiterate peasant) (1976, p. 104)....

...Much in the foregoing account of orality can be used to identify what can be called "verbomotor" cultures, that is, cultures in which, by contrast with high-technology cultures, courses of action and attitudes toward issues depend significantly more on effective use of words, and thus on human interaction, and significantly less on non-verbal, often largely visual input from the "objective" world of things. Jousse (1925) used his term *verbomoteur* to refer chiefly to ancient Hebrew and Aramaic cultures and surrounding cultures, which knew some writing but remained basically oral and word-oriented in lifestyle rather than object-oriented. We are expanding its use here to include all cultures that retain enough oral residue to remain significantly word-attentive in a person-interactive context (the oral type of context) rather than object-attentive. It should, of course, be noted that words and objects are never totally disjunct:

words represent objects, and perception of objects is in part conditioned by the store of words into which perceptions are nested. Nature states no "facts": these come only within statements devised by human beings to refer to the seamless web of actuality around them.

The cultures which we are here styling verbomotor are likely to strike technological man as making all too much of speech itself, as overvaluing and certainly overpracticing rhetoric. In primary oral cultures, even business is not business: it is fundamentally rhetoric. Purchasing something at a Middle East souk or bazaar is not a simple economic transaction, as it would be at Woolworth's and as a high technology culture is likely to presume it would be in the nature of things. Rather, it is a series of verbal (and somatic) maneuvers, a polite duel, a contest of wits, an operation in oral agonistic.

In oral cultures a request for information is commonly interpreted interactively (Malinowski 1923, pp. 451, 470–81), as agonistic, and, instead of being really answered, is frequently parried. An illuminating story is told of a visitor in County Cork, Ireland, an especially oral region in a country which in every region preserves massive residual orality. The visitor saw a Corkman leaning against the post office. He went up to him, pounded with his hand on the post office wall next to the Corkman's shoulder, and asked, "Is this the post office?" The Corkman was not taken in. He looked at his questioner quietly and with great concern: "Twouldn't be a postage stamp you were lookin' for, would it?" He treated the enquiry not as a request for information but as something the enquirer was doing to him. So he did something in turn to the enquirer to see what would happen. All natives of Cork, according to the mythology, treat all questions this way. Always answer a question by asking another. Never let down your oral guard.

Primary orality fosters personality structures that in certain ways are more communal and externalized, and less introspective than those common among literates. Oral communication unites people in groups. Writing and reading are solitary activities that throw the psyche back on itself A teacher speaking to a class which he feels and which feels itself as a close-knit group, finds that if the class is asked to pick up its textbooks and read a given passage, the unity of the group vanishes as each person enters into his or her private lifeworld. An example of the contrast between orality and literacy on these grounds is found in Carother's report (1959) of evidence that oral peoples commonly externalize schizoid behavior where literates interiorize it. Literates often manifest tendencies (loss of contact with environment) by psychic withdrawal into a dreamworld of their own (schizophrenic delusional systematization), oral folk commonly manifest their schizoid tendencies by extreme external confusion, leading often to violent action, including mutilation of the self and of others. This behavior is frequent enough to have given rise to special terms to designate it: the old-time Scandinavian warrior going "berserk," the Southeast Asian person running "amok."...

In a primary oral culture, where the word has its existence only in sound, with no reference whatsoever to any visually perceptible text, and no awareness of even the possibility of such a text, the phenomenology of sound enters deeply into human beings' feel for existence, as processed by the spoken word. For the way in which the word is experienced is always momentous in psychic life. The centering action of sound (the field of sound is not spread out before me but is all around me) affects man's sense of the cosmos. For oral cultures, the cosmos is an ongoing event with man at its center. Man is the *umbilicus mundi*, the navel of the world (Eliade 1958, pp. 231–5, etc.). Only after print and the extensive experience with maps that print implemented would human beings, when they thought about the cosmos or universe or "world," think primarily of something laid out before their eyes, as in a modern printed atlas, a vast surface or assemblage of surfaces (vision presents surfaces) ready to be "explored." The ancient oral world knew few "explorers," though it did know many itinerants, travelers, voyagers, adventurers, and pilgrims.

It will be seen that most of the characteristics of orally based thought and expression discussed earlier in this chapter relate intimately to the unifying, centralizing, interiorizing economy of sound as perceived by human beings. A sound-dominated verbal economy is consonant with aggregative (harmonizing) tendencies rather than with analytic, dissecting tendencies (which would come with the inscribed, visualized word: vision is a dissecting sense). It is consonant also with the conservative holism (the homeostatic present that must be kept intact, the formulary expressions that must be kept intact), with situational thinking (again holistic, with human action at the center) rather than abstract thinking, with a certain human-istic organization of knowledge around the actions of human and anthromorphic beings, interiorized persons, rather than around impersonal things.

The denominators used here to describe the primary oral world will be useful again later to describe what happened to human consciousness when writing and print reduced the oral-aural world to a world of visualized pages.

Orality, Community and the Sacral

Because in its physical constitution as sound, the spoken word proceeds from the human interior and manifests human beings to one another as conscious interiors, as persons, the spoken word forms human beings into close-knit groups. When a speaker is addressing an audience, the members of the audience normally become a unity, with themselves and with the speaker. If the speaker asks the audience to read a handout provided for them, as each reader enters into his or her own private reading world, the unity of the audience is shattered, to be reestablished only when oral speech begins again. Writing and print isolate. There is no collective noun or concept for readers corresponding to "audience." The collective "reader-ship"—this magazine has a readership of two million—is a far-gone abstraction. To think of readers as a united group, we have to fall back on calling them an "audience," as though they were in fact listeners. The spoken word forms unities on a large scale, too: countries with two or more different spoken languages are likely to have major problems in establishing or maintaining national unity, as today in Canada or Belgium or many developing countries.

The interiorizing force of the oral word relates in a special way to the sacral, to the ultimate concerns of existence. In most religions the spoken word functions integrally in ceremonial and devotional life. Eventually in the larger world religions sacred texts develop, too, in which the sense of the sacral is attached also to the written word. Still, a textually supported religious tradition can continue to authenticate the primacy of the oral in many ways. In Christianity, for example, the Bible is read aloud at liturgical services. For God is thought of always as "speaking" to human beings, not as writing to them. The orality of the mindset in the Biblical text, even in its epistolary sections, is overwhelming (Ong 1967b, pp. 176–91). The Hebrew *dabar*, which means word, means also event and thus refers directly to the spoken word. The spoken word is always an event, a movement in time, completely lacking in the thing-like repose of the written or printed word. In Trinitarian theology, the Second Person of the Godhead is the Word, and the human analogue for the Word here is not the human written word, but the human spoken word. God the Father "speaks" his Son: he does not inscribe him. Jesus, the Word of God, left nothing in writing, though he could read and write (Luke 4:16). "Faith comes through hearing," we read in the Letter to the Romans (10:17). "The letter kills, the spirit [breath, on which rides the spoken word] gives life" (2 Corinthians 3:6).

Words Are Not Signs

Jacques Derrida has made the point that "there is no linguistic sign before writing" (1976, p. 14). But neither is there a linguistic "sign" after writing if the oral reference of the written text is adverted to. Though it releases unheard-of potentials of the word, a textual, visual representation of a word is not a real word, but a "secondary modeling system" (cf. Lotman 1977). Thought is nested in speech, not in texts, all of which have their meanings through reference of the visible symbol to the world of sound. What the reader is seeing on this page are not real words but coded symbols whereby a properly informed human being can evoke in his or her consciousness real words, in actual or imagined sound. It is impossible for script to be more than marks on a surface unless it is used by a conscious human being as a cue to sounded words, real or imagined, directly or indirectly....

REFERENCES

Achebe, Chinua (1961) *No Longer at Ease* (New York: Ivan Obolensky).

Carothers, J.C. (1959) "Culture, psychiatry, and the written word," *Psychiatry, 22,* 307–20.

Carrington, John F. (1974) *La Voix des tambours: comment comprendre le larsage tambouriné d'Afrique* (Kinshasa: Centre Protestant d'Editions et de Diffusion).

Chafe, Wallace L. (1982) "Integration and involvement in speaking, writing, and oral literature," to appear in Deborah Tannen (ed.), *Spoken and Written Language: Exploring Orality and Literacy* (Norwood, NJ: Ablex).

Eliade, Mircea (1958) *Patterns in Comparative Religion,* trans. By Willard R. Trask (New York: Sheed & Ward).

Faik-Nzuji, Clémentine (1970) *Enigmes Lubas-Nshinga: Étude structurale* (Kinshasa: Editions de l'Université Lovanium).

Goody, Jack [John Rankine] and Watt, Ian (1968) "The consequences of literacy," in Jack Goody (ed.), *Literacy in Traditional Societies* (Cambridge, England: Cambridge University Press), 27–84.

Havelock, Eric A. (1963) *Preface to Plato* (Cambridge, Mass.: Belknap Press of Harvard University Press).

Jousse, Marcel (1925) *Le Style oral rhythmique et mnémotechnique chez les Verbo-moteurs* (Paris: G. Beauchesne).

Lévi-Strauss, Claude (1966) *The Savage Mind.* (Chicago: University of Chicago Press). Originally published as *La Pensée sauvage* (1962).

Lotman, Jurij (1977) *The Structure of the Artistic Text,* trans. By Ronald Vroon, Michigan Slavic Contributions, 7 (Ann Arbor, Mich.: University of Michigan).

Luria [also Lurriia], Aleksandr Romanovich (1976) *Cognitive Development: Its Cultural and Social Foundations,* ed. Michael Cole, trans. By Martin Lopez-Morillas and Lynn Solotaroff (Cambridge, Mass., and London: Harvard University Press).

Malinowski, Bronislaw (1923) "The problem of meaning in primitive languages," in C.K. Ogden, and I.A. Richards (eds.), *The Meaning of Meaning: A Study of the Influence of Language upon Thought and of the Science of Symbolism,* introduction by J.P. Postgate and supplementary essays by B. Malinowski and F.G. Crookshank (New York: Harcourt, Brace; London: Kegan Paul, Trench, Trubner), 451–1 0.

Ong, Walter J. (1967b) *The Presence of the Word* (New Haven and London: Yale University Press).

—— (1977) *Interfaces of the Word* (Ithaca and London: Cornell University Press).

—— (1978) "Literacy and orality in our times," *ADE Bulletin,* 58 (September), 1–7.

Opie, Iona Archibald and Opie, Peter (1952) *The Oxford Dictionary of Nursery Rhymes* (Oxford: Clarendon Press).

Oppenheim, A. Leo (1964) *Ancient Mesopotamia* (Chicago: University of Chicago Press).

10 | Pre-literacy of the Greeks
Eric Havelock

It sometimes happens in the course of scholarly investigation carried out over a long period of time that one is gradually pushed into accepting a view of the facts—an interpretation of them—which is not only contrary to received opinion but which is accepted slowly and reluctantly by the investigator himself. This has been the case with my own inquiries into the subject of Greek literacy. As some who have read my published work will know, I have concluded that the population of Athens did not become literate in our sense until the last third of the fifth century before Christ.[1] That is to say, while the historian of the time would fasten his eyes on the progress and consequences of a war—the Peloponnesian war—waged during those same years, which occupied the forefront of the historical stage, an event of greater social and cultural importance was quietly taking place behind the scenes.

Starting with an examination of the Greek alphabet and the precise way in which it functions as a symbolic system, and then proceeding to the first works inscribed in this medium, namely, the Homeric poems,[2] and then pushing on down through the course of what is called Greek "literature" (itself a misnomer), that is, rereading Hesiod, the lyric poets, Pindar, and finally Athenian drama, and asking myself fresh questions about the way these works were composed, their style and substance, and the kind of public to which it seems they were addressed, and the conditions of their performance—I have gradually approached a series of conclusions of which I have only recently appreciated the full consequences, and how drastic they may appear from the standpoint of traditional classical scholarship. At risk of appearing dogmatic, I think it will be best to expose them comprehensively, in something like their logical order, simply because the structure of the argument taken as a whole may carry greater conviction than would be true of the sum of its individual parts.

First: the invention of the Greek alphabet, as opposed to all previous systems, including the Phoenician, constituted an event in the history of human culture, the importance of which has not as yet been fully grasped. Its appearance divides all pre-Greek civilizations from those that are post-Greek. When all allowance is made for the relative success of previous systems of writing, and for the degree to which the Greek invention developed out of them, the fact remains that in the Greek system it became possible for the first time to document all possible forms of linguistic statement with fluency and to achieve fluent recognition, that is, fluent

From *New Literary History*, Vol. 8, by Havelock, pp. 369–391. Reprinted by permission of Johns Hopkins University Press.

reading, of what had been written, on the part of a majority of any population. On this facility were built the foundations of those twin forms of knowledge: literature in the post-Greek sense, and science, also in the post-Greek sense.

Second: the classical culture of the Greeks was, however, already in existence before the invention took effect. That culture began its career as a nonliterate one and continued in this condition for a considerable period after the invention, for civilizations can be nonliterate and yet possess their own specific forms of institution, art, and contrived language. In the case of the Greeks, these forms made their appearance in the institution of the *polis*, in geometric art, in early temple architecture, and in the poetry preserved in the Homeric hexameter. These were all functioning when Greece was nonliterate.

Third: to understand what we mean by a "culture," the Greek included, we have to ask what gives it a structure, what is continuous and so identifiable. This question can be answered by borrowing from the cultural anthropologists the concept of the storage of information for reuse. The information concerned is not merely technological in the narrow sense, but also covers that body of directives which regulates the behavior patterns of individuals who are members of the culture. In a literate culture, it is easy to perceive this kind of knowledge taking shape as a body of law and belief, covering religion and morals, political authority ("the constitution," as we say), legal procedures of all kinds, especially those governing property, and also rights and responsibilities within the family. The civilization of the ancient Greeks is admittedly a rather startling phenomenon, but it may become less miraculous and more understandable if we are prepared to regard it as an ongoing experiment in the storage of cultural information for reuse.[3]

Fourth: a nonliterate culture is not necessarily a primitive one, and the Greek was not primitive. Once this proposition is taken seriously, one has to ask: in the absence of documentation in a preliterate society, what was the mechanism available for the storage of such information—that is, for the continuous transmission of that body of religious, political, legal, and familial regulation which already constituted, before literacy, the Greek way of life? This information could be carried only in the form of statements imprinted upon the memories of individual brains of living Greeks. How, then, could these statements preserve themselves with alteration, and so retain authenticity? The solution to this problem is supplied if they are cast in metrical form, for only as language is controlled by rhythm can it be repeated with anything like the uniformity that is available in documentation. The shape of the words and their place in the syntax are fixed by rhythmic order. The vernacular is therefore not used for any statements that require preservation.

Fifth: what we call "poetry" is therefore an invention of immemorial antiquity designed for the functional purpose of a continuing record in oral cultures. Such cultures normally follow the practice of reinforcing the rhythms of verbal meter by wedding them to the rhythms of dance, of musical instruments, and of melody. A poem is more memorizable than a paragraph of prose; a song is more memorizable than a poem. The Greeks identified this complex of oral practices by the craft term *mousikē*, and correctly identified the Muse who gave her name to the craft as the "daughter of Remembrance." She personified the mnemonic necessity and the mnemonic techniques characteristic of an oral culture.

Sixth: while the act of imprinting, considered psychological, operates upon individual memories, its social function cannot become effective unless these memories are shared. Oral poetry therefore required for its existence an occasion which could supply a listening audience, large or small, ranging from an entire city to the company at a dinner table. Knowledge hoarded for reuse required not only rhythm, but constant performance before audiences who were invited to participate in its memorization. Truly private communication of preservable information becomes possible only under conditions of developed literacy. Only the documented word can be perused by individuals in isolation.

Seventh: the Greek alphabet, both at the time of its invention and for many generations after, was not applied in the first instance to transcribing vernacular statements but rather to those previously composed according to oral rules of memorization. That is why Greek literature is predominantly poetic, to the death of Euripides. This literature therefore will evade our understanding as long as we conduct its critique exclusively according to the rules of literate composition. These rules, whatever they are, can be said to intrude themselves by degrees, and slowly. High classical Greek literature is to be viewed as composed in a condition of increasing tension between the modes of oral and documented speech.

Eighth: the education of the Greek leisured classes throughout this period was oral. It consisted in the memorization of poetry, the improvisation of verse, the oral delivery of verse, the oral delivery of a prose rhetoric based on verse principles, the performance on instruments, string or wood, and singing and dancing. For a long time after the invention of the alphabet, letters were not included, and when they were first introduced, they were treated as ancillary to memorization and recitation. There is ample evidence that in the sixth and fifth centuries B.C. this curriculum was identified in Athens by the term *mousiké*, as previously defined, and no hard evidence that in this period it covered reading. Organized instruction in reading at the primary level, that is, before the age of ten, cannot have been introduced into the Athenian schools much earlier than about 430 B.C. It is described in Plato's *Protagoras*, written in the early part of the next century, as by then standard practice, as it indeed had become when Plato grew up.[4]

Ninth: the inventors, and for a long time the only habitual users of the alphabet, were craftsmen and traders.[5] No doubt, as time went on, the leisured classes picked up some acquaintance with letters, but the extent to which they did so must remain problematic, for they had minimal motives for employing the skill until the middle decades of the fifth century. The craftsman's children went to work in the shop before puberty, and if they learned letters, that is where they learned them.[6] The upper-class boy, prolonging education into adolescence, had time to master the polite arts, which did not include reading. There are indications that a crude literacy among craftsmen was becoming common in the age of Pisistratus and after. This is consistent with the tradition that under Solon's policies craftsmen from overseas were encouraged to settle in Athens.

Such are the general conclusions here presented as an interconnected whole. They run against the grain of several common presuppositions from which classical historians find it difficult to escape, deriving as they do from our inherited experience of two thousand years of literacy.

The dominant one, from which all others flow, is the view that a nonliterate culture must be a nonculture, or at least marks a stage in human development which is better forgotten once literacy sets in. The two belong in different worlds. The prejudice is reinforced by the modern results of contact between literate and nonliterate cultures; the latter seem to collapse before the approach, the onslaught, of what is taken to be a superior and civilized mode of life.

Hence, in estimating the character and history of Greek literacy, which began from scratch, one is tempted to ignore the possibility that there may have existed prior methods of preserving information which were oral and antique, and in the Greek instance may have reached a high level of proficiency. One is forced to ask the unbelieving question: how could a culture as high-powered as the Greek have got its start in nonliteracy? To which one is forced to replay that it could not have. It must have had a proto-literate ancestry, thus kindling a continuing dispute about the date of the introduction of writing in Greece: either the alphabet must have been in use as early as the tenth century at the latest; or the Greeks never ceased to use the Linear B system of the Mycenaeans; or if a date of around 700 B.C. be admitted for the introduction of writing, then the Dark Age, so-called, was truly a dark age. Greek civilization can only be said to begin after 700. None of these three propositions is tenable.

Today persons and people are either literate or not: if semiliterate, this condition is viewed as a failure to become literate. This is because the alphabet is available, its full use is understood, a regimen for teaching reading to children is available, as also is an adequate supply of documented speech to afford practice in reading as well as a motive for reading. These resources are either used or not used, and the result is either literacy or nonliteracy. In dealing with ancient Greece, which started from scratch and had to learn the full use of the alphabet after inventing it, this simplistic view should be abandoned. Tentatively, let me suggest in its place a progressive classification, which would identify the condition of Athenian society during the seventh and as far as the last decades of the sixth centuries B.C. as craft-literate: the alphabet written or read represents an expertise managed by a restricted group of the population. During the latter part of the sixth and the first half of the fifth, the skill begins to spread, though I would suspect that the governing classes were the last to acquire it, but the skill is one of decipherment rather than fluent reading. The use of the written word is very restricted, and any reading of it is regarded as ancillary to the central function of culture, which still is, as it had always been to memorize and recite the poets. I would classify this period as one of "recitation literacy." Only in the last third of the century is the average Athenian taught letters in such a way as to begin to pick up a script and read it through. It follows that testimonies drawn from fourth-century authors will take literacy for granted, for it has now been achieved. These chronological distinctions may seem fine-drawn, but they call attention to the basic fact that what we call the "literature" both of the sixth and fifth centuries is addressed to listeners rather than readers and is composed to conform with this situation.

Long experience of our own literate condition in the West has done more than merely convince us that all cultures depend upon achieving literacy as quickly as possible. It has had the indirect result of fostering two preconceptions about how any culture actually functions, both of which get in the way of a proper understanding of the original Greek experience. For the first of these let me quote, by way of illustration, what an eminent archaeologist has to say about one of the earliest alphabetic inscriptions we have, a craftsman's signature the lettering of which is well executed: "The fact of the signature at this very early date should imply that the artist was no humble *cheironax* but a person of social standing. On this evidence he would seem to have been a highly cultured person."[7] At first sight this statement seems perfectly natural and reasonable. Yet the way it is worded reveals a judgement unconsciously guided by the norms of our own society, in which the maximum of education is identified with the maximum of literacy. The cultivation centered today in the more privileged classes, to use a term which is snobbish but seems inevitable, is identified with a superior capacity to read and write, which diminishes as one goes down in the social scale. Therefore, if it be discovered that a Greek potter or carpenter or stonemason could use the alphabet, it is assumed a fortiori that the upper classes must have previously mastered this skill which had now filtered down to the artisan, or conversely, that the artisan was not really an artisan but a very educated type. The great bulk of the inscriptional material on which we rely for any material evidence of the alphabet's use in the early centuries is contributed by craftsmen. It may seem therefore inevitable to the historian of the period, and particularly the epigraphist, to conclude that if craftsmen wrote, then everyone did. But suppose, as I have earlier suggested, that the truth was rather the reverse of this, that the alphabet's use did not achieve what I may call cultural prestige for a very long time?

It is also a fact of life in literate societies that prose is the primary form in which experience is documented, while poetry is more esoteric and sophisticated, a medium to be reserved for special experiences outside the day's work. The notion runs deep in our consciousness, and continually colors the attitude we take up towards Greek literature in the first three centuries of its existence. Its poetic form prevents us from evaluating its functional role as preserved communication in the society of its day. More particularly, if we encounter in inscriptions a plethora of metrical statements, memorials, dedications, and the like, we are ready to read these in the light of what is believed to be an unusual degree of Greek cultivation. This conception has to be reversed if we are to understand early Greek poetry. In an oral culture, metrical language is part of the day's work....

NOTES

[1] Eric A. Havelock, *Preface to Plato* (Cambridge, 1963), p. 40.

[2] I accept the consensus, disputed by M.L. West, ed., *Theogony* (Oxford, 1966), pp. 46 ff., that "Homer" preceded "Hesiod."

[3] Havelock, "Prologue to Greek Literacy," in *Univ. Cincinnati Classical Studies,* II (Norman, Okla., 1973), 32.

[4] *Protagoras* 325e, cf. 326c-e and *Charmides* 159c. Immerwater (below n. 39) says: "The book roll is thus a mnemonic device facilitating recitation, not a real 'book' for reading alone" (p. 37). The "nuts and bolts" of Greek education have received scant attention from scholars, mainly because they were ignored by ancient historians. The handbooks cling tenaciously to the view that at the elementary level education began where we begin it. Thus Kenneth J. Freeman in his *Schools of Helios* (London, 1907), noting the Platoanic order "grammalistes" "kitharistes" "paidotribes" (*Prolag.* 312b), argues that "this system of primary education at Athens may reasonably be traced back to the beginning of the sixth century" (p. 52), placing reliance on the legend that Solon made the teaching of letter compulsory. This opinion has been recently repeated in Frederick A. Beck, *Greek Education* (New York, 1964) p. 77. Henri J. Marrou, in his *Histoire de l'Education dans l'Antiquité,* 6th ed. (1948' rpt Paris, 1965), is more cautious. He notes evidence of illiteracy in the period of ostracism: "Néarmoins, dès l'époque des guerres médiques, on peut benir pour certaine l'existence d'un enseignement des lettres (p. 77)—an opinion supported by a mistranslation of a sentence in Plutarch, Themistocles 10, where it is said that the Troizeneans supplied the children of the refugee Athenians with "teachers," not "reading-teachers."

[5] I now withdraw previous support (*Preface to Plato*, p. 51) for the hypothesis that the invention was the work of minstrels. Those supporting it (H.T. Wade-Grey, *The Poet of the Iliad* [Cambridge, 1952], pp. 13-14; Kevin Robb, *The Progress of Literacy in Ancient Greece* [Los Angeles, 1970], p. 13) rely on the assumption that composers of the first metrical inscriptions were necessarily minstrels and at the same time writers.

[6] The apprentice relationship is described at Plato, *Prolag*. 328a; cf. R.M. Cook, *Greek Painted Pottery*, 2nd ed. (1960; rpt. London, 1972), p. 271 (black figure illustration of a manager, painter, craftsman, and five assistants); and L.H. Jeffery, *The Local Scripts of Archaic Greece* (Oxford, 1961), p. 62 (masons learned to write and passed on knowledge in sons as part of craft).

[7] J.M. Cook, "A Painter and His Age," Mélanges...afférts à André Varagnac (Paris, 1971), p. 175.

PART III	Exercises

NAME _____

Outline contemporary U.S. communication practices using the list below. List each of the communication means in order of their relative symmetry from most to least symmetrical and list those that are relatively asymmetrical from most to least asymmetrical. In the third column, list the communication means in order of prevalence as a communication practice from most dominant to least. Find evidence for your list of dominant media in recent newspaper or trade journal articles.

Communication Means	Symmetrical	Asymmetrical	Dominant
face-to-face interpersonal			
hand written letters, memos			
PC computer printing			
Xerox copying			
Telephone			
Cellular phones			
Fax			
Beepers			
E-mail			
Internet			
Radio AM/FM			
Shortwave Radio			
Television UHF/VHF			
Cable television			
Satellite television			
Newspapers, magazines			
Desktop publishing			
Newsletters			
Billboards			
Book publishing			
Movies			
Home video			
Video Cassettes (VHS)			
Cassettes			
Compact discs			
Records			
Live assemblies, concerts			

Based on your lists, describe the "system" of U.S. communication practices and discuss its significance for democracy and participatory communication. Be prepared to present your description of the U.S. communications system in class.

PART IV | Literacy to Print

The previous section traced some of the changes in communication practices and their effect on social relations as a society passes from orality to literacy. The readings in this section reflect more on the character of written communication practices, including differences between individual writing and mechanical printing. Although television has largely replaced reading as the primary communication pastime, reading remains an important part of our culture and daily life—from reading the cereal box at breakfast, the morning comic strips, and personal letters to the fine print on legal documents, traffic signs, and instructions for operating machinery or equipment at home and work. In the United States, most people take written communication for granted, but it has not always been this way.

The production of written language has progressed from clerically handwritten sheets of vellum, to illuminated manuscripts of the late Middle Ages, to movable type printing beginning in the 16th century, to the mechanized printing of mass circulation books, to computer generated "typesetting" today. Significantly, the history of print indicates some important relationships between means of communication and social relations. Paper was invented in the 1200s, but printing was not invented until the 1400s and largely undeveloped until the 1600s. Although invented in China, printing was more widely employed in Europe because written Chinese employs hundreds of complex symbols, while languages based on an alphabet of 26 characters could be more easily adapted to movable type. Of course, hand lettering seemed sufficient until an emerging middle class of merchants and artisans needed improved written communication. Additionally, printing could not be fully mechanized without improvements in metallurgy, the invention of the screw and lever, and improvements in permanent ink. In other words, like other communication practices, printing developed out of the complex interaction between particular social needs and available technological innovations. As it becomes dominant, a communication practice, like printing, may in turn alter social relations and understandings.

As argued in previous readings, literate cultures understand the world differently than oral cultures. The written word isolates us from the context of the communication and lacks the non-verbal cues of orality, which themselves are imprecise indicators of desired meaning. Stated more generally, each communication "mutation" removes us from our actual experience and conditions: sounds abstractly represent things; words and letters abstractly represent sounds.

The two contributions in this section indicate that even changes *within* a particular mode of communication may affect our thought process, knowledge acquisition, and human relations. Mechanized printing, for instance, is quite different from manuscripts handwritten by scribes. The practice of mechanized print communication, as a particular form of the literacy modality, further allows and encourages abstract representations of our existence and condition. The list below indicates a few of the differences between "writing" and printing.

SOME GENERAL CHARACTERISTICS OF INDIVIDUAL WRITING AND MACHINE PRINTING

Individual Writing of Works	Mechanized Printing of Works
artistic form, language individual, unique	standardized in presentation and language
scarce, low-circulation	accessible, wide-circulation
content mostly sacred or official	content more practical, mundane
often difficult to read	more comprehensible, clearer type
audiences listen to official reader	individually read
audience of "receivers" could be illiterate	reading "receivers" needed education
authorities control of meaning, accuracy	meaning, accuracy available in other texts

---

The above characteristics should suggest that new communication practices have contradictory consequences for knowledge and society. Although printing created a new social hierarchy of literate and illiterate, it also undermined the previous authority of existing elite communication networks of priests, nobles, and scribes. As part of its need for standardization in the production process, printing encouraged the spread of the vernacular, everyday language of the people as the best means for spreading information and overcoming regional differences. James Chesebro and Dale Bertelson (1996) have related an outline of a general sociology of print cultures. Print encourages empiricism in its need for factual data. Printing changes education by making diverse knowledge more available for learning. Printing has a democratic impulse by removing the need for official interpreters of knowledge and information. Printing encourages nationalism by popularizing national language and identity. Finally, printing promotes individualism by increasing the importance of the author and by requiring individual use of the work. These "consequences" aren't necessarily that clear cut, however. For example, by removing the reader from the context, literacy may increase the value of empirical data, but it also permits the selection and manipulation of evidence. Likewise, compared to orality, literacy may enhance education, but at the same time, it may also create a new elite of "educated" literates.

The excerpt included here from *The Day the Universe Changed*, by historian James Burke, reveals many such contradictions accompanying the dramatic spread of print communication in Europe during the 16th century. While monarchies sought to use the press to enhance their control over the people, the dissident opposition also had a louder voice. Printing increased information, mitigating the need for memory. Printing eliminated the necessity for statues, stained glass, and paintings in churches as texts could now tell the stories. Finally, and perhaps most significantly, printing encouraged populations to be more progressive and future-oriented. Orality relied on the memory of past events—tradition and age were necessarily revered. Literacy, however, permitted youthful access to knowledge and individual investigations of the world. In short, changing the dominant communication practice "changed the universe."

At times, changing the application of even a seemingly insignificant communication practice can have exceptional social and political effect. In the final article of this section, Nicaraguan political activist and novelist Omar Cabezas remembers how political wall paintings altered people's consciousness and confidence in the late 1970s. Lacking access to the dominant media technology, youth opposed to the Somoza dictatorship found a creative means of communication—walls became political billboards. Cabezas refers to this political graffitti as "the voice of the people" because only with the tacit support of the citizenry could teens continue to paint anti-Somoza slogans in public places. In that sense, the "pintas" were a hybrid form of democratic communication because they expressed (non-verbally and literally) the needs and interests of the population. Unable to read newspapers and unable to buy expensive televisions, most of the population relied on radio communication (see section 5). Still, the "pintas" helped communicate the population's shared interest in democratic life. Ironically, the literacy of the "pintas" became a channel for mass communication among a largely illiterate population.

In the United States we usually think of graffitti and "tagging" as anti-social vandalism. However, understood as form of expression by disenfranchised youth who have no other means of public communication, graffitti appears as a predictable vibrant (albeit unsightly) communication practice. Graffitti in Nicaragua or the United States represents an attempt (however conscious or effective) by the powerless and the voiceless to use the written word to have some impact and control over the conditions of their lives.

As reflected in the readings in this section, literate communication has a similar impulse towards impact and control. Through language, we identify, name, explain, and thereby hope to better understand and control the conditions of our lives. As a communication practice, literacy further encourages classification, order, control. Literacy also dramatically increases the capacity for social control—those with access to resources and the means for printing can significantly influence the production and distribution of information and knowledge. However, if the means of communication are accessible to citizens, literacy can also aid in the democratic construction and distribution of knowledge, which potentially enhances our collective and individual understanding of the world. In sum, literacy can improve the quality of human life.

REFERENCES

James Chesebro and Dale Bertelsen. *Analyzing Media*. New York: Guilford, 1996.

11 | The Printing Revolution
James Burke

Somebody once observed to the eminent philosopher Wittgenstein how stupid medieval Europeans living before the time of Copernicus must have been that they could have looked at the sky and thought that the sun was circling the earth. Surely a modicum of astronomical good sense would have told them that the reverse was true. Wittgenstein is said to have replied: "I agree. But I wonder what it would have looked like if the sun had been circling the earth."

The point is that it would look exactly the same. When we observe nature we see what we want to see, according to what we believe we know about it at the time. Nature is disordered, powerful and chaotic, and through fear of the chaos we impose system on it. We abhor complexity, and seek to simplify things whenever we can by whatever means we have at hand. We need to have an overall explanation of what the universe is and how it functions. In order to achieve this overall view we develop explanatory theories which will give structure to natural phenomena: we classify nature into a coherent system which appears to do what we say it does.

This view of the universe permeates all aspects of our life. All communities in all places at all times manifest their own view of reality in what they do. The entire culture reflects the contemporary model of reality. We are what we know. And when the body of knowledge changes, so do we.

Each change brings with it new attitudes and institutions created by new knowledge. These novel systems then either oust or coexist with the structures and attitudes held prior to the change. Our modern view is thus a mixture of present knowledge and past viewpoints which have stood the test of time and, for one reason or another, remain valuable in new circumstances.

In looking at the historical circumstances which gave birth to these apparently anachronistic elements, which this book will attempt to do, it will be seen that at each stage of knowledge, the general agreement of what the universe is supposed to be takes the form of a shorthand code which is shared by everyone. Just as speech needs grammar to make sense of strings of words, so consensual forms are used by a community to give meaning to social interaction. These forms primarily take the shape of rituals.

Rituals are condensed forms of experience which convey meanings and values not necessarily immediately obvious or consciously understood by the people performing them. They relate to those elements of the culture considered valuable enough to retain. Involvement in them implies that the participants are not maverick. They conform by acting out the ritual. Each participant has a specific role to play, and one that is not invented or elaborated but laid down prior to the event.

A wedding, for instance, is a typically structured ritual act. In the Anglo-Saxon countries it represents a transition for the protagonists from one social state to another, from being members of a family to taking on the responsibility of creating another. The wedding formalises the transition, the change of state, within clearly understood terms and limits, which are witnessed by members of the public and officials of the community.

Much of the ritual is apparently anachronistic: the bride wears white; the service, whether religious or civil, involves archaic language and concepts which include the role of the woman as a chattel, to be given away. The event is infused with symbols. Flowers represent fertility, the ring is both a sexual and a business token, implying union in both senses. The bridesmaids intimate the state of virginity which the bride is about to leave. Both participants sign the contract, implying equality before the law. The honeymoon was a time when the bride and groom were removed from the pressures of daily life in order to begin their new family.

None of these elements may any longer be of direct value or meaning to the bride and groom today, but the fact that they are retained shows that marriage is still a socially important ritual. This indicates that the community considers formal and binding relationships between the sexes a necessary part of the continuity and stability of the group. The ritual remains for that reason.

Rituals which are performed widely and generally enough become institutionalised. These institutions are staffed by members of the society who are given authority and responsibility for social acts which are considered vital to the continued security and operation of the community. The institutions perform the function of social housekeepers, taking on the routine services which are necessary for the day to day functioning of the group. In some cases, such as that of government, the institution will confer real power on its members to make and enforce decisions about the future behaviour of the whole society.

In the case of the modern West, the primacy of money and possessions is indicated by the power and the institutionalised forms of those organisations whose job it is to ensure the continuity of finance and commercial transactions. Banks safeguard the means of exchange by formalising the ways in which it can be moved around. Although electronic fund transfer now makes the physical presence of bills of exchange and letters of credit unnecessary, the new medium still adheres to the system developed originally to handle the paper activity. The system is still that of seventeenth-century banking, because our society considers it to be sufficiently effective as a means of financial regulation to be retained almost unchanged.

The law is probably the institution that changes least in any society. In its codes it enshrines and protects the basic identity of the community. In its power to punish, it delineates the permitted forms of activity, those considered valuable, such as the act of innovation which is protected by patent legislation, and those which are considered to be so detrimental to the safety of the group at large that the punishment for transgression may be death. The particularly anachronistic way in which legal proceedings are carried on today—in dress, modes of speech, jury numbers, courtroom seating, and so on—indicates the value society places on the institution. The visible evidence of a continuing legal tradition enhances the impression of a community living under a permanent and consistent rule of law.

One of the principal aims of the institutions is that they free the majority of the group to do other things considered necessary for the welfare of all, such as the production of wealth, the maintenance of physical well-being and, above all, the inculcation of the community's view of life in the young. Humanity is unique in the length of time its offspring spend learning before they begin to take on adult responsibilities. Language gives us the unique ability to pass on information from one generation to another in the form of education.

The content of this kind of instruction indicates the social priorities of the group concerned, reveals in what terms it regards the world around it, and to a certain extent illustrates the direction in which a community considers that its own development should go. The very existence of formal educational institutions indicates that the community has the means and the desire to perpetuate a particular view, and shows whether that view is progressive and optimistic or, for example, static and theoretical in nature.

In our case, we use instruction to train young members of our society to ask questions. Education in the West consists of providing intellectual tools to be used for discovery. We encourage novelty, and this attitude is reflected in our educational curricula. Apparent anachronisms such as the titles of qualifications and of the teachers, as well as the conferring of formal accouterments on the graduating student, recall the medieval origins of the Organisation and at the same time show the importance our society attaches to standardised education. It is this quality-control approach to the product of the educational system that permits us to set up and encourage groups or organisations peculiar to modern Western culture, whose purpose is to bring change. In the main these take the form of research and development subdivisions of industrial or university systems. Their members are, in a way, the modern equivalent of the hunters and food-gatherers of early tribes.

In a world where few could read or write, a good memory was essential. It is for this reason that rhyme, a useful *aide-mémoire*, was the prevalent form of literature at the time. Up to the fourteenth century almost everything except legal documents was written in rhyme. French merchants used a poem made up of 137 rhyming couplets which contained all the rules of commercial arithmetic.

Given the cost of writing materials, a trained memory was a necessity for the scholar as much as for the merchant. For more specific tasks than day to day recall, medieval professionals used a learning aid which had originally been composed in late classical times. Its use was limited to scholars, who learned how to apply it as part of their training in the seven liberal arts, where memorising was taught under the rubric of rhetoric. The text they learned from was called *Ad Herennium*, the major mnemonic reference work of the Middle Ages. It provided a technique for recalling vast quantities of material by means of the use of "memory theatres."

The material to be memorised was supposed to be conceived of as a familiar location. This could take the form of all or part of a building: an arch, a corner, an entrance hall, and so on. The location was also supposed to satisfy certain criteria. The interior was to be made up of different elements, easily recognised one from the other. If the building were too big, accuracy of recall would suffer. If it were too small, the separate parts of what was to be recalled would be too close to each other for individual recall. If it were too bright it would blind the memory. Too dark, it would obscure the material to be remembered.

Each separate part of the location was to be thought of as being about thirty feet apart, so as to keep each major segment of the material isolated from the others. Once the memory theatre was prepared in this way, the process of memorising would involve the memoriser in a mental walk through the building. The route should be one which was logical and habitual, so that it might be easily and naturally recalled. The theatre was now ready to be filled with the material to be memorised.

This material took the form of mental images representing the different elements to be recalled. *Ad Herrenium* advised that strong images were the best, so reasons should be found to make the data stand out. The images should be funny, or bloody, or gaudy, ornamented, unusual, and so on.

These images were to act as "agents" of memory and each image would trigger recall of several components of the material. The individual elements to be recalled should be imaged according to the kind of material. If a legal argument were being memorised, a dramatic scene might be appropriate. At the relevant point in the journey through the memory theatre, this scene would be triggered and played out, reminding the memoriser of the points to be recalled. The stored images could also relate to individual words, strings of words or entire arguments. Onomatopoeia, the use of words that sound like the action they describe, was particularly helpful in this regard.

The great medieval theologian St Thomas Aquinas particularly recommended the theatrical use of imagery for the recall of religious matters. "All knowledge has its origins in sensation," he said. The truth was accessible through visual aids. Especially in the twelfth and thirteenth centuries the influx of new Greek and Arab knowledge, both scientific and general, made memorisation by scholars and professionals more necessary than ever.

As painting and sculpture began to appear in churches the same techniques for recall were applied. Church imagery took on the form of memory agent. In Giotto's paintings of 1306 on the interior of the Arena Chapel in Padua the entire series of images is structured as a memory theatre. Each Bible story illustrated is told through the medium of a figure or group in a separate place....

The man who is credited with inventing the process was Johannes Gansfleisch zur Laden zum Gutenberg. His new press destroyed the oral society. Printing was to bring about the most radical alteration ever made in Western intellectual history, and its effects were to be felt in every area of human activity.

The innovation was not in fact new. There had been an even earlier attempt, in China, which produced baked-clay letter founts, but these were fragile and did not lend themselves to mass-production. In any case the task would have been daunting, as the Chinese language demanded between 40,000 and 50,000 ideograms.

The next step took place in Korea. In 1126 the palaces and libraries of the country had been destroyed during a dynastic struggle. It was urgently necessary to replace the lost texts, and, because they had been so numerous, any technique for replacement had to be quick and easy. The only Korean hardwood which might have been used to replace the books using woodcut techniques was birch. Unfortunately this wood was available only in limited quantities and was already being used to print paper money. The solution to the problem did not come until around 1313, when metal typecasting was developed. The method adopted of striking out a die to make a mould in which the letter could be cast was well known at the time, as it had been in common use since the early twelfth century by coiners and casters of brass-ware and bronze.

Due to a Confucian prohibition on the commercialisation of printing, the books produced by this new Korean method were distributed free by the government. This severely limited the spread of the technique. So too did the restriction of the new technique to the royal foundry, where official material only was printed and where the primary interest lay in reproducing the Chinese classics rather than Korean literature which might have found a wider and more receptive audience. In the early fifteenth century King Sajong of Korea invented a simplified alphabet of twenty-four characters, for use by the common people. This alphabet could have made large-scale typecasting feasible, but it did not have the impact it deserved. The royal presses still did not print Korean texts.

It may be that the typecasting technique then spread to Europe with the Arab traders. Korean typecasting methods were certainly almost identical to those introduced by Gutenberg, whose father was in fact a member of the Mainz fellowship of coiners.

In Europe, prior to Gutenberg, there are references to attempts at artificial writing being made in Bruges, Bologna and Avignon, and it is possible that Gutenberg was preceded by a Dutchman called Coster or an unknown Englishman. Be that as it may, the Koreans' interest in Chinese culture and their failure to adopt the new alphabet prevented the use and spread of the world's first movable typeface for two hundred years.

The reason for the late appearance of the technique in the West may be related to the number of developments which had to take place before printing could succeed. These included advances in metallurgy, new experiments with inks and oils, the production of paper, and the availability of eye-glasses. Also significant would have been the mounting economic pressure for more written material and dissatisfaction with the over-costly *scriptoria*, as well as the generally rising standards of education which accompanied economic recovery after the Black Death.

Once introduced, however, the speed with which printing propagated itself throughout Europe suggests a market ready and willing to use it. From Mainz it reached Cologne in 1464, Basel in 1466, Rome in 1467, Venice 1469, Paris, Nuremberg and Utrecht 1470, Milan, Naples and Florence 1471, Augsburg 1472, Lyons, Valencia and Budapest 1473, Cracow and Bruges 1474, Lübeck and Breslau 1475, Westminster and Rostock 1476, Geneva, Palermo and Messina 1478, London 1480, Antwerp and Leipzig 1481 and Stockholm 1483.

It should be noted that almost without exception these were not university cities. They were centres of business, the sites of royal courts or the headquarters of banking organisations. By the end of the fifteenth century there were 73 presses in Italy, 51 in Germany, 39 in France, 25 in Spain, 15 in the Low Countries and 8 in Switzerland. In the first fifty years eight million books were printed.

The price of the new books was of crucial significance in the spread of the new commodity. In 1483 the Ripola Press in Florence had charged three florins a sheet for setting up and printing Ficino's translation of Plato's *Dialogues*. A scribe would have charged one florin for a single copy. The Ripola Press produced one thousand and twenty-five.

Not everybody took to the press with the same eagerness. Joachim Furst, Gutenberg's financial backer, went to Paris with twelve copies of the Bible but was chased out by the book trade guilds, who took him to court. Their view was that so many identical books could only exist with the help of the devil.

The new printing shops have been variously described as a mixture of sweatshop, boarding house and research institute. They brought together members of society strange to each other. The craftsman rubbed shoulders with the academic and the businessman. Besides attracting scholars and artists, the shops were sanctuaries for foreign translators, émigrés and refugees in general, who came to offer their esoteric talents.

Printing shops were, above all, centres for a new kind of intellectual and cultural exchange. Existing outside the framework of the guild system, they were free of its restrictive practices. The new printers thought of themselves as the inheritors of the scribal tradition, and used the word *scriptor* to describe themselves rather than the more accurate *impressor*.

In the earliest printed books the scribal style of lettering was maintained. This conservative approach was in part dictated by the demands of the market. A buyer was less likely to be put off by the new product if he saw familiar manuscript abbreviations and punctuation. It was only when the new printed books were well established in the next century that printers began to spell words in full and standardise punctuation.

The print shop was one of the first truly capitalist ventures. The printer or his partner was often a successful merchant who was responsible for finding investors, organising supplies and labour, setting up production schedules, coping with strikes, hiring academically qualified assistants and analysing the market for printed texts. He was also in intense competition with others who were doing the same, and was obliged to risk capital on expensive equipment.

It should not come as a surprise that these men pioneered the skills of advertising. They issued book lists and circulars bearing the name and address of their shop. They put the firm's name and emblem on the first page of the book, thus moving the title page from the back, where it had traditionally been placed, to the front, where it was more visible. The shops printed announcements of university lectures together with synopses of course textbooks and lectures, also printed by them.

In the early years each printer adopted the script most common in his area, but before long print type was standardised. By 1480, when the scribal writing styles had disappeared, texts were being printed in *cancelleria* (chancery script) style, the classical letter shape favoured by the Italian humanists who were the intellectual leaders of Europe at the time. At the beginning of the sixteenth century, in Venice, at the print shop of the great Italian printer Aldus Manutius, one of his assistants, Francesco Griffo of Bologna, invented a small cursive form of *cancelleria*. The style was designed to save space, and gave Aldus a monopoly on the market in books of a size which could be carried easily in a pocket or saddlebag. The new style of type was called "italic."

Initially the market for texts was limited. The first texts produced after the invention of printing fell into the following categories: sacred (Bibles and prayer books), academic (the grammar of Donatus, used in schools), bureaucratic (papal indulgences and decrees) and vernacular (few, mostly German).

Thereafter the content of the books became rapidly more diverse. By the end of the century there were guide-books and maps, phrase books and conversion tables for foreign exchange, ABCs, catechisms, calendars, devotional literature of all sorts, primers, dictionaries—all the literary paraphernalia of living that we in the modern world take for granted and which influences the shape and style of every aspect of our lives.

Almost immediately after its invention print began to affect the lives of Europeans in the fifteenth century. The effect was not always for the better. Along with the proliferation of knowledge came the diffusion of many of the old scriptural inaccuracies. Mystic Hermetic writings, astrologies and books of necromancy were reproduced in large numbers, as were collections of prophecies, hieroglyphics and magic practices. The standardisation made possible by print meant that errors were perpetuated on a major scale.

Apart from the Latin and Greek classics, all of which were reproduced within a hundred years, and the Bible, the greatest number of new books sold were of the "how to" variety. The European economy had desperate need of craftsmen, whose numbers had been reduced by the Black Death, the effects of restrictive practices and lengthy apprenticeships. For centuries these skills had remained unchanged and unchallenged as they were passed from generation to generation by word of mouth and example. Through the medium of the press they now became the property of anyone who could afford to buy a book. The transmission of technical information was also more likely to be accurate, since it was now written by experts and reproduced exactly by the press.

The principal effect of printing, however, was on the contents of the texts themselves. The press reduced the likelihood of textual corruption. Once the manuscript had been made error-free, accurate reproduction was automatic. Texts could not easily undergo alteration. The concept of authorship also emerged. For the first time a writer could be sure of reaching a wide readership which would hold him personally responsible for what he had written. Printing made possible new forms of cross-cultural exchange without the need for physical communication. New ways were developed to present, arrange and illustrate books. It became feasible to collect books systematically, by author or subject. But the most immediately evident effect of printing lay simply in the production of many more copies of existing manuscript texts.

A prime example of the proliferation of an already established text was the use of the press by the Church to reproduce thousands of printed indulgences. These were documents given to the faithful in return for prayer, penitence, pilgrimage or, most important of all, money. The early sixteenth-century Popes, especially Julius II, had grandiose plans for the embellishment of Rome after the fall of the rival city of Constantinople in the previous century. Rome would become the centre of the world and indulgences would help to pay for the work of expensive artists such as Michelangelo.

The widespread cynicism which greeted this ecclesiastical involvement with the world of technology was undoubtedly a contributing factor to the rebellion of the Augustinian friar of Wittenberg, Martin Luther, which sparked off the Reformation. In 1517, Maximilian I's silver jubilee year, indulgences were being hawked in great numbers near Wittenberg by one of the papal commissioners for sales, a certain Tetzel. His techniques were flamboyant, and the credulous flocked to hear him and to buy his wares. The demand for indulgences was so great that a thriving black market was generated.

Luther reacted to events by producing ninety-five criticisms of the Church, which he nailed to a notice board in his church in Wittenberg, He also sent a copy to his Bishop and one to friends. Luther's expectations of a quiet, scholarly discussion of his grievances among his friends were rudely shattered when copies were printed and distributed. Within a fortnight the "theses" were being read throughout Germany. Within a month they were all over Europe. Luther found himself at the head of a rebellious army he had never thought to command. The only way to make the rebellion effective was to use the same weapon that had started it: the press.

Three years later 300,000 copies of Luther's works were on the market. The broadsheet carried his words to every village. The use of cartoons brought the arguments to illiterates and his choice of the vernacular strongly appealed to the nascent nationalist temper of the Protestant German princes. "Print," Luther said, "is the best of God's inventions." The first propaganda war had been won.

The new power to disseminate opinion was seized early by anybody with a desire to influence others. The printers themselves had shown the way with their advertisements. Now the broadsheet radically changed the ability to communicate. Broadsheets were pinned up everywhere, stimulating the demand for education and literacy by those who could not read them. Public opinion was being moulded for the first time, fuelled by anonymous appeals to emotion and the belief that what was printed was true.

Centralised monarchies used the press to enhance their control over the people and to keep them informed of new ordinances and tax collections. Since the increasingly large numbers of directives in circulation each originated from one clearly identifiable printing house, it was easy for Church and state to impose controls on what could and could not be read.

The corollary was, of course, that dissidence now also had a louder voice, whether expressed as nationalist fervour—itself fostered by the establishment of the local language in print—or as religion. The persecution and religious wars that ravaged Europe in the sixteenth century were given fresh and continuing impetus by the press, as each side used propaganda to whip up the frenzy of its supporters.

In the political arena printing provided new weapons for state control. As men became more literate, they could be expected to read and sign articles of loyalty. The simple oath was no longer sufficient, and in any case a man could deny it. He could not deny the signature at the foot of a clearly printed text. This represented the first appearance of the modern contract, and with it came the centralisation of the power of the state.

Through the press the monarch had direct access to the people. He no longer had to worry about the barons and their network of local allegiance. Proclamations and manifestoes were issued to be read from every pulpit. Printed texts of plays were sponsored to praise and give validity to the king's policies. Woodcut cartoons glorifying his grander achievements were disseminated. Maximilian of Austria had one made entitled "The Triumphal Arch" which simply reproduced his name in a monumental setting.

Political songs emerged, as did political catch-phrases and slogans. The aim was to identify the kingdom with the ruler, thereby strengthening his position. A war became known as "the King's War." Taxes were collected for the king's needs. Prayers for his health were printed and distributed. In England they were inserted into the book of Common Prayer. For the first time, the name of the country could be seen on broadsheets at every street corner. The king's actual face would eventually appear, on French paper money.

With the press came a new, vicarious form of living and thinking. For the first time it was easy to learn of events and people in distant countries. Europe became more aware of its regional differences than ever before. As Latin gave way to the vernacular languages encouraged by the local presses, these differences became more obvious. Printing also set international fashions not only in clothes, but in manners, art, architecture, music, and every other aspect of living. A book of dress patterns in the "Spanish" style was available throughout the Hapsburg Empire.

The printing press brought Italy before the world, elected that country arbiter of taste for a century or more, and helped the Renaissance to survive in Europe longer and with more effect than it might otherwise have done.

With the spread of printing came loss of memory. As learning became increasingly text-oriented, the memory-theatre technique fell into disuse. Prose appeared more frequently, as the mnemonic value of poetry became less important.

Printing eliminated many of the teaching functions of church architecture, where sculpture and stained glass had acted as reminders of biblical stories. In the sixth century Pope Gregory had stated that statues were the books of the illiterate. Now that worshippers were literate the statues served no further purpose. Printing thus reinforced the iconoclastic tendencies among reformers. If holy words were available in print, what need was there for ornamental versions? The plain, unadorned churches of the Protestants reflected the new literary view.

Art in general began increasingly to portray individual states of emotion, personal interpretations of the world. It was art for art's sake. Printing removed the need for a common share of images and in doing so destroyed the collective memory that had sustained the pre-literate communities. There also began a new genre of printed illustrated books for children, such as Comeius' picture book and Luther's catechism. These and others served to continue the old images in new form.

One major result of printing was the emergence of a more efficient system of filing. With more than a thousand editions reproduced from the same original, book collecting became fashionable. These collections needed to be catalogued. Moreover, printers had begun to identify their books by title, as well as author, so it was easier to know what a book was about.

Cataloguing involved yet another new ability. People began to learn the alphabet, which until the advent of printing had had little use. Early printers found that their books sold better if they included an index. In scribal times indexing, when used at all, had been achieved by the use of small tabs attached to the side of the parchment leaf. Johannes Trithemius, Abbot of Sponheim, produced the first indexed catalogue in Basel, in 1494: *Liber de Scriptoribus Ecclesiasticis* (The Book of Ecclesiastical Writings).

His successor, Conrad Gesner, went further. His idea was to produce a comprehensive, universal bibliography listing all Latin, Greek and Hebrew works in their first printing, using as a source publishers' lists and booksellers' catalogues. In 1545 he published the *Bibliotheca Universalis* (The Universal Collection) of 10,000 titles and 3000 authors. He followed this in 1548 with the *Pandectae*, a catalogue with nineteen separate headings dedicated to a different scholarly discipline. Each one contained topical entries cross-referencing author and title, with dedications that craftily included the publishers' lists. The work contained more than 30,000 entries.

The new interest in indexing led to a more factual analysis of the older texts. Machiavelli's father was asked to index Livy's *Decades* for Vespasiano da Bisticci, and in doing so he made comprehensive lists of flora and fauna, place names and other such factual data, rather than taking the scribal approach of listing everything according to moral principles. The new availability of data and the novel concept of information as a science in itself made the collation and use of data easier than before.

The principal contribution to knowledge by the presses, however, lay in the establishment of accurate reproduction. When books came to be written by men whose identity was known, writers became more painstaking. After all, the text might be read by people who knew more of the subject than the author himself. Moreover, each writer could now build on the work of a previous expert in his field. Scholarship benefited from not having to return to first principles every time, so ideas progressed and proliferated.

Texts could be compared and corrected by readers with specialised or local knowledge. Information became more trustworthy. More books encouraged more inter-disciplinary activity, new combinations of knowledge and new disciplines. Among the earliest texts were tables of mathematical and navigational material, eagerly sought by an increasing number of ships' captains.

Ready-reckoners made technical and business life easier. Above all, the fact that identical images could be viewed simultaneously by many readers was a revolution in itself. Now the world was open to analysis by the community at large. The mystery of "essence" and intangible God-given substance gave way to realistic drawings which took advantage of the new science of perspective to measure and describe nature mathematically. Not only was the world measurable, it could be held in one's hand in the knowledge that the same experience was being shared by others.

New natural sciences sprang up, born of this ability to standardise the image and description of the world. The earliest examples took the form of reprints of the classics. Soon, however, Europeans began describing the contemporary world around them. In Zurich Gesner began compiling his compendium of all the animals ever mentioned in all the printed texts he knew. He published four books in 1557. Meanwhile, in 1530, Otto Brunfels had produced his book on plants, *Herbarum vivae eicones*. In 1535 Pierre Belon of Le Mans published *Fish and Birds*. In 1542 came the *Natural History of Plants* by Leonard Fuchs. Four years later Georg Bauer's work on subterranean phenomena was published under his pen-name of Agricola. In 1553, Bauer, who was inspector of mines in Bohemia, produced the great *De Re Metallica* (On Metals).

Printing changed the entire, backward-looking view of society, with its stultifying respect for the achievements of the past, to one that looked forward to progress and improvement. The Protestant ethic, broadcast by the presses, extolled the virtues of hard work and thrift and encouraged material success. Printing underlined this attitude. If knowledge could now be picked up from a book, the age of unquestioned authority was over. A printed fifteenth-century history expressed the new opinion: "Why should old men be preferred to their juniors when it is possible, by diligent study, for young men to acquire the same knowledge?"

The cult of youth had begun. As young men began to make their way in the new scientific disciplines made possible by standardisation of textual information, it was natural for them to explore new areas of thought. Thus was born the specialisation which is the lifeblood of the modern world. The presses made it possible for specialists to talk to specialists and enhance their work through a pooling of resources. Researchers began to write for each other, in the language of their discipline: the "gobbledegook" of modern science. And with this specialised interchange came the need for precision in experiment. Each author vied with his fellow-professionals for accuracy of observation, and encouraged the development of tools with which to be more precise. Knowledge became something to be tested on an agreed scale. What was proved, and agreed, became a "fact."

Printing gave us our modern way of ordering thought. It gave us the mania for the truth "in black and white." It moved us away from respect for authority and age, towards an investigative approach to nature based on the confidence of common, empirical observation. This approach made facts obsolete almost as soon as they were printed.

In removing us from old mnemonic ways of recall and the collective memory of the community, printing isolated each of us in a way previously unknown, yet left us capable of sharing a bigger world, vicariously. In concentrating knowledge in the hands of those who could read, printing gave the intellectual specialist control over illiterates and laymen. In working to apply his esoteric discoveries the specialist gave us the rate of change with which we live today, and the inability, from which we increasingly suffer, to communicate specialist "facts" across the boundaries of scientific disciplines.

At the same time, however, the presses opened the way to all who could read to share for the first time the world's collective knowledge, to explore the minds of others, and to approach the mysteries of nature with confidence instead of awe.

REFERENCES

Brown, Lloyd A., *The Story of Maps* (Dover Publications: New York, 1949).

Buck, L. P., *The Social History of the Reformation* (Ohio State University Press, 1972).

Clanchy, M. T., *From Memory to Written Record* (Edward Arnold, 1979).

Dickens, A. G., *The German Nation and Martin Luther* (Fontana, 1974).

Eisenstein, Elizabeth L., *The Printing Press as an Agent of Change*, Vols I and 11 (Cambridge University Press, 1979).

Febvre, Lucien, and Martin, Henri-Jean, *The Coming of the Book* (New Left Books, 1976).

Gilmore, Myron P., *The World of Humanism, 1453-1517* (Harvard University Press, 1962).

Ivins, William M., *Prints and Visual Communication* (Routledge & Kegan Paul, 1953).

Jemett, Sean, *The Making of Books* (Paber & Faber, 1951).

Lindsay, Jack, *The Troubadours and their World* (Frederick Muller, 1976).

Scholderer, Victor, *Johann Gutenberg: The Inventor of Printing* (British Museum Publications, 1970).

Smalley, Beryl, *The Study of the Bible in the Middle Ages* (Basil Blackwell: Oxford, 1952).

Steinberg, S. H., *Five Hundred Years of Printing* (Pelican: Harmondsworth, 1955).

Updike, D, B., *Printing Types: Their History, Forms and Use* (Oxford University Press, 1922).

Yates, Frances A., *The Art of Memory* (Penguin: Harmondsworth, 1966).

12 | The Voice of the People Is the Voice of the "Pintas"

Omar Cabezas

The "pintas" were, at first, the voices of the catacombs. They were the speakers of the clandestine struggle, the spreading of a secret which was beginning. Thus, "la pinta" was a clandestine expression, the surreptitious voice which the country suddenly perceived as an announcement of "clandestinity."

Like the voices from the catacombs, which began to announce the Front, there were walls or isolated "pintas," but they announced a complete act of conspiracy. Like the labor of an ant, secret, solitary, an awareness, an organization beginning to form itself.

I am speaking of, shall we say, from 1965 to 1968 because by 1969 the "pinta" began to become more generalized. From then on, the "pintas" were always keeping the beat, the pulse of what was happening, as much through their range and quantity as through their message. The "pintas" were the stethoscope of the Sandinista Front placed over the political heart of the people. In fact, there began to unfold an entire, yet slow, process of increasing the "pintas" which corresponded to the increase in the political forces of the FSLN, of the people organized at different levels and made into a vanguard by the FSLN. In this way, the "pintas," at one point the voices of political silence became the voice of those who have no voice—the voice of the silenced, of the quiet, of the humiliated, of the hidden, of those who cannot speak.

I remember my first "pinta." The first "pinta" that I put into my life I wrote on the run, out of fear. It was a duty to write this "pinta"; besides, I was responsible for it. It was located within the miserable frame of my own neighborhood. What can I tell these people? I asked. They are so alone, so unprotected. So I wrote on the wall, in big letters: "Vivan los pobres, mueran los ricos, FSLN" ["Long live the poor, death to the rich, FSLN"].

The people under the dictatorship didn't have a voice; in appearance they had the vote, but never a voice, and on the walls a process of regaining the word was unfolding, beginning to be expressed. The wall is the voice of a people shouting. Of course, there were different messages, but the important thing is to make clear that it was a process of regaining one's voice on behalf of the people. It was the right of the people to express themselves. The voice of the people is the voice of the "pintas." We took the walls away from the enemy; this was our property. They used the walls before the Front; afterwards, we began to use them and for some time we shared them and there was an equilibrium between "pintas"; and, finally, we displaced them from

---

From *Communicating in Popular Nicaragua*, edited by Armand Mattelart. Reprinted by permission of the editor.

the walls, just as we evicted them from power, just as we evicted from the barracks, first, we evicted them from the walls. The "pintas" gave an insurrectional character to the walls. The voice of the silenced ones took the walls by assault. The people let out a shout on the surface of the walls. From then on, the walls bore true witness to what was happening.

I don't know when, historically, the "pintas" first appeared in Nicaragua, but ever since I can remember, in my town there have been "pintas." The political "pintas" which I recall most clearly were those which appeared one day in my neighborhood, "El Laboría," in the town of León: "Viva el Frente de Liberación Nacional" or "Viva el FSLN" ["Long live the National Liberation Front," "Long live the FSLN"]. This was sometime near the end of 1966 or in the beginning of 1967, to the best of my memory. I used to leave for classes at seven in the morning and suddenly I discovered these "pintas" on the wall. My first sensation was one of fear. I felt this because this was something against the government, something dangerous that people painted in darkness, men probably armed with a gun. This is why the "pintas" signified danger. They were people who were doing this at night, unknown people. As to whether or not they would someday win...no way; the thought never crossed my mind.

Later, it was different. On the wall it said, "Abajo Somoza" or "Basta ya" ["Down with Somoza", "Enough"]. But also I remember when I saw for the first time the "pintas" "Sandino, Viva Sandino" or "Viva el Frente Sandinista" ["Long live Sandino," "Long live the Sandinista Front"]. That was possibly one of the first times that I felt again close to Sandino. Again, because my grandma used to tell me about Sandino. In Sandino's time, in the north, the Yankees had burnt down my grandfather's ranch, beat him and hung him up from a wooden beam, and then burnt down the farmhouse with him inside. These were the stories that my grandma told me when I was a child, and when I saw those "pintas," I was in my fifth year of my bachelor's degree, and it had been a long time since I had heard anything about Sandino. One morning, I leave my house and there it is, across the street: a large wall with the sign "Viva Sandino," which unexpectedly sends me back to my grandfather, to the stories of my childhood and I feel the presence in red, in red spray paint or in red paint, of Sandino and of my grandfather.

The "pintas" began with the students and afterwards they became more generalized with political work, first in Managua and later throughout the country. But the culture of the "pintas" begins with the university. The "pintas" were always the tasks of the moment. There are "pintas" painted for conjunctural moments, there are "pintas" with tactical and strategic content. There are threatening "pintas," and there are "pintas" which reflect popular humor. There are very direct "pintas," personal ones, as if the people had begun to converse by using the walls as an intermediary. The people began to become conscious of one another; messages began to have a new language all their own. The walls were always announcements.

Here, of course, never appeared: "Mientras más hago el amor, más quiero hacer la revolución, y mientras más hago la revolución, más quiero hacer al amor" ["The more I make love, the more I want to make revolution, and the more I make revolution, the more I want to make love"]. Because this "pinta" belongs in another context, that of May '68 in Paris. The "pintas" in Nicaragua reflect the political content of a concrete event, of a concrete people, of a concrete culture. Because the "pintas" also are a cultural event, a cultural/political phenomenon.

The political phrases appeared on the walls for the masses to interpret. There was, for example, a moment when the bourgeoisie was beginning to prepare a *coup d'Etat* against Somoza, after the tyrant had suffered a heart attack, in order to frustrate the revolution. At that time, this "pinta" came forth: "Golpe Militar No" ["No Military *Coup*"]. There were many preinsurrection "pintas," such as "A desarmar la guardia somocista" [Disarm the Somoza Guard"]. This precise slogan called for the neighborhoods to attack the guard's vehicles and disarm them. If a dumb guard or police watchman is found, he must be disarmed. In order to have weapons, one must take them from the guards; the goal is to get hold of weapons. Each person in his neighborhood, because one has to have weapons for the insurrection, and until now there were few. There are "pintas" which were a very practical example of their use in conjunctural moments.

The 1965 "pinta" "Viva el FSLN" ["Long live the FSLN"] announced the existence of the Front. An entire development was necessary in order for the masses to express "FSLN al poder" ["FSLN to power"]. The "pintas" are the expression of popular ingenuity. There is a saying which goes, "No hay mal que dure cien años ni cuerpo que lo resista" ["There is no illness which lasts one hundred years, nor a body which could stand it"]. Somoza intended his presidential term, which began in 1975, to last until 1981. This lead the people to say on the walls "No hay mal que dure hasta 81 ni pueblo que lo resista" ["There is no illness which lasts until '81, nor a people who could stand it"]. In this one is found the hatred of the people, where insult and obscenity become political: "Somoza hijo de puta" ["Somoza, son of a whore"]. Or this one, after the triumph: "Se fue quien nos jodió" ["The one who screwed us is gone"]. And rhyme is always present; it is one of the characteristics of spontaneous popular expression. Spontaneous rhyme is one of the poetic gifts of this people. It's the presence of Darío[1] in the middle of the insurrection; the existence of Darío in this country.

Other "pintas" give a rallying cry; Somoza must be isolated. For this, it's necessary for the people to gang up on Somoza: "El pueblo se está muriendo por culpa de Somoza" ["The people are dying and it's Somoza's fault"]. This type of "pinta" was a form of propaganda. The "pintas" had to be direct so that the people could grasp them. For that reason, at the same time that the people were acquiring a consciousness, the "pinta" began to acquire different connotations and to reflect the tasks of the moment. If you had written "Todo el poder al FSLN" ["All power to the FSLN"] in the mid-1970s, folks would have looked at you as if you were crazy. But if you wrote it in 1978-79, it is because we were really capable of taking power. That's why the "pintas" of the 1960s and early 1970s, when we were a clandestine few, were different from the "pintas" during the insurrection and the "pintas" after the insurrection. The "pintas" of the revolutionary process reflect the tasks of the class struggle which began after the triumph of the insurrection. Now they have two connotations; some are goals to be worked for—all those dealing with literacy and health—and the others concern ideological debates. Then there are always those defending our sovereignty.

In the beginning, there was very little spray paint with which to make "pintas." We had to use a bucket of paint and a brush. Then, one would always go with one's "compañeros," sometimes with a car, at night or at dawn, in darkness. One of us would stand on one corner and another on the other corner. Then one guy in the middle would paint. When the guardia came we would hide everything in the car and drive off normally. That was the "nocturnal 'pinta'." In the beginning, if they caught you painting "pintas," they would arrest you, convict you and give you six months. Later, when the repression was increasing, if the guards caught you painting, you were a dead man.

But not always. The 15th of September is our traditional patriotic holiday commemorating the battle of San Jacinto against Walker and the independence of Nicaragua, of Central America. The dictatorship always organized events on the 14th or the 15th, I don't remember which, and the mayor or a town representative would speak and a military band would parade playing marches. Well, the night before this, we left the club at the university to "pinta" the streets. We began at about two in the morning. My friend, El Gato Munguia, and I went one way as we were both on foot that night. We painted from two in the morning until dawn when we arrived at the downtown area of the city of León with our "pintas." At 5:30 in the morning we were in the central park in the plaza of León, where the events were going to take place. We did the last "pinta," to finish the job, on the wall of the circular baptismal font in the central park. El Gato and I were completely stained with paint, our hair, our shirts, our pants; everything was red and blue. Those were the only two colors which we had been able to obtain. Our hands, our faces, dripping paint from all sides, with the brushes, were worn out. We did the last "pinta" and we sat down on top of the circular wall of the font, which is across from the cathedral. We were resting there, without speaking, watching the cathedral cutting into the skyline and the large columns holding up the cathedral, when suddenly we heard the sound of a vehicle coming from the street where the National Guard is stationed. We turned our heads around and then said to ourselves, "Damn it, there's the National Guard." We were filthy and besides, in León we were "fingered." We had a certain aura of bravery; how should I know that legends that arise among the people also crop up among the ranks of the enemy. The National Guard's vehicle appeared and parked directly across from where we were sitting. El Gato and I were resolved not to move as long as they didn't approach us. They got out of the vehicle, first one, then another, then afterwards, two others. They stayed there looking at us, and we saw them taking something out. It was the flag of Nicaragua which they put at half mast to be raised for an official ceremony. The guards continued watching us, and we stared back with an air of superiority, just daring them. The best thing is that they didn't dare, and as soon as they left we took off down the street headed for the university. We almost died of fright, but what joy!

There is not only the "nocturnal 'pinta'," when one left the house clandestinely, in darkness, to leave a message for the people via the walls. When the struggle of the masses was reaching a crescendo, they took advantage of the daylight, of the demonstration, to go painting as a group. As such the "pinta" became not the expression of the voice of the silenced, but, rather the expression of struggle in the streets by the oppressed masses who became active in the streets and regained their voice. In this way, things were said publicly, in demonstrations, by means of the walls. At that time, the guards would throw paint on the "pintas", as a form of drowning out the voice of the people. Another expression of censorship of the media under the dictatorship was throwing black tar over the "pintas." But the people living in the houses became furious because they preferred to put up with the "pintas" rather than the black tar. The walls of the house would really look horrible afterwards. And besides, since the *compañeros* always painted on the recently painted houses, the prettiest ones....

The "pintas" were a voice from darkness, coming from the night, and to tell the truth, the walls were always our accomplices. They were our means of communication with the masses, the means of communication of the masses. The newspaper *Barricada* was born on the walls. The Voice of Nicaragua and Radio Sandino were born on the walls, and the television system in the hands of the people was born on the walls. All those graphic signs, those schemas, those funny drawings, are also the genesis of our means of mass communication.

The "pintas" patiently bore the pain of the masses, the rage, the happiness—I remember a "pinta" after the triumph "Por fin somos libres" ["At last we are free"]—the trust, the poetry, the humor of the masses. The "pintas" are the masses live and in color on the walls. That's why the "pinta" has been the site of a form of culture; the "pintas" were initiated when we were alone and now we even have murals by internationalists who have come to accompany us. This poses a very valid question which is both beautiful and interesting; a very symbolic question. The question of camaraderie. As the culture of the "pinta" has developed, it has given rise to an expression of camaraderie with the Nicaraguan people. We Nicaraguans are not alone and the walls tell us this.

Now that I think about it, creating "pintas" is also an impetus. Someone wrote on a sign under the motto "Una esperanza para Nicaragua—Partido Conservador" ["A Hope for Nicaragua—the Conservative Party"), "Qué clase de esperanza! " ["Some kind of hope!"] This is a great "pinta." This is Nicaraguan humor at its best. There is a sign which inspired me to paint on it. It's on the Northern highway and says, "Con el partido socialdemocrata Nicaragua va a ser república" ["With the Social Democratic Party, Nicaragua is going to be a republic"], and I added underneath, "Banana." I didn't think of this when I was in the mountains because there are no walls, but when we were going back south, it came to me.

NOTES

[1] "Pintas": any painted graffiti, usually containing a sociopolitical message (Translator's Note).

[2] Darío was a Nicaraguan poet of the late 19th and early 20th century, a leader of the Modernist movement and probably Central America's greatest poet (Translator's Note).

PART V | Journalism as a Communication Practice

Each general pattern or "modality" of communication can take many forms depending on the needs and relationships within a particular society . As noted earlier, orality can be more or less symmetrical, with a varying degree of ritual and non-verbal systems. Likewise, literacy may appear in many forms, from handwriting, to mechanical printing, to computer-generated characters on a video screen. Additionally, each of these forms may "mutate" into a variety of specific communication practices. For instance, "e-mail" is a common communication practice based on computer "print." One of the most important communication practices for generating and exchanging knowledge and information in modern society is journalism. None of the readings included detail particular journalism techniques. Rather, in keeping with the approach of this text, the readings deal more generally on the history and practice of journalism.

Journalism professor and American cultural studies scholar, James Carey enters what he calls the "dark continent" of American journalism by reflecting on its early years. Carey notes that journalism's communication practices are social conventions which developed in conjunction with clear social interests. Newspapers did not always "report" breaking stories, distinguish news from analysis and editorial, or subscribe to current "professional" practices of objectivity, fairness, and accuracy. Rather, these and other practices, arose in tandem with advertising, urban growth, class antagonisms, and new media technologies. Carey marks three key moments in early print history in the United States which shaped current journalistic practices: the decline of the partisan press, the emergence of the penny press, and the development of the telegraph as the primary transmitter of information "facts."

The "partisan" press printed news and information important to a specific political or cultural group. Carey argues that news in partisan papers made sense and had meaning because it was interpreted around clear social group interests. Most partisan papers, including those of labor and ethnic groups which were concerned with community, culture, and quality of life, have long since disappeared under the pressure of the market. According to Carey, the penny press choked off the working class partisan press by promoting inexpensive "public, non-ideological" news, human interest stories, and advertisements for consumers. The simultaneous growth of the telegraph cemented these changes advocated by the penny press. Newspapers were now able to operate in "real" time, language was standardized for telegraph communication and stripped of its regional differences. And, finally, the need to quickly and cheaply communicate "facts" about events far away promoted "objectivity," impartiality, and terseness. News became a commodity—like any other product, news could now be transported, measured, timed, and exchanged at a price. The description and explanation available in the partisan press was not feasible under such economic and communication constraints. Objectivity and neutrality became the code words for a journalism dedicated to efficiency and mass audiences.

One of the many who have challenged the presumed objectivity and neutrality of journalism in the United States, political scientist W. Lance Bennett (1988) argues that form has triumphed over substance. Despite the many news styles—tabloid, action news, happy news, public journalism—Bennett finds that the substance of the news remains much the same whether communicated through print or broadcast. It seems not a little ironic in a nation which heavily promotes individuality that the marketing goal of the mass media is to have standardized news. More importantly, Bennett's description of personalization, dramatization, fragmentation, and normalization as news biases suggests that current professional norms and practices do not meet our information needs. Bennett argues that "the news we are given is not fit for democracy; it is superficial, narrow, stereotypical, propaganda-laden" (9).

The second reading in this section describes a different kind of journalism practice, one based explicitly on community needs and perspectives. Guillermo Rothschuh Villanueva, former editor of *La Prensa*, the largest daily newspaper in Nicaragua, tells the story of the "journalism of the catacombs"—an allusion to the underground caverns early Christians used to escape persecution by the Romans. Churches in Nicaragua provided a similar sanctuary for journalists and citizens persecuted by Somoza in 1978. As the population's resistance to the dictatorship intensified, Somoza clamped down on media coverage. Journalists were fined, jailed, and even murdered by the National Guard. Somoza nationalized radio broadcasting and censored the print media. To continue their profession, radio and newspaper journalists needed another means of communication. The citizenry needed a source of news and information. Together they found a forum for reporting and exchanging news—24 churches in Managua, and others in Leon, Matagalpa, and Grenada became venues for a new form of journalism.

The interpersonal exchanges between reporters and community residents became a form of mass communication. The traditional stance of "objectivity" and "balance" became more partisan, more democratic, and in Villanueva's view "more honest, more conscientious." Certainly this new communication practice was more publicly accessible and interactive. Each of the "catacomb" churches had an editor, editorial board, community correspondents, and distributors who went to other churches to relay and receive news and information. In catacomb journalism, "transmittors" were indistinguishable from the "receivers."

Villanueva also introduces a concept not familiar to most North Americans. He refers to "social communication"—as distinct from organizational, religious, political, interpersonal, or other "types"—to emphasize that communication which surrounds and informs everyday life. Social communication expressed in movies, popular music, church services, mass entertainment and sports, art, and poetry, infuses society, the public, the citizenry with values, beliefs, accepted behaviors, and general knowledge about how the world should work. Social communication underpins much of our values, beliefs, and behaviors (see Section 2). As a veteran journalist and a participant in the democratic upheaval in Nicaragua, Villanueva understands social communication as crucial to democratic life.

The "journalism of the catacombs" would have been impossible without the existing social communication of widespread urban Christian base communities of liberation theology, neighborhood defense committees, university student service projects, the traditions of poetry and song performance, and neighborhood-based socials. Although conducted under uniquely Nicaraguan conditions, "journalism of the catacombs" dramatically demonstrates the potential for other communication practices which might advance the democratic exchange and construction of knowledge. If communication scholars, students, and practitioners turned their attention to popular social communication in the United States, it's quite possible that other new communication practices unique to the U.S. could be discovered or created that would expand democracy and citizen participation.

REFERENCES

Bennett, W. Lance. *News: The Politics of Illusion.* 2nd ed. White Plains, N.Y.: Longman, 1988.

13 | The Partisan Press, Penny Press, and Telegraph

James Carey

• • •

As a rule, the newspaper presents a disconnected and often incoherent narrative—in its individual stories and in its total coverage. If the newspaper mirrors anything, it is this disconnection and incoherence, though it contributes to and symbolizes the very condition it mirrors. In fact, journalism can present a coherent narrative only if it is rooted in a social and political ideology, an ideology that gives a consistent focus or narrative line to events, that provides the terminology for a thick description and a ready vocabulary of explanation.

The crucial events, the shaping influences, in the history of American journalism were those that stripped away this ideological context: the decline of the partisan press, the emergence of the penny papers, and the deployment of the telegraph as the nervous system of the news business.

The *Wall Street Journal* is, in a sense, the archetype of the American newspaper: a paper from a commercial class interested in and with an economic interest in the news of the day. The American newspaper of the eighteenth and early nineteenth centuries was a producer good for a commercial class rather than a consumer good for a consumer class. It reflected the economic, political, and cultural orientations of that class. News of the day was primarily news of the rudimentary and disjointed markets of early American capitalism: of prices, transactions, shipping, the availability of goods, and events which affected prices and availabilities in markets near and far. There was political news, too, but it was political news in a restricted sense: news that could influence the conduct of commerce, not news of every conceivable happening in the society. Much of what is today called news—burglaries, fires, for example— was inserted in the paper as paid advertisements; much of what is today called advertising—the availability of goods, for example—appeared in the news columns. It was no coincidence that the most popular name for American newspapers in 1800 was *The Advertiser*. But the word "advertising" had a special meaning: not the purchase of space but the unpurchased announcement of the availability of merchandise.

The commercial and trading elites and the papers and newsletters representing their interests were central to fomenting conflict with Britain when the crown hampered their commercial activities. Following independence, the commercial press retained its interest in politics; that is, it "reported" on matters affecting the fate of merchants and traders. But this

From *Reading the News*, edited by Manoff and Schudson. Reprinted by permission of the author.

class was deeply divided over issues such as the national bank. The partisan press, aligned with different factions of the commercial class, gave venomous expression to these differences. But the thing to remember is this: because the press was organized around articulate economic interests, the news had meaning, could be interpreted through the explained by those interests. A partisan press created and utilized an ideological framework that made sense of the news.

The second critical fact concerning the partisan press concerns the matter of time. The cycle of business is the cycle of the day: the opening and closing of trade. The press of the eighteenth and early nineteenth centuries was not technologically equipped to report on a timely, daily basis, but it shared with businessmen the understanding that time is of the essence of trade. As a result, the natural epoch of journalism became the day: the cycle of work and trade for a business class. The technological impetus in journalism has been to coordinate the cycle of communication with the cycle of trade.

While journalism lives by cycles ranging upward from the hour, its natural métier is the stories of the day, even if it recycles them over longer or shorter units of time. Journalism is a daybook that records the significant happenings of that day. Its time frame is not posterity, and the journalists' flattering, self-protecting definition of his work as the "first rough draft of history" does not alter that fact. The archetype of journalism is the diary or account book. The diary records what is significant in the life of a person for that day. The business journal records all transactions for a given day. The news begins in bookkeeping. Commerce lives by, begins and ends the day with, the record of transactions on, say, the stock and commodity markets. The news begins as a record of commercial transactions and a tool of commerce. Every day there is news; every day there are stories to be told because every day there is business to be done and prices to be posted. In this sense, the origins of journalism, capitalism, and bookkeeping are indissoluble.

In the 1830s, a cheap, daily popular press—a "penny press"—was created in the major cities. The penny press did not destroy the commercial press. The latter has continued down to this day not only in the *Wall Street Journal* and the *Journal of Commerce, Barron's* and *Business Week, Forbes* and *Fortune*, but in private newsletters and private exchanges that grew after the birth of the penny press. Such publications have edged closer to the popular press with the enormous expansion of the middle class. The *Wall Street Journal* doesn't call itself "the daily diary of the American dream" for nothing. But the penny press did displace the commercial-partisan press in the 1830s as the model of a daily newspaper.

While scholars disagree over the significance of the penny press, one can safely say three things about it. First, the penny press was a consumer good for a consumer society; it reflected all of society and politics, not just the world of commerce and commercial politics. The retreat from partisanship meant that any matter, however minor, qualified for space in the paper: the details not only of trade and commerce, but the courts, the streets, the strange, the common-place. The penny papers were filled with the odd, the exotic, and the trivial. Above all, they focused on the anonymous individuals, groups, and classes that inhabited the city. They presented a panorama of facts and persons, a "gastronomy of the eye"; in another of Baude-laire's phrases, they were a "kaleidoscope equipped with consciousness."

Second, the penny press displaced not merely partisanship but an explicit ideological context in which to present, interpret, and explain the news. Such papers choked off, at least relatively, an ideological press among the working class. At its best, the penny press attempted to eliminate the wretched partisanship and factionalism into which the press had degenerated since the Revolution. It tried to constitute, through the more or less neutral support of advertising, an open forum in which to examine and represent a public rather than a merely partisan interest.

Third, the penny press imposed the cycle and habit of commerce upon the life of society generally. Because in business time is money, the latest news can make the difference between success and failure, selling cheap or selling dear. Time is seldom so important in noncommercial activity. The latest news is not always the best and most useful news. Little is lost if the news of politics or urban life is a little old. Nonetheless, the cycle and habit of beginning and ending the day by reading the latest prices was imposed on social activities generally. Beginning in the 1830s, the stories of society were told on a daily basis. The value of timeliness was generalized by the penny press into the cardinal value of journalism.

The events of journalism happen today. The morning reading of the *New York Times* is important because it establishes the salience of stories for the day. It also determines salience for the television networks, the news magazines, the journals of opinion issued weekly and monthly. And the stories of books begin in the announcements in news columns: a family named Clutter was murdered in Hollcomb, Kansas, yesterday. With the penny press, all forms of writing became increasingly a parasite of "breaking news."

The telegraph cemented everything the "penny press" set in motion. It allowed newspapers to operate in "real time" for the first time. Its value was insuring that time became irrelevant for purposes of trade. When instantaneous market reports were available everywhere at the same moment, everyone was effectively in the same place for purposes of trade. The telegraph gave a real rather than an illusory meaning to timeliness. It turned competition among newspapers away from price, even away from quality, and onto timeliness. Time became the loss leader of journalism.

The telegraph also reworked the nature of written language and finally the nature of awareness itself. One old saw has it that the telegraph, by creating the wire services, led to a fundamental change in news. It snapped the tradition of partisan journalism by forcing the wire services to generate "objective" news that papers of any political stripe could use. Yet the issue is deeper than that. The wire services demanded language stripped of the local, the regional and colloquial. They demanded something closer to a "scientific" language, one of strict denotation where the connotative features of utterance were under control, one of fact. If a story were to be understood in the same way from Maine to California, language had to be flattened out and standardized. The telegraph, therefore, led to the disappearance of forms of speech and styles of journalism and storytelling—the tall story, the hoax, much humor, irony, and satire—that depended on a more traditional use of language. The origins of objectivity, then, lie in the necessity of stretching language in space over the long lines of Western Union.

Similarly, the telegraph eliminated the correspondent who provided letters that announced an event, described it in detail, and analyzed its substance. It replaced him with the stringer who supplied the bare facts. As the telegraph made words expensive, a language of spare fact became the norm. Telegraph copy had to be condensed to save money. From the stringer's notes, someone at the end of the telegraphic line had to reconstitute the story, a process that reaches high art with the newsmagazines: the story divorced from the storyteller.

If the telegraph made prose lean and unadorned and led to a journalism without the luxury of detail and analysis, it also brought an overwhelming crush of such prose to the newsroom. In the face of what was a real glut of occurrences, news judgment had to be routinized and the organization of the newsroom made factorylike. The reporter who produced the new prose displaced the editor as the archetype of the journalist. The spareness of the prose and its sheer volume allowed news, indeed forced news, to be treated like a commodity: something that could be transported, measured, reduced, and timed. News [became] subject to all the procedures developed for handling agricultural commodities. It was subject to "rates, contracts, franchising, discounts and thefts."

Together those developments of the second third of the nineteenth century brought a new kind of journalism, a kind that is still roughly the staple of our newspapers. But, as explained earlier, this new journalism made description and explanation radically problematic: "penny" and telegraphic journalism divorced news from an ideological context that could explain and give significance to events. It substituted the vague principle of a public interest for "class interest" as the criterion for selecting, interpreting, and explaining the news. It brought the newsroom a glut of occurrences that overwhelmed the newspaper and forced the journalist to explain not just something but everything. As a result, he often could explain nothing. By elevating objectivity and facticity into cardinal principles, the penny press abandoned explanation as a primary goal. Simultaneously, it confronted the reader with events with which he had no experience and no method with which to explain them. It filled the paper with human interest material that, however charming, was inexplicable. And, finally, it divorced the announcement of news from its analysis and required the reader to maintain constant vigilance to the news if he was to understand anything.

The conditions of journalistic practice and the literary forms journalists inherited together strictly limit the degree to which daily journalism can answer how and why. How something happens or how someone accomplishes something demands the journalist's close, detailed attention to the flow of facts which culminate in a happening. The dailiness and deadline of the newspaper and the television news show usually preclude the opportunity to adequately etch in the detail which intervenes between an intention and an accomplishment, a cause and its effect. Moreover, the journalist's typical tools, particularly the telephone interview, are inadequate to a task that demands far more varied resources. Journalists cannot subpoena witnesses; no one is required to talk to them. As a result, "how," the detail, must await agencies outside of journalism such as the grand jury, the common trial, the blue-ribbon commission, social surveys, congressional investigating committees, or other, more leisured and wide-ranging forms of journalistic inquiry: the extended series, magazine article, or book.

Explanation in daily journalism has even greater limits. Explanation demands that the journalist not only retell an event but account for it. Such accounting normally takes one of four forms: determining motives, elucidating causes, predicting consequences, or estimating significance. However, the canons of objectivity, the absence of a forum or method through which evidence can be systematically adduced, and the absence of an explicit ideological commitment on the part of journalists renders the task of explanation radically problematic, except under certain well-stipulated conditions.

First, the problem of objectivity. Who, what, when, and where are relatively transparent. Why is invisible. Who, what, when, and where are empirical. Why is abstract. Who, what, when, and where refer to phenomena on the surface of the world. Why refers to something buried beneath appearances. Who, what, when, and where do not mirror the world, of course. They reflect the reality-making practices of journalists. Answering such questions depends upon conventions that are widely shared, even if infrequently noted. The other essays in this volume attest to the conventionality of these elements. We no longer, for example, identify figures in the news by feminine nouns: poetess, Negress, Jewess, actress. The who, the identification, now obeys a different set of conventions which attempt to depress the importance of "race" and gender, conventions which journalists both use and legitimate. But for all the conventionality of who, what, when, and where, they are accessible and identifiable because our culture widely shares a gradient against which to measure them. As Michael Schudson's essay demonstrates, the notion of when, of time in journalism, is not as transparent as phrases like "recent," "immediate," or "breaking" seem to suggest. Nonetheless, time in journalism is measured against a standard gradient of tense, of past, present, and future, which is widely shared in the culture.

There is no accessible gradient for the measurement of causes, the assessment of motives, the prediction of consequences, or the evaluation of significance. No one has seen a cause or a consequence; motives are ghostly happenings in the head; and significance seems to be in the eye of the beholder. Explanations do not lie within events or actions. Rather, they lie behind them or are inferences or extrapolations that go well beyond the common sense evidence at hand. Explanation, then, cuts against the naive realism of journalism with its insistence on objective fact.

The first injunction of journalists is to stay with the facts; facts provide the elements of the story. But causes, consequences, and motives are not themselves facts. Because journalists are above all else empiricists, the why must elude them. They lack a framework of theory or ideology from which to deduce evidence or infer explanations. To explain is to abandon journalism in the archetypal sense: it is to pursue soft news, "trust me" journalism. Explanatory journalism is, to use an ugly phrase, "thumbsucker journalism": stories coming from the journalist's head rather than the facts.

Something is philosophically awry about all this, of course. While the first law of journalism is to stick to hard surfaces, the essays in this volume present enough evidence for the mushiness of all facts. The facts of the case are always elaborate, arbitrary cultural constructions through which who, what, when, and where are not only identified but judged, not only described but evaluated. But such constructions and identifications can be pinned down by ordinary techniques of journalistic investigation. Not so with why. For it, one must go outside the interview and the clip file. It drives one to the library, the computer, government documents, historical surveys. But there are no conventions to guide journalists in sifting and judging evidence from such sources and no forum in which conflicting evidence can be weighed.

More than the organization of the newsroom, the nature of journalistic investigations and the professional ideology of journalism suppress a journalism of explanation. The basic definitions of news exclude explanation from the outset. News focuses on the unusual, the non-routine, the unexpected. Thus, it necessarily highlights events that interest us precisely because they have no explanation. This is part of the meaning of human interest: deviation from the accepted routine of ordinary life. News of novel events must strain causality and credibility. News is when man bites dog. Unfortunately, no one knows what possessed the man who bit the dog; even psychiatrists are not likely to be much help.

Much of journalism focuses on the bizarre, the uncanny, the inexplicable. Journalism ritualizes the bizarre; it is a counterphobia for overcoming objects of fear. Such stories of the bizarre, uncanny, horrible, and unfathomable are like roller coasters, prize fights, stock car races—pleasurable because we can be disturbed and frightened without being hurt or over-whelmed. Where would we be without stories of UFOs and other such phenomena, stories at once intensely pleasing and intensely disturbing? In the age of the partisan press, such stories were consigned to folklore, the oral tradition, and other underground modes of storytelling....

14 | Notes on the History of Revolutionary Journalism in Nicaragua

Guillermo Rothschuh Villanueva

During the liberation process in Nicaragua, the last two years of the revolutionary war, 1977-1979, were the most important historical periods.

During these stages, the guerrilla organization redefined its strategy, introducing as a way of confronting "Somozismo" [the policies of the dictatorship of Anastasio Somoza], the insurrectional struggle, by means of which it achieved greater elasticity in the handling of alliances in the political field and established agreements with different social sectors of the country who assumed the revolutionary project of the FSLN as their own.

The FSLN began to give special importance to the organization and mobilization of the masses, capitalizing on armed actions, which lead to the founding of the group "Los Doce" ["The Twelve"] and the "Movimiento Pueblo Unido" (MPU) [the "United People Movement"].

This combination of events began to influence the political actions of the country's existing organizations who had accepted the FSLN's clearly-defined strategic project of struggle. The added participation of the oppositional bourgeois sectors was motivated by a different political project. The polarization of social forces was the most evident sign of these two years of political-military struggle.

Strategic and tactical redefinitions were necessary in order to avoid annihilation by the army of occupation, which had been formed at the end of the 1920s to destroy the "Pequeño Ejercito Loco del General de Hombres Libres, Augusto César Sandino" ["Little Crazy Army of the General of Free Men, Augusto César Sandino"].

It is during this period that certain events occurred in the domain of information which generated a series of historic experiences in the field of social communication. Among the most relevant were:

- The "Sindicato de Radioperiodistas de Managua" (SRPM) [the "Union of Radiojournalists of Managua"] was transformed into one of the most active and belligerent forces in the struggle;

From *Communicating in Popular Nicaragua*, edited by Armand Mattelart. Reprinted by permission of the editor.

- To be able to confront the regime and its press censorship, the SRPM managed to create one of the most ingenious and fertile forms of communication produced by the struggle: "El Periodismo Catacumbas" ["The Journalism of the Catacombs"];
- Somozismo treacherously assassinated Dr. Pedro Joaquin Chamorro, editor of the daily *La Prensa*, which sharpened the crisis and contributed to radicalizing the masses;
- After ten years of struggle, the journalists went even further, founding the "Union de Periodistas de Nicaragua" (UPN) [the "Union of Nicaraguan Journalists"], taking their greatest step forward in organizing;
- Around mid-1978, the clandestine Radio Sandino went on the air. It later played a strategic role in the agitation, organization, and combat preparation of the people;
- The national cinema was born on the war front. On the Southern Front "Benjamín Zeledón," the Cultural Brigade, "Leonel Rugama," filmed 8,000 feet of film; and
- An entire culture of resistance arose which succeeded in staying alive and reproducing itself.

These notes are a brief account of the principle events in the field of communication during the last two years of the war of liberation. Far from exhausting the subject, it is only a first approach; each event should be studied in depth. We have placed special emphasis on the links between political, military and journalistic events, since the war of liberation was the factor which unleashed these experiences in the field of social communication, and culture in general.

I. The October Offensive and Press Censorship

After the first new armed actions of the Sandinista National Liberation Front (FSLN) in October 1977, there began an uninterrupted offensive against the Somoza military dictatorship involving the country's diverse social forces.

The struggle acquired a new character militarily and politically, both nationally and internationally. The FSLN launched a permanent military offensive of insurrectional dimensions, converting the cities for the first time into the main areas of armed struggle, and began to undertake a broad policy of alliances with different sectors of national life.

From the middle of 1977, there was reactivation of the opposition struggle of the bourgeoisie against Somozismo as a result of the human rights policy of U.S. President Carter. The fundamental reason for the bourgeoisie's contradictions with Somozismo was Somoza's participation in Nicaraguan finance, tacitly reserved in the past for the two most powerful economic groups in the country, the Bank of America and the Banco Nicaragüense.

Somoza broke this formal alliance by founding the Banco de Centroamérica, the Nicaragüense de Ahorro y Préstamo company (NIAPSA), and Interfinanciera, entering with very advantageous conditions into unfair competition with these two economic consortiums.

The first note of discord within the bourgeoisie were translated as a mild questioning of Somoza's management of the state apparatus. His answer to the private sector was categoric. He called them "procesadores de aforos," meaning that they also were benefitting from the economic policies of his government.

The new situation led the FSLN to a new plan of struggle; it decided to take advantage of this favorable opportunity, and try to generate greater contradictions which would weaken

Somozismo militarily and politically. The guerrilla attack on the National Guard headquarters in San Carlos on 13 October 1977, inaugurated the insurrectional struggle as a new phase in the revolutionary war in Nicaragua.

These actions were disconcerting to the majority of political sectors in the country, who didn't know how to evaluate the military offensive. But even more surprised was Somoza's military dictatorship, which thought that the FSLN had been completely annihilated as a result of the military ground-razing actions in the north.

We should point out that since December 1974, after the assault on the home of Dr. Jose Maria Castillo Quant, Somozismo imposed martial law, a state of siege and press censorship, in order to create the conditions which would allow them to act with impunity under the supposed veil of legality to repress the guerrilla movement and its logistical support centers in the cities and the mountains. A totally merciless repression was the response to the guerrilla attack.

What surprised Somoza was that, far from having been destroyed, the FSLN reappeared with more strength, openly challenging its military power. The audacious attacks against the Somoza garrisons in San Carlos (13 October 1977), in Monzonte, Nueva Segovia (October 15th), and in Masaya (October 17th), weakened the position of Somoza's political alternative which he was seeking to renovate his regime.

The prolonged state of exception created by Somoza lasted 33 months. This situation forced the Union of Radiojournalists of Managua (SRPM) to rethink their struggle in order to be able to practice their profession. Their very livelihood was in danger. The journalists initiated a new stage marked by two forms of confronting the dictatorship: first, they emphasized their professional work (1975-1976) and demanded the end of press censorship and the abolition of the Radio and TV Code; and secondly, they adopted political forms of struggle against Somozismo (1977).

At its professional stage, the SRPM demanded among other things, that its members were covered by the Social Security system, it initiated a campaign to create its own printed material, and set up seminars on labor unions. Press censorship made them focus their demands on its elimination. Its fundamental activity was directed toward the re-establishment of freedom of the press.

All the initiatives taken by the SRPM to obtain the restitution of freedom of the press and the abolition of the Radio and TV Code were unsuccessful. Yet, these circumstances had positive effects. It served to politicize many of its members leading them to take positions which openly challenged the dynastic power. In June 1977, the SRPM, after two failures successfully led a 24-hour work stoppage, demanding the end of press censorship. Three years of constant struggle had served as a catalyst for their consciousness.

II. The Struggle to Suppress the Radio and TV Code

In this context, the struggle to end the Radio and TV Code eventually was converted into a tactical objective for confronting Somozismo. The different political parties and professional associations opted to include among their demands of the regime the abolition of the Radio and TV Code, finally incorporated into their respective programs a section on the freedom of the press.

The positive reception given by the different political, economic, religious, and professional sectors to the appeal formulated by "Los Doce" ["The Twelve"] (*La Prensa*, 21 October 1977), to hold a national dialogue to put an end to the violence, legitimized completely the struggle being waged by the FSLN. Once the basis for this dialogue was realized, the suppression of the Radio and TV Code was included in the demands.

The tactical objective had been turned into an important point of discussion on the agenda of the political parties. The lifting of press censorship (19 September 1977) was the result of the pressures by the different sectors of the country. This opportune conjuncture allowed the SRPM to use more pressure and to demand the removal of the Radio and TV Code, not as a professional demand, but rather as part of the struggle for national liberation.

The same crisis in which Somozismo was debated inhibited the Code from being modified or reformed. The Radio and TV Code, promulgated under the presidency of Luis Somoza in July 1962, was created to avoid the increasing propaganda of an armed, political and ideological struggle against Somozismo and, fundamentally, to contain the development of revolutionary ideology.

The Code, in fact, constituted a law of exception against practicing journalism and against the rise of any ideology except extreme liberalism or traditional conservativism. Its exceptional character was that the supposed violations were only known to the director of the Office of Radio and TV who was assigned to the National Guard.

The procedure established for judging the supposed infractions was by means of government order. This kept the courts from knowing about any act or circumstances which apparently violated the Code. In practice, it was converted into an expedient of force which Somozismo used in its duel against the radio and TV journalists (the written press was not covered by the Code).

The fact that the print media remained on the fringe of this judicial statute did not mean that they were outside Somoza's arbitrariness. On 28 January 1967, only six days after the bourgeoisie's "putsch," Somoza enacted a decree which authorized the Executive wing, that is, Somoza, to seize the machines used to print the newspapers. Naturally, only he had the power to determine what constituted a violation.

This decree was directed against the daily *La Prensa*, but it was also aimed at obstructing the circulation of the workers' newspapers at the time. Its purpose was to prevent the professional organizations from counting on their own media to disseminate information. The left parties were practically operating illegally. Bipartisanship was the dominant political norm in Nicaragua from independence (1821) until 19 July 1979, the year of National Liberation.

The essential content of the Radio and TV Code was oriented to exclude anything except the promotion of the electoral farce in which the two historic traditional parties (Liberals and Conservatives) participated, and to contain any political ideology founded on other principles, and obviously, to thus impede the growth of left parties. The Code was promulgated in 1962, just a year after the FSLN was founded.

In practice, the Radio and TV Code not only limited the freedom of the press, but also the exercise of political liberties. Its repressive stance forced the FSLN to be constantly creative in order to be able to deliver its message to the masses.

For this reason, no political or professional group remained on the margin of the struggle to have it repealed. Principally, the left groups actively involved themselves since they were fully aware that it was they who were most hurt by it. For the FSLN, it never went beyond a tactical objective in its struggle.

From its clandestine position, it was the FSLN who was in the worst situation. Tacitly or expressly, the social communication media omitted information about their actions, be it because they were distancing themselves from this form of struggle or because they feared Somoza's repression. From its foundation in 1961 until a short time before the triumph, the FSLN had to use their ingenuity to devise their own means of communication. In order to get their message to the people, they had to take over different radio stations by force of arms.

The FSLN was forced to attempt different types of agitation and propaganda among the popular sectors of the country. From the armed incursion of "El Chaparral" (1959), in which the founding members Carlos Fonseca Amador, Tomás Borge, Silvio Mayorga, Victor Manuel Tirado, Germán Pomares, participated, among others, special importance was given to the social communication media, since from that time on it was thought that they should rely on a clandestine radio station.[1]

The first experience the leaders had in this field was the control they exercised in directing *El Universitario*, the organ of the University Center of the Autonomous National University of Nicaragua. In order to spread their revolutionary doctrine among the students and the masses, they printed and distributed flyers, leaflets, handouts, and painted "pintas" on the walls, and managed to edit their own media (*El Sandinista, Trinchera, Rojo y Negro, Universidad Revolucionaria*) and their own magazine (*Pensamiento Crítico*).

In the beginning of the war of liberation, they founded their own radio station, "Radio Sandino" (1978), which played a fundamental role in the combat preparation of the Nicaraguan people. The broadcasts fulfilled two basic objectives: the key factor was agitation and mobilization, and the other was to transmit political and military watchwords around which the Nicaraguan people should rally their activities.

III. The Assassination of Pedro Joaquin Chamorro: The Catalyst of the Crisis

As we said, in October 1977, the group "Los Doce" ["The Twelve"] came forward as a force for establishing a national dialogue. As a result of its alliances, the FSLN tried to capitalize politically on its military actions. As part of its pre-planned strategy, the FSLN welcomed the dialogue, but warned that Somozismo should not participate. This position was based on the fact that the FSLN thought that the participation of Somoza could lead to an understanding—as had occurred earlier—between the traditional opposition and the dynastic regime.

In this way, the FSLN posed the alternative for Nicaragua: reform or revolution, reiterating a clear preference for the latter.

The possibility to establish a dialogue was eliminated on 10 January 1978, when Dr. Pedro Joaquin Chamorro, the editor of the newspaper *La Prensa*, was assassinated by the Somoza forces. His assassination touched all social sectors of the country. His death served as detonator among the masses. The first abrupt actions took place in the streets during which several properties of the Somozistas were burned. The people were in a state of insurrection during Chamorro's wake and burial.

This led to a deepening of the Somozista crisis. The breaking off of the dialogue meant his total isolation and ruled out any possibility of an understanding between the traditional political sectors and Somozismo.

As a result of the assassination of Dr. Pedro Joaquin Chamorro, a general sit-down strike was begun on 23 January 1978, in which many political, economic, and professional sectors participated. In Managua, the strike spread to business, industry, and the workers' sector of banking. It was supported and sponsored by the traditional opposition and the private sector in an attempt to capitalize on the crisis for their own benefit.

While reporting on the course of these events, the journalists from the different radio and television media in the country again felt the weight of Somozista repression. The newscasters from "Radio Mi Preferida" were the first to be suspended by the Director of the Radio and TV, Col. Alberto Luna. The suspension was due to their reporting on the development of the country's strike. On this occasion, Somozismo sought to frighten the journalists and tried to interfere in the content of their news reports.

The dictatorship's image suffered further deterioration due to the work stoppage of ten minutes throughout Latin America which was decided by the Federación Latinoamericana de Periodistas [FELAP, the Latinamerican Federation of Journalists] to protest the assassination of the editor of *La Prensa*. The stoppage of the FELAP (which had brought together by its action 60,000 journalists) occurred within the development of the strike in Nicaragua. This further isolated Somozismo internationally while internally it increased the participation of the masses behind the insurrectional focus set out by the FSLN.

The information media led by *La Prensa* changed and gradually radicalized its offensive against the regime. This situation was a determining factor in the dictatorship's again imposing a state of emergency and press censorship after 28 January 1978.

One of the most important measures adopted by the SRPM was that the communications media wouldn't actively join the work stoppage. Their functioning was vital in order to maintain a state of permanent agitation among the masses. The different media created a unified reporting policy which allowed their reports to be handled by a single editor.

Without necessarily talking on the project of revolution, *La Prensa*, from then on:

> spread the clandestine struggles, legal and semi-legal, which our people were developing to confront the dictatorship for the last time. This signified and synthesized the contribution which that newspaper gave to the struggle when all the means of communication were censored, were repressed, when silence was menacing Nicaragua.[2]

The attitude of the owners and workers at *La Prensa* had different motivations. Part of its members supported the struggle with the intention of crystallizing the reformist policy of the Frente Amplio Opositor [FAO, the Broad Opposition Front], with which they were affiliated. The other part acted in their capacity as militants or sympathizers of the FSLN. Almost all of the journalists from the social communication media in the country experienced this. The positions taken by many of the journalists put them in open contradiction with the stands taken by the media owners and particularly with the advertising agencies.

At this point, the members of the SRPM understood that the abolition of the Radio and TV Code was not the most important part of the struggle. What was fundamental was to get rid of the dictatorship. In spite of all the risks, the journalists eventually became the principal propagandists for anti-Somoza activities. The new imposition of censorship occurred in a different political context. Far from accepting the orders of the dictatorship, they contravened its orders, going to great lengths to inform the public.

The FSLN had succeeded in transforming the demands of the moment into a total questioning of Somozista power. However, the traditional opposition tried to turn the strike into a means to apply pressure for the resignation of Somoza and present themselves as a legitimate alternative to the crisis. Fundamentally, it attempted to sell that image to the United States Embassy, who was viewing with growing concern Somozismo's irreversible agony and the necessity of filling the power vacuum with a group who shared their interests in Nicaragua and in the Central American region.

IV. The SRPM and "Journalism of the Catacombs"

Censorship of the press stimulated the creative capacity of national journalism. With the tempestuous closing of the news programs "Sucesos" ["Events"], "Mundial" ["The World"], "Extra," and "Aquí Nicaragua" ["Here Nicaragua"], which broadcast on Radio Corporación, Radio Mundial, Radio Continental, and Radio Preferida, the SRPM created a commission to study a new way to keep the Nicaraguan people informed.

The commission took the name of Comité Popular de Huelga [the Popular Strike Commission]. One of its functions was to establish ties between the sectors involved in the strike and the sectors of the left organically linked to the FSLN who proposed not only the fall of Somoza, but also a radical change in the social, political, and economic structures of the country.

Besides the shutdowns, the Radio and TV Commission imposed considerable fines with the intention of putting the very existence of the information media in danger. During the last two years of the dictatorship there were more than 100 shutdowns. The SRPM proposed that the fines be paid by the people. Bank accounts were opened where people would deposit their help. In this way, the people began to actively participate in the struggle against the repressive laws and earn the right to be independently and freely informed.

With all legal forms of information closed, the sense of invention of Nicaraguan journalism and its commitment to the national liberation cause were put to the test. Leaving behind its traditional professional role of broadcasting on the radio where censorship prevented reporting, the SRPM sought in interpersonal communication a better way of informing the people. Thus was born what the world would come to know as "Journalism of the Catacombs," a reminder of what had been the persecution of primitive Christians.

Its name was derived from two circumstances: firstly, from the fact that journalism began to be practiced almost clandestinely and, secondly, that the journalists found refuge in Catholic churches, where they could bring people together to inform them about the prevailing situation in Nicaragua. Journalism of the Catacombs was begun on 31 January 1978. Participating in this experience were journalism students, editors, photographers, and head of the different media; an important contribution to national, continental, and world journalism.

Journalism of the Catacombs

can be considered as the most important and most original contribution of Nicaraguan journalists, of those who valiantly resisted remaining silent. They were the first paper barricades erected, *a parallel to the church naves, which in the dark days of Christian persecution they extended to the eaves like protecting arms and said to the executioners: "You shall not pass."* [3]

Journalism of the Catacombs showed, for the first time, that between members of the SRPM there could exist an absolute consensus to challenge the dictatorship and to join in the struggle which would overthrow it. Old academic precepts regarding the supposed nature of professional practice were thrown out. The so-called "objectivity" in the transmission of information, which some schools of social sciences argue, was put to the test and totally defeated. Never before had national journalism been more honest and conscientious in its duty to inform.

These are the periods which crystalize a class consciousness which can go on to become combative positions to question the nature of a profession whose exercise in practice had tended to be corrupted and eroded by those who proclaim that journalism calls for "objectivity." In the field of social science, this "objectivity" does not exist, since in a society divided into antagonistic classes, scientific discourse becomes ideological. [4]

Journalism of the Catacombs was a lively, flexible and dynamic journalism. It managed to create a "circuit" of language, or what Pasquali calls a "communicational relation"; transmitter and receiver intimately united, interchangeable. Journalists went to the churches to inform and to gather information. They succeeded in covering 24 churches in Managua and the experience was repeated in León, Matagalpa, Masaya, Granada, and Carazo. [5]

This was neither an isolated nor spontaneous action. For its operation, the journalists of the SRPM set up an editor-in-chief, a group of *ad hoc* editors, a distribution department, and group leaders in each church. They transmitted national and international news. La Casa del Periodismo [Journalism House] was the epicenter of their work.

In spite of its short duration—this experience ended on February 10th—it had international repercussions. Journalists on this and other continents have harvested this legacy of Nicaraguan journalism. A legacy of liberation for which some Nicaraguan journalists paid for with their lives, such as Walter Mendoza, Aura Ortiz, and Alvaro Montoya Lara, all of whom were organically connected to the FSLN.

The taking of a position against the dictatorship did not come from a specific professional field, but rather it was the result, to a greater or lesser degree, of the level of political consciousness. Periods of revolutionary upsurge are characterized by there being key moments in the clarification of consciousness and in the taking of a position for or against a given class or sector in conflict. The Nicaraguan journalists, joined together in the SRPM, took the side of the people against the regime who, when undergoing a broad crisis showed all its viciousness.

The political consciousness of the journalists was at the same level as the objective crisis which was demolishing the Somozista dictatorship. The subjective factors called for by the country's situation were unleashed by the FSLN offensive. Its constant drive and form of insurrectional struggle radicalized the consciousness of the Nicaraguan people.

A sit-down strike was not a suitable nor sufficient way to topple the Somozista military dictatorship. The reformist sectors, consistent with their traditional way of confronting the regime, never realized that their way of fighting wasn't capable of defeating tyranny. Nevertheless, it served to de-legitimatize Somoza's rule and to isolate it from the rest of Nicaraguan society.

When the bourgeoisie sectors backed down from the general strike, the FSLN again began to push forward on the military front in order to make clear that this was the only road which could lead to the defeat of the Somozista military dictatorship. On 2 February 1978, they carried out two very important guerrilla actions in the cities and another in a Somoza counter-insurgency camp in the mountains.

The military takeover of Granada and Rivas, and the attack on the antiguerrilla encampment in Santa Clara, Nueva Segovia were an important step in the Sandinista offensive. From this moment on, the FSLN imposed their form of fighting, while the political parties and traditional movements sought a different way out of the crisis which would allow them to retain power.

V. The Founding of the UPN and Radio Sandino

The journalists' struggle took a qualitative leap forward by founding, on 1 March 1978, a union organization on a national level: la Unión de Periodistas de Nicaragua [UPN, the Union of Nicaraguan Journalists]. The necessities of the struggle had pushed them to create an entity which would permit, under its aegis, the organizing of all the nation's journalists.

The leaders of the SRPM who founded the UPN were the same ones who from 1977 began a movement leading to the creation of a national organizing structure which would involve all of the journalists in the country in the struggle. At that time, the structure of the SRPM was limited to organizing the radio journalists working in Managua. The UPN was founded on the same day that Nicaragua celebrates Journalists' Day. Within the repressive conditions imposed by Somoza, a new institution was born which respected the most honorable tradition of the SRPM's struggle without implying that the journalists had sacrificed the more belligerent objectives of their combative entity.

The events of February and the Journalism of the Catacombs represent two qualitative leaps in the confrontation with the Somoza military dictatorship. The FSLN by its own armed actions had guaranteed its propaganda internally and abroad, and thus succeeded in influencing and enrolling in their ranks numerous journalists attached to the SRPM. In this way, a definitive bridge was built between the journalists and the masses. National journalism presented itself as a permanent frontal attack against the dictatorship, with an important part of its platform being the suppression of the Radio and TV Code.

Afterwards, events would happen one after another with the driving force being the FSLN. Nevertheless, the insurrection of Monimbó (20 February 1978) was a new experience for the guerrilla organization. The struggle proposed by this indigenous community went beyond the intentions of the FSLN, although their leaders were at the forefront of combat. The contact bombs and the native masks formed part of the war arsenal. This form of resistance showed the Nicaraguans they could use rudimentary homemade arms.

Afterwards came the attack on the National Palace (22 August 1978), which would liberate the FSLN prisoners and precipitate a crisis in the dictatorship. Like 1974, Somoza was forced to allow the publication of two communiques which served to propagandize the struggle and to radicalize the masses. With the attack against the National Palace, the FSLN blocked the United States manoeuvre to put a civilian—military junta at the head of the government.[6]

The evident decomposition of the dictatorship was seen by the United States, who began mediating in 1978 to seek a favorable outcome to the crisis and avoid the triumph of the guerrilla movement. The Broad Opposition Front [Frente Amplio Opositor, FAO] then became the imperialist alternative to fill the power vacuum left by Somozismo.

In the information field, internationally, the FSLN benefitted from a favorable conjuncture. Through the work of the Solidarity Committees, a journalism offensive was kept up which helped to clarify and make understood the struggle taking place in Nicaragua. Foreign correspondents from different news media set themselves up in Managua to transmit to the world the process of the war of liberation.

The evident mediating role of the FAO and its proimperialist thesis created a fracture which led to the rise of the National Patriotic Front [Frente Patriótico Nacional, FPN], in which the United People Movement [Movimiento Pueblo Unido, MPU] played a well-known leadership role as the political arm of the FSLN. From this moment on, the two groups represented different options. The FAO turned openly proimperialist and the FPN supported the revolutionary project impelled by the guerrilla group.

The Union of Journalists of Nicaragua was active in the ranks of the FPN. With its determination, it confirmed the character of its struggle and the politicizing of national journalism.

During the rest of the year 1978 the FSLN further developed its activity among the masses; in the popular neighborhoods the daily struggle grew more violent with more arms being captured, and the guerrilla force "Pablo Ubeda" attacking many National Guard quarters in the northern and central mountains.

In April 1979, a guerrilla column took Esteli and defeated the city's military forces, avoiding a double encirclement which Somoza's army had set up in an attempt to annihilate them. This military victory created anticipation nationally and once again demonstrated the vulnerability of the National Guard. It accelerated the final offensive, which was initiated in May 1979.

We should keep in mind that in mid-1978, Radio Sandino had started up, on short wave, with five watts of power and with morning and evening broadcasts, making repeated calls to struggle, teaching the people how to handle all types of arms and to prepare explosives. Radio Sandino was a strategic arm against Somozismo. Journalists of the SRPM and UPN participated in its broadcasts and in preparing its war dispatches and general news.

During the last two months of combat, the communication media began to play a critical role in the development of the war. The newspaper *La Prensa* had been bombed and destroyed by Somoza's airplanes, and the radio stations not connected with Somozismo which were still operating became part of the Radiodifusora Nacional, the official voice of the government. They were forced to rebroadcast information which tended to paralyze the masses and to sow psychological terror especially in the eastern popular neighborhoods of Managua.

As the war fronts of the FSLN reached the cities, a few radio stations began broadcasting messages and war dispatches from the victorious troops. Nicaraguans began to turn their dial to the new stations which were the prelude to the final victory of the armed population. Radio Insurreción in Matagalpa, Radio Venceremos in León, Radio Liberación in Esteli, Radio Revolución in Juigalpa, all united their voices with broadcasts of clandestine Radio Sandino.

In almost all the radio stations members of the SRPM and UPN were in the forefront. Familiar voices began to spread the good news that the triumph of the people was only a matter of hours.

In the final assessment which Commander Humberto Ortega Saavedra made of the war of liberation, he stated that:

without radio, it would have been difficult to maintain the strike...[Radio Sandino was] the principal agitational element in the insurrection and the strike....Without a radio to orient the movement of the masses...there would not have been a revolutionary triumph.[7]

VI. The Counterculture of the Resistance

The fundamental forms of communication of the FSLN with the masses were leaflets, flyers, "pintas" [wall graffiti], the seizure of radio stations, its own propaganda linked to each of its battles, and the counterculture which grew throughout the war of liberation.

On the walls in various cities in the country, one can still read the war slogans and the calls to insurrection. Flyers containing the denunciation of assassinations were covertly distributed on the buses, and the messages stuck to the lips of the people.

In the sphere of propaganda the assault of 17 December 1974, had the desired effect. As part of the negotiations, the FSLN made the dictatorship diffuse two communiques on all the radio stations in the country, in all the print media, and on television. This touched everyone and deeply affected the Nicaraguans' sensibilities.

Even more successful was the propaganda repercussions of the assault on the National Palace on 22 August 1978. In addition to forcing Somoza to distribute two communiques to all the news media in the country, this event inspired the publication of a series of books, feature articles and special reports about the audacious guerrilla *coup*. The presence of many journalists in the Camara de Diputados [House of Representatives] was used advantageously to inform the world of this action via the many news agencies and national news magazines.

In the field of social communication, the war was not only a determining factor in the politization of journalists, but also it was the stage of the struggle during which the Nicaraguan movie industry was born. It was on the southern front "Benjamín Zeledon" where there arose what would later become the Instituto Nicaragüense de Cine [Nicaraguan Film Institute, INCINE], then called the "Brigada Cultural Leonel Rugama," in homage to the militant poet who died in combat against the dictatorship on 15 January 1970.

The song was a form of struggle and an element in raising consciousness. The appearance of "Guitara Armada" ["Armed Guitar"], by Carlos and Luis Enrique Mejía Godoy, was the result of FSLN's political and cultural work. The content of their songs was an initiation into the struggle showing how to use a gun and how to make explosives. These songs had a wide-spread national exposure and penetrated profoundly into the popular consciousness. Once again the drums of Subtiava sounded, calling to war.

With good reason, Sergio Ramírez wondered during his speech at the awards for the "Casa de las Américas" prize (22 January 1982), in Havana:

I really don't know how much the revolution owes to the songs of Carlos Mejía Godoy, which organized the collective spirit of the people by extracting the themes and chords from the deepest of our roots, and preparing this feeling for the struggle.[8]

"La Misa Campesina" ["The Peasants' Mass"] had a tremendous impact on Catholics. It offered a new version of the Gospel, making it a popular re-creation of the origins of Jesus Christ as His emergence out of the hearts of the oppressed. The Somoza regime became enraged at the authors of "La Misa Campesina" and forbid its public presentation because they understood that its message had penetrated deeply into the Catholic parishioners of Nicaragua. Parallel to the testimonial song introduced by the two Mejía Godoy, other groups of singer-troubadours emerged including the outstanding "Pancasán," whose very name reminds one of the FSLN's guerrilla action of 1967 in the mountains in the north of the country, in the days when the bourgeois opposition tried to overthrow Somoza (22 January 1967) and made martyrs of hundreds of Nicaraguans.

The confrontation with Somozismo, as local representative of imperialism, took on the character not only of military and political resistance, but also of cultural resistance. The FSLN was rooted profoundly in the Nicaraguan nationality and battled in the field of culture with tremendous success.

They were convinced that all the cultural activity sponsored by the Somozista system was designed to justify and legitimize its new existence. The dictatorship had succeeded in elevating:

> a whole complex of ideological values which, through the educational system, the communication media, and the culture, in general, were aimed at developing, maintaining, and reproducing the criteria that give rise to economic injustice.[9]

In these conditions, the FSLN necessarily had to establish a front of ideological struggle and undertake a confrontation with the country's other currents. Thus a counterculture was elaborated to oppose the ruling culture. In examining this phenomenon, Commander Bayardo Arce explained:

> With popular testimonial music, music of protest, we opposed "disco" music, the deformed music which was being fed to our peasantry.
> We opposed vapid poetry which entertains itself by shuffling words to make them beautiful with a poetry of revolutionary content.
> We opposed the opulent theater with the "sketch" which would reflect the national reality.
> We opposed in the ideological field, the backward, antipopular theories of the Church, with theories from the Vatican Council which spoke of the new mentality of the Church.
> We opposed the historical lie with the historical truth, we opposed alienated journalism with the leaflets which told the truth about our revolutionary process. And on the same front of ideological struggle, we opened the political front against the institutions and the individuals holding enemy power. We fused together all these battle fronts, the economic, the ideological and the political, with the principal battle front which was the military front.[10]

Let us remember that a year after the armed incursion of "El Chaparral" (1959), and the sudden murder of the university students on 23 July 1959, the "Frente Ventana" ["Ventana Front"] arose in 1960 at the National Autonomous University of Nicaragua (UNAN) with the clear political purpose of contributing to the liberation of the country.

During the first roundtable of young Nicaragua poets which was supported by the "Frente Ventana" and held on the 28-29 October 1961 in the city of León, the poets stood out by their literary positions which were "the same as those held on a more combative, political, level, which also was developing in the early sixties."[11]

One of the fundamental tasks of one of the founders of "Frente Ventana," Sergio Ramírez; would be to summarize and spread the thought of Sandino nationally and internationally. Ramírez' work had profound political repercussions. The publication of *El Pensamiento Vivo de Sandino [The Living Thought of Sandino]* by the Editorial Universitaria Centroamericana (EDUCA) in 1974, made widely know the political content and doctrine of Augusto César Sandino who was betrayed by the Somoza military dictatorship, and assassinated on 21 February 1934, at the insistence of United States imperialism.

The literary production of two of its founders, Sergio Ramírez and Fernando Gordillo (1940–1967), are permeated with Sandinista thought. Some of their work in poetry and prose revolves around the guerrilla's exploits and, in their political militancy, they were allied with the basic principles of the FSLN.

Literature and art in Nicaragua was always stamped with political compromise. The guerrilla exploits of Sandino infused generations of writers with his nationalism. Salomón de la Selva was one of the first to sing of the "General de Hombres Libres" ["General of Free Men"], taking his songs into the very heart of the United States. The "Movimiento de Vanguardia" ["Vanguard Movement," 1929] from the very first moment was nourished by the nationalism of the anti-imperialist resistance struggle of Sandino. They hoisted their flag and fought against secular United States intervention in Nicaragua (1926). With a sharp feeling of nationalism, one of its founders, the poet and teacher Luis Alberto Cabrales, expressed clearly that, regarding Nicaragua. "She has only two saving graces in the eyes of the world: Darío and Sandino."

In the north of the country, the scene of the struggle for the defense of national sovereignty, the "Los Romances y Corridos Nicaragüenses" arose which sang of the Sandinista struggle and was transmitted orally and handed down from generation to generation. Initially this material was gathered together and published by Ernesto Mejía Sánchez in Mexico at the Imprenta Universitaria (UNAM) in 1946, and, today, reasearcher Jorge Eduardo Arellano has again undertaken this project.

Some of the songs of Mejía Godoy are re-creations of the songs which first appeared in the Segovian mountains of Nicaragua. A substantial part of "Guitara Armada" is inspired by these "canciones norteñas" ["northern songs"] and by poems of national writers. "Flor de Pino" ["Pine Flower"], "Allá va el General" ["There Goes the General"], "La Tumba del Guerrillero" ["The Guerrilla Fighter's Tomb"], blend honorably the tradition of song and popular struggle.

A testimony to this permanent confrontation between the creators and the dictatorship is found in the anthology *Poesía Revolucionaria Nicaragüense* [*Nicaraguan Revolutionary Poetry*], whose first edition in 1962 (Talleres B. Costa Amic, México City), prepared by Enesto Mejía Sánchez and Ernesto Cardenal, was stamped with "Patria y Libertad" ["Homeland and Liberty"], the seal of the Ejército Defensor de la Soberanía Nacional [Defending Army of National Sovereignty].

This anthology:

> was re-edited seven times between 1962 and 1973, without counting the offset editions done right in Nicaragua by students at the risk of their lives. In 1973, Ernesto Cardenal himself prepared another anthology, not limited to sociopolitical themes, with the title Poesia Nicaraguense [Nicaraguan Poetry] (Habana, Casa de las Américas), which included some of the poems from the earlier collection.[12]

The anthology *Poesía Política Nicaragüense [Nicaraguan Political Poetry]* (Difusión Cultural, UNAM, México City, 1979), put together by Francisco de Asis Fernández, is one of equal political and literary merit. It attempts to show a cultural colonialism and Somoza's sell out to imperialism, and is focused on showing how creativity takes on a combative character in a country resisting the loss of its personality when faced with foreign subjugation.

The novel *Trágame Tierra [Earth Swallow Me]* (1969), by Lizandro Chávez Alfaro, with which Nicaragua definitively became part of the new hispano-american narrative current, is inspired by the nationalism and transcendent anti-imperialism of Sandino.

> With a basic use of Nicaraguan history, above all of the first half of the twentieth century, Chávez Alfaro exposes the conflict (between a generation which accepts the intervention of the U.S. Marines and another which rejects it) and succeeds in stamping his work with the concept of the novel as denunciation.[13]

The Sandinista militancy of Ernesto Cardenal had its most refined expression in his *Epigramas* (1961) and in *La Hora Cero* (1960) where his blending of political and social themes rose above pamphleteering and produced one of the best political poems from Hispanic America.

In painting, the "Grupo Praxis," during its first period (1962-1967) and its second stage (1971-1972), took a political position similar to that of the "Frente Ventana." In a strictly artistic realm, this gave "rise to the most important and original art movement in Central America and elevated its art to the heights of international renown."[14]

The "Grupo Gradas" (1974), with a more defined militancy, in its short existence generated a movement which was organically tied to the FSLN. Its artistic character was multifaceted, bringing together painters, sculptors, poets, sociologists, journalists, music workshops, and actors, among others. They performed the length and breadth of the country with the development of the popular mobilizations, proposing their message to the people who would then put it into practice.

These different forms of cultural resistance later affected the consciousness of Nicaraguans, helping them to resist the accelerating and continuing transculturation process which Somozismo had forced on the national culture. The masks of Monimbó, the contact bombs, and the drums of Subtiava are indigenous forms of cultural expression whose origins go back to the colonial period. They are cultural forms which could not be destroyed by the implantation of a foreign culture which are alien to our character. The people not only learned to resist, but also to fight, to sing, and most important of all, to triumph.

NOTES

[1] Analyzing the capacity for agitation that can be achieved through clandestine broadcasting, Commander Humberto Ortega Saavedra said that the origins of Radio Sandino were connected with a radio which the first antisomozistas had used in 1960. See Humberto Ortega Saavedra, *Sobre la insurrección*, Havana: Editorial de Ciencias Sociales, 1981, p. 79.

[2] Carlos Nuñez, "El Debate entre la verdad y la infamia," *Hacia una política cultural de la revolución popular Sandinista*, Managua: Ministerio de Cultura, 1982.

[3] Carlos Tünnermann Bernheim, *La contribución del periodismo a la liberación nacional* (Lección inaugural del IV Congreso de la Unión de Periodistas de Nicaragua), Mangua: Ministerio de Educatión, March 1981.

[4] Based on the idea of ideology elaborated by Eliseo Verón, the sociologist José Antonio Alonso says that to relate the ideological with the conditions of production of messages, in the social sciences discourse as any other discourse, is necessarily ideological. "All scientific and non-scientific dialogue which are born in a class society, like capitalist society, are ideological." See José Antonio Alonso, *Metodolgía*, Mexico City: Editorial Edicol, 1981, p. 20.

[5] A detailed study on the experience of Journalism of the Catacombs has been written by journalist María Alicia Chacón Olivas in her thesis for her university degree in journalism, entitled *Refugio de noticieros radiales en las iglesias*. Managua: Universidad Nacional Autonoma de Nicaragua, September 1978.

[6] Humberto Ortega Saavedra, *op. cit.*, p. 83.

[7] Humberto Ortega Saavedra, *op. cit.*, pp. 93 and 95.

[8] Sergio Ramírez, "La revolución, el hecho cultural mas importante de nuestra historia," *Hacia una politica cultural de la revolución popular Sandinista*, Managua: Ministerio de Cultura, 1982. A similar appraisal of the importance of the song of testimony in the struggle for liberation is made by Commander Tomás Borge in his "La Cultura es el pueblo," *Hacia una politica cultural de la revolución popular Sandinista*. Managua: Ministerio de Cultura, 1982.

[9] Bayardo Arce, "El dificil terreno de la lucha: el ideologico," *Hacia una politica cultural de la revolución popular Sandinista*, Managua: Ministerio de Cultura, 1982.

[10] Bayardo Arce, *op. cit.*, p. 18.

[11] Jorge Eduardo Arellano, *Panorama de la literatura Nicaragüense*, Managua: Ediciones Nacionales, 1977.

[12] Gregorio Selser, "Hasta que pudo hacerlo con las armas, el pueblo de Nicaragua peleó con la poesía." *Apuntes Sobre Nicaragua*, Mexico City: Centro de Estudios Economicos y Sociales del Tercer Mundo (CEESTEM); Editorial Nueva Imagen, 1981.

[13] Jorge Eduardo Arellano, *op. cit.*, p. 115.

[14] Leoncio Sáenz, "Breve historia del arte Nicaragüense," *Ventana*, No. 100, *Barricada Cultural*, Vol. III, 18 January 1983.

Exercises

NAME _____

Select an article from a local newspaper and one article from a national newspaper then complete the worksheet below.

Local Newspaper _____ Title of Article _____

Date and page _____ Length of Article _____

  1. How was it personalized?

  2. How was it dramatized?

  3. How was it fragmented?

  4. How was it normalized?

In the space below, write an account of this story without dramatizing, fragmenting, or normalizing the news event.

National Newspaper _____ Title of Article _____

Date and page _____ Length of Article _____

1. How was it personalized?

2. How was it dramatized?

3. How was it fragmented?

4. How was it normalized?

In the space below, write an account of this story without dramatizing, fragmenting, or normalizing the news event.

PART
VI

Radio:
The Popular Medium

Literacy revolutionized communication and human development. It opened cognitive thinking to greater conceptualization and abstraction. Literacy also provided the means for
organizing dramatic social transformations from the Protestant Reformation (Luther's theses)
to the American Revolution (Tom Paine's "Common Sense"). Yet, as testimony to the uneven
development of human progress, millions by-passed by literacy rely on a more recent post-lit-
erate medium for their information: radio. Radio may be the most important mass communication medium in the world. Today, in the United States 6778 radio stations provide mostly
music and popular entertainment. But for millions of people in Africa, Asia, and Latin America,
radio provides their only access to international news and information.

As a communication practice, radio changes the communication process. Radio avoids
literacy's reliance on sight but depends more on sound than orality. Radio displaces orality's
non-verbal systems. By expanding communication beyond face-to-face exchanges, radio upsets
orality's sense of community and literacy's sense of permanency. Radio transmits messages,
sounds, events as they happen, over great distances to millions of listeners—immediately,
simultaneously. Through radio our conceptions of the world must be constructed and understood differently—not by ritual group communication, not by linear, analytical, individual
reading, but by transitory, distant, electronically-communicated *aural* communication. Thus,
radio communication requires us to use our different senses in new ways to understand its
transmitted representations of the world around us.

In the readings assembled here, we are not only interested in radio as a communication
practice which changes the means for human understanding, but also in how social relations
employ radio for some particular purpose.

When Guglielmo Marconi sent his first wireless transmission through the air in Bologna,
Italy in 1895 he could not have imagined the impact his invention would have on society. Radio
transformed mass communication. No longer was time or distance a problem. And in due time,
even cost became incidental for radio reception as mass production provided millions with the
new "talking box." The development of radio from Marconi's first experiments to a technology
suitable for mass production is the subject for a media technology history text or a documentary
film such as *Empire of the Air: The Men Who Made Radio* (1991). But, we might observe how much
the developments in early radio bolster Dewey's claim about self-realization depending on
collective resources and knowledge. Surely, Lee DeForest, the "Father of Radio," was a creative,
ingenious inventor. Yet, his audion tube would not have carried voice transmission so soon or
so well, if he had not borrowed from British inventors and collaborated with Canadian Reginald
Fessenden and American Edwin Armstrong (the inventor of FM radio) to fabricate his own
transmission device. As radio grew into a popular medium for news and entertainment, its use

135

also demonstrated how a dominant communication practice emerges from the intersection of social interest and available means of communication. David Sarnoff, President of NBC, legally captured control over radio technology through purchase and patent license, determining radio's subsequent commercial design as well as blocking the development of FM radio for some four decades.

Early radios were both receivers and transmitters. But in 1920, General Electric, Westinghouse, AT&T, and RCA began manufacturing only receivers—although only one radio broadcasting station existed in the U.S. The new means of communication was a big hit. By 1924, 550 stations were broadcasting to five million listeners who were tuned in to their radios at home. A truly mass communication technology had arrived. How would American society use this new means of communication?

Noted media historian Robert McChesney gives an account of how early radio broadcast and its democratic, participatory character was replaced by a distinctly commercial private network system. From 1927–1934, educators, radio broadcasters, church and community groups, lawyers, politicians, and corporate owners engaged in an intense battle over the proper social use of this new means of communication. In the early 1920s, over 40% of the radio stations in the United States were community, university, or educational stations. Within ten years, less than 2% remained. The public airwaves were captured by newspaper chains, radio manufacturers, and their networks for advertising and entertainment.

McChesney identifies three important moments in early radio history: the Radio Act of 1927, the General Order 40 of 1928, and the Federal Communication Act of 1934. At each juncture, elected officials favored commercial and network interests over educational and public uses of radio, despite laws which declared that radio stations should serve "public interest, convenience, or necessity." Joy Elmer Morgan, President of the National Committee on Education, a coalition of the largest educational associations in the country, warned of "the monopoly of ideas and information" which "strikes at the very roots of a free democratic government." We can scarcely imagine how different radio might be if the Paulists, the Chicago Federation of Labor, and countless community and educational broadcasters had prevailed.

Many years ago, noted German playwright and poet, Bertolt Brecht (1967) proposed that radio be converted from a "distribution" system to a communication system. Brecht argued that network radio merely "hands things out," but radio as a means of public communication might allow interactive discourse between receivers who could also be transmitters. Brecht's ideas might at first seem impossible in a country as large and populous as the United States, but the film *Pump Up the Volume* (1990) and the existence of micro-broadcasters such as Black Liberation Radio in Decatur and Springfield, Illinois suggest that his ideas about public access to radio are not that far-fetched. In fact, in Japan, homemakers already practice Brecht's call for building community. Using transmitters with the micro-power of garage door openers, women use radio to exchange news and information and converse with neighbors in their communities. The wide AM, FM, and short-wave radio spectrum could easily be made accessible to low-watt community broadcasting which would allow dozens of transmitters and a more participatory, democratic use of electronic technology. Such micro-radio broadcasting would not displace or interfere with higher-watt broadcasting, but would instead expand the radio dial to local civic use and return radio to its original two-way capability.

The final essay illustrates an example of successful public access, democratic radio communication. Based on extensive field research in Nicaragua during the 1980s, Lee Artz has argued that the extent of democracy in a dominant communication practice reflects the influences of a medium's ownership, professional norms, and social function. In the excerpt included here, Artz describes some of the daily practices of public access radio—practices which would delight Dewey as they express and advance the democratic impulse. Moreover, the story of community radio in Nicaragua marks social relations and communication practices which might be creatively emulated in other media, under other conditions, to help construct a more democratic society.

REFERENCES

Brecht, Bertolt. "Radio as a Means of Communication." In *Communication and Class Struggle. Vol. 2. Liberation, Socialism*. Eds. Armand Mattelart and Seth Siegelaub. New York: International General, 1983: 169-171.

15 | The National Committee on Education by Radio and the Battle for Radio Broadcasting, 1928–1935

Robert W. McChesney

Scholars almost unanimously concur that public service broadcasting, meaning radio and television operated not-for-profit and without advertising, has been, as one put it, "the starveling stepchild of 'The American System' of broadcasting."[1] U.S. broadcasting is regarded, for better or for worse, as a system dominated by a relative handful of profit-motivated corporations that earn the lion's share of their revenues from the sale of audiences to advertisers; in this sense broadcasting is a branch of the advertising industry. In this context, as one of the most accomplished scholars of U.S. public service broadcasting recently observed, "the public service notion has been institutionalized only marginally in the U.S." and, compared to most other industrial nations, "at a rather low level of social and political commitment and material support."[2] The summer 1992 campaign to eliminate federal funding for the Corporation for Public Broadcasting and the Public Broadcasting System, on what were at times transparently partisan political grounds, only highlighted the weakness of public service principles in U.S. political culture.[3]

Most U.S. proponents of public service broadcasting reveal a gloomy, almost predestinarian, belief that commercial broadcasting was the only conceivable broadcasting system for the United States and that notions of public service were logically relegated to the margins. As Robert J. Blakely put it, "by 1920 [the first year of regular broadcasting] all the ingredients were present for the development of a national commercial system of broadcasting based on the sale of time to advertising."[4] Hence the plight of public service broadcasting was inscribed in the United States from the very beginning, without any hope of there being an alternative to the capitalist structure.[5] As the second Carnegie Commission on public broadcasting observed in 1979, "The failure to provide adequately for noncommercial broadcasting at the outset has had lasting results."[6] Given these presuppositions, it is not surprising that there has been little hard examination of the movements for public service broadcasting prior to the 1940s, when the Federal Communications Commission (FCC) first formally allocated radio frequencies on the experimental FM band to colleges and universities.

I believe the paltry status of public service broadcasting in the United States was not necessarily inevitable, and it certainly was not regarded as a "given" in the 1920s and early

1930s. When the modern network-dominated, advertising-supported system did emerge, between 1927 and 1932, various elements of U.S. society reacted with outrage and organized to establish a significant non-profit and non-commercial component to the U.S. system. Educators formed the vanguard of this broadcast reform movement; in subsequent years they would continue as the primary advocates of establishing some public service component in U.S. broadcasting. The attraction of educators to broadcasting was uncomplicated; many regarded radio and other systems of communication as logically part of the nation's broader educational network and therefore fully within their purview.[7] These educators were enamored with radio's general capacity to promote a democratic political culture far more than they were interested in the medium's potential as a classroom supplement, although these interests were not negligible. They regarded the profit motive as being nearly as inimical to democratic communication as it would be to public education. Their efforts for reform were directed by the National Committee on Education by Radio (NCER), a group funded by the Payne Fund and established in 1930.

Not all educators, however, worked for structural reform. The National Advisory Council on Radio in Education (NACRE), also formed in 1930, advocated that educators should work with the two networks, the National Broadcasting Company (NBC) and the Columbia Broadcasting System (CBS), that dominated U.S. broadcasting. Educators associated with the NACRE shared the NCER's belief in the importance and potential of radio broadcasting for a democratic society, but were either sanguine about the power of NBC and CBS to dictate U.S. broadcasting or resigned to its immutability for the foreseeable future. Subsidized by the Carnegie Corporation and John D. Rockefeller, Jr., the NACRE argued that if educators cooperated with the networks, they would be able to establish public service principles in network business practices while the industry was in its infancy.

In this paper I address the activities of the NCER during what was the most tumultuous period in the development of U.S. broadcasting. It was between 1927 and 1935 that the basic institutions and regulatory and business practices were established not only for radio, but also for television when it would be developed in the 1940s and 1950s. I will review the general landscape of the period, the formation of each of the groups, their stances concerning commercial broadcasting, their visions for public service in U.S. broadcasting, and their relationships with each other and educators as a whole. I will then discuss how the NCER fared with its programs. Although it and NACRE eventually failed, each group had an impact upon the debate over broadcast policy in the 1930s. Moreover, each group, in its own manner, attempted to expand the possibilities for public service broadcasting in the United States.

The defeat of the NCER and the NACRE signaled the beginning of the modern era, in which the profit-driven, advertising-supported basis of U.S. broadcasting became politically sacrosanct, as it remains to the present. One cannot grasp the tragedy of public service broadcasting in the United States unless this period is given its due weight. Moreover, given the near ubiquity of advertising and commercial media in our culture and the movement to extend explicit commercial criteria to the educational system, this episode points to a rich and overlooked U.S. tradition of anti-market media criticism provided by educators with a striking commitment to universal public education.[8] This is a tradition we should recognize and may wish to draw from as we confront the important questions of the relationship of communication and education to democracy, and the complex problems associated with generating answers to those questions, in the years to come.

The Emergence of Commercial Broadcasting and Ferment among the Educators

Although large corporations, especially the Radio Corporation of America (RCA), dominated most aspects of the radio industry, broadcasting eluded the corporate net for much of its initial decade. Educational institutions were arguably the "true pioneers" of U.S. broadcasting, establishing over one hundred stations in the early 1920s.[9] Even those stations established by for-profit groups in the 1920s were not intended to generate profits in their own right; rather they were meant to generate favorable publicity for the owner's primary enterprise. Thus, although radio broadcasting was bustling and dynamic in the 1920s, it was uniformly unprofitable for all types of stations and therefore unstable. The core problem was the inability to determine an adequate manner to subsidize broadcasting. Direct advertising, meaning advertising with explicit sales messages rather than merely mentioning the sponsor's name, was not even considered prior to the end of the decade. As the American Newspaper Publishers Association reassured its membership in 1927, "Fortunately, direct advertising by radio is well-nigh an impossibility."[10] An American Telephone & Telegraph survey in 1926 determined that only 4.3 percent U.S. radio stations could be characterized as "commercial broadcasters."[11] Prior to the end of the decade there was no discussion of broadcasting's future in terms of what would soon follow.

Under pressure from all broadcasters and listeners, Congress passed the Radio Act of 1927, which established the Federal Radio Commission (FRC), to provide regulation of broadcasting and bring stability to the ether, as many more stations wished to broadcast than could be accommodated in the scarce electro-magnetic spectrum.[12] While there was a general consensus that broadcasting should not be monopolized by the government, as was the case in Britain, the congressional debates over the legislation did not consider advertising nor did they examine the role of NBC, established by RCA in 1926, and CBS, which followed in 1927.[13] Rather, Congress expected the new FRC to determine which stations would be permitted to broadcast and, which would not. The Radio Act of 1927 only authorized the FRC to favor those stations which best served the "public interest, convenience, or necessity," though it did not define the terms. With barely any congressional or public oversight and almost no publicity, the pro-commercial broadcasting FRC instituted a general reallocation in 1928 which effectively assigned all stations to new frequency assignments and provided them with new power allowances. This reallocation determined the shape of AM radio for the balance of the century.

NBC and CBS were the clear victors in the reallocation. Whereas they barely existed in 1927, by 1931 they and their affiliated stations accounted for 70 percent of all wattage. By 1935 only four of the 62 stations that broadcast at 5000 watts or more did not have a network affiliation; one study showed that fully 97 percent of nighttime broadcasting, when smaller stations were not licensed to broadcast, was controlled by NBC or CBS.[14] Likewise, the networks rapidly developed direct advertising as a lucrative method of support, even in the teeth of the Great Depression. From virtual non-existence in 1927, radio advertising expenditures were over $100 million in 1929.[15] It continued to grow throughout the 1930s, to the point where it nearly approached the amount of advertising in the U.S. newspaper industry.[16] The development of the networks and advertising were mutually reinforcing as over 80 percent of advertising expenditures went to 20 percent of the stations, all network owned or affiliated.[17] These developments took most Americans by surprise. "Broadcasting today is not what it was expected to be," one observer noted in 1932. "The amount of advertising on the air beyond any expectation that could have existed five years ago."[18] Another observer stated in 1930 that "Nothing in American history has paralleled this mushroom growth." This has since become a staple insight in U.S. broadcasting history.[19]

The losers in the reallocation were the educational and non-profit broadcasters. Most non-profit broadcasters thought the term "public interest, convenience, or necessity" meant the FRC was supposed to favor non-profit organizations over commercial enterprises in the allocation of licenses.[20] The FRC determined otherwise, arguing that it had to favor commercial broadcasters because non-profit groups were not motivated by profits (i.e. satisfying market demand), and therefore were more likely to spread unwanted "propaganda." The FRC also asserted that advertising was a necessary evil, as it was the only form of material support that did not have ideological strings attached.[21] As a result, the number of college broadcasters continued to plummet in the late 1920s, falling from 128 in 1925 to about 40 in 1930. Those non-profit stations that remained on the air were almost all given limited daytime hours on frequencies shared with commercial stations. Even the University of Wisconsin's WHA, the foremost college station, found its work "practically wrecked" when forced by the FRC to share its frequency with eight other stations.[22] The FRC has "taken away all the hours that are worth anything and left us with hours that are absolutely no good either for commercial programs or educational programs," wrote the director of the soon defunct University of Arkansas station.[23] In this context most university stations had difficulty developing audiences or maintaining budgets from state legislatures.

Non-profit broadcasting was effectively non-existent for most Americans by the early 1930s, but the system was not ideologically entrenched; between 1927 and 1934 commercial broadcasting was not considered innately "American" and "democratic" nor immune to fundamental attack. Indeed, the initial public response to commercial broadcasting was decidedly negative, particularly in comparison to later attitudes. Radio advertising was almost uniformly disliked. "I know that dissatisfaction with the present broadcasting system and its results is well nigh universal," one journalist wrote. "Out of one hundred persons you will not find more than five who are satisfied; of the other 95%, more than one-half are ready to support any kind of movement for drastic change."[24] This assessment was shared to varying degrees by the industry and its supporters. "Radio broadcasting," *Business Week* noted in 1932, "is threatened with a revolt of the listeners. . . . Newspaper editors report more and more letters of protest against irritating sales ballyhoo."[25] The challenge for those opposing the status quo was to convert this antipathy to commercial fare into support for structural reform, before the system became fully entrenched and listeners reconciled and conditioned to its existence.

This was a daunting task, regardless of public opinion, if only due to the strength of the radio lobby. NBC, RCA, CBS and the National Association of Broadcasters (NAB), the commercial broadcasters' trade association, comprised a lobby that was, as all acknowledged, "one of the most powerful here in Washington."[26] Network presidents could have audiences with members of Congress, even the president, almost at a moment's notice. The industry devoted lavish resources to a public relations campaign to establish the benevolence of commercial broadcasting and utilized the airwaves to further promote this vision.[27] The radio lobby also successfully cultivated the support of the newspaper industry and the legal community.[28] Perhaps most important, the networks had a policy of offering free air time to members of Congress and government officials during this period; between January 1931 and October 1933, for example,

U.S. Senators made 298 appearances over NBC. Moreover, it was the network lobbyists who were responsible for scheduling members of Congress for their broadcasts.[29] As one frustrated reformer observed, "the politicians are too eager to use radio to come out for reform."[30]

This was the situation facing the national foundations and educational organizations as they became interested in broadcasting in the second half of the 1920s. The political and business climate was such that philanthropies and non-profit groups determined that it would be incumbent upon them to provide the missing public service component to U.S. broadcasting. The Payne Fund, a small foundation established in 1926, was perhaps the first of these groups to actively pursue the educational potential of radio.

The Payne Fund's initial goal was to create a national "School of the Air," whereby educational programs for children and adults would be broadcast by educators over the commercial networks. The Payne Fund had no qualms about working with NBC and CBS, finding them "friendly" and willing to provide the necessary air time "without charge."[31] The networks also agreed, at the Payne Fund's insistence, that these educational programs should be produced by independent educational authorities and that there should be no commercial interference. The major stumbling block for this project, as it developed, came not from the networks but from educational groups and foundations. Perry spent most of 1928 attempting to find an educational group willing to undertake such a program or a philanthropist willing to underwrite it. "I see no evidence," he concluded in 1929, "that any educational organization will do so on a national basis."[32] By this time the Payne Fund was convinced that with the flood of advertising to radio, the prospects for educational broadcasting were dismal, and that, if anything, the educational programs provided by the networks would be "prepared for advertising purposes rather than educational value."[33]

Using their contacts with the National Education Association (NEA), the Payne Fund convinced Secretary of the Interior Ray Lyman Wilbur in May 1929 to convene an Advisory Committee on Education by Radio, known widely as the Wilbur Committee, to examine the crisis in educational broadcasting. The Payne Fund helped subsidize the Wilbur Committee and it assigned Perry to work for the committee until it filed its report. Perry spent the balance of 1929 traveling across the United States interviewing educators and broadcasters.

It was during this period that Perry became radicalized. First, he discovered that NBC and CBS were curtailing their commitment to educational programming as they were able to sell more and more of their time to advertisers.[34] There was the distinct possibility, he concluded, that "all the time available on stations covering any considerable territory will be sold for advertising purposes."[35] Second, Perry finally located a group of educators that seemed to grasp the importance of radio for education: the college and university broadcasters. Perry became convinced that the only hope was to protect these stations from extinction and, to create a viable non-profit and non-commercial broadcasting sector. These broadcasters convinced Perry that their enemies were the FRC and, above all, the commercial broadcasters, who, in the quest for profit, were attempting to occupy every available channel. "One thing is evident," Perry noted in June 1929, "and that is that commercial radio wants to head off any possibility of the growth and connection of stations owned by the people."[36] The NBC and CBS executives on the Wilbur Committee successfully deflected Perry's efforts to have the committee recommend that educational stations be protected and invigorated. The networks argued that they remained willing to provide whatever air time was necessary for educational and cultural purposes. The February 1930 report simply called for the educators and commercial broadcasters to work together and for the Office of Education to establish a special radio section to promote educational broadcasting and "attempt to prevent conflicts between various broadcasting interests."[37] Although the networks were elated, this was not a thorough defeat for the proponents of independent educational stations.

The Payne Fund set aside a five-year $200,000 grant to support an educator broadcast reform organization and on October 13 established the NCER as an umbrella organization of the NEA, the American Council on Education, the National Association of State Universities, and six other national educational organizations.[38] Joy Elmer Morgan, editor of the NEA's *Journal*, became chair of the NCER.[39] The NCER was formally chartered to lobby Congress for legislation to set aside 15 percent of the channels for educational stations. The NCER was established as a "fighting committee," as the Payne Fund put it. There was no pretense at the Chicago meeting or thereafter that it was possible for educators to work with commercial broadcasters; that approach was presupposed as bankrupt.[40] The Fund "emphatically" disavowed "the least intention to influence the policies of your Committee when our judgments may be at variance."[41] The Fund established the NCER so educators could defend their own interests against commercial broadcasters and congress.

The NCER and the Broadcast Reform Movement

The NCER formally commenced operations in January 1931. The nine member organizations each provided one representative for the NCER's board which met to determine basic policy four times annually. Morgan was the NEA representative and served as NCER chair until 1935, serving as the spokesperson for the campaign for broadcast reform. Based in Washington, D.C., the NCER was directed on a daily basis by Tracy F. Tyler, a Columbia Ph.D. who managed the office and edited the NCER newsletter, *Education by Radio*. Tyler also coordinated the NCER's research program and arranged a clearinghouse so educational stations could share their programs. Nonetheless, it was the campaign for broadcast reform that was the NCER's raison d'etre. In its first week the NCER sent an open letter to Congress criticizing U.S. radio as "the dollar sign's mightiest megaphone."[42] Between 1931 and 1934 Tyler, Perry and the other educators associated with the NCER made hundreds of speeches and wrote scores of articles promoting the cause.

Morgan had worked for public ownership of utilities during the progressive era, where he honed his hatred of the "power trust" and the large corporations, like RCA, that would come to dominate radio.[43] Morgan believed accessible public education was the foundation of genuine democracy; he derided college admissions tests as a "crime," claiming they created an "intellectual aristocracy."[44] He regarded education as "the most fundamental activity of the state" and in the broadest terms imaginable. "Education is no narrow academic affair. It is not confined to children. It concerns the entire population. It involves the whole life of the individual, on the one side, and the whole life of society, on the other."[45] In his capacity with the NEA Morgan became convinced that the commercial broadcasters would never provide adequate time for educational programming. "That practice has been tried for nearly a decade and proved unworkable," he stated in 1931. "It is no longer open to discussion."[46] Moreover, radio broadcasting had emerged as the most important educational influence in the United States, "more important than home, school, and church combined in the formation of human character," he asserted in 1933.[47]

Given these sentiments, Morgan regarded the fight for broadcast reform as indispensable and central to the battle for political and social democracy, casting the struggle in urgent, almost apocalyptic, terms.

As a result of radio broadcasting, there will probably develop during the twentieth century either chaos or a world-order of civilization. Whether it shall be one or the other will depend largely upon whether broadcasting be used as a tool of education or an instrument of selfish greed. So far, our American radio interests have thrown their major influence on the side of greed....There has never been in the entire history of the United States an example of mismanagement and lack of vision so colossal and far-reaching in its consequences as our turning the radio channels almost exclusively into commercial hands. [48]

Morgan argued that "whoever controls radio will in the end control the development of the human race."[49] In the depths of the Depression he wrote that the United States cannot "solve any of its major political problems without first solving the radio problem."[50]

Not surprisingly, the NCER generated an ice-cold response from the commercial broadcasters. The trade publication *Broadcasting* characterized the NCER as "a group of misguided pedagogues" who were "professional reformers" with "silly demands." One editorial described the NCER as "childish" and as "a racket by which a few zealots want to justify the jobs they are holding."[51] The industry displayed no interest in taking the NCER's concerns seriously; rather, the NAB characterized the NCER as trying to "invade the broadcast band at the expense" of the commercial stations that had been willing "to bear the trials of pioneering."[52] Morgan, in particular, was a target of derision and ridicule. *Broadcasting* dismissed him as "coming from the ranks of primary school men," and possessing an "unreasoning sort of crusading."[53]

The NCER was not the only group pursuing broadcast reform, though it was the best financed. Organized labor, religious groups, and the American Civil Liberties Union (ACLU), among others, worked throughout the early 1930s for legislation to establish a significant non-profit and non-commercial component to U.S. broadcasting.[54] In addition to organized reform efforts, the cause of broadcast reform received the nearly unconditional support of the U.S. intelligentsia.[55] As Morgan observed, it was virtually impossible to find any intellectual in favor of the status quo unless that person was receiving money or air time from a commercial station or network.[56] Among these intellectuals was John Dewey, who in 1934 stated "radio is the most powerful instrument of social education the world has ever seen. It can be used to distort facts and to mislead the public mind. In my opinion, the question as to whether it is to be employed for this end or for the social public interest is one of the most crucial problems of the present."[57] Dewey argued that freedom of the press was structurally impossible as long as broadcasting was under "concentrated capitalist control."[58]

Dewey's critique was similar to that of the NCER. Indeed, there was a striking consistency in the criticism of commercial broadcasting made by all the various elements of the broadcast reform movement. Three themes dominated this reform movement critique. First, the reformers emphasized that the system was structurally flawed on free expression grounds; a for-profit, corporate-dominated system would be inherently biased against broadcasting material critical of big business and the status quo. "Freedom of speech is the very foundation of democracy," one *Education by Radio* article stated.

To allow private interests to monopolize the most powerful means of reaching the human mind is to destroy democracy. Without freedom of speech, without the honest presentation of facts by people whose primary interest is *not* profits, there can be no intelligent basis for the determination of public policy.[59] [their emphasis]

Second, the reformers detested radio advertising and its influence over programming. In the early 1930s advertisers generally provided the programs in addition to the commercial announcements that appeared during the programs.[60] "It is a trite but ever truthful saying that he who pays the piper calls the tune," *Education by Radio* observed. "Where has it been shown to better advantage than in radio?"[61] Most commercial programs were regarded as trivial and inane, and it was seen as inevitable that advertisers would downplay educational, cultural or controversial fare to favor inexpensive, unoriginal entertainment programs. One college president associated with the NCER stated that "it is inevitable that a commercial concern catering to the public will present a service as low in standard as the public will tolerate and will produce the most profit."[62] The NCER emphasized that radio advertising was distinct from print advertising as the listener was "helpless" to avoid it, and, to enjoy radio programs, the public was forced to have "its homes turned into salesrooms."[63] Moreover, the public showed no desire for radio advertising. To the NCER, if the commercial broadcasters were genuinely interested in "giving the public what its wants," as they often proclaimed, the first thing that would happen is advertising would be stricken from the airwaves.[64]

The NCER took this critique of radio advertising one step farther than the other reformers. Morgan argued that radio advertising "is making great efforts to get into the schools."[65] He contended that "one reason why commercial interests have sought to destroy independent educational stations has been their ambition to broadcast radio advertising into the schools themselves."[66] The NCER carefully monitored incidents of commercial educational programs being used in public schools, arguing that it must "be kept out of the schools just as advertising has been kept out of textbooks."[67]

The NCER's critique of advertising harbored an element of elitism and, at times, academic contempt for the mere notion of entertainment programming. This left the educators in stark contrast to organized labor, which insisted that entertainment had to play a large role on a non-profit working class radio station, whether or not advertising was present.[68] It also undercut the populist appeal of the balance of their critique, damaging their prospects for generating popular support. "It is much more important that people be informed than that they be entertained," Morgan argued.[69] Morgan informed one 1931 audience that for the commercial broadcasters "to get the large audiences, they cultivate the lower appeals. The educational stations realize that the finer things of life have always appealed first to the few."[70] This point should not be exaggerated, however. Most of the college and non-profit broadcasters regarded their survival as dependent upon their ability to cultivate and satisfy audiences in order to win the budgets necessary to stay on the air. In their minds, they were appealing directly to listeners while the commercial broadcasters were concerned primarily with advertisers. Moreover, the broadcast reformers regarded themselves as representing the legitimate desires of the vast majority of U.S. listeners in the early 1930s; it was only later, as the system became entrenched, that educators accepted their role as one of attempting to establish a non-commercial beachhead in a popularly embraced commercial system.

The third theme in the reform movement critique was that the commercial system had been the result of a mostly secretive process in which the public and even Congress had played almost no role. This violated the reformers' democratic sensibilities. More broadly, the reformers thought the very notion of turning a vital public resource over to private interests for profitable exploitation was nothing short of "an incredible absurdity for a democracy," as one NCER member put it.[71] "So the question really is," Perry noted, "do we want to submit to the regulation of radio by the people we elect to rule over us, or do we want to leave our radio channels in the hands of private concerns and private individuals who wish to use these public radio channels for their own profit?"[72]

In sum, this was explicitly radical criticism; the reformers were unified in their belief that the FRC experience established beyond doubt that it was absurd to think a government agency could regulate private broadcasters to act against their interests and in the public interest. Structural reform was mandatory. It is "a fact that radio channels belong to the people," one NCER organizer stated, "and should not be placed in the hands of private capital."[73] While most reformers looked to basic capitalist economics to explain the seeming mad rush of capital to dominate the airwaves, they all saw this as a classic struggle of the people versus the plutocrats, where those in power were well aware of the stakes in the outcome. Some were inclined to more sinister explanations. "Candidly," one educational broadcaster observed,

> I believe there is a definite, organized conspiracy within big business to keep radio out of the hands of those who would put it to use for the people. It is such a potent agent of enlightenment that special privilege cannot tolerate its public uses.[74]

If there was unanimity among the reformers regarding the core weaknesses of commercial broadcasting and the need for structural reform, the opposite was the case when it came to generating an alternative plan for U.S. broadcasting. The NCER was never enthusiastic about the proposal to reserve 15 percent of the channels for educational broadcasters; Morgan characterized it as merely "an emergency and not a final measure."[75]

All of the NCER officers individually were enthralled by the British Broadcasting Company (BBC), a non-profit, non-commercial, quasi-governmental agency that held a monopoly over broadcasting in the United Kingdom. While none wanted to see such a monopoly in the United States, most major NCER figures thought a publicly funded non-profit system, with a dominant though not exclusive role, was a rational alternative.[76] To Perry, the BBC provided the "ideal" example of a "broadcasting service maintained primarily for the benefit of all radio listeners," and was the solution to "the whole world problem of broadcasting."[77] The NCER and the other reformers determined that it would be politically impossible to win such a system in the United States, so it was never formally proposed or advocated.

If the NCER could not apply the BBC model to the United States, it came to regard Canada as "leading the way" for the balance of North America.[78] In 1932 the Canadian House of Commons formally resolved to establish a non-profit, non-commercial, government-subsidized broadcasting system after studying both the British and U.S. experiences with radio.

The NCER hoped that Canada would expose Americans near the border to the possibilities of public service broadcasting. More important, the NCER became convinced that if the U.S. Congress established a full-blown independent study of broadcasting like Canada had done, it, too, would resolve to establish a non-profit and non-commercial system.

Fall of the NCER and Collapse of the Broadcast Reform Movement

In January 1931 the NCER convinced Senator Simeon Fess, Republican of Ohio, to introduce legislation requiring the FRC to set aside 15 percent of the channels for educational broadcasters. The very early 1930s were the high-water mark for congressional antipathy to commercial broadcasting; despite the strength of the radio lobby, one reformer estimated that fully 70 percent of the Senate and 80 percent of the House of Representatives favored broadcast reform.[79] The NAB put the figure at closer to 90 percent for both branches of Congress.[80] Unfortunately for the reformers, however, the radio lobby had the universal backing of the relevant committee chairmen, who were able to keep reform legislation from ever getting to the floor for a vote. "If it were not for a little group of reactionary leaders in both branches of Congress," the chief labor radio lobbyist observed, reform "legislation would have been passed."[81]

The reform efforts were not helped by the political incompetence of the NCER, which eschewed working with labor, the ACLU or even the *Ventura Free Press* radio campaign, which had been established by the Payne Fund specifically to assist it. The *Free Press* publicists and lobbyists were repeatedly exasperated in their attempts to get the NCER to do anything.

The NCER even took an incomprehensible position regarding its own Fess bill. Morgan informed H. O. Davis, publisher of the *Ventura Free Press*, that the only position he supported was that of the National Congress of Parents and Teachers, which resolved in 1931 for the complete nationalization and decommercialization of broadcasting, although no legislation was ever introduced to that end.[82] By the summer of 1932 it was clear that reform legislation could not get through Congress for the foreseeable future. In the autumn of 1932 the Payne Fund disbanded the *Ventura Free Press* radio campaign. At the same time it asked S. Howard Evans, the Payne Fund official who conducted the *Free Press* lobbying activities, to prepare a memorandum on whether the Payne Fund should acknowledge defeat, urge the NCER to drop the campaign for broadcast reform and, work with the commercial broadcasters.

Evans acknowledged the difficulty of reform but he argued that the "fundamental structure of broadcasting" remained "absolutely unsound" and he convinced the Payne Fund to stay the course.[83] The NCER then found a member of Congress to introduce a resolution calling for a Canada-style federal study of broadcasting to determine a new system in the public interest. Given the situation on Capitol Hill, however, the NCER never made more than a superficial attempt to lobby on the measure's behalf. In February 1933, the NCER decided to "concentrate all their forces on creating local opinion which would later be reflected in Congress."[84] The NCER pursued several courses of action along these lines, but their efforts were overwhelmed by the strength of the radio lobby and the growing public acceptance of commercial broadcasting. "I doubt if the public can be led to look to educators as administrators of a national system that includes entertainment," Perry confessed to Morgan.[85] Morgan, however, maintained his particular political perspective. "Public support is beginning to come our way," he informed Perry in April 1933. "We can afford to wait our time."[86]

A primary barrier for the NCER was its inability to receive press coverage. Most Americans were unaware that it was even within their province, or that of Congress, to determine what type of broadcasting system the United States should have.[87] In a dramatic move to bring the issue before the public, the NCER used its influence to have radio adopted as the official debate topic for U.S. high schools and colleges in the 1933-34 academic year. The question of whether the United States should adopt the British system of broadcasting was debated by some 1500 colleges and 6000 high schools in 33 states. Two and 1/2 million Americans would be exposed to the debate.[88] "The debates will arouse an enormous amount of interest in the radio problem and will bring home the nature of this problem to millions of people who have so far given it very little thought," enthused one Payne Fund official.[89] The commercial broadcasters were terrified by the debates. The trade publication *Variety* lamented that "many, perhaps most, of these people have been unaware of the existence of the question."[90] "The Radio Industry was led into these debates through an error in judgment" by an NBC executive, "who innocently enough subscribed to the idea."[91] The broadcasters shifted the debate, as much as possible, to a discussion of the limitations of the BBC rather than the nature of U.S. broadcasting. The NAB published a 191 page debate guide that consisted in large part of frontal assaults on the BBC.[92] Unfortunately, the debates had little impact upon public opinion.

The NCER's last hope was for President Franklin D. Roosevelt, inaugurated in March 1933, to come out on behalf of broadcast reform. The NCER initially was encouraged, as there were many advocates of broadcast reform in administration positions. One of Roosevelt's closest political friends, Ambassador to Mexico Josephus Daniels, wrote to the president numerous times in 1933 and 1934 urging him to nationalize radio broadcasting before the system became entrenched. "There is no more reason why communications should be privately owned than the mails," a typical letter stated.[93] As one NCER member observed, "the program of protecting radio for its best public purpose would fit admirably into his entire program."[94] Nonetheless, the president elected not to take up broadcast reform and thereby engage in a potentially costly uphill battle with the radio industry. Roosevelt also did not want to jeopardize his ability to speak on the networks whenever he pleased, which the networks granted him, and thus bypass the largely Republican newspaper industry.[95] Hence the Roosevelt administration backed the agenda of the commercial broadcasters. Whereas the radio lobby had not wanted Congress to consider radio legislation during 1931-32 when sentiment might have insisted upon reform, by 1933 the industry was committed to having a "thoroughly stabilized" industry. Specifically, the radio lobby wanted legislation to establish the permanent basis for telecommunications regulation, thereby removing fundamental broadcasting issues from Congressional consideration thereafter and eliminating the basis for annual "attacks by unfriendly groups" in Washington.[96]

Given the support of the Roosevelt administration and the key congressional leaders, one historian notes that "all signs pointed to a quick passage" in 1934 of the industry's favored Communications Act.[97] Moreover, the NCER and the other reformers had discontinued their lobbying out of frustration. Then, most unexpectedly, the Paulist Fathers religious order of New York City, whose station WLWL had recently lost a bitter hearing to a CBS affiliate before the FRC, entered the fray. Paulist Fathers Superior General John B. Harney convinced Senators Robert Wagner, Democrat of New York, and Henry Hatfield, Republican of West Virginia, to introduce an amendment requiring that the new FCC set aside 25 percent of the channels for non-profit broadcasters. With minimal media coverage, the Paulists launched a whirlwind campaign exploiting their contacts among Roman Catholic organizations and with organized labor. By the end of April *Variety* warned that the Wagner-Hatfield amendment stood "better than a 50-50 chance of being adopted."[98] The NAB proclaimed that it "brings to a head the campaign against the present broadcasting set-up which has been smoldering in Congress for several years."[99] The radio lobby attacked the amendment as if "its passage would have destroyed the whole structure of broadcasting in America," as the NAB's chief lobbyist put it.[100]

Harney spent much of April imploring the NCER to actively support the Wagner-Hatfield amendment. If educators join Catholics and labor, Harney wrote Perry, "it is almost unthinkable" that Congress would not pass the measure. "We must not let this opportunity knock at our door in vain. A better day will hardly come in our lifetime."[101] Harney's efforts were in vain. While Perry and many of the college broadcasters were enthusiastic about the Wagner-Hatfield amendment, Tyler and Morgan, the key operatives in Washington D.C., were uninterested, as they regarded the question of funding still unresolved in Harney's proposal. Tyler and Morgan offered only "silent sympathy," explaining to Harney that it would be possible to get even better legislation passed at a future session of Congress.[102] The Wagner-Hatfield amendment was defeated in the Senate 42-23 on May 15. A major weapon that defused support for the amendment was the late inclusion of a clause in the Communications Act requiring the new FCC to hold hearings on the Wagner-Hatfield proposal and then report back to Congress early in 1935 with its recommendations. The clause let supporters of the Wagner-Hatfield amendment vote against it in the belief that the experts on the new FCC would subject the topic of non-profit broadcasting to comprehensive examination. The Communications Act passed on a voice vote later the same day. In June President Roosevelt signed the Communications Act of 1934 into law. "When we read it," the NAB's chief lobbyist later stated, "we found that every point we had asked for was there."[103] Now only one opportunity remained for the reformers to advance the cause of structural reform: the FCC hearings on whether to reserve 25 percent of the channels for non-profit organizations as mandated by the Communications Act. Harney and labor refused to participate, regarding the hearings as "a pro forma affair, designed to entrench the commercial interests in their privileged position."[104] Indeed, two of the three FCC members who would conduct the October hearings informed the NAB convention in September that they would refuse to recommend any change in the status quo, regardless of the testimony.[105] Ironically, the NCER agreed to coordinate the pro-fixed percentage side of the hearings, though, as it informed the FCC, it "had not suggested the enactment of the specific legislation under discussion." As Tyler conceded, the FCC hearings "would be better than no study at all."[106]

Unfortunately for the NCER, the hearings went disastrously. The reform side was poorly organized, presenting numerous contradictory schemes for reorganizing U.S. broadcasting. The commercial broadcasters, on the other hand, devoted considerable resources to establish the industry's unequivocal commitment to broadcast educational and cultural programs. As NBC's chief lobbyist reported to New York headquarters, the broadcasters' case was "done to perfection" and "simply overwhelming."[107] To nobody's surprise, in January 1935 the FCC recommended against the fixed percentage proposal. When Congress reconvened it showed no interest in broadcast reform legislation. The matter was deemed as settled with the passage of the Communications Act of 1934 and the formation of the FCC, which regarded commercial broadcasting as the legally authorized system unless informed otherwise by Congress. The political battle for the control of U.S. broadcasting, including television as well as radio, as much as it ever existed, was now concluded. The various elements of the broadcast reform movement unraveled and disappeared in short order.

By the end of the decade, with the demise of organized opposition, the economic and political consolidation of commercial broadcasting was followed by its ideological consolidation. "Our American system of broadcasting," Sarnoff informed an NBC audience in 1938, "is what it is because it operates in American democracy. It is a free system because this is a free country."[108] CBS president William S. Paley received little comment when he informed a meeting of educators in 1937 that "he who attacks the American system" of broadcasting, "attacks democracy itself."[109] A few years earlier such a statement would have been met by derision. The system was now off-limits to fundamental attack. Not only was the capitalistic basis of U.S. broadcasting off-limits to structural criticism, it was elevated to the point where such criticism was becoming unthinkable.[110]

In these changing currents the Payne Fund had no interest in devoting resources to quixotic assaults upon an increasingly respectable and politically inviolable industry. For the balance of the 1930s the NCER concentrated on two tasks. First, under new chairman Arthur G. Crane, the University of Wyoming president, the NCER helped establish the Rocky Mountain Radio Council, a clearinghouse meant to assist non-profit groups providing non-commercial educational programming to commercial stations. Crane made it clear that the NCER had no interest in creating non-profit stations, and that the NCER accepted the commercial broadcasters as the legitimate and rightful stewards of U.S. broadcasting. "Private enterprise has succeeded in making exceptionally fine broadcasts available to American listeners," a typical NCER pamphlet observed.[111] S. Howard Evans, whom the Payne Fund assigned to run the new NCER office, attempted to encourage the FCC to aggressively regulate the networks. Unlike Crane, Evans never abandoned his hatred for commercial broadcasting or his belief in the need for radical change, describing himself in 1936 as "advocating Christianity in a world that is decidedly pagan."[112] Evans eventually quit when he became frustrated with the NCER's inability to even have minor influence over policy. Crane did not fare much better with his programs. When the Payne Fund terminated the NCER in 1941, it went virtually unnoticed, even in the educational community.

The late 1930s were far from halcyon days for the proponents of educational and public service broadcasting in the United States. By 1936, only 30 educational stations remained, and most of these were in dire financial straits that seemingly were irreversible. Moreover, with the consolidation of the status quo, educators had almost no leverage to exact concessions from either the networks or the FCC.[113] The only recourse left to educators and proponents of public service broadcasting was to accept channels on experimental bands yet to be developed for commercial purposes. This was not a novel strategy. In early 1934, for example, just before Congress was to consider permanent broadcasting legislation, the FRC attempted to convince educators to accept slots on a newly established section of the AM band between 1500 and 1600 kilocycles, a band that few radio receivers could pick up. The NCER rejected the proposal emphatically. "The administration felt the need of shutting up every discordant element in broadcasting," Armstrong Perry explained at the time, "and is just trying to find the easy way out."[114] As Perry put it, the FRC "would let the educational stations do the experimental work," just like the college stations that had largely pioneered radio broadcasting in the early 1920s, "and then perhaps would take away the channels and allocate them for commercial use."[115]

With the consolidation of the status quo, educators were in no position to bargain. In the early 1940s, they rejoiced when the FCC granted them the exclusive right to develop the new FM band.[116] This was characterized as "educational radio's second chance," and educators were cautioned not to fumble this opportunity as they had with AM broadcasting in the 1920s.[117] This and all subsequent campaigns to reserve space for non-profit broadcasting in the United

States, however, provided pale comparisons to the lofty ambitions of the early 1930s reformers. They could be successful or secure only to the extent that they did not interfere with the profitability, existing or potential, of commercial broadcasters; i.e. to the extent they were ineffectual.

Moreover, the ante for admission for those that wished to remain active in pursuing educational and public service broadcasting in the United States was to accept the premise, as a one-time advocate of a BBC-style system put it in 1946, that commercial broadcasting "is basically sound."[118] Even those like Robert Hutchins, who could barely conceal his contempt for commercial broadcasting, accepted the capitalist basis of the industry as irreversible, adopted an elitist stance, and worked only to reserve a niche for intellectuals and dissidents on the margins.[119] The industry solidified its standing with educators by launching an aggressive program of funding academic research on broadcast communications in the late 1930s.[120] The major foundations, too, devoted their largesse to broadcasting in earnest only after the consolidation of the status quo; beginning with the Rockefeller Foundation and later with the Ford Foundation and Carnegie Corporation, these philanthropies consciously worked with the industry, even when proposing non-profit channel allocations.[121] All the movements for non-profit television in the 1950s and 1960s were decidedly establishment operations; nary a word evoking the populist legacy of the NCER is anywhere to be found in their records.[122] Since these are the people and institutions responsible for most of what passes as U.S. public service broadcasting history, it is no surprise that the NCER and other reform organizations play such an inconsequential role, and are often dealt with inaccurately, in the dominant histories.

Conclusion

U.S. broadcasting histories, mainstream and critical, tend to regard the U.S. system as naturally one dominated by profit-motivated corporations and supported by advertising. In this dominant perspective, proponents of educational and public service broadcasting were logically shunted to the margins at the outset. As this paper reveals, this is an erroneous interpretation. The U.S. system emerged nearly a decade after broadcasting developed in the United States, and its development was hardly the result of any sort of public referendum. A strident and principled opposition to commercial broadcasting emerged concurrent with the system itself. Based on deep-seated U.S. political traditions, these reformers argued that a commercial broadcasting system was inimical to the communication requirements of a democratic society. Although the NCER failed, to no small extent because it was never able to generate a broad-based public discussion of the issues involved, it left an important legacy of anti-market media criticism for future generations.

Some might argue that the concerns of the NCER and the 1930s broadcast reformers are no longer relevant, as revolutionary new technologies and competition in the marketplace have asserted consumer sovereignty, reduced corporate power, and decentralized telecommunications.[123] Indeed, much of the momentum of the past two decades has been for deregulation, to discard any notions of public service in U.S. broadcasting and let the profit motive be the unabashed yardstick for resource allocation. The results of this deregulation movement appear to be far from the much-ballyhooed democratic Valhalla once promised. Perhaps the passage of the bill to re-regulate cable broadcasting in October 1992 suggests that the pendulum is begin to swing in the other direction.[124] In fact, a significant body of research suggests that the U.S. mass media are more highly concentrated and less capable of providing a basis for democratic communication than at any time in their history.[125] If that is the case, we may need to seriously evaluate the capacity of the existing broadcast media to satisfactorily serve a self-governing society. Rather then use the new technologies as a rationale for abandoning notions of public service, it might be more rational to use the new technologies to establish a vital non-profit sector previously unimaginable. In such a public discussion, it is incumbent that we draw from the experiences of the early 1930s educators and reformers, to learn from both their strengths and weaknesses.

Finally, much as the NCER feared, the same forces advocating the deregulation of broadcasting are leading the campaign to extend market criteria and commercial principles to the education system. Although public service principles are far more deeply ingrained for U.S. education than they are for U.S. broadcasting, the democratic ideals of free, universal, public education are nonetheless under severe attack.[126] Increasingly, the debate and arguments surrounding media and education are becoming intertwined, with the stakes going directly to the future vitality of our polity and culture. If nothing else, those concerned primarily with educational policy should take one lesson from the experience of the educational broadcasters in the early 1930s: The notion that the market is innately American or democratic is exaggerated if not downright inaccurate. Until that point is made clear, the campaign to preserve and promote public service principles in education, like broadcasting, will be on the defensive in the United States.

NOTES

Abbreviations:

BBC—British Broadcasting Corporation Papers, BBC Written Archive Centre, Reading, England.

CC—Carnegie Corporation of New York Papers, Butler Library, Columbia University, New York, N.Y.

GS—Graham Spry Papers, Manuscript Group 30, D297, National Archives of Canada, Ottawa, Canada.

NBC—National Broadcasting Company Papers, State Historical Society of Wisconsin, Madison, Wis.

OE—Office of Education Papers, Record Group 12, National Archives, Washington, D.C.

PF—Payne Fund, Inc. Papers, Western Reserve Historical Society, Cleveland, Oh.

SHSW—State Historical Society of Wisconsin, Madison, Wis.

[1] Eugene E. Leach, *Tuning Out Education: The Cooperation Doctrine in Radio, 1922-39* (Washington D.C.: Current, 1983), 2.

[2] Willard D. Rowland, Jr., "Public-Service Broadcasting in the United States: Its Mandate, Institutions and Conflicts," in *Public-Service Broadcasting in a Multi-Channel Environment*, ed. Robert K. Avery (New York: Longman, forthcoming), first page of draft copy.

[3] See Martin Tolchin, "Senate Rejects Efforts to Cut Fund for Public Broadcasting," *The New York Times*, June 4, 1992, 1; for an examination of the alleged left-wing bias in U.S. public broadcasting, see "PBS' Missing Voices," *Extra!*, June 1992, 15-18.

[4] Robert J. Blakely, *To Serve the Public Interest: Educational Broadcasting in the United States* (Syracuse: Syracuse University Press, 1979), 38.

[5] For three recent critical histories of U.S. broadcasting that effectively make this argument, see Susan J. Douglas, *Inventing American Broadcasting 1899-1922* (Baltimore: The Johns Hopkins University Press,

1987), 317; James Schwoch, *The American Radio Industry and Its Latin American Activities, 1900-1939* (Urbana and Chicago: University of Illinois Press, 1990), 76; Michele Hilmes, *Hollywood and Broadcasting: From Radio to Cable* (Urbana and Chicago: University of Illinois Press, 1990), 49.

[6] Cited in Leach, *Tuning Out Education*, 2.

[7] For these reasons, I use the terms educational and public service interchangeably in this paper. I realize that in other contexts one can draw useful distinctions between the terms.

[8] For recent works that point to the convergence of concerns regarding the communication and education policy, see Jeffrey C. Goldfarb, *The Cynical Society: The Culture of Politics and the Politics of Culture in American Life* (Chicago: University of Chicago Press, 1991); William Greider, *Who Will Tell the People: The Betrayal of American Democracy* (New York: Simon & Schuster, 1992).

[9] See Werner J. Severin, "Commercial Vs. Non-Commercial Radio During Broadcasting's Early Years," *Journal of Broadcasting* 20 (Fall 1978): 491-504; S. E. Frost, Jr., *Education's Own Stations* (Chicago: University of Chicago Press, 1937).

[10] "Report of the Committee on Radio," *American Newspaper Publishers Association Bulletin*, No. 5374, 5 May 1927, 285; see also John W. Spalding, "1928: Radio Becomes a Mass Advertising Medium," *Journal of Broadcasting* 8 (Winter 1963-64): 31-44.

[11] Broadcasting Station Survey, 1 January 1926, 07 01 02, Box 77, Edwin H. Colpitts Papers, American Telephone & Telegraph Archives, Warren, N.J.

[12] This period is discussed in detail in Robert W. McChesney, *Telecommunications, Mass Media, and Democracy: The Battle for the Control of U.S. Broadcasting, 1928-1935* (New York: Oxford University Press, 1993), ch. 3.

[13] See Donald G. Godfrey, "The 1927 Radio Act: People and Politics," *Journalism History* 4 (Autumn 1977): 78; Erik Barnouw, *A Tower in Babel* (New York: Oxford University Press, 1966), 281.

[14] "The Menace of Radio Monopoly," *Education by Radio*, 26 March 1931, 27; "The Power Trust and the Public Schools," *Education by Radio*, 10 Dec. 1931, 150; "Radio Censorship and the Federal Communications Commission," *Columbia Law Review* 39 (March 1939): 447; 97 percent figure cited in William Boddy, *Fifties Television: The Industry and Its Critics* (Urbana and Chicago: University of Illinois Press, 1990), 36.

[15] Martin Codel, "Networks Reveal Impressive Gains," undated, sometime in January 1931. In vol. 61, Martin Codel Papers, SHSW.

[16] See Robert W. McChesney, "Press-Radio Relations and the Emergence of Network, Commercial Broadcasting in the United States, 1930-1935," *Historical Journal of Film, Radio and Television* 11 (1991): 41-57; McChesney, *Telecommunications, Mass Media, and Democracy*, ch. 7.

[17] Cited in Hilmes, *Hollywood and Broadcasting*, 52.

[18] S. Howard Evans to Walter V. Woehlke, 29 February 1932, folder 1138, container 69, PF.

[19] Henry Volkening, "Abuses of Radio Broadcasting," *Current History* 33 (December 1930): 396-400; see also Barnouw, *Tower*, 270; Philip T, Rosen, *The Modern Stentors: Radio Broadcasting and the Federal Government 1920-1934* (Westport, Conn.: Greenwood Press, 1980), 12.

[20] This is a common theme among educational and non-profit broadcasters during this period. See, for example, John Henry McCracken, "The Fess Bill for Education by Radio," *Education by Radio*, 19 March 1931, 21; George H. Gibson, *Public Broadcasting: The Role of the Federal Government, 1919-1976* (New York: Praeger Publishers, 1976), 8; Armstrong Perry, "The College Station and the Federal Radio Commission," in *Education on the Air: Second Yearbook of the Institute for Education by Radio*, ed. Josephine H. MacLatchy (Columbus: Ohio State University, 1931), 33.

[21] Federal Radio Commission, *Third Annual Report of the Federal Radio Commission to the Congress of the United States Covering the Period from October 1, 1928 to November 1, 1929* (Washington, D.C.: United States Government Printing Office, 1929), 32-36.

[22] Jos. F. Wright to Sam Pickard, 25 October 1928, Substance of Telegram to Congressman, 29 May 1928, file 001, box 1, series 2-4, WHA Papers, University of Wisconsin Archives, Madison, Wis.

23 W. S. Gregson to B. B. Brackett, 25 February 1932, box 1a, general correspondence, National Association of Educational Broadcasters Papers, SHSW.

24 Walter V. Woehlke to S. Howard Evans, 22 December 1932, folder 1147, container 60, PF.

25 "Neither Sponsors Nor Stations Heed Listeners' Grumbling," *Business Week*, 10 Feb. 1932, 18-19.

26 Tracy Tyler to Roger Baldwin, 26 October 1933, vol. 599, American Civil Liberties Union Papers, Princeton University, Princeton, N.J.

27 For a discussion of the radio lobby, see McChesney, *Telecommunications, Mass Media, and Democracy*, ch. 5; for two example of commercial broadcasters' promotional material, see National Association of Broadcasters, *Broadcasting in the United States* (Washington, D.C.: National Association of Broadcasters, 1933); National Broadcasting Company, *Broadcasting. Volumes I-IV* (New York: National Broadcasting Company, 1935).

28 For a discussion of the relationship of commercial broadcasters to the legal community, see Robert W. McChesney, *Telecommunications, Mass Media, and Democracy*, Ch. 6.

29 Paul F. Peter, NBC Chief Statistician, "Appearances by U.S. Federal Officials Over National Broadcasting Company Networks, 1931-1933," November 1933, folder 26, box 16, NBC.

30 Joy Elmer Morgan to John Henry McCracken, 2 August 1932, folder 801, container 43, PF.

31 Report of B. H. Darrow, 7 March 1928, folder 1368, container 70, PF; Armstrong Pery, "The Ohio School of the Air and Other Experiments in the Use of Radio in Education," 29 May 1929, folder 1353, container 69, PF.

32 Armstrong Perry to H. M. Clymer, 6 April 1929, folder 1067, container 56, PF.

33 ibid.

34 Armstrong Perry to Ella Phillips Crandall, 9 July 1929, folder 1068, container 56, PF.

35 Armstrong Perry to J. L. Clifton, 21 August 1929, folder 1068, container 56, PF.

36 Armstrong Perry to H. M. Clymer, 14 June 1929, folder 1353, container 69, PF.

37 Advisory Committee on Education by Radio, *Report of the Advisory Committee on Education by Radio Appointed by the Secretary of the Interior* (Colubus: The F. J. Heer Printing Company, 1930), 35-37, 76.

38 The other six groups were the National University Extension Association, the Association of Land Grant Colleges and Universities, the Association of College and University Broadcasting Stations (which renamed itself the National Association of Educational Broadcasters by the middle 1930s), the National Council of State Superintendents, the Jesuit Education Association, and the National Catholic Education Association.

39 Minutes of the Conference on Educational Radio Problems Stevens Hotel, Chicago, October 13, 1930, At the Invitation of the U.S. Commissioner of Education, Box 31, OE.

40 Memorandum re: General Situation of Radio in Education, 29 December 1930, folder 1352, container 69, PF.

41 Frances Payne Bolton to Joy Elmer Morgan, 17 June 1932, folder 1071, container 42, PF.

42 "Congress is Asked for Radio Freedom," *The New York Times*, 6 Dec. 1931, sec. 2, 8.

43 See Joy Elmer Morgan and E. D. Bullock, *Selected Articles on Municipal Ownership* (Minneapolis: Wilson, 1911); see also Joy Elmer Morgan, "The Corporation in America," *Journal of the National Education Association* 23 (December 1934): 227-229.

44 "Intelligence Tests Called a Crime," *The New York Times*, 22 June 1930, sec. 2, 3.

45 Joy Elmer Morgan, "Education's Rights on the Air," in *NACRE 1931*, 122.

46 ibid., 128.

47 Cited in *Education by Radio*, 2 Feb. 1933, 11.

48 Morgan, "Education's Rights," in *NACRE 1931*, 120-121.

49 ibid., 128.

0

[50] Joy Elmer Morgan to Dr. William McAndrew, 20 September 1932, drawer 3, FCB 2, Joy Elmer Morgan Papers, National Education Association, Washington, D.C.

[51] "The Fittest Survive," *Broadcasting*, 15 Jan. 1933, 16; "Listeners Society," *Broadcasting* 1 April 1933, 14.

[52] "Mass Action is Imperative," *Broadcasters' News Bulletin*, 14 Feb. 1931.

[53] "Exit Mr. Morgan," *Broadcasting*, 15 Sept. 1935, 30.

[54] See Robert W. McChesney, "Labor and the Marketplace of Ideas: WCFL and the Battle for Labor Radio Broadcasting, 1927-1934," *Journalism Monographs* 134 (August 1992): 1-40; McChesney, *Telecommunications, Mass Media, and Democracy*, Ch. 4.

[55] ibid., Ch. 4, 5; Robert W. McChesney, "An Almost Incredible Absurdity for a Democracy," *Journal of Communication Inquiry* 15 (Winter 1991): 89-114.

[56] Joy Elmer Morgan, "The New American Plan for Radio," in *A Debate Handbook on Radio Control and Operation*, eds. Bower Aly and Gerald D. Shively (Columbia, Mo.: Staples Publishing Co., 1933), 82. [hereafter *Debate Handbook*]

[57] Cited in *Education by Radio*, 24 Dec. 1931, 156; see also *School and Society*, 15 Dec. 1934, 805.

[58] John Dewey, "Our Un-Free Press," *Common Sense* 4 (November 1935): 6-7; see also Robert B. Westbrook, *John Dewey and American Democracy* (Ithaca and London: Cornell University Press, 1991), 429-462.

[59] "Public Interest, Convenience, and Necessity in a Nutshell," *Education by Radio*, 28 April 1932, 61. The industry countered this criticism by asserting its complete neutrality on political and social issues and its willingness to broadcast the entire range of legitimate opinion.

[60] See J. Fred MacDonald, *Don't Touch That Dial: Radio Programming in American Life, 1920-1960* (Chicago: Nelson-Hall, 1979), 29-34.

[61] "Improve Radio Programs," *Education by Radio*, 22 June 1933, 29.

[62] "Report of the Committee on Radio Broadcasting," in *Transactions and Proceedings of the National Association of State Universities in the United States of America 1931, Volume 29*, ed. A. H. Upham (National Association of State Universities, 1931), 150.

[63] Morgan, "New American Plan," in *Debate Handbook*, 88.

[64] *Education by Radio*, 23 June 1932, 73.

[65] *Education by Radio*, 4 Feb. 1932, 18.

[66] Morgan, "New American Plan," in *Debate Handbook*, 95.

[67] "Advertising Invades the Schools," *Education by Radio*, 10 Sept. 1931, 103.

[68] See McChesney, "Labor and the Marketplace of Ideas," *Journalism Monographs*; Lizabeth Cohen, *Making a New Deal: Industrial Workers in Chicago, 1919-1939* (Cambridge and New York: Cambridge University Press, 1990), 136-142.

[69] Morgan, "New American Plan," in *Debate Handbook*, 81.

[70] Morgan, "Education's Rights," in *NACRE 1931*, 130.

[71] Arthur G. Crane, "Safeguarding Educational Radio," in *Education on the Air . . . and Radio and Education 1935*, eds. Levering Tyson and Josephine H. MacLatchy (Chicago: University of Chicago Press, 1935), 118-119.

[72] Armstrong Perry, Comments following talk by C. M. Jansky, Jr., in *Radio and Education: Proceedings of the Second Annual Assembly of National Advisory Council on Radio in Education, Inc., 1932*, ed. Levering Tyson (Chicago: University of Chicago Press, 1932), 223.

[73] Eugene J. Coltrane, "A System of Radio Broadcasting Suited to American Purposes," in *Radio Control and Operation*, ed. E. R. Rankin (Chapel Hill: University of North Caroline Extension Bulletin, 1933), 36.

[74] Gross W. Alexander to Graham Spry, 2 September 1931, folder 7, volume 95, GS.

[75] Joy Elmer Morgan to H. O. Davis, 8 March 1932, folder 901, container 47, PF.

[76] See, for example, Joy Elmer Morgan, "The Radio in Education," in *Proceedings of the Seventeenth Annual Convention of the National University Extension Association 1932, Volume 15* (Bloomington, In.: Indiana University Press, 1932), 83.

[77] Armstrong Perry to British Broadcasting Company, 17 December 1935, folder 1110, container 58, PF.

[78] Joy Elmer Morgan to Alan B. Plaunt, 9 June 1932, drawer 3, fcb 2, Joy Elmer Morgan Papers, National Education Association, Washington, D.C.

[79] Edward N. Nockels, "Labor's Rights on the Air," *Federation News*, 7 Feb. 1931, 2.

[80] "Labor Resolution Presented," *Broadcasters' New Bulletin*. 12 Jan. 1931.

[81] Nockels, "Labor's Rights," *Federation News*, 2.

[82] Telegram, Joy Elmer Morgan to H. O. Davis, 8 March 1932, folder 901, container 47, PF.

[83] Memorandum concerning Payne Fund cooperation with commercial radio stations, 15 November 1932, folder 783, container 41, PF.

[84] Ella Phillips Crandall to William John Cooper, 19 February 1933, folder 1337, container 68, PF.

[85] Armstrong Perry to Joy Elmer Morgan, 15 April 1933, folder 1077, container 56, PF.

[86] Joy Elmer Morgan to Armstrong Perry, 18 April 1933, folder 1062, container 55, PF.

[87] For a discussion of this topic see the sources cited in endnote 16.

[88] Tracy M. Tyler to T. M. Beaird, 14 April 1933, folder 916, container 47, PF; "Radio Question Popular," *Education by Radio*, 22 June 1933, 24.

[89] H. O. Davis to Cranston Williams, 27 July 1933, folder 1147, container 59, PF.

[90] "British Vs. American Radio Slant, Debate Theme in 40,000 Schools," *Variety*, 29 Aug. 1933, 1. Cited in Joel Spring, *Images of American Life: A History of Ideological Management in Schools, Movies, Radio, and Television* (Albany: State University of New York Press, 1992), 97.

[91] Merlin H. Aylesworth to David Sarnoff, 20 August 1934, folder 7, box 32, NBC.

[92] See endnote 27 for citation to NAB debate guide.

[93] Josephus Daniels to Franklin D. Roosevelt, 12 July 1933, reel 59, container 95, A,C, 18416, Josephus Daniels Papers, Library of Congress, Washington, D.C. See also Robert W. McChesney, "Franklin Roosevelt, His Administration, and the Communications Act of 1934," in *Media Voices: An Historical Perspective*, ed. Jean Folkerts (New York: Macmillan, 1992): 334-352; McChesney, *Telecommunications, Mass Media, and Democracy*, ch. 8.

[94] A. G. Crane to Tracy F. Tyler, 19 March 1934, folder 785, container 41, PF.

[95] Martin Codel, "President Aided by Chains," undated, March 1933. North American Newspaper Alliance dispatch (see endnote 15). In volume 61, Martin Codel Papers, SHSW; "F.D.R.'s Radio record," *Broadcasting*, 15 March 1934, 8.

[96] Sol Taishoff, "'War Plans' Laid to Protect Broadcasting," *Broadcasting*, 1 March 1933, 5.

[97] Rosen, *Modern Stentors*, 177.

[98] "Air Enemies Unites Forces," *Variety*, 8 May 1934, 37, 45.

[99] "Wagner Amendment Up Next Week," *NAB Reports*, 5 May 1934, 375.

[100] Henry A. Bellows, "Report of the Legislative Committee," *NAB Reports*, 15 November 1934, 618.

[101] John Harney to Armstrong Perry, 3 April 1934, folder 1132, container 59, PF.

[102] John Harney to Tracy F. Tyler, 3 April 1934, folder 850, container 44, PF.

[103] Bellows, "Report," *NAB Reports*, 618.

[104] "Commercial Control of the Air," *Christian Century*, 26 Sept. 1934, 1196-1197.

[105] "Government Interference Fears Groundless, Say Commissioners," *Broadcasting*, 1 October 1934, 18.

[106] Tracy F. Tyler to Clarence C. Dill, 5 June 1934, folder 824, container 43, PF.

[107] Frank Russell to William Hard, 23 October 1934, folder 28, box 26, NBC.

[108] Cited in "In Their Own Behalf," *Education by Radio*, June-July 1938, 21.

[109] William S. Paley, "The Viewpoint of the Radio Industry." in *Educational Broadcasting 1937*, ed. C. S. Marsh (Chicago: University of Chicago Press, 1937), 6.

[110] For a discussion of the broader implications of this process, see Robert W. McChesney, "Off-Limits: An Inquiry Into the Lack of Debate over the Ownership, Structure and Control of the Mass Media in U.S. Political Life," *Communication* 13 (1992): 1-19.

[111] Arthur G. Crane, *A Plan for an American Broadcasting Service and Proposals for the Immediate Establishment of Two Regional Units* (Laramie, Wy.: National Committee on Education by Radio, 1937), 1.

[112] S. Howard Evans to A. G. Crane, 19 June 1936, folder 1147, container 69, PF.

[113] See Willard D. Rowland, Jr., "Continuing Crisis in Public Broadcasting: A History of Disenfranchisement," *Journal of Broadcasting and Electronic Media* 30 (Summer 1986): 251-274.

[114] Round Table Discussion, "The Problems of College and University Stations," in *IER 1934*, 201.

[115] ibid., 200.

[116] *Education by Radio*, Second Quarter 1940, 12.

[117] C. M. Jansky, Jr., "FM - Educational Radio's Second Chance - Will Educators Grasp It," 5 August 1946, folder on educational FM, box 59, Edwin H, Armstrong Papers, Butler Library, Columbia University, New York, N.Y.

[118] Charles A. Siepmann, *Radio's Second Chance* (Boston: Little, Brown and Company, 1946), x.

[119] Robert M. Hutchins, "The State of American Radio," *The B.B.C. Quarterly* 4 (Winter 1949-50): 193-197; see also The Commission on Freedom of the Press, *A Free and Responsible Press* (Chicago: University of Chicago Press, 1947), 97-98.

[120] See, for example, Paul F. Lazarsfeld, *The People Look at Radio* (Chapel Hill: University of North Carolina Press, 1946), vii-ix.

[121] William Buxton, "The Rockefeller Foundation, Communications Research/Policy, and the American State: 1930-1937," paper presented to Annual Meeting of the Canadian Political Science Association, 2 June 1991, Kingston, Ontario.

[122] For a discussion of the futility of those who continued to lobby to generate a commitment to public service in the regulated commercial system after World War II, see Willard D. Rowland, Jr., "The Illusion of Fulfillment: The Broadcast Reform Movement," *Journalism Monographs* 79 (December 1932), 36.

[123] For a euphoric presentation of this argument, see George Gilder, *Life After Television: The Coming Transformation of Media and American Life* (New York: W. W. Norton and Company, 1992).

[124] John B. Schwartz, "The Future of Non-Profit Telecommunications," unpublished paper, October 1992.

[125] For major statements along these lines, see Ben H, Bagdikian, *The Media Monopoly*, third edition (Boston: Beacon Press, 1990); Edward S. Herman and Noam Chomsky, *Manufacturing Consent: The Political Economy of the Mass Media* (New York: Pantheon, 1988); Douglas Kellner, *The Persian Gulf TV War* (Boulder, Col.: Westview Press, 1992).

[126] See Spring, *Images of American Life*, 1-10.

16 | Community Radio in Nicaragua, 1979–1990
Lee Artz

Competitive economic demands, journalistic occupational standards, political preferences of media owners, and societal cultural norms have largely determined a limited and one-way public information flow in most societies. Bagdikian (1987) and Herman and Chomsky (1988) have demonstrated that a handful of "senders" relay their chosen messages to hundreds of millions of "receivers," few of whom have access to similar mass audiences. For most people, opportunity for information distribution on a scale even remotely approaching that of the mass media remains illusory, and the debatable polysemic power of resistive audiences (Fiske 1987, Morley 1980) cannot substitute for the woeful lack of direct media access. Replacing the transmission model of communication is not simply a theoretical gesture: in the end, the sheer weight of the media monopoly crushes pluralist conceptions of democratic communication (Bagdikian 1987, Turow 1990, Wirth 1986).

Of course, one's conception of democracy colors the ensuing critique of communication. Dianne Rucinski outlines a "participatory communication" which emphasizes how the "shared activity and interdependence" of citizen participation informs "collective decision-making and the enactment of shared goals" (1991, 187). Obviously, to get from unidirectional, limited access mass communication to participatory, democratic communication requires an adjustment in existing relations and practices. At issue for mass communication theory is whether the loss of community, the lack of democracy, and the organization of the mass media according to the transmission model is an inherent and necessary consequence of technology and mass society.

The development of radio in Nicaragua illustrates the organic relationship between media and society. Nicaragua was chosen because its revolution was the most striking "rupture" in the status quo in this hemisphere in the last three decades (Black 1981; Borge 1986; Melrose 1985; Petras 1981; Walker 1991; Weber 1981). Radio was chosen because it has been the dominant form of mass media in Nicaragua (Artz 1989; Läpple-Wagenhals 1984; Mattelart 1986)—in part due to the population's illiteracy, in part because its distribution and reception are more affordable than other media.

Communication and change in Latin America have long attracted the interest of North Americans (Alisky 1981; Mattelart and Siegelaub 1983). At least since the advent of broadcast technology in the 1930s, which opened up new opportunities for advertising, propaganda, and exchange between North and South, U.S. communication scholars have been intimately involved in Latin American media. Aided by U.S. government subsidy and intervention in the post-WW II period, texts by Lasswell, Merton, Parsons, and especially Wilbur Schramm have mightily influenced the study and practice of mass communication throughout the Southern hemisphere (Mattelart and Siegelaub 1983, 30-31). Of course, along with technical and professional direction, media workers there received theoretical training from their Northern professors, including instruction on the transmission model of communication. In keeping with the prevailing mass communication theory, political and social realities were assumed to be favorable to an extension of democratic communication, susceptible to the leveling effects of the mass media, or of secondary concern.

Nevertheless, numerous attempts to develop media which would be accessible, democratic, and economically viable have had a sorry history given the voracity of burgeoning commercial forms and the accompanying political institutions. According to Beltran, communication and culture in Latin America have been dominated by "oligarchic elites subduing and exploiting" their various national populations, reinforcing the transmission model of communication (Beltran 1988, 2). Throughout Latin America, media reform has continually confronted an intervening state apparatus tied to ruling elites and military staffs (Mosco and Herman 1981). Even in Mexico and Venezuela, where democratic media reforms were attempted, public interest broadcasting and public access policies were "aborted under pressure from private interests, opposition and government politicians" (Beltran 1988, 4). In practical terms, it has proven difficult to separate the media from other socio-economic and political realities because they are tied together through complex social structures and relations (e.g. government institutions, universities, electoral and party politics, economic markets, entertainment industries, etc.). Thus, the transmission model of communication from the exceptional few to the receptive many nicely complements the hierarchical social and political structures of national elites in Latin America.

Consequently, each stage in the development of mass media in Latin America has contradicted the democratic implications of traditional mass communication theories, "which built a barrier between politics and science" (Mattelart and Siegelaub 1983, 34). Ironically, the experiences of mass media in Latin America suggest that indigenous political institutions and international socio-economic pressures have built a barrier *around* communication science, while proving the efficacy of the transmission model in dozens of media systems. Of course, there is a strong tradition of popular alternative radio in Latin America, for example, the Radio Mineras in Bolivia, popular-based opposition radio during the Pinochet dictatorship in Chile, church-run radios in Brazil, radio in pre-revolutionary Cuba, and Radio Venceremos in El Salvador. The Nicaraguan example, however, is unique. In no other case, has a government supported, financed and promoted community-based and controlled radio broadcasting. So-called "grass-roots" democratic media lacks the capacity to compete with non-democratic state run media or profit-driven mass media. The evidence indicates that popular broadcasting was raised to a qualitatively higher level in Nicaragua from 1979-1989. In other words, the predominant vision of media development in isolation from the social relations, political conditions, and economic realities of Latin America has proven theoretically and practically inadequate for instituting democratic communication.

Summarizing the results of more than a decade of UNESCO plans for democratic media systems, Fox writes that all the "dreams of cultural development and autonomy of access and participation have come to nothing" because of the "social rigidity and concentration of social and political power" (Fox 1988, 171). Fox finds media firmly attached to their respective socio-political bodies: "by and large commercial enterprises run by small groups for personal gain that generally ignore larger development goals and social services" (Fox 1988, 9). Schiller further contends that a "global hierarchy of power" in the mass media, advertising, public relations and satellite communication systems precludes any substantial national reform (Schiller 1991, 62). These conclusions undergird my thesis that the construction of more democratic and accessible media must come as part of a nation's overall social transformation.

In our increasingly mediated world, discourse depends largely on the use of media technology. At the same time, the anatomy of society is not so simple as to allow the severing of its mass communication limb. Indeed, monopoly ownership of major media outlets (Bagdikian 1987), normative professional practices of production (Schudson 1978; Tuchman 1978), functional social roles of the media (Herman and Chomsky 1988; Lasswell 1971; Lazarsfeld and Merton 1971), governmental media regulations (Becker 1987), public patterns of media use (Morley 1980), media dependency on advertising (Ewen 1989; Williams 1980), acceptable cultural norms of interpersonal communication, literacy, public access, and other existing practices and conditions weave media deep within the complete fabric of any social order. Consequently, theorizing on communication practices must consider social relations which dictate control over and access to communicative forms. In light of the above assessments of media reform in Latin America, three aspects seem most central and interrelated: media ownership; production norms (especially news sources, format, content, controls); and the social role of the media. As investigative tools, each of these levels of analysis could be applied descriptively to any media institution, form, or system. For instance, Bagdikian has looked at media ownership, Schudson and Tuchman have analyzed news making, and Lazarsfeld and Merton, Lasswell, and Herman and Chomsky have addressed the social functions of the media.

If fundamental change in media institutions and practices cannot be expected separate and apart from fundamental changes in the social order, then changes in identifiable characteristics of media operations should roughly coincide with significant changes in the social order. Conversely, ownership and control of media institutions, media practices, and the social role of the media are unlikely to change independent of dramatic political events leading to disruption in the status quo.

Mattelart (Mattelart and Siegelaub 1983) has suggested that "moments of rupture" in the social order provide unique opportunities for investigating fundamental relations between media and society, which are obscured during periods of social stability. Certainly, the organic connections between phenomena are more apparent when the exterior is removed or when transitional periods are observed. Similarly, relational elements in society may be more apparent at moments of birth, transformation, climax or disruption than at times of quiescence when inner workings are often more difficult to discern. The social history of radio communication in Nicaragua is a case in point: each period exists between distinct moments of rupture with the adjacent period. The categories of ownership, production norms, and social role provide identifying characteristics of the period and illustrate the interrelations between media and society....

*

Radio broadcast was first established out of military necessity during the U.S. Marine occupation in the 1920s (Millet 1977). Guerrilla forces of the nationalist rebel General Augusto Sandino were cutting down telegraph and telephone wires, disrupting communication for the

Marines and General Anastasio Somoza's National Guard (Millet 1977). In response, the Marines established the first transcontinental radio system in Nicaragua on December 22, 1931, headquartered at the American-owned mining center in Bonanza (Millet 1977, 76). Subsequently, as head of the National Guard and later dictator of the country, Anastasio Somoza and his sons were sole owners of this, the largest broadcasting facility in Nicaragua (Läpple-Wagenhals 1984). The next radio project also originated in the U.S. La Voz de Nicaragua was established in 1934 as part of NBC's Panamerican Network, one of the embryonic radio networks that American businesses initiated in Latin America in the 1930s (Läpple-Wagenhals 1984)....

In short, a government-run radio station and an NBC-affiliate produced a narrow communication service exclusively for the needs and interests of the dictatorship and the small urban merchant classes....

At the end of four decades, Nicaraguan radio was still wedded to its restrictive socio-political system (Cf. Alisky 1981, e.g.). Given the low literacy of the populace and ubiquitousness of radio broadcasting at the end of the 1970s, this medium remained an important social and cultural support for the dictatorship. Despite the proliferation of numerous small stations, the medium was dominated by three major interests (Somoza, Valle, COSEP) which wholeheartedly adopted the North American mass communication paradigm of "objectivity," consumerism, and entertainment. Additionally, economic constraints and government censorship assured that radio served the social and political order. This model readily served as a social lubricant for the needs of the dictatorship and its allies....

*

Nicaraguan society's stable condition [was] partially shaken in the aftermath of the 1972 earthquake in Managua, which destroyed the entire business district, took thousands of lives, and exposed the narrow social base of the dictatorship (Black 1981; Weber 1981). The internation recession of 1974-75 further exacerbated underlying social contradictions. Adopting a "liberation theology" that sought God's kingdom on earth, Catholic leaders took their moral distance from the dictatorship. The rhetoric of the FSLN found a new, larger audience. Peasants occupied land. Workers went on strike. The brittle social structure began to crack under pressure. Faced with increased rural and urban unrest, Somoza predictably turned to increased repression. This time the repression triggered a response, not an acquiescence. Somoza had isolated himself from society and this isolation quickly became apparent in the media...[Guillermo Rothschuh Villanueva relates a valuable account of this period—see his article in Section 5).

In the midst of the rising tide against the dictatorship, radio was simultaneously a communicative form, a source of information, an instrument of struggle, and a spoil of war. The struggle within and over society corresponded to the struggle within and over the medium of radio broadcasting. The results of those intertwined struggles transformed the character of both.

At the beginning of this period, radio was still dominated by Somoza, Valle, and COSEP. By the end of this period, some 40% of the radio stations had passed over to control by local committees of journalists and community activists (Corporación de Radiodifusion del Pueblo 1989; Frederick 1986). Under pressure from the economic and social crisis, exacerbated by

Somoza's repression, the traditional norms of "objectivity," source credibility, and other journalistic practices gave way to political partisanship and class judgments by working journalists (Corporación de Radiodifusion del Pueblo 1989; Rothschuh 1986). News became a weapon in the war against the dictatorship; reporters sought "facts" for the battle. Consequently the medium underwent a radical change from mass entertainer, to social critic, to movement organizer. In the words of Humberto Ortega, "without radio...there would have been no revolutionary triumph" (Rothschuh 1986, 34).

*

The July 19, 1979 overthrow of the dictatorship, popularly referred to as "the Triumph" in Nicaragua, also toppled much of the infrastructure of Nicaragua. The new government immediately issued decrees returning land to thousands of peasants (Collins 1982), legalizing union organizing, launching a literacy campaign (Hirshon 1983), and ending censorship of the press (Aguirre and Soto interviews with author). What was resistance became power. The embryonic relations between democracy, technology, and social institutions (which had been symbolically initiated in the "catacombs") became the law of the land. Like most of society after the triumph (Martin 1989), journalism discovered a new, creative life.

At first, public access to the media was handicapped because only half the population could read and write (Hirshon 1983; Melrose 1985). Notably, within six months the new government organized a successful literacy campaign raising the national literacy rate to almost 90%—the highest in Central America. In 1980, UNESCO recognized Nicaragua for its historic achievement. The literacy drive reflected the real commitment of the new government towards the poor and underprivileged. It also reflected the government's attitude towards democracy: an educated population can participate more fully in decision-making. From day one of the revolution, the new government of workers and peasants led by the FSLN strived for a pluralist society with a mixed economy (Black 1981; Borge 1986; Melrose 1985). This new democratic attitude extended to the media institutions as well.

Media in the new Nicaragua exemplified the pluralism and "mixed" economy espoused by the FSLN: privately-owned media (including those owned by a variety of political parties), government-owned radio and television stations, church-owned radio, and a publicly-owned radio network (Centro de Investigaciones y Estudios de la Reforma Agraria *n. d.*, Läpple-Wagenhals 1984)

The April 1981 founding of the public radio network marks the most significant change in the history of radio ownership in Nicaragua. Sixteen stations were brought together as public-access radio under Decree #709 which established Corporación de Radiodifusión del Pueblo (CORADEP), the Corporation of Popular Radio Broadcasting (Corporación de Radiodifusion del Pueblo 1989; Frederick 1986) (See 1-3). CORADEP comprised broadcasting facilities in Nicaragua which had belonged to Somoza or his supporters who had fled during the insurrection leaving their stations in various states of operation or inoperation. In some cases, journalists and technicians who had prevented employer sabotage kept their stations on the air. In others, operation only passed into the hands of radical journalists and community activists during the insurrection. Thus, CORADEP filled one of those institutional fissures that occurred following the political and social upheaval of the revolution. The generalized societal rupture had created severe breaks in the transmission-oriented communication patterns, allowing experimentation with new forms. CORADEP represented the clearest expression of the new government's interest in democratic communication: radio stations "owned" by the people. A fuller look at the productive norms and social role of CORADEP will illustrate what public possession meant for access and participation.

In his speech to the First Seminar on Participatory Radio in 1984, Minister of the Interior Tomás Borge said that the goal of publicly-owned radio in Nicaragua was to establish "horizontal communication" based on the public's right to communicate and to counteract the "vertical dissemination" of commercial radio and its consumerist ideology (Borge 1986, 110). To realize this goal, the government provided the financing but left the daily operation and programming decisions to the discretion of independent CORADEP directors, chosen by local radio staffs. National conferences attended by elected delegates from each station made decisions on production of special programs, staff training, national campaigns, etc. Delegates included reporters, volunteers, and community correspondents from cultural groups and cooperatives.

Each CORADEP station had its own participatory organizational structure established to facilitate public access and public service. Most followed some form of democratic decision-making or consensus, collectively negotiating how to meet the needs of its particular community. The specific forms and results varied from station to station.

Radio Paz, which aired ballads, instrumental music, poetry, literary vignettes, and other cultural and intellectual commentary to serve professionals and small businesses. At 5000 watts, Radio Paz became the station of choice in office buildings and government agencies in Granada, León, Managua and Matagalpa. In Managua, Radio Cachorras (Little Cubs) carried children's music, games, stories and features on health and literacy. On the Atlantic Coast, Radio Zinica broadcasted from Bluefields in English and Creole for the predominately Afro-Nicaraguan community, and Radio Tasbra Pri programmed in Miskito from Puerto Cabezas. Financially-solvent stations would cooperatively aid others, particularly rural stations (Santos interview). When Radio Zinica was destroyed by Hurricane Joan in October 1988, CORADEP dismantled Radio Futura in Managua and transported the equipment to Bluefields so that community could continue to have their own public communication system. When the contras destroyed Radio Tasbra Pri, CORADEP made similar arrangements to rebuild the Miskito station (Areas interview).

Other stations, like Radio Liberación in Estelí and Radio Insurrección in Matagalpa, catered to the rural audiences of northern Nicaragua. Broadcast days began at 4 a.m. with five-hour segments featuring traditional campesino music, agricultural reports, health news, and regular news broadcasts which covered "all political factions, including various political parties, the Chamber of Commerce and [the private industry association] COSEP" (National Lawyer's Guild 1986, 27). Government support for health, literacy, cultural, labor and other social programs provided money for radio commercials, especially during the first few years when social welfare programs received almost 60% of the national budget (Black 1981, Melrose 1984). For example, in 1980 a UNESCO award-winning campaign against diarrhea (the leading cause of infant mortality under Somoza) used radio spots on sanitation and child health care to augment classes and home visits (Melrose 1984, Santos interview).

Throughout the morning, peasants and housewives used the radio by calling or hand-delivering comments and announcements. Although lively debates occurred between listeners/receivers, this right to communicate was not limited to important political or social issues.

For example, I heard one farmer's message on Radio Insurrección which said, "Please tell my wife, Maria, to put the horse in the barn if it rains."

Throughout the day, a variety of music, including romantic Nicaraguan ballads, was interspersed with entertainment and community programming—literacy classes, health shows, self-help programs, and call-in talk shows. Radio Insurrección and other CORADEP stations also presented their own *radionovelas*. Plots for these stories recounted the lives of national heroes and stories with social morals, as well as stories based on the lives of community residents and their ancestors. Radio Insurrección, for instance, solicited newly literate listeners to write their own stories. Radio editors then adapted these real-life experiences for *radionovelas*. Thus, one of the simplest genres of Latin American radio served to reciprocally interchange sender and receiver, as listeners became producers through the microphones of CORADEP.

Late afternoon programming returned to news and commentary. A striking characteristic was the lack of sensationalist crime and disaster stories. Instead, information privileging the interests of organized workers and peasants prevailed, reflecting the predictions of the new government: "as the informative organs break with individual control of news media and begin to express the opinions of the workers to their vast audiences more objectivity will be reached in their transmissions" (Centro de Investigaciones y Estudios de la Reforma, 121). CORADEP featured unions, farmer's groups, women's organizations and neighborhood committees reporting on their own programs, achievements, demands, and conflicts. Reporters no longer relied solely on AP wire releases or government and industry press statements (Aguirre interview). News was now being made by mass organizations and, because of CORADEP, workers and peasants reported their own news on their own community radio stations.

Nationally CORADEP worked with the journalist's union and farmworker's organizations to develop "community correspondents." Cooperatives, unions, and women's organizations established courses on writing and reporting for radio and print correspondents. "These amateur reporters [were] farmers, health workers, soldiers, and educators who, having acquired basic news gathering skills, [could] provide up-to-date, accurate reports of what [was] happening in the communities" (Twichell 1988, 9).

On market days CORADEP stations set up broadcast booths outdoors in the market and citizens aired classified ads and made comments—like products brought to the market, personal and political perspectives were brought to the media. Often, broadcasts were conducted from town squares with an open microphone for local listeners/receivers (Twichell 1988, 9). When citizens stepped up to the microphone, "they [began] to feel that the power of radio is accessible to them," said Radio Insurrección director Marlin Stewart (Twichell 1988, 9).

Thus, while the social revolution overthrew an entrenched dictatorship, the CORADEP revolution in radio overthrew the authoritarian "top-down" transmission model of mass communication. CORADEP made public communication more democratic, interactional and meaningful for the average Nicaraguan citizen.

There was no singular social role of the radio medium after the "triumph." Instead, pluralism was on-the-air: formerly locked-out journalists from all political persuasions had willing advertisers for their programs. In one corner, COSEP campaigned against the social agenda of the new government (Orosco interview). In another, the religious stations provided spiritual direction (Santos and Soto interviews with author). In a third, numerous political parties had their journalists working overtime promoting various political agendas (Fuentes interview). Finally, CORADEP promoted the "horizontal communication" model espoused by the FSLN and the new government. As UPN President Lilly Soto put it in 1989, "No one exercises hegemony in communication in Nicaragua, because our chief concern is with guaranteeing the people's 'right to communicate'."

In this period, public discourse arose and expanded in Nicaragua through many media outlets including Radio Universidad, Radio Noticias and Radio Sandino. The partisan media outlets directed by the Sandinistas expressed this new spirit of openness towards public communication. The FSLN's Radio Sandino, the government-run La Voz de Nicaragua, the newspaper *Barricada* and the two TV stations each provided a platform for criticism and debate. Face-to-face contact between citizens and government became institutionalized in weekly radio and TV programs such as "Face the People," "Direct Line," and "Context 6.20." These programs brought local and national leaders to public community meetings which were broadcast live nationwide.

Even given the diversity of perspectives offered by private and partisan media, CORADEP played a unique social role—it was primarily CORADEP which enacted the people's right to communicate. CORADEP stood apart as an open advocate of radio for social change. It was CORADEP that served as a medium for the civic exchange of news and information, ways of dealing with daily life, and discussions on public policy issues. Based on the ongoing process of communicative interaction among the general populace, CORADEP publicly proclaimed that it defended the interests of workers and peasants.

In tandem with the social and political changes instituted by mass organizations, radio communication moved towards participatory democracy via CORADEP. It was radio on the side of its listeners, under the control of its listeners. CORADEP was radio that rejected impartiality in favor of programs resulting from collective decisions. In the words of Bertolt Brecht, CORADEP represented the "employment of the apparatus in interest of the community" (Brecht 1983, 171).

The successful overthrow of the Somoza dynasty by a broad front of Nicaraguan social classes resulted in the formation of a pluralist society. Ownership of radio outlets reflected this mixed economy: major media outlets remained under the ownership and control of their former owners (with the notable exception of Somoza's Radio X, which the FSLN appropriated); churches continued their broadcasting; and most importantly, a national network of publicly-owned and locally-operated radio stations was established under CORADEP. Production norms instituted by CORADEP privileged public access and citizen participation in the production and transmission of radio communication. Consequently, the social role of CORADEP radio became an important part of the impulse towards community building. Although other opportunities developed for public access to radio communication, CORADEP was the most significant institutional change.

Each period of the social history of Nicaragua—from the U.S. installation of Somoza and the National Guard, to the growth of the urban middle classes in the 1960s, to the breakdown in the social order following the 1974-75 world-wide recession, to the "triumph" over the dictatorship—found a corresponding pattern of media ownership, journalistic productive practices, and social role for radio communication appropriate to the social and political relations of each period. This historic connection between the media and the social order partially explains the absence of any substantial media reform in other Latin America countries that have not undertaken social reconstruction. Radio reform in Nicaragua only came with the popular upsurge. Through the revolution the people found their voices; on radio those voices gathered in debate.

The new positions staked out by the victories in media developed from the particular political and cultural experiences within Nicaragua over several decades. The cultural norms of the dictatorship tied to North American consumerism had dictated the form and content of information that was disseminated through Radio Mundial, Radio Nacional, *La Prensa* and the other dominant media outlets. Alternatives to the dominant mass media in Nicaragua were severely restricted. Only the power of the massive social movement which erupted in 1977-78 allowed the radical democratic opposition to use mass communication.

At first participatory communication appeared like the social protests—sporadic, even clandestine. But as the movement grew, the public sphere grew. Radio transmission supplemented, then surpassed, the political wall paintings (called *pintas*, see Cabezas 1986), leaflets and newsletters in communicating information and propaganda. In essence, the battle for hegemony of the airwaves coincided with the battle for political and military control of the state, symbiotically growing with the mass movement. Changes in the production norms and social role of radio broadcasting during the revolution reflected the changing of the guard in ownership and control. Thus, when Radio Insurrección and the other popularly-expropriated stations joined Radio Sandino in demanding Somoza's abdication months before he fled, mass communication presented itself as a well-earned reward won for the new Nicaragua.

Those stations that passed into the hands of radio journalists and community residents, as precursors of CORADEP, reflected the triumph of decision-making audiences. Information flow through those media outlets was fundamentally transformed. Workers, peasants and students, who had made and reported the news to journalists in the catacombs, continued to make and report life resurrected under the new social order. CORADEP only institutionalized an actual social practice. It reflected the changed relationships between social forces: Somoza was gone; the elite were temporarily neutralized; and workers and peasants had empowered a new government. Once the restrictions of the totalitarian regime were removed and the occupational norms instituted by profit-driven owners were dismantled, the collective voices of workers and peasants rose crisply over the airwaves.

This process seemed headed towards institutionalizing participatory communication, but like any organism, specific social relations have no guarantee of survival—especially in an environment of limited resources and predators. Media reform depended on societal reform and both processes were interrupted. On one front, the U.S.-backed contra army assaulted Nicaraguan gains, targeting schools, teachers, clinics, healthcare workers, and trade unionists. At the same time, social forces sympathetic to the old order organized internal opposition; the media outlets they owned sowed confusion and distortion, ultimately resorting to scare tactics (Osejo interview). Although the new government responded with sporadic media controls, ironically, it was the very policy of pluralism which left ample airspace for such conservative voices opposed to the new society.

If any doubt about the social dependency of participatory communication remained, it was routed in the aftermath of the February 1990 elections. Violeta Chamorro (widow of Pedro Joaquin Chamorro) and chosen candidate of the United Nicaraguan Opposition—a coalition including COSEP, the pro-Somoza Liberal party, the Catholic hierarchy, and other conservative interests—was elected president and immediately made deep cuts in social spending (Walker 1991, 1992). The new government cancelled the TV show "Extravisión" for its political views, raised fees for independently-produced shows, instituted censorship on radio news, and fired hosts of locally-produced radio programs. In response, and not long after Chamorro was elected, CORADEP was disbanded "to preserve space to protect points of view that are not those of the government" (*Envio* 1990, 13). The fourteen stations outside of Managua were turned over to the newly-elected local governments. Two of the Managua stations were sold to private individuals and La Primerísima became the property of its radio workers. Meanwhile, Mariano Valle has returned to Nicaragua, claiming 11 CORADEP stations belong to him and UNO delegates to the National Assembly have recently demanded the confiscation of CO-RADEP stations from their local committees. Of course, Radio Sandino continues to broadcast, but popular access to radio communication is under attack. Simultaneously, the U.S. is providing significant aid to conservative media outlets which supported the Chamorro campaign (Central American Resource Network 1991).

A democratic media cannot flourish and grow in a climate of social reaction. Combined with the dismantling of numerous mass organizations by the FSLN (Benjamin and Mackler 1989, Walker 1991, 1992), the return of the government to Nicaragua's economic elite precipitated the dissolution of most social programs. Without supportive political institutions and lacking a socially-active and politically-organized populace, the experiment in participatory communication lost its material basis. Thus, Nicaraguan radio communication was curtailed, again reflecting the ongoing interrelationship between politics and media.

The institutionalization of media forms always depended on the relationship between the state and civil society. Under Somoza, radio was predominately uni-directional, monistic, and undemocratic. In the course of the Nicaraguan revolution, radio became more accessible and more integrated into the daily lives of the population. With the triumph over the dictatorship, public access to the means of communication became institutionalized with the formation of CORADEP. Since the election of Chamorro, radio broadcasting in general has been largely restored to the transmission model favored by the elite.

To conclude, while the above discussion of the Nicaraguan experience has been substantially a concrete description of a particular situation, it has illustrated that media technology *per se* neither advances nor retards participatory communication or democratic social forms. Rather, this particular history implies that communication technology provides the machinery for improving or retarding social communication and organization, depending on which social force employs it. Attention to ownership, production norms, and social role indicate a symbiotic relationship between media and the social order. In the hands of a democratic majority, society can create a mass media which is accessible, participatory, and interactional. As a medium moves from being a unidirectional transmission channel to a medium for exchange and negotiation, decisions on meaning, social policy and human goals become more connected to community needs. Radio in Nicaragua broadcasted to the world that as part of a democratic social transformation, mass communication *can* become more democratic, accessible, and meaningful to community and nation.

REFERENCES

Aguirre, Danilo, editor *El Nuevo Diario*. 1989. Interview by author. 7 January. Managua, Nicaragua. Transcript.

Alisky, Marvin. 1981. *Latin American media: Guidance and censorship*. Ames: Iowa State University Press.

Areas, Pepe, program director Radio Sandino. 1989. Interview by author. 12 January. Managua, Nicaragua. Transcript.

Artz, Lee. 1989. Public access and censorship. *Nicaraguan Perspectives.* Summer/Fall, 29-32.

Bagdikian, Benjamin H. 1987. *The media monopoly.* 2d Ed. Boston: Beacon.

Bayón, Beatriz Parga. 1983. Freedom of press in Nicaragua: Sergio Ramírez Mercado and Pedro Joaquín Chamorro Barrios. *Caribbean Review.* Winter, 20-21.

Becker, Samuel L. *Discovering mass communication.* 2d Ed. Glenview: Scott, Foresman.

Beltran, Luis. Foreword. 1988. In *Media and politics in Latin America,* ed. Elizabeth Fox, 1-5. Newbury Park: Sage.

Benjamin, Alan and Jeff Mackler. 1989. *Dynamics of the Nicaraguan revolution.* San Francisco: Walnut.

Black, George. 1981. *Triumph of the people: The Sandinista revolution in Nicaragua.* London: Zed.

Borge, Tomás. 1986a. Marginal notes on the propaganda of the FSLN. In *Communicating in popular Nicaragua,* ed. Armand Mattelart, 46-54. New York: International General.

Borge, Tomás. 1986b. Participatory communication. In *Communicating in popular Nicaragua,* ed. Armand Mattelart, 109-12. New York: International General.

Borge, Tomás. 1985. This revolution was made to create a new society. In *Nicaragua: The Sandinista people's revolution,* ed. Bruce Markus, 22-38. New York: Pathfinder.

Brecht, Bertolt. 1983. "Radio as a means of communication: A talk on the function of radio. In *Communication and the class struggle: Liberation, socialism,* Volume 2, eds. Armand Mattelart and Seth Siegelaub, 169-71. New York: International General.

Cabezas, Omar. 1986. The voice of the people is the voice of the 'pintas'. In *Communicating in popular Nicaragua,* ed. Armand Mattelart, 37-40. New York: International General.

Central America Resource Network. 1991. NicaNet hotline. In Institute for Global Communications Computer Network, PeaceNet. October 16, 3.

Centro de Investigaciones y Estudios de la Reforma Agraria. n.d. *Participatory democracy in Nicaragua.* Managua: INRA.

Collins, Joseph. 1982. *What difference could a revolution make? Food and farming in the new Nicaragua.* San Francisco: Institute for Food and Development Policy.

Corparación de Radiodifusion del Pueblo. 1989. *Solicitud de financiamiento para la adquisición de repuestos para las radios de CORADEP.* Managua: CORADEP.

Ewen, Stuart. 1989. Advertising and the development of consumer society. In *Cultural politics in contemporary America,* eds. Ian Angus and Sut Jhally, 82-95. New York: Routledge.

Fiske, John. 1987. *Television culture.* London: Methuen.

Fox, Elizabeth, ed. 1988. *Media and Politics in Latin America.* Newbury Park: Sage.

Frederick, Howard H. 1986. The radio war Against Nicaragua." In *Communicating in popular Nicaragua,* ed. Armand Mattelart, 70-81. New York: International General.

Fuentes, Agustin, program director Radio Noticias. 1989. Interview by author. 11 January. Managua, Nicaragua. Transcript.

Herman, Edward S. and Noam Chomsky. 1988. *Manufacturing consent: The political economy of the mass media.* New York: Pantheon.

Hirshon, Sheryl. 1983. *And also teach them to read.* Westport: Lawrence Hill.

Läpple-Wagenhals, Doris. 1984. *A new development model — a new communication policy?* Frankfurt: Peter Lang.

Lasswell, Harold D. 1971. The structure and function of communication in society. In *The process of mass communication,* eds. Wilbur Schramm and Donald F. Roberts, 84-99. Urbana: University of Illinois Press.

Lazarsfeld, Paul M. and Robert K. Merton. 1971. Mass communication, popular taste and organized social action. In *The process and effects of mass communication*, eds. Wilbur Schramm and Donald F. Roberts, 554-78. Urbana: University of Illinois Press.

Martin, Michael T. 1989. On culture, politics and the state in Nicaragua: An interview with Padre Ernesto Cardenal, Minister of Culture. *Latin American Perspectives* 16 (Spring): 124-33.

Mattelart, Armand. 1986. Communication in Nicaragua between war and democracy. In *Communicating in popular Nicaragua*. New York: International General.

Mattelart, Armand, ed. 1986. *Communicating in popular Nicaragua*. New York: International General.

Mattelart, Armand and Seth Siegelaub, eds. 1983. *Communication and the class struggle*, Two Volumes. New York: International General.

McLuhan, Marshall. 1964. *Understanding the media*. London: Routledge.

Melrose, Dianna. 1985. *Nicaragua: The threat of a good example*. Oxford: Oxfam.

Millet, Richard. 1977. *Guardians of the dynasty*. Maryknoll: Orbis.

Morley, David. 1980. *The "Nationwide" audience*. London: BFI.

National Lawyers Guild Central America Task Force Delegation to Nicaragua. 1986. *Freedom of expression in Nicaragua*. New York: National Lawyers Guild.

Orosco, Raul, program director at Radio Universidad. 1989. Interview by author. 18 January. Managua, Nicaragua. Transcript.

Osejo, José, program director and co-owner at Radio Corporación. Interview by author. 9 January. Managua, Nicaragua. Transcript.

Petras, James. 1981. Nicaragua: The transition to a new society. *Latin American Perspectives* 8 (Spring): 74-94.

Rothschuh, Guillermo V. 1986. Notes on the history of revolutionary journalism in Nicaragua. In *Communicating in popular Nicaragua*, ed. Armand Mattelart, 28-36. New York: International General.

Rucinski, Dianne. 1991. The centrality of reciprocity to communication and democracy. *Critical Studies in Mass Communication* 8 (June): 184-194.

Santos, Mayra, program director at Radio Paz. 1989. Interviews by author. 3-5 January. Managua, Nicaragua. Transcripts. Selzer, Gregorio. 1981. *Sandino*. New York: Monthly Review.

Schiller, Herbert I. 1991. Not yet the post-imperialist era. *Critical Studies in Mass Communication* 8 (March): 13-28.

Schudson, Michael. 1978. *Discovering the news: A social history of American newspapers*. New York: Basic Books.

Soto, Lilly, president of Unión de Periodistas de Nicaragua 1989. Interview by author. 10 January. Managua, Nicaragua. Transcript.

Tuchman, Gaye. 1978. *Making news: A study in the construction of reality*. New York: Free Press.

Turow, Joseph. 1990. Media industries, media consequences: Rethinking mass communication. In *Communication Yearbook*, Volume 13, ed. James A. Anderson, 475-501. Newbury Park: Sage.

Twichell, Peter. 1988. Community radio championed in Managua." *Maine Progressive* November, 8-9.

Update. 1990. *Envio* July, 12-14.

Walker, Thomas W. 1992. What happened to Nicaragua? Public address at University of Iowa, Iowa City. 21 February. Transcript.

Walker, Thomas W. 1991. *Revolution and counter-revolution in Nicaragua*. Boulder: Westview.

Weber, Henri. 1981. *Nicaragua: The Sandinist revolution*. London: Verso.

Williams, Raymond. 1980. *Problems in materialism and culture*. London: Verso.

Wirth, Michael O. 1986. Economic barriers to entering media industries in the United States. In *Communication Yearbook*, Volume 9, Margaret L. McLaughlin, 423-42. Beverly Hills: Sage.

PART VI | Exercises

NAME _____

In the course of the next week, listen to three radio stations that you do not normally listen to for at least an hour each. Complete the worksheet below and then write a short essay on the next page.

Station Call Letters _____ Station Frequency _____
Programming and Format _____

Audience _____
Frequency of News _____
Length of News _____
Format and Source of News _____

Frequency of Advertisements _____
Length of Commercial Breaks _____
Type of Advertisements _____
Public Affairs Programming _____

Station Call Letters _____ Station Frequency _____
Programming and Format _____

Audience _____
Frequency of News _____
Length of News _____
Format and Source of News _____

Frequency of Advertisements _____
Length of Commercial Breaks _____
Type of Advertisements _____
Public Affairs Programming _____

Station Call Letters _____ Station Frequency _____

Programming and Format _____

Audience _____

Frequency of News _____

Length of News _____

Format and Source of News _____

Frequency of Advertisements _____

Length of Commercial Breaks _____

Type of Advertisements _____

Public Affairs Programming _____

Write a short essay on your "research." Consider public interest, commercial interest, and public access to communication. What does your listening experience indicate about the character of these stations and suggest about the status of radio communication in the United States?

PART VII | Social Communication through Television

Television appeared in the late 1940s under the direction of the big three radio networks, NBC, CBS, and ABC. Early television broadcasting replicated radio programming and its emphasis on entertainment. Network producers simply moved existing radio formats like comedy, crime drama, game show, and soap opera to television, often airing the same series. Popular radio programs such as "Jack Benny," "Red Skelton," "Gunsmoke," and "Amos 'n' Andy," became standard television fare. Under network direction, the amazing new audio-visual technology drifted into American living rooms with the same stories and styles established by commercial radio.

Yet, television seduced America. Within two decades, television had replaced print communication as the primary source of news and information and exiled radio communication to cars and elevators. Eventually, television became the primary means of entertainment for American families. Today, some 98% of American homes have at least one television set. TV is now a centerpiece for home decor and central to social communication.

Television dramatically changed how we learn about the world, radically altering dominant communication practices. Some scholars (see Carpenter in Section One, e.g.) have further argued that like previous changes in communication technologies, televison effects how we perceive the world and how we think about it. Foremost in this approach, Marshall McLuhan, Canadian media historian and author of *Understanding Media* (1964), popularized notions of "technological determinism." McLuhan divided history into epochs determined by developments in media: orality was the Tribal Age; the alphabet brought the Literate Age; invention of the printing press led to the Print Age; and the telegraph ushered in the Electronic Age. According to McLuhan, television takes us "back to the future" with instant audiovisual images which return us to the pre-literate oral traditions of sound and touch. More than radio, television overcomes space and time, making the world a simultaneous, "all-at-once" world. Television requires active participation by the viewer, who must make sense of shifting contexts and incomplete images. While communication scholars now dispute McLuhan's formulas as too schematic and mechanical, most have accepted some of his more general claims about how different means of communication prompt different sensory comprehensions and agree that television as a dominant mode of communication has tremendous social consequence.

Television merges many of the characteristics of other communication forms. Television expands immediacy beyond the aural presence of radio by recovering sight. Because television lets the viewer attend events as they happen it also incorporates much of the non-verbal communication present in orality. Further, as an aural and visual medium, television employs many of the techniques present in film communication which help construct meaning,

175

including: contrast, color, camera angle and distance, timing, and music. As it unites multiple communication forms for audiovisual broadcast, television above all presents imagery. Orality communicates through speech as social ritual, literacy through printed word and language, radio through sound, but television communicates by transmitting audiovisual *images*.

To successfully function as a means of communication which broadcasts understandable messages and meanings, television must present easily recognizable images. Thus, network television airs images "coded" by dominant social rituals, practices, and relations. Further restricted by the structure of network broadcasting—such as thirty-minute programming with periodic interruptions for advertising—television relies on conventional storylines, plots, endings and stereotypical characters. Of course, images chosen based on recognition, convention, and entertainment value also deliver social communication as they reflect the mores and norms of a nation.

In his analysis of television, technology, and cultural form, British culture studies scholar Raymond Williams (1974) rejected the term "mass communication." Like Dewey, Williams expected communicators to actively participate in the process, but network television simply "broadcasts" messages to a mass of receivers who have no means for entering the conversation or producing their own communication via television.

More importantly, for Williams, this new broadcast medium has become the primary means of social communication—the communication of everyday life which educates and socializes us to accepted values, beliefs, and practices. Acceptable behavior and knowledge gets passed on to each generation (or immigrant group) through observable practices, relations, and factual information along with accompanying stories, rituals, anecdotes, and symbols which express what is good or bad, right or wrong, a right or responsibility. Historically, youth, immigrants, and other newcomers, have been socialized largely through institutions such as school, church, work, and family. Increasingly, mass society has fractured the socializing power of these traditional institutions which were built in homogeneous communities over decades. Industrialization, urbanization, mass migration, and immigration transformed communities. Existing social values and authorities faced a growing crisis of legitimation. As Williams sees it, by the late 1950s, television rescued civil society, supplanting all other social institutions. Television now functions as the premier means of socialization.

Television entertains while informing and educating its mass audiences to current values, lifestyles, and behaviors. "90210" popularizes an upscale youth culture; "NYPD Blue" relates and defends law enforcement problems; talk shows showcase unacceptable behavior for family and personal relations. These and other popular shows attract millions of viewers and communicate a fairly homogenous set of messages. Coast to coast, Americans watch the same shows, with the same themes, and the same outcomes, night after night, day after day—on average four hours each day. It's not hard to understand William's claim about the socializing effects of television in contemporary society. Indeed by reaching mass audiences that use few other means for information or entertainment, television homogenizes U.S. culture.

In the first reading in this section, Douglas Kellner finds that television's homogenizing messages have followed leading cultural trends since the first days of broadcast. The '40s echoed radio in every detail, including the integration of advertisers into the very content of the program. Television in the 1950s grew in tandem with consumer society and suburbanization, reflecting the individualism and consumerism of a prospering white middle class. TV programs in the 1960s reflected the Cold War and Kennedy liberalism, according to Kellner, but by the 1980s shows expressed a renewed conservatism. Despite the arbitrary marking of TV history according to decade, Kellner offers a convincing argument about how television's social communication fit the prevalent socio-political outlook of the time.

An enlightening excerise might be to consider what are the themes and messages of TV in the '90s. Why does WB (the Warner Brother's network) feature so many sit-coms with predominantly black casts, while the big three have largely dropped blacks from sit-com programming? Why extra-terrestial programs, such as "X-files," "Profilers," "Millenium," and "3rd Rock from the Sun"? How has network television adjusted to cable and its target marketing (ESPN, MTV, BET, Disney, and shopping, cooking, and gardening "networks")?

Kellner's analysis moves away from labelling TV as either liberal or conservative and positions it as "centrist." In its push to increase audience share and maximize advertising revenue, television producers are "reluctant to embrace any controversy" and gravitate to whatever is popular at the moment. Whatever is predominant is best. Thus, TV promotes consensus, harmony, and normalization under the status quo. Consequently, creativity is also curtailed. Even the most innovative or controversial shows—from "Mary Hartmann" and "All in the Family" to "Murphy Brown" and "Roseanne"—revolve around family values, individual solutions, and mild critiques of the status quo. At the same time, network television does not broadcast monolithic messages. Certain genres (talk, soaps, news, music) permit more diversity and standard formats frequently have challenging variations: "Ellen," "Frank's Place," and "TV Nation," for example. Ultimately, however, television programming in the United States rarely advances images which might inspire a collective or broadly social response in the Deweyian sense.

Kellner also indicts governmental support of commercial television. Congressional deregulation in 1984 increased the centralization of broadcasting and its commercialization (including increasing the number of advertisements per hour!). Legislative action also removed all public service requirements and all fairness and equal time rules. Unfortunately, the trend identified by Kellner gained momentum: the 1996 Telecommunications Bill further removed broadcasting from public access and participation (see Section 8).

One of the few genres of television programming targeted for women, soaps began as 15-minute radio programs in the 1930s, migrated to television, and by the 1970s were drawing audiences of 20 million. Soap operas—with their serialized, multi-plot story form—are a major part of many women's cultural lives (Dines and Humez, 1995). Deborah Rogers notes the strong female characters on shows like "All My Children" and "Days of Our Lives," she argues however, that successful career women are usually punished and seldom happy in the soap opera world. Women may be independent and competent on the soaps, but only as mother and spouse will they be happy and "complete." In short, one of the most popular genres of daytime television presents images of contemporary professional women while promoting traditionally gendered roles.

Elayne Rapping examines another popular daytime programming fare: talk shows. Talk shows hosted by Geraldo Rivera, Jerry Springer, Ricki Lake, and Richard Bey have long been ridiculed as "trash TV," castigated for "ambush" interviews which humiliate guests, and even denigrated as a form of entertainment. Others, such as Oprah Winfrey and Phil Donahue, have acquired a more respectable reputation. In either case, in Rapping's judgment, talk shows mark off a small site for public discourse. Serving as a national "back-yard fence," talk shows let millions of Americans "gossip" about the outrageous behavior of "other" people, simlutaneously reassuring viewers of their own moral standards and alerting them to challenges to existing norms. In the midst of this discourse, some serious issues are actually being discussed—sexual harassment, sex education, drug and alchohol abuse, family, work, and race relations, and other social concerns. The problem as Rapping sees it is not the "sleaziness" of talk shows but their complete failure to elicit any practical solution. Because talk shows are contained in the "immobilizing structure of the political status quo," they demonstrate participatory discourse in form, not substance.

As Kellner has argued, television images reflect and reinforce the status quo in many ways. The selection by Herman Gray uncovers the social communication carried by televized representations of African-Americans. With the exception of "Amos 'n' Andy" and a few comic sidekicks to white stars in the 1950s, Blacks were largely invisible on American television until the mid-1970s. Following the civil rights movement and the increased purchasing power of African-Americans, television producers found a place for Blacks on television—situation comedy. With the exception of a few "buddy" roles, Blacks have pretty much remained segregated in comedy series. Of course, over the years, some images of Blacks have been more favorable than others, as Marvin Rigg's documentary *Color Adjustment* (1990) has illustrated. For instance, Cliff Huxtable as a doctor and loving father on "The Cosby Show" presents a more positive image than J.J. as a bumbling, irresponsible fool on "Good Times." Nonetheless, even in "positive" programs, Gray finds subtle messages which marginalize and subordinate African-Americans. The standing broadcast conventions of format, plot, narrative structure, and character type provide codes which only allow "partial and incomplete" images of African-Americans. Gray discovers assimilationist themes in shows as diverse as "Benson," "Webster," "Different Strokes," and "The Jeffersons." These themes, according to Gray, reinforce the value of cooperation, harmony, and social management and more importantly assume Black social mobility, affluence, and success. Such assumptions disguise the actual conditions of life in America, short-circuiting public understanding and informed, democratic discussions about race.

While the comfortable affluence of Benson, the Jeffersons, and the Huxtables reassures white (and Black) audiences that all's well in the United States, such images belie the reality of continuing race inequality. In 1991, the Population Reference Bureau released *African-Americans in the 1990s*, a 600-page detailed report which concluded that Blacks lag behind whites in nearly every measure of economic and physical well-being because racism and discrimination remain. The prominent National Research Council (NRC) also found continued segregation in housing, inequality in income and employment, and discrimination in education (Jaynes, 1991). The NRC concluded that there has been an overall relative decline for the majority of blacks in America. In terms of employment and income, young blacks are worse off now than young blacks were twenty five years ago. In Chicago, Detroit, Newark, and most other major cities, almost half of black youth from 18-25 years old are unemployed. Some will never have a job. Even finding a job is no guarantee of upward mobility: the real average hourly wage rate is lower than at anytime since 1964. Eight million workers work full-time and are still poor. The tenets of the American Dream—work hard, play fair, be rewarded—have no meaning, no reality for most of Black America—except on television.

As Gray recognizes, the unrealistic portrayals of American life broadcast by network TV are not necessarily intentional, but occur due to existing industry conventions and practices which themselves are infected by previous social communication. Richard Butsch takes this insight further in his inquiry into television images of working class characters. Butsch details how the culture and shared world views of producers, writers, and sponsors constrains television programming in a structure marked by middle class professional norms, values, and stereotypes.

Based on the depictions of workers on television, American audiences see little of working class conditions and know even less about working class views. Television characters, in general, live in an upper middle class professional world of abundance—well-dressed, well-fed, and for want of little. As doctors, lawyers, and cops, television characters generally have their needs met by workers hidden from view. Network images feature workers as gas station attendants, bartenders, shopkeepers and the like. In his study of the twenty most popular prime time TV shows, Ralph Johnson (1981) found that working class characters were obedient to superiors, often comic and inept, usually dispensible, and "mostly silent and nameless" (203). Labor unions are even more marginal on prime time and have a mostly negative image. Can the value judgment of such social communication be clearer? Even as the lives of American working people (defined as anyone who lives by hourly wage or salary) are confronted with downsizing, mergers, and rationalization of production, televized representations of U. S. social life and relations suggest that we are all middle class.

In production and content, dominant communication practices of network television (striving for ratings and profits) legitimize popular cultural trends, established authority, and the status quo. The social communication of television champions middle class consumerism and frames the problems of women, Blacks, and working people as individual deficiencies (such as drugs, crime, poor choice) rather than structural or relational symptoms (such as unemployment, inequality, or use of resources). Information useful to citizen deliberation on community and societal issues is largely absent. Those who have access to production and decision-making are not representative of the majority of Americans or our diversity. In short, current communication practices through television technology are highly asymmetrical and not conducive to interaction, democratic participation, or community building.

The technology of television, however, has incredible democratic potential—admittedly deeply hidden within talk show formats and audience "voting" on "America's Funniest Home Videos." Available to citizens and outside market pressures, television could provide immediate access to local, national, and international information, enhance more direct citizen participation, and increase collective, democratic-decision making. Brecht's proposal for radio communication applies directly to television. Indeed, as the most important mass medium of the contemporary world, television could help realize Dewey's call for democratic communication in a mass society.

REFERENCES

Dines, Gail, and Jean M. Humez, eds. *Gender, Race and Class in Media: A Text-Reader*. Thousand Oaks: Sage, 1995.

Jaynes, Gerald David and Robin M. Williams, Jr., eds. *A Common Destiny: Blacks and American Society: Committee on the Status of Black Americans, Commission on Behavioral and Social Sciences and Education, National Research Council* . Washington: National Academy P, 1989.

Johnson, Ralph Arthur. "World without Workers: Prime Time's Presentation of Labor." *Labor Studies Journal* 5.3 (Winter 1981): 199-206.

McLuhan, Marshall. *Understanding Media*. New York: McGraw-Hill, 1964.

Population Reference Bureau. *African-Americans in the 1990s*. Washington: Population Reference Bureau, 1991.

Williams, Raymond. *Television: Technology and Culutral Form*. New York: Schocken, 1974.

17 | Broadcasting and the Rise of Network Television
Douglas Kellner

· · ·

Network television emerged in the late 1940s from within the same framework as radio. The radio networks continued to dominate television, and many top radio stars (e.g., Jack Benny, Red Skelton, Perry Como, and Patti Page) and programs (e.g., "Gunsmoke," "Dragnet," and "Amos and Andy") migrated to television. During this transition period, beginning around 1946, the three major television networks utilized the same series formats already developed by radio and film (e.g., soap operas, situation comedies, cop and crime dramas, quiz shows, and suspense thrillers). Television thus contributed to the process of cultural homogenization decried by theorists of the so-called mass society. (For further discussion of the "mass culture" and "mass society" debate, see Rosenberg and White 1957 and Swingewood 1977.)

Television and the Affluent Society

The advent of television and the emergence of a consumer society were part of the same historical conjuncture. At the end of World War II, corporate capitalism was geared up to produce a large variety of mass consumption goods, which needed to be sold to consumers. Corporate capital might have created a consumer society earlier, except that the Depression and war intervened (Ewen 1976); it was only during the postwar period that conditions were ripe. Industrial firms had been operating at full capacity to support the war effort, and corporations were preparing to switch from war production to consumer production. During the war, unions had gained in strength and workers had struggled for higher wages. When servicemen returned home, having accumulated large savings, they were eager to marry, raise families, and enjoy the benefits of the new age of affluence that was promised and to some extent realized.

The same period witnessed massive migrations to the suburbs. New suburban housing developments promised clean air, a wholesome environment in which to raise children, and a new mode of affluent living. Television fit smoothly into this great transformation, and its ubiquitous entertainment provided a new mode of leisure activity for suburban dwellers cut off from city culture. At the same time, television advertising and entertainment presented the new artifacts of consumer culture and promoted consumer life-styles that eventually encompassed suburban, urban, and rural life. New shopping malls provided the goods and services advertised on television, and television itself quickly became both a privileged source of advertising revenue and an important manager of consumer demand (Siepmann 1950, 328ff.; Bogart 1956, 184ff.).

As suburbanization mushroomed during the late 1940s and 1950s, the new "talking furniture" became a fixture in U.S. society. Rarely before had any new technology so rapidly and successfully taken hold in society. In 1946, when the networks were beginning to develop a regular television service, only a small number of homes had television sets. By 1950, 96 television stations were broadcasting to 3.1 million homes (Bogart 1956, 10, 12), and by 1956–1957, 500 stations were broadcasting to 40 million homes, 85 percent of which were equipped with television sets that were turned on an average of 5 hours per day (Barnouw 1975, 198). Thus, in little more than a decade, television had become a central feature of life in the United States.

At this time, transnational capitalism achieved world dominance. The United States had emerged after World War II with its economy intact, and its aggressive corporations were ready to develop a worldwide system dominated by U.S. transnational corporations. Television was a crucial element in this boom period because its advertisements promoted consumption and its programs celebrated the joys of the consumer society. Although the networks broadcast some socially critical news programs and documentaries, they tended to put their corporate interest in maximizing profit before the public interest of providing stimulating and thought-provoking information and entertainment.

In the last 1940s opportunities still existed to diversify television and to produce a more informative, complex, and challenging system. The new technology known as Ultra High Fidelity television (UHF) would have made it possible to greatly expand the television spectrum. But under pressure from interests in the television industry, the government in 1948 sanctioned development of a Very High Fidelity (VHF) television system, which restricted the available television spectrum to twelve channels and thus enabled the networks to dominate American television. If the UHF system had originally been mandated, however, a much more diverse and pluralistic system could have evolved (Mosco 1979).[1]

In 1948 the FCC declared a freeze on new television licenses that lasted until 1952, when a veritable television boom period began. Indeed, leisure has been organized around television watching ever since. TV henceforth became the electronic hearth in the suburbs and the city alike. The flickering TV screen was the most dazzling spectacle in the home, and the entire family was drawn to it with great fascination. In record numbers families watched the new situation comedies such as "I Love Lucy" and the variety shows put on by Ed Sullivan, Milton Berle, and Jackie Gleason. New celebrities emerged overnight and a fascinated audience viewed more than ever: In 1955, for instance, one out of every two people in the United States watched Mary Martin play Peter Pan (Bogart 1956, 1). Never before had so many people engaged in the same cultural experience at the same time. TV culture had arrived.

By the late 1940s it was clear to leaders in the industry that television would have to be an advertiser-supported medium. Its executives accordingly undertook the task of convincing corporations and advertising agencies of the virtue of television advertising. NBC President Pat Weaver led this effort and tirelessly sold television advertising, telling one group of executives:

[T]he automated business needs a constant, dependable, unfluctuating demand for its out-put....This and other solutions to steady demand mean a new kind of selling—a complete change in emphasis—educational selling to wean consumers from old habits into new ways of keeping with a new era....The Post-War Era which created new selling problems which might have caused a recession, evened up the score by providing business with the very instrument it needed to meet the challenge and the needs of the new selling concepts and methods. That instrument—the greatest mutation in communications history...man's greatest communication invention—television. A medium that proved itself, from the first, to be also the most powerful, exciting, flexible of all advertising media. (Weaver, cited in Boddy 1987, 353; emphasis in original)

Television advertising had thus come to be the vanguard of the consumer society, educating people about the new consumer goods and services that they would need as up-to-date members of the affluent society. Television also began to emerge as a mega-business and as a major cultural and political force. The ratings system, established by the 1950s, fixed advertising revenues according to the number of people watching a particular program at a given time. So much money was involved that only popular shows with good ratings survived. From the beginning, TV became a "copy-cat" medium, repeating and imitating its own biggest successes. Consequently, successive waves of variety entertainment shows, situation comedies, westerns, action/adventure series, and quiz shows came to dominate network television in the 1950s.

Television, like radio before it, increased the power and prestige of corporations, which presented themselves as benevolent and powerful providers. The announcement "NBC presents" pegged members of the audience as the recipients of entertainment provided by the powerful TV network; the slogan "General Electric brings to you" showcased GE as a friendly benefactor whose personal "to you" suggested that the programming was specially produced for the benefit of individual viewers.

The commercial format determined the form and structure of television programming. During the first decade of television, when production was primarily live, commercials were woven into the programs in a variety of ways, ranging from "Mama's" use of Maxwell House Coffee during the broadcast of "I Remember Mama" to the various characters on "Burns and Allen" who interrupted the story line to talk about the sponsor's product (Hay 1989). These practices ended with the advent of taped television, at which time a "magazine programming" concept was adopted in which programs were regularly interrupted for advertising "breaks" or "spots." Since that time, series television programs have been edited into 30- and 60-minute segments with well-structured interruptions for advertising.

During the 1950s the sponsors literally produced the shows themselves and thus had complete control over programming form and content. Early on, they perceived that "popular entertainment" created the most favorable climate for their advertising messages. Popular shows like "Ozzie and Harriet" and "Milton Berle" made the audiences feel good, and the sponsors hoped that these good feelings would be transferred to their products. In short, the sponsors wished to eliminate unpleasant programming or programs that "confused" or "alienated" the audiences in any way. Accordingly, simple, formulaic programs quickly became the norm.

In the mid-1950s the television networks attempted to take over control of programming, either producing the programs themselves or contracting programming from production companies, thus eliminating full sponsor control. But, as Boddy argues, this move—rather than improving programming—was decisive in the transformation from the so-called "golden age of television" to the "vast wasteland" (1987, 347ff.). One of the first effects of this move was a switch in programming from anthology series to episodic series—a switch that, as Barnouw has argued, was influenced by commercial considerations (1978, 102ff.). The individual dramas in anthology series often featured disturbing problems and controversial material, thereby creating friction between the executives, on the one hand, and producers and writers who wanted to produce more socially critical programs, on the other. Many of the anthology dramas dealt with working-class life ("Marty") and even with the underclass ("Requiem for a Heavy-weight"), whereas sponsors came to prefer programs with a more up-scale ambience. In addition, some of the dramas that dealt with upper-class, corporate life (e.g., "Patterns") were critical of the business culture. Moreover, the anthology dramas, which were influenced by theater, often took place in a closed, interior space, whereas the sponsors generally preferred the open outdoors as an environment for the action and adventure spectacles that came to dominate television by the late 1950s.

From the mid- to late 1950s a shift took place from live to filmed television and from anthology drama to episodic series as the basic type of entertainment programming; meanwhile, the center of television production moved from New York to California. Commercial imperatives dictated these changes as television more aggressively reproduced the ethos and values of corporate capitalism. Later, during the 1950s and early 1960s, an ever-closer fit between television and U.S. society occurred. The famous situation comedies of the era (e.g., "Ozzie and Harriet," "Father Knows Best," "The Donna Reed Show," "Leave It to Beaver") presented idealized images of American life by portraying nuclear families and middle-class values and norms. The commercial ambience of television thus tended to replicate the commercial ambience of life in affluent society during an era when the consumer society was established as the specific form of social organization in the United States.

Sponsors also preferred fast action and quick, often violent resolution of problems. Indeed, both the situation comedies and the action/adventure programming generally followed a conflict-resolution model similar to the ads, which frequently depicted a problem and then offered a product as the solution. As sponsors seemed to prefer programming that guaranteed a resolution of problems (as did the ads), a happy ending for the program was likewise guaranteed. In addition to controlling both the format and structure of television programming, sponsors relentlessly controlled and censored program content in line with their interests (for examples, see Barnouw 1970, 3ff.; Brown 1971, 65; and Lee and Solomon, 60ff.). In a very literal sense, then, network television became the voice of corporate capitalism and the instrument of its hegemony—a hegemony firmly established in the United States during the 1950s.

Advertisers had earlier produced most radio and television entertainment and had total control over its content. In the late 1950s, however, television networks assumed control over programming in the wake of disclosures regarding quiz show "fixes" that ensured the victory of "likable" contestants (Anderson 1978). Henceforth, the networks and production companies (most of which were located in Hollywood) produced television shows, and the networks took responsibility for their content with "standard and practice" offices—a euphemism for censorship agencies, which ensured that nothing would appear on television that contradicted the interests of the corporate behemoths who controlled broadcasting. All disturbing problems such as juvenile delinquency, racism, alcoholism, and the divisive communist witch-hunts were excluded from television entertainment....

...the networks constantly attempted to discern new trends, social developments, and issues to attract an audience.

As a consequence, Kennedy liberalism began to appear in 1960s television in such programs as "East Side/West Side," "The Defenders," "Ben Casey," "Dr. Kildare," and "Mr. Novak." As the United States became more interventionist and the Vietnam War escalated, more and more spy shows and anticommunist programming began appearing, including "Mission: Impossible," "I Spy," "The Man From U.N.C.L.E.," and other spy dramas. But the networks also broadcast the satire "Get Smart," which spoofed the deadly seriousness and cold war Manichaeism of the heavy-handed anticommunist dramas.

Cold war drama was the dominant mode, nevertheless: The 1960s saw more military series (in the form of both war dramas and situation comedies) than did any other epoch in TV history (MacDonald 1985, 191ff.). Such anticommunist entertainment was hardly incidental, given that this was the era of Vietnam.

At the same time, however, TV began depicting social conflicts at home to a much greater extent than previously. For one thing, the expansion of television news from 15 to 30 minutes in 1963 accelerated the amount of news coverage during a period when political struggle was intensifying. After the quiz scandals of the late 1950s and the political pressure applied by Newton Minow and other liberal FCC commissioners to improve the quality of television, the networks greatly expanded their news operations and increased not only the length and quality of the prime-time news programs but also the number of documentaries. Audiences thus began to see dramatic images of the civil rights struggle: Filling their TV screen were pictures of demonstrations, bombed churches, and blacks beaten and hosed by Southern police, chased by dogs, and brutally arrested. The 1960s also witnessed such high-quality documentaries as "Harvest of Shame," "Hunger in America," and "The Tenement," which dramatized the plight of the poor. By the mid-1960s, coverage of Vietnam had also increased and the networks began showing images of the antiwar movement and the new counterculture.

As the 1960s exploded into social conflict, television entertainment found it increasingly difficult to keep up with the unprecedented cultural change and rebellion. Television's ideological functions and conservative reluctance to embrace controversy as a consequence of its total commercialization rendered TV entertainment increasingly irrelevant to the vast process of social and cultural change that was occurring. Curiously, the only entertainment programs to portray directly the new radicalism, the experimentation with sex and drugs, and the new counterculture were cop shows like "Mod Squad" and "Dragnet"—and they generally portrayed the new ethos quite negatively. The few programs that attempted to give even a slightly positive spin to the 1960s spirit of nonconformity and rebellion were programs like "The Smothers Brothers," "Laugh-In," and "The Monkees." "The Smothers Brothers" was ultimately eliminated from television because its stars were presumably too sympathetic to 1960s radicalism and too critical of U.S. Vietnam policy; but this show appears somewhat mild and innocuous today, as do "Laugh-In" and "The Monkees."

"Star Trek" probably went to the outer limits of what was possible for network television in the 1960s. The program might be interpreted as the "starship" of Kennedy liberalism, given its theme of exploring new frontiers and going where no man (or TV program) had ever gone before. Produced by Kennedy liberal Gene Roddenberry, the series exhibited the cold war liberalist ideology associated with the Kennedy administration. The show presented allegories of the intervention in Vietnam, the cold war, U.S. imperialism, and life in the 1960s. It and other series began featuring blacks, women, and other minorities in the role of heroes, thus reflecting the integrationist liberalism and UN cosmopolitanism that became widespread in the 1960s. The series presented one of the first positive portrayals of intellectuals on network television (Dr. Spock) as well as positive images of racial integration and harmony. However, its vision of world hegemony featured a white male leader, Captain Kirk, benevolently ruling over other races and worlds, under the reign of the *U.S.S. Enterprise*, a barely disguised code for American capitalism. And although the Starship Enterprise was given the directive not to intervene in foreign cultures, Kirk and his team seemed to intervene virtually each time they encountered a culture with significantly different values.

On the whole, television's narrow vision in a period of expanding consciousness and cultural experimentation rendered it a highly retrograde culture force. Its inability to come to terms with the 1960s was evident in its coverage of one of the most divisive events in U.S. history, the Vietnam War. At first, television was generally supportive of the U.S. intervention in Vietnam. Its proclivity for cold war dramas had reinforced the anticommunist ethos in which support for U.S. intervention against communism could thrive, and this mindset was evident in talk shows, news programs, and documentaries that exhibited a strong anticommunist and pro-interventionist bias (MacDonald 1985). The major news commentators of the day—Chet Huntley and Walter Cronkite—actually made films for the Defense Department that were used to warn recruits of the dangers of world communism. In short, during the first few years of the Vietnam War, network coverage was almost uniformly favorable to U.S. intervention (Hallin 1985).

Negative images of this intervention began appearing in 1965, when Morley Safer narrated a report on CBS that showed U.S. troops setting fire to a Vietnamese village. Reports during the next several years depicted growing U.S. losses and increasing protests against the war from various sectors of U.S. society, thereby promoting a national debate over Vietnam. TV's role in this debate was quite ambiguous. Until around 1968 few dissenting voices were broadcast on television. When intra-ruling-class opinion on the war became increasingly divided, television displayed this division, allowing "responsible" liberal voices to articulate the antiwar position while marginalizing the more radical antiwar movement as being communist infiltrated or "sympathetic to the enemy" (Gitlin 1980). Yet when Walter Cronkite began speaking critically about U.S. aims in Vietnam and cited the improbability of a U.S. victory, public opinion began to shift toward the antiwar position. Lyndon Johnson decided not to run for reelection in 1968 after he discerned that the antiwar forces were growing in popularity and militancy.

In 1968, clearly one of the most tumultuous years in contemporary history, television was swept along with the dramatic events it was covering. Television news portrayed the vicissitudes of Vietnam and the growing antiwar movement, the antiwar campaigns of Eugene McCarthy and Robert Kennedy, the assassinations of Robert Kennedy and Martin Luther King, the black ghetto insurrections, and the bloody police riots at the 1968 Chicago Democratic Convention. As the drama intensified, television circulated images of struggle and upheaval; these images became political forces, which in turn inspired and thus circulated further struggle, as when students in one part of the country observed campus take-overs of buildings in another area and replicated the acts. Even when the network frames and commentaries attempted to contain and defuse these images, the dramatic spectacles of upheaval persisted in carrying their own meanings. But television was attracted to such spectacles, which it circulated and amplified. Television, it seemed, *might* very well televise the revolution.

It has often been remarked that television is primarily an imagistic medium, inasmuch as its images remain most vividly in the memory. Such "compelling images" present dramatic events that break with the normality of everyday life. For instance, the images of police brutality against blacks during the civil rights struggle powerfully portrayed the inhumanity of racism and oppression. Images of antiwar demonstrators chanting "The Whole World Is Watching!" as Chicago police attacked protestors during the 1968 Democratic convention presented a critical vision of the dominant culture, which was carrying out an increasingly unpopular Vietnam War while repressing its opponents on the home front. Compelling images of blacks struggling for civil rights and of antiwar protesters struggling against the Vietnam intervention legitimated and circulated the ideas behind these movements.

In particular, live events often produce images that are not subject to manipulation and control. The increasingly competitive television environment of the 1960s drove the network news divisions to seek dramatic imagery of conflict and struggle. The quest for "compelling images" resulted in pictures of contestation and opposition that helped to promote oppositional movements, even when the television discourse and framing attempted to present these movements negatively. By appearing on television, oppositional movements acquired legitimacy and attracted audiences to their struggles. Such images also inspired other oppositional groups to emulate the actions and tactics portrayed and thus circulated the messages and struggles of the antiwar movement and counterculture.

At the same time, television's proclivity for dramatic imagery often led oppositional groups to undertake spectacular, sometimes violent, actions to attract television coverage. Such tactics ultimately had the effect of deflecting attention from the antiwar movement and from the New Left critiques of the existing society; they also led some demonstrators into dangerous adventurism and violence. Thus, television's portrayal of oppositional movements was ambiguous in its effects. Although it helped to circulate contestation and to legitimate oppositional movements, it also presented negative images of these movements and sometimes undermined their attempts to develop a mass base for social change.

With the election of Richard Nixon in 1968, however, television coverage again became highly conservative, generally reproducing the administration line and only occasionally presenting more critical positions toward the Vietnam imbroglio, which continued year after year and eventually expanded into Cambodia and Laos during the early 1970s (this despite Nixon's promise of "peace with honor"). Still, the antiwar movement grew and establishment opposition to the war proliferated. Eventually it became clear to the Nixon administration that the United States could not win the war with Vietnam. A "Vietnamization" of the war was thus implemented and U.S. troops were pulled out, leading to the eventual collapse of the South Vietnamese military in 1975 and to victory by the National Liberation Front and its North Vietnamese allies.

Thus, television never really came to terms with either the Vietnam War or the tumultuous social upheavals of the 1960s. Many among the generation of the 1960s rarely watched television during this era because it had become totally irrelevant to their experience and concerns. This generation turned instead to rock music, film, and other forms of cultural expression. Television was seen as a highly conservative, culturally retrograde, and generally banal social force and institution. The Left and the counterculture mounted intense critical attacks on television, inaugurating a vigorous tradition of cultural and media criticism that continues to this day.[2] Conservative and liberal critiques of television began to proliferate at the same time.

Conservatives began complaining of a liberal bias in television following Spiro Agnew's attack on the medium in 1969. And in her book *The News Twisters*, Edith Efron (1972) argued that television was sharply biased in favor of Hubert Humphrey and against Richard Nixon in the 1968 election. Indeed, there may have been some truth in the conservative critique of the media's liberal bias during this period, but the conservatives greatly exaggerated the degree of bias.[3]

It has been argued (Hodgson 1976, 368ff.) that, following the turmoil of the 1968 Democratic convention, the news networks reconsidered their policies of covering demonstrations and social upheaval, and moved to a more conservative terrain, backing off from controversy. The election of Nixon certainly accelerated television's centrist slide, and government harassment of the media during the Nixon years clearly had a "chilling effect" on critical news coverage (Powledge 1971; Lashner 1984). Yet even during this period, "compelling images" of social reality circulated spectacles of struggle and upheaval, even if the network texts and commentary were conservative or markedly apolitical. Moreover, as the 1970s began, television entertainment began dealing with social conflicts that the network news divisions were trying to ignore or downplay.

Contested Terrain: Television in the 1970s

In the early 1970s television entertainment finally recognized and attempted to deal with the struggles and upheavals of the 1960s. New, and largely unsuccessful, series featured young professionals working for change within the system (e.g., "The Young Lawyers," "The Bold Ones"). But these programs failed in the ratings because they pleased neither the large (still conservative) audience who constituted the mainstay of television viewers nor the young radicals. New comedy programs that dealt with the conflicts of the 1960s, especially Norman Lear's "All in the Family," did become highly popular and brought into the United States' living rooms the sort of debates that had indeed been taking place in the real world of struggle and conflict. These fierce, generational conflicts dramatically contradicted TV's world of harmonious resolutions of trivial or unreal problems. (For a discussion of programming in the early 1970s, see Brown 1971 and MacDonald 1990, 191ff.)

It was as if the audiences could face the turmoil wrought by the 1960s only in the medium of comedy, as if laughter provided both the best shield against and the easiest access to the upheavals of the day. Indeed, television pursued the time-honored tradition of using comedy and satire to deal with society's most difficult and divisive problems. Interestingly, the Lear comedies became popular with conservative, liberal, and radical constituencies alike: The conservatives identified with Archie Bunker, and the liberals and radicals identified with Archie's son-in-law Mike. In fact, the decade of the 1970s was one of genuine contestation in the political, social, and cultural spheres (Kellner and Ryan 1988). This decade was perhaps the most interesting period in the history of television, precisely because television reproduced in various programs the ideological struggles of the day and literally became a contested terrain— a terrain in which the competing liberal and conservative forces struggled for power and the radical position became increasingly marginalized in both the TV world and the actual political arena.

Intense struggles raged during the 1970s. The antiwar movement gained in force and influence, eventually contributing to the United States' decision to give up its Vietnam adventure. Although television arguably promoted the government intervention during the 1960s (Hallin 1985; Herman and Chomsky 1988), one might also contend that significant forces within the ruling elites eventually came around to the position that the war could not be won without great and intolerable domestic costs and that U.S. policy thus had to be abandoned. Television reflected this opposition and circulated the debate, thereby raising doubts concerning the Vietnam intervention. Moreover, although it is arguable that television rarely presented fully articulated antiwar positions, its images—whatever their ideological content—may well have contributed to the formation of a significant antiwar majority, which forced the U.S. government to give up its venture.

By the same token, it was the sheer length of the war and the sheer amount of coverage that dispirited the American public and created a negative response to the war. Saturation TV coverage of Vietnam, week after week, year after year, created the impression that Vietnam was a "downer." Even if the coverage had been more positively framed from the viewpoint of the administration, it might have contributed to the antiwar consensus. Yet, although television provides material that suggests what people should see, think, and do, it cannot determine *how* people will appropriate and use that material. There is always a distance between network intentions (the encoding of television texts) and its actual effects (the ways in which the audience decodes and uses the material). In the case of Vietnam, I would suggest that even if television did not actively contribute to promoting the aims of the antiwar movement, it eventually helped produce the antiwar consensus that led the political/military establishment to abandon the war.

The corporate establishment was obviously uncomfortable with the liberal candidacy of George McGovern during the 1972 election, and network television did little to promote his campaign, thus helping Richard Nixon win his second term as president. McGovern went beyond the boundaries allowed by consensualist centrism (which had increasingly become television's ideological stance) with his criticism of the military-industrial complex and U.S. interventionist policy, as well as with his mobilization of young and not-so-young radicals and liberals. If they had wished to, the networks could easily have done Nixon in during the 1972 campaign. The networks and other mainstream media had the essential facts concerning the Watergate break-in before the election; but, except for a two-part series on CBS, television avoided the issue until after the election, thus effectively ensuring Nixon's victory. Yet after his reelection, new facts surfaced to implicate the Nixon White House in a variety of political scandals; intense conflicts broke out concerning Nixon's subversion of the democratic political process during the Watergate affair and in related activities, including dirty tricks throughout the 1972 election that went beyond the boundaries of established political rules and propriety.

Revelations of an "enemies list," which included prominent members of the television industry, also elicited widespread liberal revulsion and might have helped turn the television industry against Nixon. It was during the Watergate affair that television's rise to megapower became ratified. Television took on and then eliminated a president. It gained in prestige and legitimacy what other institutions had lost. The Watergate hearings and the Nixon impeachment hearings demonstrated that television was both a mediator of political power in the United States and the arena in which battles for hegemony took place. Of course, reporters of the *Washington Post* and other newspapers broke and stuck to the Watergate story, and congressional figures ultimately maneuvered Nixon out of office; but it was television through which the drama was eventually played out. The Watergate hearings in particular fascinated the nation and showed how television could involve its audience in complicated political drama. The process exposed scandal after scandal in the Nixon administration and portrayed television as a crucial instrument in democratic society. Ultimately, television emerged as the real winner when it eased Richard Nixon into early retirement and celebrated the ascension of Gerald Ford as his successor.

In a battle between conservatism and mild liberalism, Jimmy Carter won the 1976 presidential election. Yet Carter was a member of the centrist Trilateral Commission, and he filled his administration with key members of that organization (see the articles in Sklar 1980, especially 197ff.). His membership in the commission and consequent relationships with dominant elites may help explain the positive media coverage of Carter's campaign, which enabled him to rise from being almost unknown nationally to successfully winning his party's nomination and then the national election. Yet the center couldn't hold. After initially favorable TV coverage and popularity with the electorate, Carter became increasingly unpopular and battles between liberals and conservatives intensified in Congress and throughout the country.

For the rest of the decade, intense struggles between liberals and conservatives continued. Television mediated these contests and began producing more aggressively liberal as well as conservative programming. It even permitted successful television producers and stars to use their series to promote their views—within certain well-defined limits, of course. Still, much programming was markedly apolitical; many producers wished to avoid all controversy and refrained from offending any segment of the audience. Nonetheless, some of the most progressive television programs ever to appear surfaced during this era.

A new "miniseries" form employed both the conventions of television melodrama and "critical realism," following the example of the British Broadcasting Corporation's presentation of dramas in a limited series form. The miniseries broke with the series form and used the expanded time frame to treat issues hitherto excluded from network television, such as class conflict, racism and anti-Semitism, imperialism, and the oppression of the working class and blacks while presenting capitalists and right wingers as oppressors and exploiters. Docudramas criticized Joe McCarthy, J. Edgar Hoover, the FBI, and other right-wing forces while vindicating Martin Luther King as well as victims of McCarthyism and FBI persecution. "Kill Me If You Can" sympathetically depicted the plight of a victim of capital punishment, Caryl Chessman, while presenting as strong a case against capital punishment as ever appeared on television.

These programs represent an important revision of idealized images of history and a reversal of conventional good guy/bad guy roles. Formerly, in programs like "The FBI" and in numerous police and spy series, the FBI, CIA, and police were portrayed as heroic saviors, whereas radicals or anyone failing to conform to the rules of the system were depicted as incarnations of evil. The U.S. economic and political system, as well as social institutions such as the family, were almost always idealized in television culture. During the mid- and late 1970s, however, television dramas exposed brutal racism in "Roots," "King," and "Roll of Thunder, Hear My Cry"; portrayed the corruption of the political system in "Washington: Behind Closed Doors" and "Blind Ambition," a fictionalized version of the Watergate scandals; displayed the evils of McCarthyism and 1950s blacklisting in "Fear on Trial" and "Tailgunner Joe"; and revealed class conflict and attacked two venerable institutions of corporate capitalism —the banks and the automobile industry—in "The Moneychangers" and "Wheels." The "critical realist" miniseries represent a form of popular culture as popular revenge (Kellner 1979). Blacks were avenged against their oppressors in "Roots," "King," and other series that portrayed racists as evil and the struggles of blacks as legitimate. "Holocaust" took revenge against Nazi oppression in its harsh portrayal of fascism and its sympathetic presentation of Jewish victims and resistance. "Fear on Trial" and other TV portrayals of McCarthyism and blacklisting gained a retrospective cultural victory for victims of political oppression by portraying the injustice, irrationality, and pettiness of right-wing oppression. And, finally, victims of FBI persecution gained revenge against J. Edgar Hoover in the representations of Hoover and the FBI in "King," "Washington: Behind Closed Doors" and in later miniseries dealing with the Kennedys. In all of these programs, the oppressed were portrayed in positive images and the oppressors in negative ones, thus providing a critical perspective on political institutions and on views previously presented positively.

A satiric form of critical television emerged in 1975 with "Saturday Night Live!" The first few seasons exhibited some of the cleverest satire in television history, focusing on television and politics. The "news" segment made great fun of political figures and policies, and Chevy Chase's stumbling and fumbling imitations of Gerald Ford helped circulate a popular image of Ford as comedic bumbler that contributed to his defeat in the 1976 presidential election.

Norman Lear's 1970s series, "Mary Hartman, Mary Hartman," subverted the forms of both the soap opera and the situation comedy while engaging in social critique and satire. Whereas soap operas generally trivialize serious problems through pathos, sentimentality, and moralistic melodrama, "Mary Hartman" approached some of the same problems more critically. Often starting with apparently common everyday problems, it used humor and self-reflective irony to suggest that something was profoundly wrong with patriarchy and consumer capitalism. Whereas situation comedy generally follows a conflict-resolution model in which problems are humorously solved in 30 or 60 minutes, the problems on "Mary Hartman" were endlessly multiplied and appeared insolvable within the present way of life. In the process, authority figures of all types were ruthlessly satirized. Such reversal of television codes and stereotypes provoked reflection on social institutions and their workings. Further, "Mary Hartman," more than any previous television show, constantly reflected on television's view of the world and its impact on American life. It confronted TV ideology with contradictory experiences and showed both the false idealizations and distortions of television by contrast to the real problems and quandaries of working-class women.

"Mary Hartman" also dealt with topics that were previously taboo, including impotence, venereal disease, union corruption, alienated industrial labor, and religious fraud. In fact, most Norman Lear series presented subjects previously eliminated from the world of television. "All in the Family," for instance, confronted bigotry and generational conflict more powerfully than ever before on television; "Maude" treated women's liberation and middle-class malaise in a provocative manner; "The Jefferson's," "Sanford and Son," and "Good Times" dealt with middle-class and working-class blacks more effectively than did previous series; "All's Fair" featured more political debates (between the conservative male and the liberal women) than did any previous TV comedy; and Lear's syndicated comedies—"All That Glitters," "Fernwood Tonight," "America Tonight," and "Fernwood Forever"—were imaginative shows that contained some of the most striking satires of television and American society ever broadcast.

To be sure, Lear's programs also had their limitations. "Mary Hartman" collapsed into cynicism and despair when the series ended after two years with Mary back in the kitchen, repeating her former way of life with her new lover. Evidently, the show was unable to offer any positive alternatives. Most of Lear's other situation comedies, moreover, were structured according to the standard conflict/resolution model, which manages to resolve the problems and issues confronted without serious change. "All in the Family," for instance, often implied that most problems of everyday life could be settled within the family and established society. (Of course, it also demonstrated that racism and bigotry resisted easy solutions and were serious and enduring problems.) In short, although Lear's programs presented real problems never before portrayed in the television world, they never offered solutions that transcended the limits of liberalism and the current organization of society. Individuals solved their problems through correct action, not by struggling together. Indeed, television entertainment has rarely depicted collective action and political movements as legitimate modes in which to deal with social problems.

Lear's liberalism represented the cutting edge and outmost boundary of what was permissible in 1970s network television, but it also revealed the limits of commercial television in the United States. Television liberalism does not go beyond individualism, and it rarely deals with problems of inequality, justice, poverty, or acute suffering, which arguably have their roots in the current organization of society. Television thus accepts this organization as given, and either idealizes and celebrates it in conservative forms or depicts liberal critiques and reform measures for all problems.

Nevertheless, much markedly apolitical as well as conservative programming also appeared during the 1970s. Some of the most popular programs during this decade were predominantly conservative crime dramas. In the mid-1970s another trend emerged; known as "T & A," it exploited women as sex objects. Programs like "Charlie's Angels," "The American Girls," and "Three's Company" debased women's liberation and sexual freedom, robbing these movements of their progressive elements. Silly situation comedies, mindless action/adventure shows, and vapid specials continued to dominate the network television schedules and ratings.

Yet there was probably more diversity in network television in this period than during any other in history. The decade of the 1970s was one of struggle, during which television became a contested terrain. Liberals and conservatives fought for control of U.S. society, and representatives of both groups were in the television industry. But the right wing and its prime political actor, Ronald Reagan, won the contest. Indeed, television turned sharply to the right in the Age of Reagan.

Conservative Hegemony: Television in the 1980s

The 1960s and 1970s were bad times for conservatives. Barry Goldwater, the Right's darling, suffered the most massive political defeat in history in the 1964 election against Lyndon Johnson. Soon after, the movements of the 1960s challenged all of the values in which the Right believed. But in the 1970s the Right counterattacked. It blamed liberals, Democrats, and radicals for the political and economic decline of the United States, for the growth of a cumbersome welfare state, and for the decay of morals and traditional values. Ultraconservative groups such as Jerry Falwell's "moral majority" and Richard Viguerie's New Right organization, used direct-mail campaign tactics to help elect Ronald Reagan and unseat prominent liberal senators such as George McGovern, Birch Bayh, and Frank Church in the 1980 election. The moment of the New Right had arrived.

Reaganite Entertainment

Network television wasted no time in responding to the new political hegemony of the Right. In the season after Reagan won, a set of crime drama series appeared. Such programs as "Strike Force," "McClain's Law," "Today's FBI," "Code Red," and "Magnum P.I." featured strong male heroes who represented conservative law-and-order values. They were played by long-time patriarchal movie and TV stars such as James Arness, Robert Stack, and Lorne Green, who earlier had starred in conservative TV series such as "Gunsmoke," "The Untouchables," and "Bonanza." These shows sought to tap into perceived audience needs for reassurance from strong male authority figures and a return to conservative values. Yet most of these series flopped, whereas the one new "liberal" cop show, "Hill Street Blues," became a major critical and audience success of the decade. Perhaps the public wasn't buying all of Reagan's conservative agenda after all.

Other new 1981 shows, during the first prime-time season of the Reagan era, included "Dynasty," "Falcon Crest," "Flamingo Road," and "King's Crossing," which joined "Dallas" in their depictions of wealth, greed, and power. These programs were dual edged: They can be seen as celebrating the values of wealth and power or as portraying the emptiness and corruption of upper-class life. Indeed, some people may identify with the wealthy protagonists and be reinforced in their materialist values and yearnings for the trappings of wealth. Others may perceive the corruption in a negative light and enjoy the sufferings of the wealthy. In its search for a mass audience, television does indeed often produce shows with contradictory ideological tendencies that appeal to as many people and groups as possible.

The 1982 season saw the (mercifully brief) appearance of two neoimperialist epics, "Tales of the Golden Monkey" and "Bring 'Em Back Alive," which pastiched Indiana Jones, Frank Buck, and the white man's burden in tales depicting Third World villainy and white male heroism. Then 1983 witnessed two military soap operas, "For Love and Honor" and "Emerald Point, N.A.S." The first featured the lives and loves of young male and female recruits who, fittingly, were advertised as "Fit to Fight—Anywhere, Anytime." Both series—like the movies *Private Benjamin* (also made into a TV series), *Stripes, An Officer and a Gentleman, The Great Santani,* and *Tank,* among others—portrayed the military as an institution where love, honor, and good times were to be had, thus providing free advertisements for the free-enterprise volunteer army that Reagan and his administration were rebuilding.

The miniseries during the first years of the Reagan administration included "The Winds of War," "The Blue and the Grey," "George Washington," and, in case these past wars and their glories became boring, "World War III." Forgetting that the media are supposed to be relatively autonomous in relation to the state and economic system, network producers also presented a slew of series that advanced Reagan's political agenda. His demand for a military buildup found support in the series "From Here to Eternity," based on the popular World War II novel and film, and "Call to Glory," which dealt with military life at the time of the Cuban missile crisis. Both humanized the military at a point when the military's image needed refurbishing. Both dealt with eras during which the military either wasn't properly prepared (as in the Pearl Harbor debacle, which is the centerpiece of "From Here to Eternity") or was enjoying a moment of glory (as when U.S. military power forced Khrushchev to withdraw Soviet missiles from Cuba in 1962). The cumulative message seemed to be that without a strong military we might be subject to enemy attacks (like that at Pearl Harbor), but with a strong military we can dictate policies to the Soviets (as we did during the Cuban missile crisis); therefore, we need a strong military buildup.

Now, I am not claiming that the networks planned and orchestrated this message. Rather, they were and remain business machines seeking to maximize profits by maximizing their audiences. This policy leads them to produce programs that they believe resonate with present trends, audience desires, fears, and fantasies, and will thus be attractive to mass audiences. Obviously, the networks believed that Reagan and his policies were popular, and they attempted to capitalize (literally) on this supposed popularity by producing programs that tapped into the conservative mindset. Consequently, as Reagan built up and unleashed the CIA, series began to heroize intelligence work. In "Masquerade" (1984), for instance, ordinary Americans, like Cibyl Shepherd, were enlisted as intelligence operatives on the assumption that the KGB knew who all the American spies were. Thus ordinary members of the audience could fantasize about being spies, too—and about fighting the nasty Reds. Another short-lived spy fantasy, "Cover-Up" (1984), featured a woman fashion photographer who was accompanied by a handsome ex-Special Forces agent. The woman became an "out-rider" (i.e., an undercover trouble shooter) after her intelligence agent husband was killed by a villainous French corporation hoping to steal U.S. technology and, undoubtedly, to sell it to the "evil empire."

As Reagan and his cronies contemplated and carried out military intervention in the Third World, series emerged that promoted macho interventionism or high-tech weaponry (e.g., "The A-Team," "Blue Thunder," "Airwolf," "Riptide," "Knightrider"). A series on the heroic exploits of the CIA was often announced but did not appear. In 1985, perhaps in celebration of the second Reagan administration, one miniseries portrayed Mussolini as a tragic hero and another celebrated the Russian tyrant, Peter the Great; in the meantime, Ronald Reagan's preferred class of the rich and powerful was lionized in movies and series too numerous to mention.

Analysis of episodes from some of these Reaganite fantasies reveals certain audacious revisions of history and advancements of blatantly right-wing ideology. A 1984 episode of the TV series "Blue Thunder," a spin-off of the movie, featured a high-tech surveillance helicopter, a trip to an island in the Caribbean, an American medical school, and a black population suffering under a communist dictatorship. In this rewriting of Grenada, a group of white American mercenaries, funded and directed by the KGB, plan to assassinate the black leader Maurice Priest so that a military coup led by Soviet-oriented Marxist Leninists can take over. (The Grenadan leader Maurice Bishop was evidently demoted to a priest in this episode.) The Blue Thunder team connects with democratic resistance forces and prevents the Soviet coup from taking place. On the way out, the helicopter crew disobeys orders and blows up a Soviet-Cuban arms depot (a more glamorous target than the mental institution that the U.S. forces accidently bombed during the actual Grenada invasion). Then, upon returning home, the crew learns that the Soviet-Cuban clique had taken over the government and that the U.S. president had heroically undertaken a counteraction to liberate the island—an intervention facilitated in this fantasy by the Blue Thunder bombing of the arms depot.

Historical revisionism continues in a "Call to Glory" episode of 1984. Here, after documenting the existence of Soviet missile bases in Cuba during the Cuban missile crisis, an Air Force Captain (Craig T. Williams) suddenly becomes a diplomat sent to Vietnam to investigate the Diem regime. The regime is shown to be extremely repressive and inept, thus retrospectively justifying CIA involvement in Diem's assassination so that a more effective government could be formed. (It wasn't.) The Vietnamese were, for the most part, depicted as corrupt, repressive, or ineffectual victims needing help from strong, well-meaning Americans, whereas the American hero was shown to be totally decent, strong, and heroic. To be sure, in the Vietnam episode there were questions raised as to what the United States was doing there in the first place, but the cumulative (and chauvinistic) message was that Americans are basically good and decent people who, out of misguided idealism, sometimes make minor mistakes.

I am not claiming that these series were necessarily part of a right-wing conspiracy; nor were they devastating indications of a long-term turn to the Right. Indeed, most of the right-wing series failed or, like "The A-Team," were not unambiguously conservative. One series, "The Equalizer," frequently depicted CIA types as villains, as did the highly popular "Miami Vice." In a famous episode of the latter, G. Gordon Liddy played a totally unscrupulous and unsavory representative of the U.S. intelligence service who provided illegal weapons to the Nicaraguan Contras engaged in a dirty war to overthrow the Sandinista government. Here, the Contras were depicted as a terrorist force armed and guided by the CIA. Moreover, the action was accompanied by the musical score of Jackson Browne's "Lives in the Balance," which sharply attacks U.S. intervention in Central America. The episode thus provides a leftist critique of a central policy of the Reagan administration (Best and Kellner 1987; Kellner 1990).

In short, the Reganite entertainment did not go uncontested. Embattled liberalism continued to be voiced in such shows as "Hill Street Blues," "St. Elsewhere," and, until it was terminated in 1983, "Lou Grant" (Gitlin 1983). Sophisticated modernism made an appearance in "Moon-lighting," and Yuppie liberalism was exhibited in "L.A. Law" and "Thirtysomething." "Miami Vice" turned to the Left in the 1980s and featured episodes sharply critical of the CIA and state policy while depicting the role of the banks and capitalist financial institutions in the drug trade. Other series, such as "Frank's Place," "Cagney and Lacey," "Murphy Brown," and "Designing Women," also tended to promote a liberal view of the world, whereas "Max Headroom" promoted a left post-modernist view.

In the final analysis, Reagan never really did forge a strong and enduring conservative majority. His policies continued to be contested by liberals and radicals, and on many issues the majority of the population continued to support more liberal positions.

Deregulation and Corporate Hegemony

Meanwhile, back in Washington, in line with Reagan's attack on all regulatory agencies (Horowitz 1989), the Federal Communications Commission was doing everything possible to take apart the regulatory structure that had been built up over the past few decades.[4] FCC commissioner Mark Fowler undertook a systematic deregulation of broadcasting. By the end of 1984 Fowler's FCC had (1) increased the number of radio and television stations that a company could own nationally from seven (AM and FM) radio and TV stations to twelve of each; (2) exempted radio and television stations from government-imposed limitations on the number and extent of commercials during a given hour; (3) eliminated the requirement that broadcasters must carry a certain amount of public service broadcasting and provide a minimum amount of educational material for children; (4) extended license renewal periods from three to five years while eliminating requirements to keep either programming logs and financial records for public inspection or FCC ascertainment for license renewal, which would presumably be automatic in the future; (5) exempted broadcasters from the requirement that they own a television station three years before selling it, thus triggering mergers and take-overs among television stations; and (6) promoted the deregulation of cable. The FCC later eliminated the Fairness Doctrine, which mandated that television networks present a diversity of controversial issues of public importance. Also eliminated was the "equal-time rule," which stipulated that opposing sides would be fairly treated; that is, representatives of different positions would be allowed to express their opinions, and qualified candidates for public office would be permitted to answer opponents.

Fowler's deregulation agenda attempted both to remove all major structural constraints on the broadcasting business in terms of ownerships, licenses, and business practices, and to eliminate as many restraints on programming as possible. (Fowler's FCC did, however follow the right-wing agenda of the day in attempting to regulate obscenity; and Fowler himself once sternly lectured broadcasters to "get it right" when they meekly criticized Reagan for his lax "management style.") Consequently, the Reagan FCC dramatically redefined the relation between government and television, and attempted to undo decades of regulatory guidelines and programs.

Since the late 1970s groups both in Congress and in the communications industry have been attempting to pass a new bill to update the Communications Act of 1934. Although Congress, the courts, and the FCC had amended the 1934 bill over the years, no successful effort had been made to deal with new communications systems such as cable television. Although the much-discussed new communications bill never reached the floor of Congress, both the House and the Senate, in October 1984, approved by voice vote a new cable bill after a series of compromises to resolve disputes over versions previously passed in each chamber. In November of the same year, Reagan signed the Cable Franchise Policy and the Communications Act of 1984, thus signaturing the trend toward deregulation in the communications industries that he and many of his supporters had been advocating for years.

The Senate followed the deregulation line as well. The bill it passed in 1985 (SB66) further deregulated cable television and, in effect, validated Reagan's deregulation policies. Following the trend toward deregulation, the cable television bills shifted power away from the public and cities and toward cable operations. Although the legislation allowed the cities to continue regulating cable fees, programming, and adherence to franchise agreements for two more years, the cities will have little effective power after that time to regulate rates and programming or to play a significant role in franchise renewal. Critics of the cable bill, however, described it as "an industry wish list in which Congress had given cable system owners a free hand to control every program and service they carry. Rather than establish a coherent national policy on cable television access, Congress succumbed to heavy lobbying by cable operators. The public, as usual, will be the loser" (Schmuckler and Dean 1985). Cathy Boggs, policy analyst for the Telecommunications Research and Action Center, claims that "[i]t was seen as a cities and industry battle, with consumers and third-party programmers needs not taken into account. The bill reflects the lack of input by citizens and cable users." Indeed, by now it is clear that one effect of the bill was to produce a dramatic rise in prices for cable subscription rates during the following years. For example, "Between 1986 and 1989...the monthly rate for basic cable service surged sevenfold in Denver; more than threefold in Louisville, Ky., and Shreveport, La.; and nearly threefold in Gary, Ind. On average, monthly rates for basic cable service have jumped 39 percent since 1986, according to the General Accounting Office" (*New York Times*, July 14, 1990, p. 18A).

Although the 1934 Communications Act mandated that the airwaves belonged to the public as a public good and that broadcasting was to serve the "public interest, convenience, and necessity," Reagan's deregulation policies subverted the notion that broadcasters were public trustees and, in effect, stipulated that the networks were simply businesses that would allegedly benefit from deregulation. The whole notion of broadcasters as public trustees who must serve the public interest was thrown out, along with accountability to the public. The result was a drastic reduction of news, documentary, and public affairs broadcasting. A Ralph Nader-affiliated public interest group, Essential Information, carried out a survey indicating that programming in 1988 carried 51 percent less local public affairs programming than that in 1979; that 15 percent of all stations carried no news at all; and that program-length commercials, prohibited until the 1980s, constituted about 2.6 percent of airtime (Donahue 1989).

Deregulation also led to dramatic conglomerate take-overs of radio stations and curtailment of radio news operations. Research in Florida revealed that there was an average 30 percent decrease in weekday public affairs programming and a 24 percent decrease in the number of locally prepared newscasts (Edward 1986). In practice, this major curtailment of local news deprived communities lacking a local daily paper of news concerning their area. Previously, radio was the voice of these communities, but with the take-over of local radio stations by corporate conglomerates, local news and public affairs programs were often cut back significantly and sometimes even eliminated completely.

Other studies indicated an increased amount of commercial interruptions, a dramatic deterioration of children's television, large cutbacks in the news and public affairs programming departments at the networks, and large increases of "reality programming" in which dramatic simulations of sensationalistic topics masqueraded as "news." Furthermore, …the era saw not only a sharp turn to the right in television entertainment but also saw television actively help to forge the conservative hegemony of the period.

The Reagan/Bush years also witnessed the merging of major networks with giant conglomerates. (In this connection, the Reagan administration's attack on antitrust laws was as significant as its moves toward deregulation [Gomery 1989].) In 1985 ABC merged with Capital Cities Communications and RCA merged with GE. The latter was a $6.3 billion dollar deal that reconstituted the mega-conglomerate as one of the biggest corporations in the world. CBS fought off a hostile take-over in 1985 and merged with the Tisch corporation in 1986, producing another mega-communications giant. And in March 1989 Time Inc. proposed a merger with Warner Communications Inc. that would form the largest media conglomerate in the world. The combined company, Time Warner Inc., has a total value of $18 billion and a projected yearly revenue of $10 billion from its magazine and book publishing empire, its film and television production companies, its cable systems and networks, and its subsidiary businesses. (See Bagdikian 1989 for documentation of the worldwide trends toward multinational communications giants being created by this "merger mania.")

Consequently, television networks are now entrenched as a central force within the transnational corporate power structure and have served capitalist interest even more directly during the 1980s. Indeed, during this era, television and popular culture have helped produce a climate in which a movie actor who had skillfully internalized the world views of Hollywood film and network television could be twice elected president of the United States. As television had shaped the world views of the U.S. electorate, Reagan and his audience shared the common terrain of television and film. Television helped promote Reaganism during much of the 1980s, but it also limited Reagan by exposing the excesses of his presidency during the Iran/Contra affair.

Reflecting on the historical and political trajectory of network television since its introduction at the end of World War II should give rise to some insights into the social and political functions of television in the United States. Television has become a central economic force that manages consumer demand and sells consumption as a way of life. The salient facts concerning network television are its blatant commercialization and its relentless promotion of the interests of capitalist corporations. Indeed, television has become a major political, social, and cultural force; its information and entertainment programming are saturated with ideologies, messages, and values that promote the interest of dominant elites and legitimate their rule. Thus, television plays a dual role; as both a business machine and an ideological apparatus, it has assumed crucial functions in the development of contemporary capitalism and the process of capital accumulation. Yet it also mediates (and is caught up in) class conflict and antagonisms as well as the contradictions between capitalism and democracy that have constituted the American experience.

During the late 1940s and 1950s television helped promote the consumer society and sold the conservative, centrist view of middle-class life that was to become the norm during the era of the consumer society. Its action/adventure series promoted anticommunism and the view that violence was justified in resolving conflict and in advancing the "good"—a view that replicated official U.S. ideology during the cold war and may have served as a defense of an increasingly interventionist foreign policy.

During the 1960s television promoted Kennedy's liberalism and then became a center of heated controversy when it began covering the turmoil and intense social conflict of the era. Television was thrust into the role of mediator of social conflict and crisis manager. At this time, the simplistic middle-class ideology that saturated its entertainment became increasingly laughable and even repugnant to many of the new generation who turned away from television and toward other cultural forms.

During the 1970s television took on a more contradictory role as it attempted to mediate the struggles between liberals and conservatives that continued throughout the decade. With the victory of Reagan and the New Right, television tentatively promoted a conservative hegemony. In a sense, then, television has been locked into a framework bound by liberalism and conservativism but has also taken on different ideological positions at various times. The ideological hegemony it has helped to create is constantly appropriating new contents—shifting and transmuting in response to changing social conditions, political struggles, and the vicissitudes of history itself.

NOTES

[1] This pattern was repeated later, when the networks and government delayed the introduction of cable and then pay television (Mosco 1979). By the mid-1980s dominant corporate interests, once again supported by the government, were able to hamper the development of satellite television by allowing HBO and other cable networks to scramble signals. In so doing, they precluded the development of a direct-broadcast system from satellites to home owners, instead forcing consumers to pay for each channel, ensuring corporate control of the satellite system, and maximizing exploitation of consumers.

[2] Television was at the center of the Left's cultural critique. Former SDS President Todd Gitlin (1972) wrote a provocative article entitled "Sixteen Notes on Television and the Movement," while more radical

and theoretically sophisticated works from Europe wee translated and disseminated during the 1970s. Discussed in these latter works were the theory of the cultural industries of Horkheimer and Adorno (1972 [orig. 1947]), the theory of radical intervention and reconstruction of the media of Brecht (1967) and Benjamin (1969), and the media theory of Enzensberger (1974), who attempted to synthesize these positions. A group of radical media critics based at Columbia University, collectively called The Network Project, published a series of pamphlets critizing corporate control over the broadcast media and the lack of adequate alternative broadcast media (see The Network Project's Notebooks 1-11 [1972-1975]).

[3] Efron's analysis was criticized by Steveneson et al. (1973). The conservative critique began in the 1950s, when William Buckley (1951) and others began attacking the "liberal bias" in the media—a trend that accelerated with the founding of the conservative *National Review*. In the 1960s conservatives became angry over television's depiction of Nixon and then of Goldwater in his 1964 race for the presidency. The "liberal bias" position became the official stance of the Nixon administration and was religiously taken up by conservative commentators of the era. Conservatives became increasingly hysterical in their attacks on television during the period in which Nixon was driven out of office and Jimmy Carter defeated Gerald Ford. For instance, Efron, Phillips, Buchanan, and others who were published in *TV Guide*, owned by Ronald Reagan's good friend Walter Annenberg, claimed that television was promoting the agenda of "new class" ultraliberals and the New Left. The deep conservative hatred for television was also apparent in remarks by Oliver North and Richard Secord during the Iran/Contra hearings and in Reagan's 1988 "Iron Triangle" speech in which he attacked the media, the government, and the intellectual elite.

[4] Reagan's deregulation policies provided an impetus for liberals to criticize conservative free-market ideology and to express outrage at the dismantling of decades of regulatory structures. See Brown (1981, 1982, 1984).

REFERENCES

Anderson, Kent (1978) *Television Fraud*. Westport, Conn.: Greenwood Press.

Bagdikian, Ben (1987) *The Media Monopoly*, 2nd ed. Boston: Beacon Press.

Barnouw, Erik (1975) *Tube of Plenty*. New York: Oxford University Press.

———. (1978) *The Sponser*. New York: Oxford University Press.

Best, Steven, and Douglas Kellner (1987) "(Re)Watching Television: Notes Toward a Political Criticism." *Diacritics* (Summer), pp. 97–113.

Boddy, William (1987) "Operation Frontal Lobes Versus the Living Room Toy: The Battle Over Programme Control in Early Television." *Media, Culture and Society*, Vol. 9, pp. 347–368.

Bogart, Leo (1956) *The Age of Television*. New York: Ungar.

Brown, Les (1971) *Television: The Business Behind the Box*. New York: Harcourt Brace Jovanovich.

Edwards, Mickie (1986) "FCC Changes Cut Public's Access to News." *Miami News* (September 2), p. 15A.

Ewen, Stuart (1976) *Captains of Consciousness*. New York: McGraw-Hill.

Faulk, John Henry (1964) *Fear on Trial*. New York: Simon and Schuster.

Friendly, Fred (1967) *Due to Circumstances Beyond Our Control*. New York: Random House.

Gitlin, Todd (1980) *The Whole World's Watching*. Berkeley: University of California Press.

Gomery, Douglas (1989) "The Reagan Record." *Screen* (Winter-Spring), pp. 92–99.

Halberstam, David (1979) *The Powers That Be*. New York: Knopf.

Hallin, Daniel (1985) "The American News Media: A Critical Theory Perspective." In Forester 1985.

Hodgson, Godfrey (1976) *America in Our Time*. New York: Random House.

Horowitz, Robert (1989) *The Irony of Regulatory Reform*. New York: Oxford University Press.

Kellner, Douglas (1979) "TV, Ideology, and Emancipatory Popular Culture." *Socialist Review*, Vol. 45, pp. 13–53.

———. (1990) "Postmodernism and Identity." In Jonathan Friedman and Scott Lash, eds., *Modernity and Identity*. London: Basil Blackwell.

Kellner, Douglas, and Michael Ryan (1988) *Camera Politica: The Politics and Ideology of Contemporary Hollywood Film*. Bloomington: Indiana University Press.

Lashner, Marilyn A. (1984) *The Chilling Effect in TV News*. New York: Praeger.

MacDonald, J. Fred (1990) *One Nation Under Television*. New York: Pantheon Books.

Mosco, Vincent (1979) *Broadcasting in the United States*. Norwood, N.J.: Ablex.

Powledge, Fred (1971) *The Engineering of Restraint*. Washington, D.C.: Public Affairs Press.

Rosenberg, Bernard, and David White (1957) *Mass Culture*. Glencoe, Ill.: Free Press.

Siepmann, Charles A. (1946) *Radio's Second Chance*. Boston: Little, Brown and Company.

Sklar, Holly, ed. (1980) *Trilateralism*. Boston: South End Press.

Swingewood, Alan (1977) *The Myth of Mass Culture*. London: Macmillan.

18 | Daze of Our Lives:
The Soap Opera as Feminine Text
Deborah D. Rogers

S oap operas are the only fiction on television, that most popular of mass cultural media, specifically created for women. This genre can therefore provide us with a valuable opportunity to examine the complexities of feminine cultural codes the more easily as they are writ large in feminine popular culture.... I argue that the fragmentation of soap narrative form reinforces the status quo with respect to the nature of sex roles and of interpersonal relationships in a patriarchal culture. Although the mixed messages of soap operas may allow scholars to construct subversive readings, actual viewers fail to respond in this manner....

Since they appeal to so many women, soap operas have naturally attracted the attention of feminists.... One major problem in dealing with soap operas is the historical denigration not only of television, but also of forms of feminine popular culture. Indeed, the very term "soap opera" has become so pejorative that it is applied condescendingly to a variety of genres and situations to indicate bathetic superficiality and kitsch. This is so much the case that one of the respondents to a recent survey I conducted attempted to justify her enthusiasm for *Days of Our Lives* by denial, insisting, "I really don't consider this show a soap opera."[1] Many feminists are similarly ambivalent about the genre: We desperately *want* to like a form that is popular with so many women but are repulsed by the conservative ideology. This ambivalence manifests itself when the same scholars who criticize soaps for promoting patriarchal stereotypes praise them for being "in the vanguard...of all popular narrative art" (Modelski, 1984, p. 13). In countering the denigration of feminine forms, however, we must be wary of going in the opposite direction, celebrating them just because they are female genres—especially when they might be potentially harmful....

The cumulative effect of introducing in a fragmented text messages that reconcile women to traditional feminine roles and relationships is to reinforce patriarchal cultural behavior in a way that is difficult to identify during a typical—that is, casual—viewing experience. Perhaps the easiest way to demonstrate this process is by isolating soap tenets, abstracting them from the disjointed context in which they are embedded.

If soaps are featuring more career women, their romances and families take precedence over jobs, which may simply provide sites for gossip and personal relationships. The same could, of course, be said of the portrayal of male professionals. (Victor Newman, CEO of the multi-million

From *Gender, Race and Class in Media*, edited by Gail Dines and Jean Humez. Reprinted by permission of Sage Publications, Inc.

dollar Newman business empire, recently announced, "Generally I don't discuss business matters over the phone"—and generally he does not, and neither does anyone else.) Although soap jobs are hardly portrayed realistically, male professionals are depicted as superior beings who often transcend specialties. The same male doctor who handles AIDS patients, trauma victims and neonatal care also delivers babies. Male corporate lawyers handle homicides. When we do see women engaged in professional activities, they are usually subordinate to men. For example, on one soap a young female lawyer is solely responsible for a murder case until shortly before it goes to trial, when she feels compelled to hire a more seasoned (male) co-counsel.

Women who devote too much time to jobs at the expense of their relationships and families are usually punished. For example, the son of one career woman who spent little time with him turns out to be a rapist. Another strong, aggressive, competent and well meaning career woman, *All My Children*'s Barbara Montgomery, glanced away while she was babysitting for a friend whose child was consequently hit by a car and killed. Is it pure coincidence that this accident occurred even as Barbara was composing an updated resume? Here we can ask of the soaps what Rosenblum (1986) asks concerning the "careerless career women" of other media who make a mess of their personal lives: "Is there a hidden message here, namely that women had better stay out of the corner office or they'll get what's coming to them?" [2]

All this should not be surprising since in the soap world pregnancy within a marriage has always been the supreme state and children the ultimate "achievement" for women (Rogers, 1988)....

Mother Moran, a character in a radio soap, early elaborated the soaps' endorsement of patriarchal marriage and parenting ideas: "A cake ta bake, and a floor ta sweep. And a tired little babe ta sing ta sleep. What does a woman want more than this—A home, a man, and a child ta kiss" (quoted in Allen, 1985, p. 194). Similarly, on contemporary soaps, if childbearing is necessary for completeness, having both a child (or children) and a "good marriage" constitutes true bliss. (This sentiment may present some problems for women in the audience who, while they have their husbands and their babies, are still miserable.) For example, on *The Young and the Restless* Nikki tells her husband, Victor, "I am so lucky. I have everything a woman could want.... I have a beautiful daughter and a loving husband, and a wonderful marriage...."

... In the fictionalized representation of motherhood on daytime soap operas, the myth of maternal omnipotence conceals the subordination and marginalization of women.

Employing the rhetoric of female apotheosis, soaps define having a baby as "the single most important thing in a woman's life." As one soap character remarked on the day she discovered she was pregnant: "This is what I've wanted all of my life, and now it's all coming true.... This is the most important day of my life." Male dominance is ideologically reinforced by the belief that women are gloriously suited for child care because they are by nature cheerfully domestic, nurturing and self-sacrificing. This "innate" selflessness, essential to fulfilling their roles as wives and mothers, allows for the happiness of women to reside in being constantly attentive to the needs of other family members. For example, after being told sarcastically "Lucky you—you get to listen to everybody's problems," one soap mother responded in all seriousness, "That's part of being a mother. You'll find out about it some day." Other soap mothers have recently made statements like "I'm here whenever you want to talk" and "I only want what's best for him" and have been asked such rhetorical questions as "what kind of mother are you, to put your feelings before the feelings of your child?"...

Without offspring, women are incomplete. Take, for example, the case of *General Hospital's* Bobbie Meyer, who acknowledges the terrible emptiness of her barren state: "I'm thinking about the babies that I'm never going to have.... I just feel empty... [My husband] is a man who *deserves* to have a child." Since failure to comply with moral norms is usually punished on soaps, and Bobbie is a former prostitute, her sterility may be no accident.

On another soap a new father extends this baby ethic to men:

[H]aving a child of my own was one dream I just could never turn loose of. And when [my wife] became pregnant, I thought...the gods are smiling on me. And there was nothing left for me to ask for because there was nothing else I wanted. Ya know, I was—complete.

If such sentiments of completeness imply more male sensitivity, they never seem to extend to beliefs about shared parenting. It is therefore likely that these expressions may simply be a variation of the traditional male fantasy of procreation as immortality. This myth is stressed repeatedly on the soaps, where men "deserve" to have children and, as one character puts it, "any man...would just go crazy to have a son that would carry on your name and follow in your footsteps."

...Although women are overtly respected for bearing children and for being mothers, ironically, men treat them like children. For example, one soap husband tells his wife she should go "sleepy-bye," while another calls his baby daughter his "other little good girl," equating his wife and his infant. On *One Life to Live*, at the very moment she tells her husband, Cord, the results of her pregnancy test, Tina is infantilized:

Tina: *Well, aren't you the least bit interested in whether you and I made a baby?—we didn't. What are you smiling for?*
Cord: *Well, to tell you the truth, I kinda' didn't think we did, but I tell ya—I think it's real cute you being so excited about it.*

Another soap wife gets worked up because she has tried to serve "the most important dinner of my life—and I blow it....I spill the appetizers....I burn the dinner.... Her husband predictably responds, "I think you're cute."

Although it is difficult to see how women can be taken seriously as long as they are being treated like children, their subordination may be obfuscated, as they collude in this pattern, decoding it in terms of "cuteness" and male protection. Soap women are repeatedly imaged as children: like children, they frequently "flood out," losing control in gales of laughter or in tears. They are playfully fed by men and are the objects of mock-assault games (of the food- or pillow-fight variety) that are usually reserved for children. Although on the soaps these "attacks" usually collapse into lovemaking, sociologist Erving Goffman (1979) has pointed out in another context that such "games" suggest what men could potentially do, should they ever get serious about it.

Unsurprisingly, on the soaps men give more orders and advice than women. This often extends to female topics (Turow, 1974). Women have no relief from this ubiquitous male instructors—a de facto role of authority that demands subordination even during commercial "breaks," when they are subject to predominantly male voice-overs.[3] Not only do male voiceovers dominate the commercials themselves, in what Robert Allen (1985, pp. 154–170) considers to be a vestige of the omnipotent male announcers of radio soaps, today's an-nouncers—all of whom are male—seem to control the networks' programming. They point to commercials, promise that the soap will resume after interruptions, signal the end of the commercial segments and urge us to continue watching or to tune in tomorrow. While all these little expressions of male dominance and female submission may seem insignificant in and of themselves, they add up to create an effect that is overwhelming. Unfortunately, typical viewers do not seem to regard this behavior as suspect....

Applying reader-response theories specifically to soaps, Jane Feuer (1984) finds *Dallas* and *Dynasty* "potentially progressive" because their serial form with its multiplicity of plot lines admits to unchallenged ideological stances: "Since no action is irreversible, every ideological position may be countered by its opposite" (p. 15). John Fiske (1987, pp. 179–197) argues that such a variety of reading positions allows for an interrogation of patriarchy. Ellen Seiter (1982) is hopeful about the progressive potential of the soaps for similar reasons:

> The importance of small discontinuous narrative units which are never organized by a single patriarchal discourse or main narrative line, which do not build towards an ending or closure of meaning, which in their very complexity cannot give a final ideological word on anything, makes soap opera uniquely "open" to feminist readings. (p. 4)

Although I find that the dominant ideology of the soap is patriarchal and that any challenges implicit in contradictory readings are regularly trounced on as patriarchy continually rears its ugly head, the potential that Feuer, Fiske and Seiter posit for constructing feminist interpreta-tions of soaps from their inconsistencies certainly exists. But let me raise a crucial question: What if viewers fail to identify the subtext?...For example, most of the respondents to my survey are partially attentive viewers likely to gossip about soap characters for fun but unlikely to read or analyze soap operas as texts, watching with the rapt attention of the critic....

When asked whether soaps contain messages, most of my respondents said yes and pointed to blatant messages about issues like sex and alcoholism. Many remarked that soaps teach about relationships and practical matters. One respondent, who credits the soaps with helping her get pregnant, first heard of ovulation prediction kits on *All My Children*, where they were mentioned obliquely—"It's blue. Let's get into bed"—when Brooke was trying to conceive. Some even mentioned world view and distinguished between the obvious and the subtle. For example, an especially thoughtful respondent wrote:

> A "say no to sex before you are ready" (married was the suggested time to be "ready") campaign was written into one story line in hopes of preventing teenage pregnancies and the spread of sexually transmitted diseases. I also see the message that being rich and powerful is not synonymous with happiness. There are both obvious and subliminal messages. The subliminal messages are male dominated and family oriented, but the blatant messages may have in some cases redeeming social value.

Now consider one of the messages widely praised in the press and by respondents as having this "redeeming social value." An astonishing number of respondents mentioned the rape story on *Santa Barbara*, recognizing the obvious moral: report rapes to the authorities. They were totally oblivious to the subtext which undercut this message, insidiously destroying the social value of this plot. On the soap Eden Castillo is raped. While this story line is developed, daily after the program we see the constructedness of the fiction, which is rare in the soap world (usually reserved for occasions like the death of an actor). At the end of each episode, Marcy Walker steps out of the frame, announcing that she is the actress who plays Eden and advising victims to report rapes. Perhaps part of the reason for this strategy is that the rape sequences are so gripping the audience needs to be reassured that this is a fiction. The ostensible reason—to promote the message—is, however, vitiated. In the story Eden does indeed report the rape and undergoes a pelvic examination. Our perspective is of her raised knees covered with a sheet. In the end we discover that the rapist is the very same gynecologist who performed the examination.

Unfortunately, the subtext here—the authorities we should report rapes to are equivalent to the rapists themselves—went unnoticed, even as it subverted the blatant message. This could create considerable anxiety for viewers who may find themselves unwilling to report male violence and brutality. The whole misogynistic plot may speak to women's fear of trusting male authority....

Another familiar soap plot with a subtext that often goes unrecognized concerns the reformed rake. In perhaps the most famous example, *General Hospital*'s Luke raped—and later married—Laura, who subsequently referred to the event as "the first time we made love," perpetuating the fiction that women really want to be raped. (*General Hospital* producer Gloria Monty described the rape as "choreographed seduction"; Dullea, 1986). Luke and Laura became a romantic super-couple, as Luke underwent a transformation, eventually becoming not only mayor of Port Charles, but heartthrob to countless teenage girls. As Janice Radway (1984) found in her study of romances, in a society where male violence against women is a constant, women may deal with their fears by decoding male brutality as love. Such a strategy, however, fails to remedy the problem. In a recent cartoon in *Soap Opera Digest,* a woman tells a man, as they watch a male image on the screen, "For your information, he's now a sweet, sensitive person. You're not supposed to remember he used a chain saw on his sixth wife in 1982" (July 11, 1989, p. 59). Such transformations of soap villains are obviously recognized. Unfortunately, however, most viewers are oblivious of the fact that reinterpreting soap rapes and brutality as romance denies—if not legitimates and glorifies—male violence by reading it as love. Instead of constructing subversive readings of soaps, many viewers simply fail to recognize latent discourses....

NOTES

[1] This ongoing survey, which is composed of seventy-one multiple-choice questions and eleven additional questions requiring a written response, has been completed by over 100 viewers.

[2] Rosenblum (1986) argues that if movies, theatre and prime time are now featuring women professionals, their careers are like "touches of trendy window dressing to spruce them up for the late 80s." From Glenn Close's Alex in *Fatal Attraction* to Heidi in Wendy Wasserstein's *Heidi Chronicles,* the portrayal of professional women of the eighties with their "toy careers" is far removed from the depiction of 1940s career women like Katharine Hepburn in *Woman of the Year* and Rosalind Russell in *His Girl Friday.* Although the message of such movies is that what a woman really needs is a good man, the women were consummate professionals.

[3] According to Butler and Paisley, 90% of voice-overs in television commercials are male (cited in Cantor & Pingree, 1983, p. 202).

REFERENCES

Allen, R. C. (1985). *Speaking of soap operas*. Chapel Hill: University of North Carolina Press.

Cantor, M., & Pingree, S. (1983). *The soap opera*. Beverly Hills, CA: Sage.

Dullea, G. (1986, July 11). As Gloria Monty's world turns. *The New York Times*, p. Y19.

Feuer, J. (1984). Melodrama, serial form, and television today. *Screen, 25*(1), 4–16.

Fiske, J. (1987). Television culture. New York: Methuen.

Goffman, E. (1979). *Gender advertisements*. New York: Harper.

Modleski, T. (1984). *Loving with a vengeance: Mass-produced fantasies for women*. New York: Methuen.

Radway, J. (1984). *Reading the romance*. Chapel Hill: University of North Carolina Press.

Rogers, D. D. (1988, September 23). The soaps: Do they support or undermine the family? *Christian Science Monitor*, p. 21.

Rosenblum, C. (1986, February 26). Drop-dead clothes make the working woman. *The New York Times*, p. 1H.

Seiter, E. (1982). Eco's TV guide—the soaps. *Tabloid, 5*.

Turow, J. (1974). Advising and ordering: Daytime, prime time. *Journal of Communication, 24*, 138–141.

19 | Daytime Inquiries
Elayne Rapping

"On Oprah today: Women who sleep with their sisters' husbands!"
"Donahue talks to women married to bisexuals!"
"Today—Sally Jessy Raphäel talks with black women who have bleached their hair blond!"

These are only three of my personal favorites of the past television season. Everyone's seen these promos and laughed at them. "What next?" we wonder to each other with raised eyebrows. And yet, these daytime talk shows are enormously popular and—more often than we like to admit—hard to stop watching once you start.

As with so much else about today's media, the knee-jerk response to this state of affairs is to hold one's nose, distance oneself from those who actually watch this stuff, and moan about the degradation and sleaze with which we're bombarded. But this doesn't tell us much about what's really going on in America—and television's role in it. Worse, it blinds us to what's actually interesting about these shows, what they tell us about the way television maneuvers discussions of controversial and contested topics.

It's no secret that television has *become* the public sphere for Americans, the one central source of information and public debate on matters of national import. Ninety-eight per cent of us live in homes in which the TV set is on, and therefore in one way or another being experienced and absorbed, an average of seven-and-a-half hours a day; 67 per cent of us get *all* our information from TV. This is not a matter of laziness, stupidity, or even the seductive power of the tube. It is a tragic fact that illiteracy—actual and functional—is rampant. It is difficult if not impossible for more and more of us to read, even when we try. Television, in such cases, is a necessity, even a godsend.

In the early 1950s, when TV emerged as the dominant cultural form, it presented to us a middle-aged, middle-class, white-male image of authority. Network prime time *was* TV, and what it gave us, from dusk to bedtime, was a series of white middle-class fathers—Walter Cronkites and Ward Cleavers—assuring us night after night that they knew best, that all was in good hands, that we needn't worry about the many scary, confusing changes wrought by postwar capitalism.

Network prime time still plays that role, or tries to. The fathers sometimes are black now, the authority occasionally shared with mothers, a voice from the ideological fringes invited

From *Gender, Race and Class in Media*, edited by Gail Dines and Jean Humez. Reprinted by permission of Sage Publications, Inc.

from time to time to be a "guest" (and behave appropriately or not get asked back). But prime time is still the home of Official, Authoritative Truth as presented by experts and institutional power brokers. Whatever oppositional voices are heard are always controlled by the Great White Fathers in charge, who get paid six- and seven-figure salaries for their trouble.

The money value of these guys to the media—the Koppels, the Jenningses—is so high because their jobs are increasingly difficult. TV, in a sense, was developed to put a reassuring, controlling facade over the structural fault lines of American life.

Ever since the 1960s, however, this has been harder and harder to manage. The breakdown of the family, the crises in education, religion, and the credibility of the state, the growing visibility and vocality of minority groups and ideas—all these took the country and media by storm. The most recent dramatic proof of the impact of social crises and the progressive movements they spawned is the amazing media hullabaloo over "multiculturalism" and "political correctness" on campuses. The Left, people of color, women, gays, and lesbians are apparently making the old white men extremely nervous.

At night, all of this tumult is being handled more or less as it has always been handled. Things seem to be under control. *MacNeil/Lehrer* and *Nightline* have their panels of experts, which now often include women, blacks, and—on rare occasions—"leftists" who really are leftists. But the structure of these shows makes it impossible seriously to challenge the host and, therefore, seriously to challenge TV hegemony.

A much juicier and, in many ways, more encouraging kind of ideological battle rages before 5 P.M., however. Daytime, women's time, has always been delegated to "domestic matters." If Father Knew Best in the evening, on the soaps the women always ruled the roost and what mattered were family and relationship issues—sex, adultery, childbirth, marriage, and the negotiating of the social and domestic end of life in a class- and race-divided society.

This is still true on daytime. In fact, the soaps are more likely to treat such social issues as rape, incest, aging, and interracial relationships with depth and seriousness than any prime-time series. In the sexual division of labor, these matters of emotional and relational caretaking and socialization have always been seen as "women's domain." And so it goes in TV Land. Daytime equals women equals "soft" issues. Prime time equals men and the "hard" stuff.

Except that what used to be soft isn't so soft anymore. The social movements of the 1960s—especially feminism, with its insistence that "the personal is political"—changed all that. Everyone who isn't brain-dead knows—and feels with great intensity—that all the old rules for living one's life are up for grabs. Relations between the sexes, the generations, the races, among co-workers, neighbors, family members—all of these are matters of confusion and anxiety.

What is the line, in the workplace, between being friendly and sexual harassment? How do we deal with our children, who are increasingly media-savvy and street-savvy and whose social environments are radically different from ours? What about sex education? Drugs? Condoms? Interracial dating? How do we handle social interactions with gay men and lesbians, now that more and more people are out and proud?

These are just the obvious issues. But they grow out of changes in the larger political and economic environments and they resonate into every crevice of our lives in far stranger, more confusing ways. In the breakdown of accepted views about things, and of the ties that kept us on the straight and narrow in spite of ourselves, unconventional behavior is both more common and more visible.

Women do, in fact, sleep with their sisters' husbands or find themselves married to bisexuals. Or perhaps they always did these things but never dreamed of discussing it, never saw it as a social topic, a matter for debate and disagreement about right and wrong. The same is true of something as seemingly trivial as one's choice of hair color. For black women, such tensions are rife, reflecting divisions brought on by political and cultural issues raised by black liberation movements.

The personal is ever more political, and inquiring minds not only want to know, they need to know. Or at least they need to talk and listen about these things. And so the coming of daytime talk shows, a financial gold mine for the media and a sensationalized, trivialized "political" event for confused and frightened people everywhere.

The political roots of this form are apparent. In structure, in process, and in subject matter, they take their cues from an important political institution of the 1960s: the women's consciousness-raising movement. In those small groups, through which hundreds of thousands of women passed during a brief, highly charged four- or five-year period starting in about 1968, we invented a democratic, emotionally safe way of bringing out in the open things we never before spoke of. We found we were not alone in our experiences and analyzed their meanings.

Of course, the purpose of these consciousness-raising groups was empowerment, political empowerment. The idea that the personal was political led to a strategy for social change. We hoped that when previously isolated and privatized women recognized common sources of our unhappiness in the larger political world, we could organize to change things.

The words "political" and "organize" do not, of course, occur on daytime TV. The primary goal of talk shows as a television form is to lure curious audiences and sell them products, not revolution. Thus the circus-like atmosphere and the need for bizarre and giggle-inducing topics and participants.

Still, the influence of feminism (and other social and cultural movements) is there, and the result is more interesting and contradictory because of it. Donahue, Oprah, and pals have reproduced, in a plasticized format, the experience of being in a group and sharing deeply personal and significant matters with others in the same boat. Consciousness-raising, unfortunately, is long gone. But from 9 to 11 A.M. and from 3 to 5 P.M. on weekdays, there is a reasonable facsimile thereof.

One reason these shows appeal is because, in line with the democratic thrust of 1960s feminism, their structure approaches the nonhierarchical. The host is still the star, of course. But in terms of authority, she or he is far from central. The physical set enforces this fact. Audiences and participants sit in a circular form and—this is the only TV format in which this happens—speak out, sometimes without being called on. They yell at each other and at the host, disagree with experts, and come to no authoritative conclusions. There is something exhilarating about watching people who are usually invisible—because of class, race, gender, status—having their say and, often, being wholly disrespectful to their "betters."

The discussion of black women with blond hair, for example, ignited a shouting match between those for whom such behavior meant a disavowal of one's "blackness," a desire to "be white," and those who insisted it was simply a matter of choosing how one wished to look, no different from the behavior of white women who dye their hair or tan their bodies. The audience, selected from the black community, took issue with everything that was said. Both participants and audience members attacked the "expert," a black writer committed to the natural—to BLACK IS BEAUTIFUL.

This is as close as television gets to open discourse on serious issues. But it is only possible because the issues discussed are not taken seriously by those in power. And that is why the sensationalism of these shows is double-edged. If they were more respectable in their style and choice of issues, they'd be reined in more. By allowing themselves to seem frivolous and trashy, they manage to carry on often-serious discussions without being cut off the air or cleaned up.

This may seem contradictory, but it's not. The truth is that the fringy, emotional matters brought up on Oprah, Donahue, Sally, and the others are almost always related in some way to deep cultural and structural problems in our society. Most of us, obviously, wouldn't go on these shows and spill our guts or open ourselves to others' judgments. But the people on these shows are an emotional vanguard, blowing the lid off the idea that America is anything like the place Ronald Reagan pretended to live in.

A typical recent program, for instance, featured a predictably weird ratings lure as topic: FAMILIES WHO DATE PRISONERS. It featured a family of sisters, and some other women, who sought out relationships with convicts. The chance for humor at guests' expense was not spared; Procter & Gamble doesn't care if people watch just to feel superior, as long as they watch. But in the course of the program, important political points came out.

Two issues were of particular interest. The "expert," a psychologist, pushed the proto-feminist line that these women had low self-esteem "women who love too much." Some admitted to it. Others, however, refused to accept that analysis, at least in their own cases. They stressed the prejudice against prisoners in society and went on to discuss the injustices of the criminal-justice system and to insist that their men were good people who had either made a mistake or were treated unfairly by the courts.

Our discomfort on watching what seems to be gross exhibitionism is understandable. We are taught, as children, that we don't air our dirty laundry in public. We learn to be hypocritical and evasive, to keep secret our own tragedies and sorrows, to feign shock when a public official is exposed for his or hers. It is not easy, even today, for most of us to reveal difficulties to neighbors. We are rightly self-protective. But the result of this sense of decorum is to isolate us, to keep us frightened and alone, unwilling to seek out help or share problems.

And so we sit at home, from Omaha to Orlando, and watch Oprah in order to get some sense of what it all means and how we might begin to handle it, whatever it is. These talk shows are safe. They let it all hang out. They don't judge anyone. They don't get shocked by anything. They admit they don't know what's right or wrong for anyone else. They are, for many people, a great relief.

Let me give one final example of how these shows operate as forums for opposing views. A recent segment of *Donahue* concerned women and eating disorders. This show was a gem. It seems Phil had not yet gotten the word, or understood it, that eating disorders are serious matters from which women suffer and die. Nor had he grasped that this is a feminist issue, the result of highly sexist stereotypes imposed upon women who want to succeed at work or love.

Donahue's approach was to make light of the topic. His guests were actresses from Henry Jaglom's film *Eating*, which concerns women, food, and body image, and he teased them about their own bouts with food compulsions. After all, they were all beautiful and thin; how bad could it be?

First the call-in audience, then the studio audience, and finally the actresses themselves, rebelled. Women called in to describe tearfully how they had been suicidal because of their weight. Others rebuked the host's frivolous attitude. Still others offered information about feminist counseling services and support groups. And finally, one by one, those downstage and then those on stage—the celebrities—rose to tell their stories of bulimia, anorexia, self-loathing, many with tears streaming down their faces.

Donahue was chastened and, I think, a bit scared. Ted Koppel would never have allowed such a thing to happen. He would have several doctors, sociologists, or whatever, almost all of them white and male, answer *his* questions about what medical and academic professionals know about eating disorders. There would be no audience participation and very little dialogue among guests. Certainly none would yell or cry or show any other "excessive" emotional involvement in the matter. If they did, Koppel, the smoothest of network journalists, would easily take control and redirect the show. For that matter, only when such a subject as eating disorders is deemed nationally important by the media gatekeepers will it ever get on *Nightline* anyway. Daytime is less cautious.

I have been stressing the positive side of these shows primarily because of their differences from their highbrow, primetime counterparts, which are far more reactionary in form and content. It is, in the grand scheme of things as they are, a good thing to have these arenas of ideological interaction and open-endedness.

But, finally, these shows are a dead end, and they're meant to be. They lead nowhere but to the drug store for more Excedrin. In fact, what's most infuriating about them is not that they are sleazy or in bad taste. It is that they work to co-opt and contain real political change. What talk shows have done is take the best insights and traditions of a more politicized time and declaw them. They are all talk and no action. Unless someone yells something from the floor (as a feminist did during the eating discussion), there will be no hint that there is a world of political action, or of politics at all.

This makes perfect sense. It is the nature of the mass media in a contradictory social environment to take progressive ideas, once they gain strength, and contain them in the large, immobilizing structure of the political status quo.

We are allowed to voice our woes. We are allowed to argue, cry, shout, whatever. We are even allowed to hear about approved services and institutions that might help with this or that specific bruise or wound. But we are not allowed to rock the political or economic boat of television by suggesting that things could be different. That would rightly upset the sponsors and network heads. Who would buy their Excedrin if the headaches of American life went away?

Ralph, Fred, Archie and Homer:
Why Television Keeps Recreating the
White Male Working-Class Buffoon

Richard Butsch

S trewn across our mass media are portrayals of class that justify class relations of modern
capitalism. Studies of 50 years of comic strips, radio serials, television drama, movies and
popular fiction reveal a very persistent pattern, an underrepresentation of working-class
occupations and an overrepresentation of professional and managerial occupations among
characters.[1]

My own studies of class in prime-time network television family series from 1946 to 1990
(Butsch, 1992; Butsch & Glennon, 1983; Glennon & Butsch, 1982) indicate that this pattern is
persistent over four decades of television, in 262 domestic situation comedies, such as *I Love
Lucy, The Brady Bunch, All in the Family* and *The Simpsons*. In only 11% of the series were heads
of house portrayed as working-class, that is, holding occupations as blue-collar, clerical or
unskilled or semiskilled service workers. Blue-collar families were most under represented:
only 4% (11 series) compared with 45% of American families in 1970.

Widespread affluence was exaggerated as well. More lucrative, glamorous or prestigious
professions predominated over more mundane ones: 9 doctors to one nurse, 19 lawyers to 2
accountants, 7 college professors to 2 school teachers. Working wives were almost exclusively
middle-class and in pursuit of a career. Working-class wives, such as in *Roseanne*, who have to
work to help support the family, were very rare. Particularly notable was the prevalence of
servants: one of every five series had a maid or butler.

The working class is not only underrepresented; the few men who are portrayed are
buffoons. They are dumb, immature, irresponsible or lacking in common sense. This is the
character of the husbands in almost every sitcom depicting a blue-collar (white) male head of
house, *The Honeymooners, The Flintstones, All in the Family* and *The Simpsons* being the most
famous examples. He is typically well-intentioned, even lovable, but no one to respect or
emulate. These men are played against more mature, sensible wives, such as Ralph against Alice
in *The Honeymooners*.

In most middle-class series, there is no buffoon. More typically, both parents are wise and
work cooperatively to raise their children in practically perfect families, as in *Father Knows Best,
The Brady Bunch* and the *Bill Cosby Show*. In the few middle-class series featuring a buffoon, it

From *Gender, Race and Class in Media*, edited by Gail Dines and Jean Humez. Reprinted by permission of
Sage Publications, Inc.

is the dizzy wife, such as Lucy. The professional/managerial husband is the sensible, mature partner. Inverting gender status in working-class but not middle-class sitcoms is a statement about class.

How Does It Happen?

The prevalence of such views of working-class men well illustrates ideological hegemony, the dominance of values in mainstream culture that justify and help to maintain the status quo. Blue-collar workers are portrayed as requiring supervision, and managers and professionals as intelligent and mature enough to provide it. But do viewers, and particularly the working class, accept these views? Only a handful of scattered, incidental observations (Blum, 1969; Gans, 1962; Jhally & Lewis, 1992; Vidmar & Rokeach, 1974) consider how people have responded to portrayals of class.

And why does television keep reproducing these caricatures? How does it happen? Seldom have studies of television industries pinpointed how specific content arises. Studies of production have not been linked to studies of content any more than audience studies have. What follows is an effort to make that link between existing production studies and persistent images of working-class men in domestic sitcoms. In the words of Connell (1977), "No evil-minded capitalistic plotters need be assumed because the production of ideology is seen as the more or less automatic outcome of the normal, regular processes by which commercial mass communications work in a capitalist system" (p. 195). The simple need to make a profit is a structural constraint that affects content (see also Ryan, 1992).

Let us then examine how the organization of the industry and television drama production may explain class content in television series. I will look at three levels of organization: (a) network domination of the industry, (b) the organization of decisions within the networks and on the production line, and (c) the work community and culture of the creative personnel. I will trace how these may explain the consistency and persistence of the portrayals, the underrepresentation of the working class and the choice of the particular stereotypes of working-class men in prime-time domestic sitcoms.

Network Domination and Persistent Images

For four decades ABC, CBS and NBC dominated the television industry. Of television audiences, 90% watched network programs. The networks accounted for over half of all television advertising revenues in the 1960s and 1970s and just under half by the late 1980s (Owen & Wildman, 1992). They therefore had the money and the audience to dominate as almost the sole buyers of drama programming from Hollywood producers and studios.[2]

During the 1980s, the three-network share of the audience dropped from about 90% to 60%; network share of television ad revenues declined from 60% to 47% (Owen & Wildman, 1992). These dramatic changes have generated many news stories of the demise of the big three. Cable networks and multistation owners (companies that own several local broadcast stations) began to challenge the dominance of the big three. They became alternative markets for producers as they began purchasing their own programs.

But program development is costly; even major Hollywood studios are unwilling to produce drama programs without subsidies from buyers. Nine networks have sufficient funds in the 1990s to qualify as buyers of drama programming: the four broadcast networks (ABC, CBS, Fox and NBC) and five cable networks (Disney, HBO, Showtime, TNT and USA Network) (Blumler & Spicer, 1990). But ABC, CBS and NBC still account for the development of the overwhelming majority of new drama series, the programming that presents the same characters week after week—and year after year in reruns.

This is the case in part because the broadcast networks still deliver by far the largest audiences. Even in 1993, the combined ratings for the 20 largest cable audiences would still only rank 48th in ratings for broadcast network shows. The highest rated cable network, USA Network, reached only 1.5% of the audience, compared to an average of 20% for ABC, NBC and CBS. The larger audiences translate into more dollars for program development.

And producers still prefer to work for the broadcast networks. When sold to broadcast networks, their work receives much broader exposure, which enhances their subsequent profits from syndication after the network run and increases the likelihood for future purchases and employment.

Moreover, whether or not dominance by the big three has slipped, many of the same factors that shaped their programming decisions shape the decisions of their competitors as well. The increased number of outlets has not resulted in the innovation and diversity in program development once expected. Jay Blumler and Carolyn Spicer (1990) interviewed over 150 industry personnel concerned with program decision making and found that the promise of more openness to innovation and creativity was short-lived. The cost of drama programming limits buyers to only a handful of large corporations and dictates that programs attract a large audience and avoid risk. How has this affected content?

Using their market power, the networks have maintained sweeping control over production decisions of even highly successful producers from initial idea for a new program to final film or tape (Bryant, 1969, pp. 624–626; Gitlin, 1983; Pekurny, 1977, 1982; Winick, 1961). Their first concern affecting program decisions is risk avoidance. Popular culture success is notoriously unpredictable, making decisions risky. The music recording industry spreads investment over many records so that any single decision is less significant (Peterson & Berger, 1971). Spreading risk is not a strategy available to networks (neither broadcast nor cable), because only a few programming decisions fill the prime-time hours that account for most income. Networks are constrained further from expanding the number of their decisions by their use of the series as the basic unit of programming. The series format increases ratings predictability from week to week. Each decision, then, represents a considerable financial risk, not simply in production costs but in advertising income. For example, ABC increased profits from $35 million in 1975 to $185 million in 1978 by raising its average prime-time ratings from 16.6 to 20.7 (personal communication, W. Behanna, A.C. Nielsen Company, June 1980).

Because programming decisions are risky and costly and network executives' careers rest on their ability to make the right decisions, they are constrained, in their own interest, to avoid innovation and novelty. They stick to tried-and-true formulas and to producers with a track record of success (Brown, 1971; Wakshlag & Adams, 1985). The result is a small, closed community of proven creative personnel (about 500 producers, writers, directors) closely tied to and dependent on the networks (Gitlin, 1983, pp. 115, 135; Pekurny, 1982; Tunstall & Walker, 1981, pp. 77–79). This proven talent then self-censor their work on the basis of a product image their previous experience tells them the networks will tolerate (Cantor, 1971; Pekurny, 1982; Ravage, 1978) creating an "imaginary feedback loop" (DiMaggio & Hirsch, 1976) between producers and network executives.

These same conditions continue to characterize program development in the late 1980s (Blumler & Spicer, 1990), as the new buyers of programming, cable networks, operate under the same constraints as broadcast networks.

To avoid risk, network executives have chosen programs that repeat the same images of class decade after decade. More diverse programming has appeared only in the early days of an industry when there were no past successes to copy—broadcast television in the early 1950s and cable in the early 1980s—or when declining ratings made it clear that past successes no longer worked (Blumler & Spicer, 1990; Turow, 1982b, p. 124). Dominick (1976) found that the lower the profits of the networks, the more variation in program types could be discerned from season to season and the less network schedules resembled each other. For example, in the late 1950s, ABC introduced hour-long western series to prime time to become competitive with NBC and CBS (Federal Communications Commission [FCC], Office of Network Study, 1965, pp. 373, 742). Again, in 1970, CBS purchased Norman Lear's then controversial *All in the Family* (other networks turned it down) to counteract a drift to an audience of undesirable demographics (rural and over 50). Acceptance by networks of innovative programs takes much longer than conventional programs and requires backing by the most successful producers (Turow, 1982b, p. 126). *Roseanne* was introduced by Carsey-Werner, producers of the top-rated *Cosby Show*, when ABC was trying to counter ratings losses (Reeves, 1990, 153–154). Hugh Wilson, the creator of *WKRP* and *Frank's Place*, described CBS in 1987 as desperate about slipping ratings; "Consequently they were the best people to work for from a creative standpoint" (Campbell & Reeves, 1990, p. 8).

Network Decision Making—Program Development

The second factor affecting network decisions on content is the need to produce programming suited to advertising. What the audience wants—or what network executives imagine they want—is secondary to ad revenue. (Subscriber-supported, pay cable networks, which do not sell advertising, also do not program weekly drama series.) In matters of content, networks avoid that which will offend or dissatisfy advertisers (Bryant, 1969). For example, ABC contracts with producers in 1977 stipulated that

> no program or pilot shall contain…anything…which does not conform with the then current business or advertising policies of any such sponsor; or which is detrimental to the good will or the products or services of…any such sponsor. (FCC, Network Inquiry, 1980, Appendix C, p. A-2)

Gary Marshall, producer of several highly successful series, stated that ABC rejected a story line for *Mork & Mindy*, the top rated show for 1978, in which Mork takes TV ads literally, buys everything and creates havoc. Despite the series' and Marshall's proven success, the network feared advertisers' reactions to such a story line.

An advertiser's preferred program is one that allows full use of the products being advertised. The program should be a complimentary context for the ad. In the 1950s, an ad agency, rejecting a play about working-class life, stated, "It is the general policy of advertisers to glamourize their products, the people who buy them, and the whole American social and economic scene" (Bamouw, 1970, p. 32). Advertisers in 1961 considered it "of key importance" to avoid, "irritating, controversial, depressive, or downbeat material" (FCC, Office of Network Study, 1965,

p. 373). This requires dramas built around affluent characters for whom consuming is not problematic. Thus affluent characters predominate, and occupational groups with higher levels of consumer expenditure are overrepresented.

A third factor in program decisions is whether it will attract the right audience. Network executives construct a product image of what they *imagine* the audience wants, which surprisingly is not based on actual research of audiences in their homes (Blumler & Spicer, 1990; Pekurny, 1982). For example, Michael Dann, a CBS executive was "concerned the public might not accept a program about a blue collar worker" when offered the pilot script for *Arnie* in 1969 (before *All in the Family* proved that wrong and after a decade in which the only working-class family appearing in prime time was *The Flintstones*). On the other hand, in 1979 an NBC executive expressed the concern that a couple in a pilot was too wealthy to appeal to most viewers (Turow, 1982b, p. 123).

With the exception of the few anecdotes I have mentioned, almost no research has examined program development or production decisions about class content of programs. My research found no significant differences between characters in sitcom pilots and series from 1973 to 1982, indicating that class biases in content begin very early in the decision-making process, when the first pilot episode is being developed (Butsch, 1984). I therefore conducted a mail survey of the producers, writers or directors of the pilots from 1973 to 1982. I specifically asked how the decisions were made about the occupation of the characters in their pilot. I was able to contact 40 persons concerning 50 pilots. I received responses from 6 persons concerning 12 pilots.

Although this represents only a small portion of the original sample, their responses are strikingly similar. Decisions on occupations of main characters were made by the creators and made early in program development, as part of the program idea. In no case did the occupation become a matter of debate or disagreement with the networks. Moreover, the choice of occupation was incidental to the situation or other aspect of the program idea; thus it was embedded in the creator's conception of the situation. For example, according to one writer, a character was conceived of as an architect "to take advantage of the Century City" location for shooting the series; the father in another pilot was cast as owner of a bakery after the decision was made to do a series about an extended Italian family; in another pilot, the creator thought the actor "looked like your average businessman." The particular occupations and even the classes are not necessitated by the situations that creators offered as explanations. But they do not seem to be hiding the truth; their responses were open and unguarded. It appears they did not think through themselves why this *particular* class or occupation; rather, the occupations seem to them an obvious derivative of the situation or location or actors they choose. The choice of class is thus diffuse, embedded in their culture.

This absence of any awareness of decisions about class is confirmed by Gitlin's (1983) interviews with industry personnel about social issues. Thus the process of class construction seems difficult to document given the unspoken guidelines, the indirect manner in which they suggest class and the absence of overt decisions about class. Class or occupation is not typically an issue for discussion, as are obscenity or race. To examine it further, we need to look at the organization of the production process and the culture of creative personnel.

The Hollywood Input—Program Production

Within the production process in Hollywood studios and associated organizations, and in the work culture of creative personnel, we find factors that contribute to the use of simple and repetitious stereotypes of working-class men.

An important factor in television drama production is the severe time constraints (Lynch, 1973; Ravage, 1978; Reeves, 1990, p. 150). The production schedule for series requires that a finished program be delivered to the networks each week. Even if the production company had the entire year over which to complete the season's 22 to 24 episodes, an episode would have to be produced on the average every 2 weeks, including script writing, casting, staging, filming and editing. This is achieved through an assembly line process in which several episodes are in various stages of production and being worked on by the same team of producer, writers, director and actors, simultaneously (Lynch, 1973; Ravage, 1978; Reeves, 1990).

Such a schedule puts great pressure on the production team to simplify the amount of work and decisions to be made as much as possible. The series format is advantageous for this reason: When the general story line and main characters are set, the script can be written following a simple formula. For situation comedy, even the sets and the cast do not change from episode to episode.

The time pressures contribute in several ways to the dependence on stereotypes for characterization. First, if ideas for new series are to be noticed, they cannot be "subtle ideas and feelings of depth" but, rather, "have to be attention getters—loud farts," in the words of a successful director (Ravage, 1978, p. 92).

Also, time pressure encourages type-casting to obtain casts quickly. The script is sent to a "breakdown" agency, which reads the script and extracts the description of characters that need to be cast. One such agency, employing six persons, provided this service for the majority of series (Turow, 1978). These brief character descriptions, not the script, are used by the casting agency to recommend actors, particularly for minor characters. Not surprisingly, the descriptions are highly stereotyped (Turow, 1980). Occupation—and by inference, class—was an important part of these descriptions, being identified for 84% of male characters.

Producers, casting directors and casting agencies freely admit the stereotyping but argue its necessity on the basis of time and dramatic constraints. Type-casting is much quicker. They also argue that to diverge from stereotypes would draw attention away from the action, the story line or other characters and destroy dramatic effect. Thus, unless the contradiction of the stereotype is the basic story idea—as in *Arnie, a* blue-collar worker suddenly appointed corporate executive—there is a very strong pressure, for purposes of dramatic effect, to reproduce existing stereotypes.

The time pressures also make it more likely that the creators will stick to what is familiar to them whenever possible. Two of the most frequent occupations of main characters in family series were in entertainment and writing, that is, modeled on the creators' own lives (Butsch & Glennon, 1983). The vast majority of producers grew up in middle-class homes, with little direct experience of working-class life (Cantor, 1971; Gitlin, 1983; Stein, 1979; Thompson & Burns, 1990). Moreover, the tight schedules and deadlines of series production leave no time for becoming familiar enough with a working-class lifestyle to be able to capture it realistically. Those who have done so—for example, Jackie Gleason, Norman Lear—had childhood memories of working-class neighborhoods to draw on.

Thus the time pressure encourages creative personnel to rely heavily on a shared and consistent product image—including diffuse and undifferentiated images of class—embedded in what Elliott (1972) called "the media culture." The small, closed community of those engaged in television production, including Hollywood creators and network executives (Blumler & Spicer, 1990; Gitlin, 1983; Stein, 1979; Tunstall & Walker, 1981; Turow, 1982a) shares a culture that includes certain conceptions of what life is like and what the audience finds interesting. According to Norman Lear, the production community draws its ideas from what filters into it from the mass media (Gitlin, 1983, p. 204). From this, they try to guess what "the public" would like and formulate images of class they think are compatible (Gitlin, 1983, pp. 225–226).

Although the consistency of image, the underrepresentation of the working class and the use of stereotypes can be explained by structural constraints, the particular stereotypes grow from a rather diffuse set of cultural images, constrained and framed by the structure of the industry. Any further specification will require a close examination of the construction of the consciousness of the program creators and network executives from, among other things, their exposure to the same media they create—a closed circle of cultural reproduction. Whether one can indeed extract the process of class image making from the totality of this occupational culture remains a challenge to researchers.

NOTES

[1] Subordinate statuses, generally, race and gender as well as class, are underrepresented and/or presented negatively.

[2] The sellers, the production companies, on the other hand, are not an oligopoly. Market concentration is low compared to the buyers (broadcast and cable networks); there was high turnover in the ranks of suppliers and great year-to-year fluctuation in market share; and collusion between suppliers is very difficult (FCC Network Inquiry Special Staff, 1980; Owen & Wildman, 1990).

REFERENCES

Barnouw, E. (1970). *The image empire: A history of broadcasting in the U.S. from 1953*. New York: Oxford University Press.

Blum, A. (1969). Lower class Negro television spectators. In A. Shostak (Ed.), *Blue collar world* (pp. 429–435). New York: Random House.

Blumler, J., & Spicer, C. (1990). Prospects for creativity in the new television marketplace. *Journal of Communication, 40*(4), 78–101.

Brown. L. (1971). *Television: The business behind the box*. New York: Harcourt, Brace Jovanovich.

Bryant, A. (1969). Historical and social aspects of concentration of program control in television. *Law and Contemporary Problems, 34*, 610-635.

Butsch, R. (1984, August). *Minorities from pilot to series: Network selection of character statuses and traits*. Paper presented at the annual meeting of Society for the Study of Social Problems, Washington, DC.

Butsch, R. (1992). Class and gender in four decades of television situation comedy. *Critical Studies in Mass Communication, 9*, 387–399.

Butsch, R., & Glennon, L. M. (1983). Social class: Frequency trends in domestic situation comedy, 1946–1978. *Journal of Broadcasting, 27*(l), 77–81.

Campbell, R., & Reeves, J. (1990). Television authors: The case of Hugh Wilson. In R. Thompson & G. Burns (Eds.), *Making television: Authorship and the production process* (pp. 3–18). New York: Praeger.

Cantor, M. (1971). *The Hollywood TV producer*. New York: Basic Books.

Connell, B. (1978). *Ruling class, ruling culture*. London: Cambridge University Press.

DiMaggio, P., & Hirsch, P. (1976). Production organization in the arts. *American Behavioral Scientist, 19*, 735–752.

Dominick, J. (1976, Winter). Trends in network prime time, 1953–1974. *Journal of Broadcasting, 26*, 70-80.

Elliott, P. (1972). *The making of a television series: A case study in the sociology of culture*. New York: Hastings.

Federal Communications Commission, Network Inquiry Special Staff. (1980). *Preliminary reports*. Washington, DC: Government Printing Office.

Federal Communications Commission, Office of Network Study. (1965). *Second interim report: Television network program procurement* (Part 2). Washington, DC: Government Printing Office.

Gans, H. (1962). *The urban villagers*. New York: Free Press.

Gitlin, T. (1983). *Inside prime time*. New York: Pantheon.

Glennon, L. M., & Butsch, R. (1982). The family as portrayed on television, 1946–78. In National Institute of Mental Health, *Television and social behavior: Ten Years of scientific progress and implications for the eighties* (Vol. 2, Technical Review, 264–271). Washington, DC: Government Printing Office.

Jhally, S., & Lewis, J. (1992). *Enlightened racism: The Cosby Show, Audiences and the myth of the American dream*. Boulder, CO: Westview.

Lynch, J. (1973). Seven days with *All in the Family*: A case study of the taped TV drama. *Journal of Broadcasting, 17*(3), 259–274.

Owen, B., & Wildman, S. (1992). *Video economics*. Cambridge, MA: Harvard University Press.

Pekurny, R. (1977). *Broadcast self-regulation: A participant observation study of NBCs broadcast standards department*. Unpublished doctoral dissertation, University of Minnesota.

Pekurny, R. (1982). Coping with television production. In J. S. Ettema & D. C. Whitney (Eds.), *Individuals in mass media organizations*. Beverly Hills, CA: Sage.

Peterson, R. A., & Berger, D. (1971). Entrepreneurship in organizations: Evidence from the popular music industry. *Administrative Science Quarterly, 16*, 97–107.

Ravage, J. (1978). *Television: The director's viewpoint*. New York: Praeger.

Reeves, J. (1990). Rewriting culture: A dialogic view of television authorship. In R. Thompson & G. Burns (Eds.), *Making television: Authorship and the production process* (pp. 147–160). New York: Praeger.

Ryan, B. (1992). *Making capital from culture: The corporate form of capitalist cultural production*. New York: Walter de Gruyter.

Stein, B. (1979). *The View from Sunset Boulevard*. New York: Basic Books.

Thompson, R., & Burns, G. (Eds.). (1990). *Making television: Authorship and the production process*. New York: Praeger.

Tunstall, J., & Walker, D. (1981). *Media made in California*. New York: Oxford University Press.

Turow, J. (1978). Casting for TV parts: The anatomy of social typing. *Journal of Communication, 28*(4), 18-24.

Turow, J. (1980). Occupation and personality in television dramas. *Communication Research, 7*(3), 295-318.

Turow, J. (1982a). Producing TV's world: How important is community? *Journal of Communication, 32*(2), 186–193.

Turow J. (1982b). Unconventional programs on commercial television. In J.S. Ettema & D. C. Whitney (Eds.), *Individuals in mass media organizations*. Beverly Hills, CA: Sage.

Vidmar, N., & Rokeach, M. (1974). Archie Bunker's bigotry: A study in selective perception and exposure. *Journal of Communication, 24*, 36–47.

Wakshlag, J., & Adams, W. J. (1985). Trends in program variety and prime time access rules. *Journal of Broadcasting and Electronic Media, 29*(1), 23–34.

Winick, C. (1961). Censor and sensibility: A content analysis of the television censor's comments. *Journal of Broadcasting, 5*(2), 117–135.

21 | Benson and the Jeffersons
Herman Gray

· · ·

"**B**enson" is based on the character of Benson Dubois played by Robert Guillaume. In the series "Soap" from which it was created, Guillaume was cast as a witty and quietly subversive butler to a wealthy white family. By the beginning of ABC's "Benson," Guillaume's character has changed jobs but not professions; he appears as the head housekeeper in the governor's mansion. Significantly, with the show's success and evolution, Benson was eventually promoted to State Budget Director and later elected Lt. Governor.

For a clearer understanding of "Webster," consider the origins of the series and especially Emanuel Lewis's involvement. Lewis established himself in the United States and Japan as the cute kid in a series of Burger King television commercials. His size and natural ability made him an instant success among advertisers and audiences. Lewis was spotted and subsequently approached by ABC executive Lew Erlicht, who not only liked what he saw in the commercial but wanted to build a series around the young Lewis. "Webster" was thus born from a network-initiated idea, which meant commitment, development, promotion and effective scheduling.

"The Jeffersons" is the longest-running prime-time series featuring a predominantly black cast. The programme is the brainchild of Norman Lear and Bud Yorkin, an imaginative team of writers and producers who pushed on the conventional boundaries of situation comedy with programmes like "Maude," "Mary Hartman, Mary Hartman," and "All in the Family." In its ten-year history the show has gone from a highly charged, often explicit platform for addressing social issues through a focus on family development to its most recent emphasis on neighbourhood, friendship and social responsibility.

Themes of success and affluence are central elements that define the television representations of the new black male as assimilated, Where these characters live, work and with whom they interact in the routine conduct of their lives therefore contains generalized visions and definitions of racial interaction in American society.

The emphasis on material affluence is certainly present in the social setting of "Webster," who lives with a white, upwardly mobile professional couple. The family's living environment and lifestyle explicitly convey upper-middle-class status. They live in an apartment (later a large

Victorian house) liberally decorated with expensive furniture and art objects. Webster's room contains a full collection of toys and emblems of a child's space (games, stuffed animals, books and posters).

Of all the shows, the most explicit celebration of success and affluence is "The Jeffersons." Each programme begins with a long shot of a moving van transporting the upwardly mobile family to their "deluxe apartment in the sky." The show's popular theme song simultaneously reinforces the message of social mobility with the lyric "well, we're moving on up..." The Jeffersons' apartment is decorated with plants, artwork, modern furniture and other symbols of material affluence. Most of the activity is set in their apartment, though action sometimes occurs in other locations including George's laundry or public settings like a nightclub or bar, where the settings establish the values of affluence and link them to the more general idea of assimilation. Black male characters are exceptionally competent, articulate, attractive and agreeable. With the exception of the Jefferson family, they exemplify the notion of fitting in and the ideal of invisibility or colourblindness.

When combined with the circumstances of middle-class affluence, these characteristics are presented in ways that soften elements of the character's personality, history and world-view which define them as black Americans living in a multiracial society. Indeed, there is little about these characters and the shows to suggest the presence of a multiracial society. What remains (and the reasons the shows are successful) are preferred and acceptable white, middle-class definitions of racial interactions

Consider Guillaume's Benson for instance. He is an attractive well-dressed gentleman who is the quintessential (black) middle-class professional. He is not only competent, but always cool under pressure. Bordering on the "super-Black," the ideology of competence and invisibility is reinforced in Benson's relationship with the other characters on the show.

James Noble is cast as Benson's boss: an absent-minded and mildly competent governor. Occasionally assertive, Noble's character is forgetful, uncertain and usually on the fringes of activity. Rene Auberjonois is cast as Clayton, the governor's administrative assistant and Benson's chief rival. He offers a striking contrast to Benson's studied rationality. Arrogant and abrasive, Clayton is an opportunist while Benson is the patient and loyal organization man who works his way slowly through the system.

Inge Swenson's Krauss is, like Benson, a consummate professional. By wearing her ethnicity on her sleeve (in the form of a thick European accent), Krauss and Benson symbolically reinforce the ideology of assimilation—in this case women, ethnic groups and racial groups. The bond between Krauss and Benson is characterized by a potential but forbidden sexual attraction. Their relationship is rooted in mutual respect and co-operation, though it is often marked by argument and a ritual trade of insults.

The interaction between Benson, Krauss, Clayton and the governor showcase Benson, highlighting his competence, compassion and intellect. He can be counted on to put down Clayton's arrogance, comfort the governor's daughter, collaborate with Krauss and provide solutions to the governor's political problems. That the entire cast is white simply adds to the ideological significance of Benson's presence.

At twelve Emanuel Lewis is unusually small (forty inches). However, Lewis's size quickly became one of the unique features of the show. By casting Alex Karras and Susan Clark in the role of Webster's parents, the writers emphasized Lewis's size. Karras is cast as a former professional football player who works as a sports announcer. Clark is the self-employed and assertive mother who relies on her confidence to overcome insecurities about parenting.

Against the backdrop of Karras and Clark, Lewis is especially cute and lovable. He is also intelligent, witty and fits into the household with little difficulty. As we'll see, problems of membership that do emerge are presented as routine issues of growing up rather than issues of racial difference, cultural background or social class. Aside from Webster, his uncle, and a best friend, the remainder of the cast is white.

Where Webster and Benson emphasize racial invisibility, the Jeffersons seem to move in the opposite direction. The two leading cast members and members of the supporting ensemble are black. None the less, the theme of fitting in and assimilation remains. These characters are simply more explicit and tenacious in their attempts to remain black and upwardly mobile. In the face of assimilationist ideals this explicitness and tenacity seem contradictory.

"The Jeffersons" central characters are George played by Sherman Hemsley, his wife Louise played by Isabell Sanford, and their housekeeper Florence played by Maria Gibbs. Frank Cover and Roxy Roker are cast as the married interracial couple, the Jeffersons' neighbours and closest friends.

Hemsley's robust George is a successful dry-cleaning entrepreneur who worked his way up from a small Harlem cleaner to ownership of a profitable chain of dry-cleaners. Arrogant and abrasive, George has evolved from the caricature of an angry black nationalist to a model citizen whose tolerance of racial difference (white folk) has increased considerably. For instance, George has softened (matured) in his relationship with his neighbour Willis; a relationship previously built on antagonism and contempt has evolved into an intimate friendship based on understanding and respect.

George disagrees with Louise in most things. Like "Kingfish" from another era, George is often wrong, left out or the object of someone's jokes. Also in the tradition of "Kingfish," George maintains a ritualized trade of insults with the female characters. When not exchanging insults or talking his way out of a difficult situation, George is passive, sometimes to the point of invisibility. Though a competent and successful businessman, George is often incompetent in his personal life. Ironically, it is with George's personal life that we are the most familiar. The idea of competence remains, but it, along with George's work life, recedes.

If George prances through each episode pouting, insulting and demanding, Louise moves with plan and control. Always smartly dressed, she projects the image of competence and control. She spends her leisure time on vacations, shopping and as a volunteer for various community groups. As the responsible member of the family, Louise spends a lot of time getting and keeping George out of trouble. For Louise, competence in personal life abounds.

Aside from George, the show's main source of humour is Florence. As the smart domestic, she provides the context for Louise's (and Helen's) middle-class elegance. In manner and dress, Florence is direct and simple. As the chief foil (and disciplinarian) for George, much of the series displays Florence's common sense and ability to trade insults with George.

The remaining cast includes Helen and Tom Willis, the interracial couple. The writers use Helen to instruct Tom in the subtleties of black culture. Helen is also the target of George's insults and like Florence spars with him regularly. Though other white characters are in the cast, Tom is portrayed as the native and misplaced token white. This role defines Tom's relationship with Helen, George and Louise, and it reduces him to a spectator rather than a major participant.

Situation comedies featuring black males routinely address issues such as life in the workplace, social relationships and family life. Though they sometimes treat explicit racial themes, the dominant representations of race relations reinforce the values of co-operation and harmony, individual adjustment and social management. Significantly, these values are played out in the social context of mobility, affluence and success.

On reflection, none of this is surprising, since this general framework defines much of the genre of situation comedy in American commercial television. However, the treatment of race (and other expressions of social difference) reveals the pervasiveness of assimilationist ideology in American society. The vitality of this ideological viewpoint remains because these programmes appear to invite and confirm the view of the United States as an open multiracial social order, one where racial, ethnic and cultural differences are encouraged. I want next to show how, in the world of television, this apparently open and multiracial society operates within a carefully defined social, cultural and economic assumption that keeps alive the assimilationist assumptions of racial interaction.

At the most explicit level "Benson" revolves around the theme of interpersonal harmony and co-operation in the workplace. Benson's character and the settings in which he operates suggest in clear terms that he has arrived—he is successful, competent, professional, attractive and middle class. His class position (as opposed to his racial position) is the predominant social experience that shapes his outlook. The subjects of race and racial interaction are rarely treated explicitly. Indeed, what seems to make Benson such a popular character is his apparent invisibility (as a black man). His unique experience, interests and attitudes, to the extent that they are shaped by his racial and cultural circumstances, are never explicitly addressed. More than anything else Benson is a member of the "family"; he is the centre that keeps it all together.

Benson is the culmination of all of the servant and helping roles that blacks have historically played in television and the movies. There is one major qualification: Benson is uniquely modern—sophisticated, competent and arrogant when necessary. He openly maintains his integrity and his personal pride. He counsels members of the staff (the workplace family) through social and personal crises. And he does so with the sarcasm established by Hattie McDaniel and Eddie Anderson from earlier periods. Because he is so modern and middle class, this moment of potential defiance remains muted, and Benson emerges as the perfect American vision of racial assimilation.

The episode of 2 February 1984 illustrates this vision of assimilation. Here Benson not only lives up to the role of the reliable advisor/servant, but he also "refuses" to be used by those around him. The major action revolves around the governor and the staff's misuse of Benson's friendship, a situation which occurs because the governor puts Benson in the position of having to chose between friendship and responsibility. Benson is selected to judge a beauty contest where one of the contestants is the daughter of an old friend of the governor.

In the show's final segment an angry Benson scolds the governor for violating their friendship and putting him in a compromising position. With Benson's integrity intact and the friendship secured, the mansion family return to a conventional state of balance and happiness. What is significant about this narrative is that Benson represents the moral conscience of the family. He reaffirms the ideals of responsibility, fairness and loyalty by judging the contest without yielding to pressure.

The one episode of "Benson" that came close to explicitly addressing public social issues focused on the demolition of a hotel for the indigent and homeless. This programme is significant because it shows the limits of Benson's public power as a government official. The opening segment involved an excited Krauss persuading a reluctant Benson to get involved in the issue. The remainder of the segment focused on Benson and Krauss's exploration of a series of strategies to save the hotel including a meeting between Benson and the developer responsible for razing the hotel. As a last resort, Krauss and a reluctant Benson occupy and subsequently refuse to vacate the hotel. In the process of trying to remove Benson and Krauss from the property, the developer learns about the historical significance of the hotel and agrees not to destroy the building.

This episode is particularly curious because it was one of the few to make explicit reference to Benson's social position and potential influence as a public official. Also, with the episode's resolution there was no return to the theme of the homeless people who initially occupied the property. The developer's change of heart (on the basis of personal interests) rather than Benson's influence or persuasion lead to the survival of the hotel. Through it all Benson survives and in the process helps a family member.

For a contrast to Benson's racial invisibility, we turn to George Jefferson. George's style is quite a bit more explicit and enthusiastic than Benson's; George celebrates the virtues of status, affluence and social mobility. Although the Jeffersons share with Benson the affirmation of mobility and affluence, they offer a different way of experiencing these circumstances. The explicit message is that blacks also value and live middle-class lives. Therefore, black and white experiences of social life in the middle class are not all that different. In this context "The Jeffersons" is the least bashful about explicitly addressing racial situations and issues.

The episode of 18 March 1984 illustrates the programme's treatment of an explicit racial theme. This episode examined the costs, responsibilities and conflicts that come with social mobility and affluence. The show presented these complex issues by contrasting the material and social excesses of the black middle class against the common sense, struggle and restraint of the black working class.

In the first segment we learn of George and Louise's selection for a magazine feature about them as outstanding community members. Preparation for the interview and photo session provides the context in which the action develops. The Jeffersons are not immediately drawn to media exaggerations (of themselves), but they are flattered by all the attention. George is especially excited by the attention, but he is also the most ambivalent about the situation. Some of George's ambivalence stems from his large appetite for power and from his simultaneous desire to remain close to those friends and employees who helped him up the ladder to success. This ambivalence is the source of the episode's major tension. It becomes explicit when George tries to include in the feature a photo with his friends and employees.

The image of George's friends and his roots is symbolized in the character of Otis, an older black man who operates a shoeshine stand outside the laundry. Like Florence, Otis is dignified, confident and hard-working. Predictably, the episode's major tension is heightened by the magazine's refusal to include George's friends because they do not represent the image of blacks that they (the magazine) wish to project. The second segment is devoted almost exclusively to George's attempt to manage this major conflict. With his mood alternating between anger and sadness, we follow George through confrontations with the magazine writer, family and friends, and Otis.

Finally, apologetic and hurt, George explains to Otis that the magazine will not publish a photo of them together. Otis responds by turning the issue of black images back on George;

"Who's the stereotype, you or me?" Otis asks. This unexpected twist forces George to examine more closely his own circumstance and values. For Otis, the magazine represents a case of "...niggers stereotyping niggers." Otis reminds George that for all his success he does little more than take in laundry.

With the confrontation into its downward phase, Otis advises George to make his own image and follow that. In a final assimilationist plea for racial unity, Otis calls for every one, rich and poor, to work together. At this exchange, the episode's closing scene moves back to the Jeffersons' apartment where Louise, Tom, Helen and the magazine writer wait for George's return. The closing shot returns to the shoeshine stand where, dressed in a three-piece suit, George is shown giving Otis a shoeshine.

Several features of this episode require comment. That the issue of differences within the black community is acknowledged is admirable. This is one of the few episodes that treated George Jefferson as a complex and multi-dimensional adult character. We see George do more than insult, hoard and pout. His responses cover a range of emotions and intellectual responses. For a brief moment viewers are capable of respecting and empathizing with George as a black man. Less laudable is the exaggerated way in which these complex and long-standing issues were framed. The representation of the black middle class is never developed and at best provides a backdrop against which to focus on George's individual plight. (Why don't other characters have problems with the magazine?) The episode never suggests that other, more pervasive, political and economic factors may influence both George's and Otis's circumstances. The issues are all posed and explored at the level of individuals.

Just as the adult-focused programmes treat the question of race and racial interaction on a continuum from invisibility to visibility, so too do the programmes featuring black male children. "Webster" and "Different Strokes" settle closer to the model of racial invisibility than visibility in both setting and thematic content. The pattern that emerges from these shows suggests that race and racial issues exist primarily as a context in which other issues are developed. Race itself is not a central issue....

These programmes are predominantly assimilationist in tone and texture. They continually reinforce the importance of success, professionalism, competence and individualism. They represent predominantly white circumstances with upper-middle-class orientations and situations. Attractive black characters operate in largely white worlds where references to blacks and racial interactions are seldom addressed. Aside from "The Jeffersons," few of the episodes of any show made any explicit reference to blacks in different class situations or circumstances.

At the same time the contexts, mannerisms and behaviours of these individual black characters promise to address the unique features of the black experience in America. Occasionally the audience is taken inside black cultural and social institutions and situations. In some cases viewers learn about significant black heroes. With closer examination, however, the themes, settings and characters that anchor these shows stop short of the promise. The symbols and images are familiar enough to attract attention but too superficial to illuminate or explore complex issues of racial interaction or the black experience. Audiences learn little about the meanings, definitions and perspectives of these characters. We learn little about what they believe in, are committed to, and how their experiences as black Americans shape their outlook.

The issue of cross-racial adoption, for example, is presented on "Webster" as an individual family matter rather than a public or social issue. This view stresses racial invisibility and individual adaptation. By confining the issue to personality and to specific family circumstance, little attention to more social interpretations and consequences is necessary. We also see Webster manage the routine problems—responsibility, trust, friendship, death—of growing up in an upper-middle-class home, a home where nothing of the anxiety or confusion of cultural isolation, alienation, identification which face black children in similar situations is present. This happy and adjusted child, moreover, lives in a world where the primary adult figures are white. This interaction of character and setting suggests rather explicitly that white adults offer security, protection, direction and discipline. This representation does not imply that black adults do not provide these things. Black adults were present. But presentations of black adults focused on a close but transient relationship and Webster's momentary infatuation with his teacher.

The case where racial issues were explicitly addressed, "The Jeffersons" was framed as an individual moral conflict between George and Otis. Other situations where racial themes emerged provided comic relief or distractions from more normal circumstances. A predominant theme in all of these shows is that these are normal (assimilated) individuals who happen to be black. They encounter situations and issues that transcend race. It matters little what the intensity or circumstance of the issue—saving a hotel, launching a career, romantic mischief, cross-racial adoption or bed-wetting —they are all managed and conquered with equal vigour.

The television world of situation comedy is one where race and racial issues are simply points of personal difference and not sites of social, cultural and political organization and interaction. The complexity of racial identity as a basis of social interaction and struggles in modern societies like the United States is simplified and rendered invisible. In those cases where racial interaction is examined, it is defined within the framework of assimilationist assumptions that emphasize racial harmony and an open society.

In section I, I offered a production explanation for the emergence and persistence of black images in commercial television. To this production explanation I want to add a social and political account that stresses the social and legal context in which images of black males operate.

Television images of racial assimilation and individualism appear at a time when public debate in the United States over racial inequality has receded from the national agenda. A significant expression of this shift is the subtle but far-reaching changes in the legal and social definition of racial inequality and discrimination. In major action by the executive, judicial and legislative branches of the United States federal government, the social definition and legal basis for racial discrimination has shifted from the group to the individual. This redefinition has made it legally more difficult for racial minorities to challenge the basis for legal definitions of discrimination; it has also made it more difficult for those who suffer most from the group basis of racial discrimination to obtain legal redress,

These television images and presentations, then, must be considered against the present legal and social circumstances of racial interaction in the United States. Against the upper-middle-class conception of "Benson," "The Jeffersons" and "Webster," black unemployment remains epidemic, especially among black teenagers. Black infants continue to die at a rate greater than white infants, and blacks continue to live in poor and segregated housing at a rate far greater than whites (Mathey and Johnson, 1983). Black income continues to lag behind white income by two to one. These patterns are rooted in group and not individual circumstance.

Television's idealization of racial harmony, affluence and individual mobility is simply not within the reach of millions of black Americans. To the extent that different realities and experiences are not mentioned or addressed in television programmes featuring blacks, the effect is to isolate and render invisible social and cultural experiences of poor and working-class black Americans. In those instances where racial issues are addressed, they are often presented as expressions of deviance and function to confirm existing definition of normal middle-class experience. With their emphasis on individualism and individual achievement in a supposedly colourblind society, the present generation of black male images offers popular legitimation for a narrow and conservative definition of race relations and racial interaction. The major impact of this narrow conception is to deflect attention from the persistence of racism, inequality and differential power.

PART VII

Exercises

NAME _____

During the next week, watch at least six network television programs—two comedies, two dramas, and either two soap operas or two talk shows. Complete the worksheet below.

Program Title _____

Program Genre _____ Station, Day, Date, Time_____

Setting and context _____

Lead character types _____

Supporting character types _____

Episode story line _____

Themes of program and episode _____

Social Communication (Values and Norms) of program:

Program Title _____

Program Genre _____ Station, Day, Date, Time _____

Setting and context _____

Lead character types _____

Supporting character types _____

Episode story line _____

Themes of program and episode _____

Social Communication (Values and Norms) of program:

Program Title _____

Program Genre _____ Station, Day, Date, Time _____

Setting and context _____

Lead character types _____

Supporting character types _____

Episode story line _____

Themes of program and episode _____

Social Communication (Values and Norms) of program:

Program Title _____

Program Genre _____ Station, Day, Date, Time _____

Setting and context _____

Lead character types _____

Supporting character types _____

Episode story line _____

Themes of program and episode _____

Social Communication (Values and Norms) of program:

Program Title _____

Program Genre _____ Station, Day, Date, Time _____

Setting and context _____

Lead character types _____

Supporting character types _____

Episode story line _____

Themes of program and episode _____

Social Communication (Values and Norms) of program:

Program Title _____

Program Genre _____ Station, Day, Date, Time _____

Setting and context _____

Lead character types _____

Supporting character types _____

Episode story line _____

Themes of program and episode _____

Social Communication (Values and Norms) of program:

List any themes, values, or norms which appear in several programs and genres:

Can you discern any thematic unity in contemporary television?

PART VIII | Political Economy of Communication

All communication studies must answer some fundamental questions: what are we studying? How and why do we study it? This text began with a clear rationale for why we should study communication. Communication is essential for community and democracy. Selected readings have also argued that communication is an essential component of all human practice—from how we materially produce our way of life, to how we understand that process, and how we treat each other.

This section introduces an important critical perspective for understanding communication in society: political economy. Political economy sees a connection between the material production of goods and services and the symbolic production of how we talk about that "stuff" and what it means to us. The interaction between the material, physical conditions of life and the symbolic, representational conditions of life are understood to mutually determine our social reality. A political economy of communication then investigates the complex connections between the form and content of symbols and representations and the material conditions and social relationships which produce those symbols.

In his definitive critical overview of political economy of communication, Vincent Mosco (1996) defines political economy as "the study of the social relations, particularly the power relations, that mutually constitute the production, distribution, and consumption of resources" (25).

Consider the "political economy of milk," for example. Milk comes from cows, the primary resource. Farmers own and raise cows. But the process of producing, distributing, and consuming milk involves myriad resources and social relations. The farmer has loans from the bank, which is regulated by state and federal laws, which are written by appointed and elected officials—all of whom have multiple social relations with bankers, farmers, and others. The farmer uses feed and fertilizer resources and thus has relations with grain producers and chemical manufacturers, all of whom have relations with government agencies, researchers, marketing firms, transportation companies (which are regulated by Interstate Commerce and state and federal transportation laws). The farmer may belong to a co-op, which establishes production, price, and regulations for its members—do we use the BgH growth hormone or go organic?. The co-op sells its milk to distributors who process, package, and wholesale the milk to grocers and supermarkets. The processors are regulated by the FDA and have agreements with advertisers, marketing firms, and industry councils like the National Dairy Council. Supermarkets enter into relations with customers, citizen action groups, the FDA, advertisers, the media, and state and federal inspectors. All of these operations have their own political economy construction, production, distribution and consumption which include social relations among citizen-workers—farmworkers, truckdrivers, machine operators, retail clerks,

231

typists...Moreover, none of these relations are distinct from the others. And, more importantly, all communicate via recognizable symbols and ideologies. Nostalgia for the family farm, children's toy farm animals, and media images of healthy living with fresh milk combine with an ideology of hard work, fair trade, cleanliness, and convenience to give meaning to these practices. Of course, this quick description of milk only marks some ingredients in its political economy which must be placed in the context of larger socio-economic and symbolic relations.

Likewise, the political economy of communication is complex, even more so, because of the variety of media products and the importance of communication to the functioning of everyday life. We may live a day without milk, but not without communication. No group of readings or even an entire text could fully explain the production, distribution, and consumption of "communication." Here we introduce some concepts and categories and provide some examples.

Communication resources include: newspapers, books, videos, films, television programs and audiences. But the political economy of media in the United States encompasses much more than the material production of goods and services as commodities. As in milk production, the processes and practices in the production of communication include multiple social relations. Social relations of communication include at least: ownership and control of media institutions, government regulations, production practices, and corresponding distribution and consumption circuits. The political economy of communication has a further dimension: Communication and culture are important as decisive material practices which make up our way of life—our personal relations, our rituals, our knowledge and beliefs, our values. Thus, the social relations of capitalism and its media reflect and reinforce a way of life expressed through a dominant ethos: This ethos is often expressed as "The American Dream" with its promotion of individualism, hard work, and white-Christian-middle-class values, including consumerism. Dominant communication practices, including mass media practices, can only be understood in a social totality which includes this dominant ethos and its practices as well as ongoing contradictions and challenges—which is why readings on the political economy of the media are included in this text on communication practices.

According to Mosco, contemporary political economy perspectives have several characteristics, including 1) attention to social change; 2) awareness of the social totality; 3) concern for social values; and 4) commitment to social practice. Political economy views society as dynamic, full of contradictions, multiple tendencies, and conflicting impulses. While recognizing the imposing power to Time-Warner, Sony, Disney, and other media giants, political economists do not view existing communication practices and social relations as invariant but as being "constantly constituted" through battles and negotiations among social groups (Connell, 44). Conditions of life are historically contingent and always subject to social change. Moreover, communication studies informed by political economy do not look at communication or media in isolation from the larger world because communication exists in a web of political, economic, and cultural practices. How we work, how we play, how we decide what to make, do, or value, how we live are all intertwined in the complex fabric of society. This attention to the social totality concretizes Dewey's concern for self in community and communication. A third characteristic of political economy is a concern for social values, specifically a preference for the social and collective good. In the words of Adam Smith, a founding economic theorist, the harmony of humanity and perfection of human nature compels us "to feel much for others, and little for ourselves, to restrain our selfish, and to indulge our benevolent affections" (in Mosco 35). In terms of issues raised in this text, political economists are concerned with democracy, equality, participation, decision-making and community. Finally, a commitment to social change in a social totality with clear social values directs political economy to conscious social practice. When pressed, humans can provide reasons for what we do, how we act. On the other hand, we generally do only what we already know. Of course, acting from an awareness of the relationship between knowledge and action permits us to make more conscious choices about ourselves and the world. Social practice based on this dual process—taking action based on existing knowledge and constructing knowledge with attention to existing social action—is called *praxis*. *Praxis*, as conscious social practice, guides political economy.

The political economy of communication approach has a long and respected tradition in the United States, beginning with Dallas Smythe (1957) and Herbert Schiller (1973) through Thomas Guback (1969), to Janet Wasko (1994), Vincent Mosco (1996), and Robert McChesney (1993) to name a few. Much of the early research focused on media ownership, power, and concentration. Edward Herman and Noam Chomsky's *Manufacturing Consent* (1988) went further by providing a "propaganda model" which identified how the media's political economy affected media content. The selection included here from Herman illustrates some of their discoveries.

Whatever the particular media industry at issue, each of these political economists have "decentered" the media by investigating their social, economic, political, cultural and other material constituents (Mosco 71). Situating the media in the framework of the production and reproduction of society recognizes the institutionalized communication practices of the media have parallels in education, religion, work, family and other social practices. While each are distinct, all are mutually constituted within a wider social totality. Using different terms, the political economy approach to communication essentially regards communication as a social product, social tool, and social process (see Introduction) in all of its social, cultural, political, and institutional arrangements.

The best studies do not solely deal with media concentration and power, but find that dominant communication practices have inconsistencies, internal contradictions, and external challenges which may require or allow possible alternative communication practices. Thus, U.S. media is marked by heavy monopolization *and* significant decentralization, by concentrated ownership and production circuits *and* small, yet significant variations in content (the occasional "TV Nation," National Public Radio, and independent book publishers like Verso, Common Courage and Southend). The use of literacy for democratic discourse (see Section 3), the battle for public non-commercial radio in the 1930s (see McChesney, Section 6) and democratic opportunities for the Internet today confirm that power over communication is never monolithic.

Of course, like the earlier article by McChesney, and articles in this section by Husseini, Naureckas, and Stadtmiller reveal, the political resolve and influence by economic powerhouses has consequence for communication practice. Indeed, the easy alliance between business and government does not inspire expectations of forthcoming democratic communication practices in the U.S. The refusal by most political economists to regard Americans as simply consumers or media use as primarily a leisure activity helps prepare us to be thoughtful, engaged citizens. It also forces us to recognize the media as socio-economic entities that have more than just owners, but operate only with the steady cooperation of journalists, reporters, copy editors, computer programmers, technicians, grips, camera operators, graphic artists, truck drivers, publicists, and more.

A political economy of communication finds four distinct, but interrelated, roles for the media in capitalist society. First, media businesses directly produce commodities for sale: movies, videos, books, newspapers, compact discs, television programs, and so on. Secondly, media also directly produce audiences as commodities to be "sold" to advertisers. By attracting readers, listeners, or viewers, media businesses construct potential consumers for producers of other goods and services. Advertisers purchase print space and electronic time because media space and time materially delivers audiences to producers of goods and services. Thirdly, then, media indirectly contribute to the production of major goods and services which depend on consumers because they attract and organize consumers in ready-made demographic groups. Finally, media directly contribute to the production, reproduction, and adjustment of consumer society by manufacturing and distributing educational, informational, and ideological messages. These messages come in the form of images, representations, symbols, and themes which carry values, beliefs, and knowledge about the world and how it should be. In short, the media produce the social lubricant necessary for a smooth-running society.

GOODS AND SERVICES ADVERTISED IN THE U.S.

Category	Ad Spending in Millions $
Retail	8,082
Auto	7,754
Services	5,249
Entertainment	3,749
Food	3,442
Cosmetics	2,608
Medicine	2,294
Hotels and Travel	2,030
Direct response companies	1,404
Candy, snacks, soft drinks	1,286

Source: *Advertising Age*, January 2, 1995.

In understanding the media as producer, advertiser, and promoter of commodities, the political economy approach affords a more thorough appreciation of the integral relationship between communication and society. It moves us to look at communication practices in the context of technology, its social use, and the social relationships that effect and arise from that use. Political economy of communication elevates the significance of media to society by admitting the complexity of media productions, including images, ideologies, and audiences. Finally, political economy approaches encourage the possibility for improved communication practices by locating points in need of more democracy and citizen participation. These are big claims with many precise applications, but political economy paints communication in broad strokes with some very concrete details.

The readings assembled in this section do not do justice to a political economy of communication. Indeed, they were not selected because they express theoretical claims or explicate research methods. Some of the authors would not even consider their contribution to be political economy. Yet, each reading addresses a particular instance of the political economy of the media in the United States today. Moreover, each makes the political economy of the media more understandable by furnishing a brief account of a timely issue for democratic communication.

According to University of Pennsylvania Professor of Finance, Edward Herman, commodification, deregulation, and privatization all but ensure that every aspect of culture will be "For Sale." Already, eating, sports, child care, entertainment, even dating have become product markets. The trend to McDonaldization in television programming, for instance, has had a lethal effect on non-commercial values: sit-coms, light entertainment, and sex and violence have elbowed out more thoughtful, creative, and profound offerings. Herman argues that privatization further increases inefficiency (recall Sarnoff's hold on FM broadcasting!) and reduces competition (see Bagdikian in Part One). Corporate downsizing and government deregulation exacerbate concentration of industry, including the media. Herman opens the first selection with a summary of cultural production under capitalism, followed by a short account of five "filters" which regulate the construction of mass information: media ownership, advertising, news sources, public relations "flak," and a free market ideology. Herman's selections conclude with a critique of commercial broadcasting and its adverse impact on public discourse, children's programming, and social values.

Doug Henwood's series from *Extra!*, a publication of the watch-dog group Fairness and Accuracy in Reporting, are somewhat dated but deliver relevant details about the ownership structures of major media in the United States. Cross-listing the directors of the media Henwood investigates reveals that a number of corporations "share" seats at CBS, NBC, ABC and other media (and other corporate and government institutions not presented here). These "interlocking" directorships suggest a "community" of directors who also likely share economic and political interests, world views, cultural sensibilities, and social values. What happens to democracy if the major media players agree with the *Washington Post*'s publisher Katherine Graham that its best if the media keep secrets from the public?

Less-than-public decisions cannot expand democratic communication. Four short readings submitted here target several important changes in communication practice in the U.S. "Net Loss" warns of the encroaching commercialization of the Internet. "Info-bandits" and "Give-away of the Century" highlight the cause and consequence of the 1996 Telecommunications Act which reinforces and expands the control and influence of network and cable companies over broadcasting, including the new HDTV technology.

There are 6778 radio stations, 1520 television stations, 25,000 theater screens, 1570 daily newspapers, and 11,143 periodicals distributing millions of media products (Alleyne 1996). The chart included here from *The Nation* magazine maps the ownership structure of this industry, which produced $224 billion in total spending in 1993 (Alleyne 1996). In his articles, Mark Crispin Miller articulates what he recognizes as the result of this monopoly: "the universal sleaze and 'dumbing down,' the flood-tide of corporate propaganda, and the terminal inanity of U.S. politics" have arisen from "the inevitable toxic influence of those few corporations that have monopolized culture."

Commenting on the media ownership chart, Herbert Schiller (1996) said, "No matter how many editors, producers, filmmakers, artists, photographers, musicians et al. labor in cultural factories…in the end they are all subject to the overriding corporate imperative—make a profit, indeed, make a steadily increasing profit…the inevitable outcome is a cultural product that is short on bite and long on safe formulas for crowd control" (18). Would a different political economy of the media produce and distribute a different cultural product? Would it have different structures, practices, and themes? Miller believes so and argues that the sameness of the choices from a monopolized media are insufficient for a functioning democracy.

The growth of book publishing supplies one cogent example. In 1994, readers in the U.S. bought a record 1 billion books, a 31% increase over 1994 (Alleyne). However, many of the best sellers were not novels, biographies, or traditional creative literature. Rather, leading sellers were inspirational books, cookbooks, and celebrity "tell-alls" by Seinfeld, Leno, Oprah, and Ellen, and other "marketable" texts. According to Miller, the quality and diversity of book choice has not kept pace with the quantity: books are "low intellectually" and "poor materially, because of editorial neglect." Two bookstore chains: Barnes and Noble and Borders (discussed by Statdmiller here); two book distributors: Ingram and Baker & Taylor; and a handful of publishers, including Random House, Bantam, and Simon & Schuster (see Chart) are squeezing out artistic, cultural, and political creativity and choice. Miller writes, "For those who like to read the prospect is frightening."

In keeping with the political economist's commitment to *praxis*, each of the contributions in this section encourage citizen action as a means for changing communication practices and expanding democratic discourse. Miller, for instance, argues that we need to "teach everyone, ourselves included, that this whole failing culture is an oversold dead end, and that there might be a way out." Political economists are undaunted by the sheer power and size of the media monopoly because it must continually—daily and hourly—attract, seduce, and persuade millions to purchase its disposable products and perspectives. Given what the readings in this text have already shown, that is no easy task. Every dominant communication practice has been subject to democratic intervention, even as it appeared other interests might triumph. The historical experience of changing communication practices also indicates that the democratic majority has found and will continue to find creative and participatory means for identifying and organizing their social interest in community.

REFERENCES

Alleyne, Mark. "The Economics of Mass Communication: The Media in a Free Enterprise System." In *Mass Communication in the Information Age*. Ed. David Sloan. Northport, AL: Vision P, 1996: 93–109.

Connell, Rob. *Power and Gender*. Stanford: Stanford U P, 1987.

Guback, Thomas. *The International Film Industry*. Bloomington: Indiana P, 1969.

Herman, Edward and Noam Chomsky. *Manufacturing Consent*. New York: Pantheon, 1988.

McChesney, Robert. *Telecommunications, Mass Media, and Democracy*. New York: Oxford, 1993.

Mosco, Vincent. *The Political Economy of Communication*. Thousand Oaks: Sage, 1996.

Schiller, Herbert. *The Mind Managers*. Boston: Beacon P, 1973.

Schiller, Herbert. "On That Chart." *The Nation* 3 June 1996: 17–18.

Smythe, Dallas. *The Structure and Policy of Electronic Communication*. Urbana: U Illinois, P, 1957.

Wasko, Janet. *Hollywood in the Information Age*. Boston: Polity, 1994.

22 | The Commercialization of Broadcasting

Edward Herman

. . .

Every aspect of culture is in a process of commodification and linkage to the sale of goods. Sports events have been seized by commercial interests as vehicles for marketing, and the force of the market has diminished the element of play in sport. Players as well as managers and owners are increasingly becoming businesspersons/celebrities, and the sports page more and more belongs in the business section of the newspaper. Big-name players make as much or more money via endorsements and commercial appearances as in contracts to play.

The games themselves are increasingly dominated by the demands of the market—the National Football League (NFL) has reportedly been considering moving to an eighteen- instead of a sixteen-week schedule to "better position the product," in the words of one NFL official. Pauses in the game are dictated as much by advertising needs as by the demands of the participants, and advertisers' logos steadily increase their presence—extending to the names of the events, the ads shown in the stadiums and on players' attire, as well as in the increasingly frequent ads within the TV programs. Tennis, formerly a gentlemanly amateur sport, has been transformed by television and money into a professional entertainment vehicle, with playing time schedules and venues dictated by market (and especially TV) demands.

The Olympic Games held in Los Angeles in 1984 were a turning point in the commercialization of that traditional international competition. With television and radio audiences for the games now reaching several billion, the aggressive selling of the audience and marketing of events, heroes, teams, logos, and tied-in merchandise has inevitably followed. The winter games have been shifted so that there will be an Olympics every two years, in accord with the demands of television and the Olympic Committee's drive for greater TV revenue and sponsorship. As Stuart F. Cross, marketing vice-president of Coca-Cola, stated recently, "The Olympics is *all* business." Nations and cities bid for the right to host the games, with a 60 percent cut of broadcasting rights proceeds; transnational corporations (TNCs) buy ad time and rights to market logos and merchandise; and thousands of locals who stand in the way are forced out of their homes to make room for temporary facilities and progress.[1]

In movies and television, brand-name products are used, for a price, in program materials. Since 1982, "product placement" has become institutionalized in movies, with the price now averaging about $50,000 per item/incident.[2] By 1994 product placement had entrenched itself in video games, where "the new advertising is being embraced by game makers as a possible cash cow." A report on this development cites critics saying that "the arrival of advertising in computer games is wiping out one of the last havens children have against commercial messages."[3]

In a further advance of the market into TV, in 1994 a weekly program called "Main Floor" "[took] viewers into department stores to show them the latest fashion and beauty trends, while quietly steering them to specific merchandise that sponsors have paid to promote on the show." There were commercial breaks as well, but the body of the show displayed Paloma Picasso talking about "her new men's fragrance" and "a Lee representative [talked] about the problems women have buying jeans that fit, while also pushing its fall line." That Lee (etc.) paid for time on the show is only disclosed when the final credits are displayed.[4] In magazines, also, the distinction between advertising and editorial material has been eroding under the force of competition for ads, and advertisers' pressures for editorial "support" that will "add value" to the space they buy. Beyond "advertorials," in which ads mimic editorials, we now have "funded journalism," in which articles are paid for by advertisers who gear the story's topic and tone toward the needs of their advertisements.

The market has had a significant effect on culture through the broader impact of commercialization and sponsorship on TV programming. Advertisers want large audiences and a congenial environment for selling goods, and owners strive to provide these, with "lethal effects" on noncommercial values.[5] The long-term drift of programming has been away from the thoughtful, profound, and controversial (which would disturb the sales pitch), away from serious public affairs programming (which draws relatively small audiences), and toward light entertainment. Sex and violence, which sell well both at home and abroad, have been given a large place in TV, just as children's programming has steadily eroded in quantity and quality.

The global market has been enormously receptive to U.S. movies, rock music, and other U.S. expressions and dreams of individual freedom and rebellion, and wealth and power. In some respects these elements of popular culture *have* been liberating, both ideologically and as a release from suffocatingly narrow environments. But these products are mere entertainment in the form of fun, games, and fairy tales; and to a great extent their huge global audience reflects the global decline in family and civil life, and loss of faith in politics. As Barnet and Cavanagh express it,

> Popular culture acts as a sponge to soak up spare time and energy that in earlier times might well have been devoted to nurturing and instructing children or to participating in political, religious, civic, or community activities or in crafts, reading, and continuing self-education. But such pursuits sound a bit old-fashioned today, although political theory still rests on the assumption that these activities are central to the functioning of a democratic society. Yet increasingly, vicarious experience via film, video, and music is a substitute for civic life and community. As it becomes harder for young people in many parts of the world to carve out satisfying roles, the rush of commercial sounds and images offers escape.[6]

The market has moved slowly but steadily into the schools, where the business community has long offered educational aids in the form of printed and video materials on their companies, products, and industries, and on the principles of free enterprise. More recently, companies have entered into "partnership" relationships with schools, some 40 percent of all public schools now receiving modest assistance on this basis. The business community vigorously supports political parties and leaders who defund the schools, and bargains and fights for lower local taxes, but then gallantly offers small change to alleviate the troubling "crisis in the schools!"[7]

A notable development of recent years was Whittle Communications' offer of free equipment to schools in exchange for the right to show students a news broadcast containing advertising. This camel's nose under the tent has been accepted by thousands of financially strapped schools,[8] and the advertisement as part of the formal educational package has thus found a home. Schools are also selling advertising space on school buses, sport scoreboard logos, and on acrylic-faced billboards in school restrooms, as well as the right to blare music with commercials into hallways and lunchrooms.[9]

Even more important has been the powerful thrust toward "school choice" via vouchers and an enlargement of the private sector in competition with public schools. Entrepreneurs, including Whittle, have come forward to take over schooling responsibilities on a contract basis. These privatizing developments weaken support for public schools, leaving many of them to service the urban poor without adequate resources, while the more affluent attend better financed suburban public schools or private schools.

Playgrounds have been increasingly commodified, providing "security zones" as well as an array of entertainment and food attractions for children and their anxious parents. In a polarizing society, where crime is an important and rational choice for large numbers at the bottom, and safe community play space is not supplied by the state, those who can afford it simply *buy* it. Private playgrounds are smaller versions of theme parks, which are controlled environments heavily oriented toward selling goods. A major playground provider is Discovery Zone (DZ). Selling under the brand name Discovery Zone Fun Centers, it plans to expand globally in the next five years. DZ is affiliated with Blockbuster Entertainment Corporation, which operates music stores, game stores, movie studios, and home entertainment centers, as well as playgrounds. Its head, Wayne Huizenga, states that "our goal is to drive traffic from one Blockbuster business to another."[10]

Museums and libraries have also been integrated more closely into the market. Debora Silverman's *Selling Culture* featured the coordination of the New York Metropolitan Museum of Art's exhibits on China and pre-revolutionary France with Bloomingdale's featured sales of items of the same genre.[11] Both the department store and the museum were being advised by the late Diane Vreeland, a longtime editor of *Vogue* magazine and consultant to both Bloomingdale's and the museum's exhibitions. The latter lacked historical or social context, and seemed like museum versions of sales campaigns.

More generally, museums have increasingly felt the need to obtain corporate sponsorship for exhibits, and thus to adjust their overall orientation to attract this primary source of funding. Corporate expenditures on the arts rose from under $100 million in 1970 to more than $500 million in the early 1990s. One curator noted that "most corporate sponsors finance exhibitions based on centrist ideals and uncontroversial subject matter." Artist and radical critic of museums, Hans Haacke, has stated that "shows that could promote critical awareness, present products of consciousness dialectically and in relation to the social world, or question relations of power, have a slim chance of being approved. . .self-censorship is having a boom."[12]

Commodification of Information

The technological revolution in "informatics" has not only made it possible to use information more extensively and intensively within the business world and for social control, it has made information itself more marketable. The result has been a further commodification of information. Data bases in all kinds of fields have multiplied. This "for sale" information is collected and formatted in accordance with the needs of the parties best able to buy it. Public libraries are increasingly by-passed as repositories of information, and they have had to subscribe to some of the new private information services. The "free" library is thus on its way out, as libraries are compelled to impose charges for access to privately controlled information. They are also suffering from severe financial stringency as a result of servicing a disproportionately non-elite clientele in financially stressed urban areas.

Another important development has been the tendency to reduce and privatize information collected by the government, much of which was traditionally subsidized as valuable to the public and fitting the concept of a "public good." For a public good, one person's use does not interfere with that of another person, so that imposing a price restricts use unnecessarily and the market "fails" when price is used as a rationing device.[13] In the 1980s, government-collected information was increasingly turned over to private users to sell on their own terms (even back to the government at a price). So in this "information age" information has been more and more privatized and commodified, its public good quality ignored, in the interest of serving "the market." This strengthens the position of those able to control and pay for such information (i.e., the business sector, especially its larger units), and weakens the position of the general public.

Internet provides a significant new, partially noncommercial means of communication that has a global reach and potentially links together millions of people. It does, however, require ownership of a computer, technical knowhow, means of access to Internet through a linked provider, and knowledge of other users sharing common interests. It is therefore a system serving relatively isolated and elite individuals and small groups, not large numbers of unorganized and non-elite people. Furthermore, its commercial exploitation is being aggressively explored and experimented with by commercial interests, who are likely to make major inroads (and help inundate the system) over the next decade.[14]

Advertising and Public Relations

While traditional, hard information is being commodified and subject to rationing by price, advertising and public relations (PR) expenditures have been growing at a steady clip. We may crudely generalize: hard data is being reserved for business and the "cognitive elite"; the information sector made increasingly available to the masses as public goods (with no direct charge) is *so* "soft" it is hokum.

Advertising is the subsidized message provided by sellers of goods to facilitate sale. PR is its institutional counterpart. These self-serving and inherently biased forms of communication are dominant in modern market economies and are geared to the demands of the owners/managers of firms that pay for them. They reinforce the values of acquisition, consumption, and accumulation, and marginalize values of noncommercial interest (community, equality, ethical concerns, the sacredness of life and nature) although advertisers regularly make opportunistic use of these values for their own advantage. They have had a profound effect on the broadcasting media and the political process, as will be discussed....

...the evolution of the structure of the communications industries, has yielded a system in which private rights of free expression are protected, but rights to public access, insofar as these entail outreach through privately owned communications facilities, are not. Decisions on access are left to the "marketplace" and those who control it. This means that individuals with facts, ideas, and proposals important to the public interest may be effectively ignored (or relegated to marginal forums) if the controllers of the marketplace disapprove of and refuse to disseminate their messages. But in the frame of freemarket thought and ideology, competition among media already operating, and freedom of entry, assure that all views that are important to substantial numbers—and to the truth—will be expressed. As stated in A.J. Liebling's famous irony: We are all free to start our own newspaper if we don't like those available to us.[15]

The Free-Market Model

A free market model can readily be constructed, however, that shows how market processes naturally constrain free expression and marginalize dissent. And there is evidence that such constraints and processes are operative and have large effects. It is well known that the market "rations" goods by price, and that people without "effective demand" will be excluded from, that is, priced out of, the market. The point is not often applied to the media and free expression, possibly because those who might make the point have already been priced out of the market and denied access!

Access is restricted, first, by the requirement that one have capital to enter the media industries.[16] From the earliest times, capital requirements ensured that the media "gatekeepers" are members of the economic elite, with associated class biases; other interest groups, some with enormous constituencies but without substantial capital, like trade unions, racial and ethnic minorities, environmentalists, and consumer organizations, have to depend on the elite gatekeepers for access to the general public.[17]

This control mechanism has been strengthened over the years as the scale of production and capital requirements have steadily grown, the wealth of mass media owners has greatly increased;[18] newspaper chains and television and cable networks have grown in importance, the media have become parts of conglomerates, and the media industries have spread beyond single country borders. The media have been further integrated into the market by increasing competition and an active takeover market. The result of all this has been both delocalization and steadily greater pressure to focus on profitability.

The bias of the media toward the status quo and the interests of the corporate system is assured by this set of considerations alone.[19] But beyond this, profit-oriented media are extremely sensitive to advertiser, governmental, and other powerful interest group wants, needs, and pressures, and tend to avoid controversy and oppositional views even more comprehensively than government-funded media enterprises.[20]

While the owners of the media are wealthy individuals and companies, their operations are funded mainly by advertisers; that is, by business firms trying to sell goods and corporate messages. These have a powerful impact on the media, especially on television but also on the print media.[21] Their influence is exercised under a competitive system mainly by advertisers' demands for a suitable "program environment" for their commercial messages, and their power to choose among stations and programs according to these preferences.[22] The biases of corporate advertisers, whose ideological assumptions and fondness for the status quo is similar to that of the media's owners, should reinforce establishment positions and tend to marginalize dissent.

A third factor that causes market forces to limit free expression arises from the media's quest for cheap, regular, and credible sources of information. Dissident sources are expensive to locate and their claims must be checked out carefully. Claims of the Secretary of State and other high officials, or police officers in charge of investigating an act of violence, are readily available, are newsworthy in themselves, are supplied by credible sources, and do not require careful checking (although a media concerned seriously with truth and *substantive* objectivity would treat all sources with the same degree of scrutiny). A symbiotic relationship develops between dominant sources and the media, which makes the latter more reluctant to transmit dissident claims, as these would embarrass and annoy the media's primary sources.

The dominant sources within the government and corporate system also finance and otherwise support quasi-private institutes and think-tanks, where experts who will preempt further space in the mass media for proponents of establishment views are funded and accredited.[23] Dissidents have no comparable endowed funding and accrediting agencies[24] and are therefore further limited in access to the mass media.

A fourth route through which the market limits free expression is by the generation and use of "flak." Flak is negative feedback that threatens, imposes costs upon, and therefore constrains the media. The importance of flak to the media is a function of money and power, which allow monitoring and serious media challenges, including advertising boycotts, threats of libel suits, congressional hearings, and FCC and anti-trust actions. Just as the American Enterprise Institute, Hoover Institution, and Georgetown Center for Strategic and International Studies serve the establishment by providing accredited experts, so Accuracy in Media, the American Legal Foundation, and Capital Foundation are funded to discipline the media by systematic challenges for "liberal bias," unfairness, and libel.

A final factor in media control by market forces is the ideological premises of the system, which reflect a culture centered in private property. The merits of free enterprise, the threat of state ownership and intervention, the benevolent role of the government in international affairs, and anti-communism are central. Anti-communism has been especially strategic as a disciplinary device, keeping the media and Democratic Party in line by their fear of being tagged unfaithful to the national religion, when they might otherwise be inclined to respond to mass demands by raising questions about tax equity, the size of the military budget, and the propriety of destabilizing and attacking countries not governed in accord with U.S. establishment interests and demands.[25]

These free-market mechanisms, working in concert, and on foreign policy matters usually geared closely to a government agenda, provide a powerful means of filtering out dissident and inconvenient information and opinion. One of the great merits of this system of control is that it operates so naturally, without collusion or explicit censorship, merely by the decentralized pursuit of a set of micro-interests. It "just works out that way." If Poland, a Communist power aligned with a then-hostile Soviet Union, cracks down on the Solidarity union, this is extremely newsworthy, whereas if at the very same time Turkey (a U.S. client state) is cracking down on its trade unions, the filters work to keep this out of the news. If it is serviceable to the Reagan administration to inflate the Libyan menace, the market causes Qadaffi to become a featured "terrorist," while at the same time if state policy toward South Africa and Guatemala is accommodation and "constructive engagement," their far more severe terrorism is found not newsworthy, is largely suppressed, and the word terrorism is not applied to these states and their leaders.[26] If it serves state propaganda needs to focus on the abuses of the Khmer Rouge in Cambodia, the market does this energetically and with great indignation; and if at the same time client state Indonesia invades East Timor and decimates its population with at least equal ferocity, the market-based media avert their eyes.[27] The ease and naturalness with which this is done by uncoordinated self-censorship makes for extremely effective propaganda and allows the creation of a virtually Orwellian world of doublespeak via free-market processes.

A second great merit of the evolving market system of control is that it is not total and responds with some flexibility to the differences that frequently crop up among elite groups. This allows controversy to rage within the mass media, but confined almost entirely to tactical matters, and not challenging fundamental premises. Thus, during the Vietnam War, it was fiercely debated whether we could win, how this could be done, and whether the costs (to us) were too great. The premises: that we had a right to be there, were not invaders and aggressors, and were seeking self-determination and "protecting South Vietnam," were rarely questioned in the mainstream media.[28]

Similarly, in the case of the subversion and proxy warfare against Nicaragua in the 1980s, the view that this was plain aggression and international terrorism, and that the U.S. design was to oppose independence, self-determination, and the pursuit of the "logic of the majority," was simply not addressed in the mainstream media. The access to the mass media of individuals and groups anxious to make such points, in both news columns and opinion pages, was so low as to approach total exclusion.[29]

With the mainstream "Left" lauding our benevolent ends and the eventual achievement of a "democratic election" through "patience" (i.e., not invading Nicaragua with large U.S. forces)[30] following the destruction of the Nicaraguan economy, and with the election held under the ongoing threat of more of the same in the absence of a U.S.-approved outcome,[31] the market system of control performed a propaganda feat that a system of state censorship could hardly improve upon.

A third merit of the market-based system is that a dissident media is allowed to function, but without the capacity to reach large numbers. This is interpreted in the mainstream as evidence that the public does not want the excluded products. But their producers can rarely raise the capital or attract advertising support sufficient to allow a valid product test. For those products that do come into existence, advertiser disinterest, and the benefits of advertiser support for rival publications in price charged, promotion, technical quality, etc., make the survival of dissident media difficult. In Great Britain, the *Daily Herald*, with a large working class audience, failed in the 1960s despite a circulation larger than *The Times, Financial Times* and *Guardian* combined; but its 8.1 percent of national circulation yielded it only 3.5 percent of advertising revenue.[32]

Furthermore, the excluded dissident "product" is a complex of products that often includes elements of the news and perspectives that are highly relevant to issues discussed by mainstream media, but which simply fail to meet their criteria of newsworthiness. This means that literal lies may in institutionalized in the mainstream media, with corrections in the *samizdat* press.[33] More important is the fact that unpalatable matters may be ignored or downplayed, while system-supportive facts, developments, and claims (including fabrications) may be pushed front and center to mobilize the citizenry.[34] But, meanwhile, the establishment points triumphantly to the *samizdat* press, free to operate, but not reaching a mass audience allegedly for reasons of "insufficient demand."

In sum, a market system of control limits free expression largely by market processes that are highly effective. Dissident ideas are not legally banned, they are simply unable to reach mass audiences, which are monopolized by profit-seeking large organizations offering advertising-supported programs, from which dissent is quietly and unobtrusively filtered out. Excluded individuals are free to say what they want, and may have access to a marginalized media, but do not have the power to contest the market-dominated mass media's system-supportive selectivity and propaganda with the larger public.

This system is extremely difficult to attack and dislodge because the gatekeepers naturally do not allow challenges to their own direct interests to reach the public consciousness. Nonetheless, structural change is imperative for increasing freedom of expression in the United States. This will only happen with greater public understanding of the stakes and important grassroots support for a democratic media.

...Although many democratic and progressive critics of the media have been harsh on public broadcasting, most of them have looked upon its decline as a distinctly adverse and threatening development. The most common view is that while public broadcasting has never realized its potential, it has nevertheless contributed modestly to a public sphere of debate and critical discourse and has provided information and viewpoints essential to the citizenship role. By contrast, commercial broadcasting is viewed as an entertainment vehicle that tends to marginalize the public sphere in direct proportion to its increasing dominance and profitability.[35]

Commercial Broadcasting and "Market Failure"

Commercial broadcasting, in fact, offers a model case of "market failure" in both theory and practice, although you will rarely see this point discussed in the mainstream media. But broadcasting has important "public goods" properties, with a potentially important yield of positive externalities; and negative externalities, such as the effects of the exploitation of sex and violence to build audiences, are a likely (and observable) consequence of commercialization.

Externalities are, by definition, things that the market does not take into account, like pollution, worker injuries (when the employer can escape liability), and, on the positive side, aesthetic beauty in well planned and maintained private gardens and buildings, and greater productivity from technological advances that serve industry in general. Broadcasting can be a powerful educational tool and contributor to democratic participation and citizenship. From the time of the Communications Act of 1934, and even earlier, its "public service" possibilities were widely recognized in the United States, and it was accepted even by the broadcasters that their grant for rights to use public air channels was in exchange for their serving "the public convenience, interest, and necessity." In the 1934 hearings, the National Association of Broadcasters acknowledged that it is the "manifest duty" of the Federal Communications Commission (FCC) to assure an "adequate public service," which "necessarily includes broadcasting of a considerable proportion of programs devoted to education, religion, labor, agricultural and similar activities concerned with human betterment."

The 1946 FCC report, *Public Service Responsibilities of Broadcast Licensees*, contended that "sustaining programs" (i.e., those put on at the station's expense, unsupported by advertising) are the "balance wheel" whereby "the imbalance of a station's or network's program structure, which might otherwise result from commercial decisions concerning program structure, can be redressed." It even quotes CBS's Frank Stanton to the same effect. The report referred to the sustaining programs as an "irreplaceable" part of broadcasting, and public service performance in the interest of "all substantial groups among the hearing public" as a fundamental standard and test in approving and renewing licenses.

Commercialization and the Decline of Public Service

But a funny thing happened as the commercial system matured. It became possible to sell time to advertisers for all hours of the day, and the price at which time could be sold depended on "ratings," which measure the audience size (and from 1970, its "demographics"). As time became salable and its price rose, the pressure for high ratings increased; and as Erik Barnouw noted in *The Sponsor*, "The preemption of the schedule for commercial ends has put lethal pressure on other values and interests."[36] One effect was the steady trend away from "controversial" and modestly rated public service programs and toward entertainment. Richard Bunce found that by 1970, public affairs coverage had fallen to 2 percent of programming time, and the entire spectrum of public interest programming was far below that provided by public broadcasting systems in Canada, Great Britain, and elsewhere in the West.[37]

The decline in public service performance of the U.S. commercial broadcasters paralleled a steady increase in broadcasting station and network profitability. By 1970 the profits of major station owners were in the range of 30-50 percent of revenues, and much more on invested capital. Bunce estimated that for the period 1960–72, the ratio of pretax income to depreciated tangible investments for the broadcast networks never fell below 50 percent a year.[38] These staggering profits did not alleviate broadcaster pressure for additional profits, as the workings of the market cause profits to be capitalized into higher stock values, which become the basis of calculation of rates of return for both old and new owners.

The force of competition and stress on the rate of return on capital, which comes to prevail in a free market, compels firms to focus with increasing intensity on enlarging audience size and improving its "quality," as these will determine advertising rates. A recent audience decline for NBC's morning "Today Show," moving it a full rating point behind ABC's "Good Morning, America," was reportedly the basis of a $280,000-a-day advertising income differential between the shows. Managements that fail to respond to market opportunities of this magnitude will be under pressure from owners and may be ousted by internal processes or takeovers. There will be no room for soft-headed "socially responsible" managers in a mature system, and in the United States, the three top networks have in fact been taken over by strictly market-driven corporate owners.[39]

The maturing of commercial broadcasting not only steadily reduces the public service component, the U.S. experience also suggests that maturation brings with it a decline in variety of viewpoints and increased protection of establishment interests. A telling illustration was in the coverage of the Vietnam War, where, as Erik Barnouw notes, "The Vietnam escalation of 1965-67 found commercial network television hewing fairly steadily to the administration line. Newscasts often seemed to be pipelines for government rationales and declarations...Though a groundswell of opposition to the war was building at home and throughout much of the world, network television seemed at pains to insulate viewers from its impact...Much sponsored entertainment was jingoistic." The U.S. networks not only made none of the seriously critical documentaries on the War, during the early War years they barred access to outside documentaries. As Barnouw points out "this policy constituted de facto national censorship, though privately operated."

But while the mass protest against the War rarely found any outlets in commercial TV, it "began to find occasional expression in NET [National Educational Television, precursor to the Corporation for Public Broadcasting] programming in such series as *Black Journal, NET Journal, The Creative Person*, and—explosively—in the film *Inside North Vietnam*, a British documentarist's report on his 1967 visit to 'the enemy'"[40] This pattern helps explain why President Johnson and Nixon fought to rein in public broadcasting, with Nixon quite openly seeking to force it to de-emphasize public affairs. The commercial systems did this naturally.

In depth news presentations on commercial TV reached their pinnacle with Edward R. Murrow's "See It Now" programs in the mid-1950s. There was a resurgence of news documentaries in the early 1960s, in the wake of the quiz-show scandals of 1959, but subsequently the decline continued, despite occasional notable productions. Sponsors don't like controversy and depth—in either entertainment or non-fiction. In the years when environmental issues first became of national concern, NBC dropped the environmental series "In Which We Live" for want of sponsorship, although the major companies were all busily putting up commercials and other materials on the environment. Their materials, however, reassured, and did not explore the issue in depth and with any balance, as had the NBC series. More recently, a program with Barbara Walters on the abortion issue was unable to obtain sponsors, who openly rejected participation for fear of controversy.

Fear of "Fairness Doctrine" requirements of balance also made serious programs that took a stand on an issue a threat to broadcasters; and watering them down to obviate challenges for lack of balance made them lifeless. Documentaries that appealed to sponsors were about travel, dining, dogs, flower shows, life styles of the rich, and personalities past and present. In short, under the system of commercial sponsorship, the documentary was reduced to "a small and largely neutralized fragment of network television, one that can scarcely rival the formative influence of 'entertainment' and 'commercials.'" The form survived mainly in an aborted quasi-entertainment form called "pop doc," specializing in brief vignettes, with a focus on individual villains pursued by superstar entertainers, and settling "for relatively superficial triumphs." "Infotainment" has also come to the fore, with entertainers titillating audiences with "information" about other entertainers.

Other public affairs programs, like discussion panels, with lower ratings were placed in weekend ghetto slots, and consisted mainly of unthreatening panels asking unchallenging questions of officials. In the years before the death of the Fairness Doctrine, the "public service" obligation was met largely by public service announcements cleared through the Advertising Council, which provided a further means for the broadcasters to establish a record of public service without addressing any serious issue.

Public broadcasting, by contrast with commercial, is likely to provide programs that give substantial weight to positive externalities. This is because the broadcasting media were recognized from the beginning as potentially valuable tools of education and citizen training, capable of universal outreach and service to both mass audiences and minorities, and public broadcasting took an early responsibility for realizing this potential. Most important, public broadcasting has not been driven by the profit motive or funded primarily by advertising, so that its functional role has not been as incompatible with its funding source or institutional linkage as the market-tied and profit-oriented commercial systems have been. It should be noted, however, that insofar as public broadcasting is forced to compete with growing commercial systems for a mass audience, with limited funding, there should be an erosion of original purpose and quality.

The evidence from Western Europe on the treatment of public service and positive externalities by commercial and public broadcasters is similar to that from the United States. Public broadcasting systems offer wider ranges of choice and significantly more national news, discussion programs, documentaries, cultural, and minority programs than commercial systems in the United States or in any other country.[41] The spread of commercial systems within Europe has not increased diversity and in fact threatens it through its damaging effects on the capabilities of public broadcasters. The first commercial broadcast channel in Italy offered literally zero news and public affairs programming, and Murdoch's Sky Channel provided 95.6 percent entertainment and under 1 percent information.[42] French commercial TV has been notable for "the lack of variety...the tendency of the stations to align their programming on each other; the excessive screening of films and the neglect of the documentary; and...the haziness of the frontier between the commercial and the programme..."[43]

Children's Programming

Broadcasting offers a potentially major and efficient vehicle for educating and entertaining children. Children, however, are not very important buyers of goods, especially small children, and are therefore of little interest to advertisers. The positive social benefits of quality radio and TV to children are externalities, and U.S. experience demonstrates that they will be ignored or marginalized by commercial broadcasters.

As in the case of public affairs programming, the U.S. commercial system eventually ghettoized children's programming with Saturday and Sunday morning fare that was largely cartoon entertainment with very heavy doses of commercials. Between 1955 and 1970, weekday programming for children on network affiliated TV stations in New York City fell from 33 to five hours. Only on Saturday did the children continue to get substantial time, but not with any new or non-entertainment programs.[44] A major FCC study of children's television published in 1979 concluded that children are "drastically underserved."

The failure of commercial TV in children's programming was so severe that a number of citizens groups were formed during the 1960s to fight the commercial system. One, Action for Children's Television (ACT), formed in 1968, lodged a protest with the FCC in 1970 demanding reform. The FCC response in 1974 admitted the industry's failures and responsibilities, but left the resolution to the voluntary actions of the broadcasters. In 1983, the Reagan-era FCC, in a further response to the ACT petition, declared that the broadcasters had *no* responsibility to children. The situation deteriorated thereafter. Programming of substance for children was left to public broadcasting, but there was no national policy or regular funding of children's programs. The poor performance of U.S. school children is often noted in the mass media, and is sometimes attributed in part to the underfunding of schools, but the foregone potential of TV broadcasting is rarely mentioned.

Negative Externalities

While the failure of commercial broadcasting to produce public affairs, cultural, and children's programs that promise important positive externalities has been subject to only modest study and even less publicity, its exploitation of the audience-enlarging vehicles of sex and violence has aroused important elements of the mainstream and has received greater attention. The aggressive use of themes of sex and violence, often in combination, can produce externalities in the form of distorted human and sexual attitudes, insecurity and reduced ability to function in a social order, and aggressive and violent behavior.

Television violence builds audiences. It therefore tends to dominate the TV screen under the pressure of commercial imperatives. Since 1967, Professor George Gerbner and his associates have compiled an annual television program Violence Profile and Violence Index. They have found that on average seven of ten prime-time programs use violence, and the rate of violent acts runs between five and six per hour. Some half of prime-time dramatic characters engage in violence and about 10 percent in killing, as they have since 1967. Children's weekend programming "remains saturated with violence," clocking more than 25 acts of violence per hour, as it has for many years.[45]

Violent programming has grown in Western Europe, along with the new surge in commercialization and in direct relation to the shift to action-adventure movies. With the proliferation of commercial channels and the high cost of original programming, there has been a heavy demand for mainly foreign movies and series to fill the program gap.[46] Sepstrup points out that the great increase in use of U.S. movies and serials is not based on a special preference for U.S. products, it is grounded in commercialization and the proliferation of commercial channels with slots to fill and sell.[47] With market-based imperatives in place, violence as an important ingredient of programming follows. In reference to their transnational study of TV violence, Huesmann and Efron point out that "of the violent programs evaluated in the first wave of the study in Finland, Poland, and Israel, about 60 percent have been imported from the United States."[48]

While there has been little dispute that commercial broadcasting has been associated with a large diet of violence, there are ongoing debates over the effects of violent programs. There are problems of causality: does alienation and aggression come from watching violence on television, or do alienated and violence-prone people tend to watch programs that express their world view? Is TV violence an incitement and stimulus to violence or a catharsis? Despite continuing debate, the overwhelming consensus of experts and studies over several decades, covering a number of countries and supported by a variety of models of behavior and controlled experiments, is that TV violence makes a significant contribution to real world violence by desensitizing viewers, making people insecure and fearful, and habituating, modeling, and sometimes inciting people to violence.[49]

Commercial Broadcasting and Anti-democratic Power

The threat of a centralized, monolithic, state-controlled broadcasting system is well understood and feared in the West. What is little recognized or understood is the centralizing, ideologically monolithic, and self-protecting properties of an increasingly powerful commercial broadcasting system. U.S. experience suggests that once a commercial system is firmly in place it becomes difficult to challenge, and as its economic power increases so does its ability to keep threats at bay and gradually to remove all obstacles to commercial exploitation of the public airwaves and without any charge for their use. Commercial broadcasters do compete with one another, but this competition is for large audiences through offering entertainment fare under the constraint of advertisers, and it ignores externalities as a matter of structural necessity and the force of competition.

As one illustration of the power of the industry to fend off virtually any threat, in the liberal environment of 1963 the FCC leadership decided to try to impose a formal restraint on commercial advertising, but only to the extent of designating as the regulatory standard the limits suggested by the broadcasters' own trade association. This enraged the industry, which went quickly to work on Congress, and the FCC quickly backed down.[50]

Another important illustration of the commercial broadcasting industry's self-protective power is found in the area of children's television. The country claims to revere children, and child abuse is given frequent and indignant attention. But although the erosion of children's programming, and the commercial exploitation of the residual ghettoized programs, occurred as the commercial networks were making record-breaking profits, and although substantial numbers of adults have been angered by this programming, it has taken place with only a muted outcry. The FCC has been pressed hard to do something about the situation by organized groups like ACT, but the mass media have not allowed this matter to become a serious issue. When, after a 13-year delay in dealing with an ACT petition to constrain abuses in children's television, the FCC decided in December 1983 that commercial broadcasters had no obligation to serve children, this decision was not even mentioned in the *New York Times*. In fact, between 1979 and 1989, although many important petitions were submitted by ACT and decisions were made by the FCC that bore significantly on the commercial broadcasters neglect and abuse of children, the *New York Times*, *Washington Post*, and *Los Angeles Times* had neither a front-page article nor an editorial on the subject. The dominant members of the press, most of them with substantial broadcasting interests of their own, simply refused to make the huge failure of commercial broadcasters in children's programming a serious issue.

It is also enlightening to see how the principles of broadcasters' public service responsibility were gradually amended to accommodate broadcaster interests, without discussion or debate. As advertised programs displaced sustaining programs, and the "balance wheel" disappeared, what gave way was any public interest standard. The industry defense was in terms of "free speech" and the Alice-in-Wonderland principle that if the audience watches, the public interest is served. But the industry hardly needed a defense: raw power allowed the public interest standard to erode quietly, the issues undiscussed in any open debate, even as regards the enormous abuses and neglect in children's programming.

NOTES

[1] The Atlanta Olympic Conscience Coalition estimates that the 1996 Atlanta games will displace over 9,700 low-and moderate-income residents (Metro Atlanta Task Force for the Homeless, *Homelessness in Metropolitan Atlanta*, 1994, Appendix B). And a Greek restaurant in Atlanta was forced to change its name from Olympic to Olympia to ensure exclusive name benefits to the sponsors (Karen Heller, "Selling the Olympics," *Philadelphia Inquirer Magazine*, June 23, 1995).

[2] An internal audit of Brown Williamson Tobacco Company made public in 1994 showed that the company had spent a million dollars over a four-year period to get its cigarettes exhibited in movies.

Sylvester Stallone was paid $500,000 to use its cigarettes in five feature films (including *Godfather III, Rambo,* and *Rocky IV*); Paul Newman got a $42,307 car and other amenities for helping advance cigarette images. (Philip Hilts, "Company Spent $1 Million to Put Cigarettes in Movies, Memos Show," *New York Times,* May 20, 1994, p. A26.)

[3] Kyle Pope, "Product Placements Creep Into Video Games," *Wall Street Journal,* Dec. 5, 1994, p. B1.

[4] Teri Agins, "Is It a TV Show? Or Is It Advertising?," *Wall Street Journal,* May 10, 1994, p. B1.

[5] Barnouw, *The Sponsor,* p. 95.

[6] Richard Barnet and John Cavanagh, *Global Dreams: Imperial Corporations and the New World Order,* New York: Simon and Schuster, 1994, pp. 37–38.

[7] An illustration of bargaining down at the expense of schools is given in Chapter 27, note 10.

[8] The number of schools involved was approximately 12,000 at the end of 1994; some eight million children were reached by Channel One.

[9] "Selling To School Kids," *Consumer Reports,* May 1995, pp. 327–329.

[10] Leah Brumer, "Up the Sandbox: Safe Fun in 'America's Playground,'" *Express,* Aug. 26, 1994.

[11] Debora Silverman, *Selling Culture: Bloomingdale's, Diana Vreeland, and the New Aristocracy of Taste in Reagan's America,* New York: Pantheon, 1986.

[12] These quotes are taken from Herbet Schiller's important book *Culture, Inc.: The Corporate Takeover of Public Expression,* New York: Oxford, 1989.

[13] This concept is applied to the broadcasting field in Chapter 22, below.

[14] In the spring of 1995, the advertising fraternity's leading newspaper, *Advertising Age,* was exceptionally preoccupied with the advertising and sales possibilities of the Internet, reflecting the interests of the industry. For further discussion of the Internet, and citations, see Chapter 26.

[15] A.J. Liebling, *The Press,* New York: Ballantine, 1964, p. 15.

[16] The five factors to be discussed here are elements of the "propaganda model," spelled out in greater detail in Herman and Chomsky, *Manufacturing Consent: The Political Economy of the Mass Media,* New York: Pantheon, 1988.

[17] Back in 1947, A.J. Liebling said that "I cannot believe that labor leaders are so stupid they will let the other side monopolize the press indefinitely." (*The Press,* p. 23). Liebling was not thought to have been an optimist, or to underestimate human stupidity. He may have underrated the economic costs of starting and maintaining a newspaper, however.

[18] The median value of the wealth of the control groups of the largest media corporations in the mid-1980s, as measured by the value of stock they owned in the controlled mass media corporation alone, was approximately $450 million. See Herman and Chomsky, *Manufacturing Consent,* pp. 8–10.

[19] Exponents of the neo-conservative view that the mass media have a liberal bias always avoid the question of ownership and control, implying that lower echelon personnel set their own agendas, without rules from above. Wallace (*Reader's Digest*), Katherine Graham, Arthur Hays Sulzberger, Robert Sarnoff, and Rupert Murdoch have had definite policy agendas that they have enforced in their organizations is simply not discussed. The effects of profitability rules, and policies based on advertiser interests and sensitivity, are not discussed either. The neo-conservative analysts also don't do much in the way of analyzing actual news and opinion outputs. Their main focus is on whether the reporters and copy editors vote Republican or Democratic. For the neo-conservative view, see Michael Ledeen, *Grave New World,* New York: Oxford University Press, 1985, chap. 5, and Lichter, Rothman and Lichter, *The Media Elite,* Bethesda, MD: Adler & Adler, 1986. For critiques, see Herbert Gans, "Are U.S. Journalists Dangerously Liberal?," *Columbia Journalism Review,* Nov.-Dec., 1985; Herman and Chomsky, *Manufacturing Consent,* chap. 1.

[20] See Barnouw's discussion of the evidence for this in Vietnam War coverage, *The Sponsor: Notes on a Modern Potentate,* New York: Oxford university Press, 1978, pp. 62–66.

[21] On the huge impact of advertisers on the editorial content of women's magazines, see Gloria Steinem's account of her experiences with *Ms. Magazine* during the years in which it depended on advertising. "Sex, Lies and Advertising," *Ms. Magazine*, July-Aug. 1990, pp. 18–28.

[22] See Barnouw, *The Sponsor*, pp. 79–121. The finding that advertisers don't very often actively intervene in programming misses the point: the main route for advertiser intervention lies in the nature of their demand and ability to choose.

[23] For an examination of how this has been done on the subject of terrorism, see Edward Herman and Gerry O'Sullivan, *The "Terrorism" Industry: The Experts and Institutions That Shape Our View of Terror*, New York: Pantheon, 1990.

[24] The largest of the dissident institutes, the Institute for Policy Studies, has a budget less than a fifth that of the Georgetown Center for Strategic and International Studies, the Hoover Institution, or the American Enterprise Institute.

[25] Declaring that the Sandinista government of Nicaragua was "Marxist-Leninist" played an important role in obtaining mass media and Democratic Party cooperation in the economic and military warfare carried out against Nicaragua in the years 1981–1989. As in the case of the overthrow of the democratically elected government of Guatemala by proxy invasion in 1954, both the press and Democrats accepted the false claim that the objective of the U.S. government in its actions was to bring about "democracy." See Peter Kornbluh, *Nicaragua: The Price of Intervention*, Washington, DC: Institute for Policy Studies, 1987, chap. 4; Herman and Chomsky, *Manufacturing Consent*, pp. xii–xiii.

[26] See Herman and O'Sullivan, *The "Terrorism" Industry*, preface, chaps. 1–3, and 8.

[27] These two cases are discussed at length in Chomsky and Herman, *The Washington Connection and Third World Fascism*, chap. 3.

[28] Herman and Chomsky, *Manufacturing Consent*, chap. 5.

[29] For details, see ibid., pp. xii–xiii and 116-42; Chomsky, *The Culture of Terrorism*, Boston: South End Press, 1988, pp. 39–61, 203–211; Jack Spence, "The U.S. Media: Covering (Over) Nicaragua," In Thomas Walker, ed., *Reagan Versus the Sandinistas*, Boulder, Colorado: Westview, 1987, pp. 182–201.

[30] David Shipler, "Nicaragua, Victory for U.S. Fair Play," *New York Times*, Op. Ed., March 1, 1990; Anthony Lewis, "Out of This Nettle," *New York Times*, March 2, 1990.

[31] At a press conference with Mrs. Chamorro in Washington, D.C., in early November 1989, President Bush stated explicitly that the U.S. embargo would be lifted only if her UNO party won the election. See Lauter, "Nicaragua's Opposition Candidate at White House," *Los Angeles Times*, Nov. 9, 1989, p. A15.

[32] James Curran, "Advertising and the Press," in Curran, ed., *The British Press: A Manifesto*, London: Macmillan, 1978, pp. 252–55.

[33] Sometimes these lies are corrected belatedly and in muted fashion in the mainstream press. The *New York Times* entitled an editorial of January 18, 1988, "The Lie that Was Not Shot Down," referring to the Reagan administration lie that the Soviet Union knowingly shot down a Korean civilian plane in September 1983. That lie *was* shot down, in the marginalized press; the mainstream press, including the *New York Times*, allowed it to survive and gave it intense coverage, based on maintaining a high gullibility quotient and refusing to investigate or question a lie convenient to ongoing state demands.

[34] This was the basis of the distinction drawn in Herman and Chomsky between "worthy" and "unworthy" victims. See *Manufacturing Consent*, chap. 2. An important case of remarkable but system-supportive gullibility was the mainstream media's handling of the alleged Bulgarian-KGB connection to the 1981 shooting of Pope John Paul II. See ibid. chap. 4.

[35] See Philip Elliott, "Intellectuals, the 'information society' and the disappearance of the public sphere," *Media Culture & Society*, July 1982; Graham Murdoch and Peter Golding, "Information poverty and political inequality: Citizenship in the age of privatized communications," *Journal of Communication*, 1989; Erik Barnouw, *The Sponsor: Notes on a Modern Potentate*, New York: Oxford University Press, 1978, pp. 113–52, 179–82; P. Sepstrup, "Implications of Current Developments in West European Broadcasting," *Media Culture & Society*, 1989; P. Scannell, "Public Service Broadcasting and modern

public life," *Media Culture & Society*, 1989. Scannell believes that the contribution of public broadcasting to the public sphere is more than modest.

[36] Branouw, *The Sponsor*, p. 95.

[37] *Television in the Corporate Interest*, New York: Praeger, 1976, pp. 27–31.

[38] Ibid., p. 97.

[39] In the first half of the 1980s, NBC was taken over by General Electric Company, a huge multinational important in weapons and nuclear reactor manufacture; ABC was acquired by Capital Cities, a media conglomerate famous for its bottom-line orientation; and control of CBS was assumed by Lawrence Tisch of Loews, a large conglomerate in the cigarette, hotel and other businesses. A fourth network that has emerged in the 1980s and 1990s, Fox, is controlled by Rupert Murdoch, owner of a global media empire not known for its socially forward-looking policies.

[40] *The Sponsor*, p. 138.

[41] Jay Blumler et al, "Broadcasting Finance and Programme Quality: An International Review," *European Journal of Communication*, 1986, pp. 348–50.

[42] A. Pragnell, *Television in Europe: Quality and Values in Time of Change*, Media Monograph No. 5, Manchester: European Institute for Media, 1987, p. 6.

[43] Statement of Gabriel de Broglie, the departing head of the French national supervisory organization CNCL, in January 1989, quoted in G. Graham, "Never mind the quality," *Financial Times*, June 28, 1989.

[44] Edward Palmer, *Television and America's Children: A Crisis of Neglect*, New York: Oxford, 1988.

[45] George Gerbner and Nancy Signorielli, "Violence Profile 1967 through 1988–89; enduring patterns," mimeo, Jan. 1990.

[46] This is an important reason for the surge in cross-border and vertical mergers in the communications business, as the value and importance to broadcasters of gaining access to old stocks of movies and TV series, and to the ongoing production of such programs, has risen sharply.

[47] P. Sepstrup, above, note 1.

[48] L. Huesmann and L. Efron, *Television and the Aggressive Child: A Cross-National Comparison*, Hillsdale, NJ: Erlbaum Associates, 1986.

[49] Gerbner and Signorielli, above note 11; Huesmann and Efron, ibid; Frank Mankiewicz and Joel Swerdlow, *Remote Control*, New York: Ballantine, 1979; G. Barlow and A. Hill, *Video Violence and Children*, New York: St. Martin's, 1985; National Institute of Mental Health, *Television and Behavior: Ten Years of Scientific Progress and Implications for the Eighties*, vol. 2: Technical Reviews. Washington: Department of Health and Public Services, 1982.

[50] E. Kransnow, E. Longley and H. Terry, *The Politics of Broadcast Regulation*, New York: St. Martin's, 1982, pp. 194–96.

| # Corporate Media Profiles
Doug Henwood

NBC: *The GE Broadcasting Co.*

In 1986, when GE bought RCA, and thereby *NBC*, it returned things to a state not unlike the early 1920s. The Radio Corporation of America was founded in 1919, as a joint venture of General Electric and Westinghouse; *NBC* itself was born in 1926, as a joint venture of RCA, GE, and Westinghouse. Trustbusters forced the giants to divest RCA in 1931, and the company did nicely on its own for over four decades. But by the 1970s, it was faltering badly; though new management in the early 1980s cleaned up RCA's act somewhat, it was still vulnerable to a takeover. GE paid $6.4 billion for RCA and swallowed it with nary a burp.

Ge is an industrial and financial powerhouse with 1988 sales of $50.1 billion and profits of $3.4 billion. (*NBC* contributed 7.3% and 9.1% of these totals, respectively.) Among other things, GE makes refrigerators, light bulbs, conventional and nuclear power plants, plastics, robots, aircraft engines, and medical equipment. Its highly aggressive GE Capital subsidiary offers financing for leases and leveraged buyouts; the Kidder Peabody subsidiary is a major securities broker-dealer. GE is consistently listed among the top Pentagon contractors; its detonators reside in every hydrogen bomb in the US arsenal.

Under chair John "Neutron Jack" Welch, GE has pledged that it will be number one or two in whatever markets it competes in worldwide. If a line of business can't shape up, it will be sold or terminated. (Welch is called Neutron Jack—like the neutron bomb—because he makes people disappear but leaves the buildings standing.) While *NBC* has been the top-rated network for four years now, and is by far the most profitable of the three networks, the news division is rated last, and is the only money loser in the network pack. Since it's unlikely *NBC News* will be extinguished, it must shape up.

Political Connections

GE—which employed Ronald Reagan as its PR spokesperson from 1954 to 1962—has long cultivated political connections. GE's board has traded personnel with the Pentagon, and former GE president Charles "Electric Charlie" Wilson was one of the architects of the permanent war economy." With the support of public opinion, as marshalled by the press," Wilson said in 1951, the public must be "convinced that the only way to keep disaster away from our

---

From EXTRA!, May–June 1989. Reprinted with permission.

shores is to build America's might." Now, of course, GE doesn't have to marshall the press; GE owns the press, or at least a chunk of it.

Shortly after taking over *NBC*, GE installed Robert Wright, a veteran financial executive, as network president. Wright immediately created a stir by urging network employees—including news staffers—to contribute to the company's political action committee to help the network buy some friends in Congress. He suggested that employees who failed to contribute to the PAC were of dubious loyalty to the firm—a heavy charge, given Wright's stated intentions of heavy layoffs. The resulting uproar from news employees and the public caused him to drop the suggestion, but Wright left little doubt as to where he and GE stood. (Wright gave money to the Bush campaign, as did "Neutron Jack" Welch, and Cap Cities/ABC chair Thomas Murphy.)

Though it's hard to trace a change in *NBC* news coverage since GE took over, who knows what the future holds? GE has taken a liking to conservative commentator John McLaughlin and his crew of rightwing loudmouths; it sponsors the *McLaughlin Group* and promotes it heavily. Not content with his 2 weekly programs, GE's new cable network, *CNBC*, recently launched a nightly talkshow for McLaughlin.

Chairman Welch, in turn, is a favorite of right-wing media scourge Reed Irvine. In a cost-cutting environment, will correspondents want to keep their visibly conservative bosses happy?

From Bad to Worse?

In 1987, *NBC* provoked a strike, by putting forth a take-it-or-leave-it deal that would reserve the right to transfer operations to non-union subsidiaries, hire over 100 temporary low-wage and benefit-free staffers on a day-to-day basis, robotize operations, and rely more heavily on network pools for visuals. *NBC* won, and proceeded to cut the staff by 25%.

The president of *NBC News* is ex-newspaperman Michael Gartner, a deceptively folksy, bow-tied Iowan. While editor of the *Des Moines Register*, Gartner tried to buy the paper from the Cowles chain; though he failed, his attempt put the paper "into play," leading to its takeover by Gannett. He joined Gannett shortly thereafter, first as the hatchet man assigned to "clean house" at the newly purchased *Louisville Courier-Journal*, then as a consultant to *USA Today*. Thus he has valuable experience in closing papers and laying people off—always a plus when you're in GE's employ. Gartner still owns the *Ames Tribune* (IA), notorious for its low pay scales. "He's very good with a balance sheet," says a former colleague.

Morale is reportedly awful at *NBC News*, where the workforce has been reduced from 1400 to 1000, and the budget cut from $300 million to about $250 million.

Global Reach

In December 1988, *NBC* joined with *Cablevision*, a large Long Island-based system, to create at least one national cable network and several regional news and sports channels. *Cablevision* is the 10th-largest system in the country; it owns *Bravo* and five regional sports networks, and produces a local news show for Long Island.

Cablevision offers another outlet for the 1992 Olympics, for which *NBC* paid heavily—$400 million. Recalling the flak it took for excessive commercials during the Seoul games, *NBC* promises not to clutter up the airwaves next time around; instead, they hope to offer some events, probably the less-popular ones, on the *NBC-Cablevision* channels, on a pay-per-view basis. By reserving popular events for broadcast, *NBC* will keep its affiliates happy.

The *Consumer News and Business Channel*, a nonunion operation that is *NBC*'s first cable network, premiered in April. *CNBC*, in which *Cablevision* holds a 50% share, is billed as having more of a consumer twist than its principal rival, the established but low-rent *Financial News Network*. How much can consumers expect form a GE-owned network featuring a nightly *John McLaughlin Show*? *CNBC* programmers told *Extra!* they had considered and rejected a Ralph Nader show.

Unsatisfied by merely extending its domestic reach, *NBC* wants the world. Last year, it bought 5% of a New Zealand network, 38% of the London-based *Visinews*, and an option on an Australian network. *Visinews*, which *NBC* shares with *Reuters* (51%) and the *BBC* (11%), produces news reports for 84 countries. *NBC* not only wants the footage—*Visinews* is staffed by lower-paid employees than *NBC*—it sees *Visinews*' 84 countries as virgin territory for its own news products. At first, *NBC* said *Visinews* meant no staff cutbacks, but there have been, along with demotions.

At home, to cut costs, *NBC*'s Chicago news bureau was merged with the local station's, and the Houston bureau has been closed. With Houston's demise, Louisiana—not to mention Texas—is now covered from Burbank.

While reporting is expensive, fluff is cheap: A new prime-time program, *Yesterday, Today, Tomorrow*, co-produced by the entertainment and news divisions, will include dramatic re-creations of appropriately titillating events. News can be fun! And why not—after all, Gartner has said that *Cheers* serves the public interest as much as *NBC Nightly News*. Maybe he's right.

Of course, *NBC* wasn't exactly an iconoclastic wonder in news or entertainment before GE came on the scene, nor is *NBC* the only network that has zealously stuck it to the workforce. But GE parentage adds both zip and force to the transformation, and increases pressure on other networks to follow suit. *NBC*'s profitability is one of the highest of any GE business lines. If Gartner can just get the news division whipped into shape, Neutron Jack will beam with pride.

THE BOARD

GE's board is a conservative cross-section of the power elite—corporate executives, bankers, retired cabinet members and generals, an Ivy League president and several Ivy boardmembers. There are multiple ties with the Morgan bank, Citicorp, Manufacturers Hanover. GE boardmembers also serve on several media industry boards—Harper & Row, **Reuters**, the **Washington Post**. They are well-represented in the branches of the permanent government, too: according to INFACT, three (Preston, Welch, and Sigler) belong to the Business Roundtable; three (Preston, Welch, Wriston) to the Council on Foreign Relations; two (Michelson, Wriston) to the Rand Corp. Six (Hood, Jones, Sigler, Smith, Welch, Wriston) either belong to or visit the all-male Bohemian Club, which owns the California retreat where a naked George Shultz might be seen pissing on a tree next to an equally naked Harold Brown.

OUTSIDE (not GE employees)

- **H. Brewster Atwater, Jr.** Chair and CEO, General Mills. Other board/memberships: Norwest, Sun Co.

- **Richard T. Baker.** Consultant to Ernst & Whinney (accountants). High-profile Clevelandite. Other boards/memberships: International Paper, Louisiana Land & Exploration, Pacific Construction.

- **Charles D. Dickey.** Retired Chair and director, Scott Paper. Other boards/memberships: J.P. Morgon/Morgan Guaranty Trust.

- **Lawrence E. Fouraker.** Business educator and fellow, Kennedy School of Government, Harvard. Other boards/memberships: Citicorp, Gillette, R.H. Macy, The New England, Texas Eastern; Museum of Fine Arts, Boston.

- **Henry H. Henley, Jr.** Retired chair and CEO, director, Cluett, Peabody & Co. Other boards/memberships: Bristol-Meyers, Manufacturers Hanover, Home Life, Olin, West Point-Pepperell.

- **Henry L. Hillman.** Chair, Hillman Company ("diversified operations and investments"). Other boards/memberships: Chemical Bank, Cummins Engine, PNC Financial; Business Council.

- **Gen. David C. Jones (Ret.).** Retired Air Force general and former chair, Joint Chiefs of Staff. Criticized the Carter/Brown military budget as inadequate; strident promoter of the Soviet Threat. Other boards/memberships: U.S. Air, USX.

- **Robert E. Mercer.** Chair, Goodyear Tire & Rubber. Other boards/memberships: CPC Intl., Manufacturers Hanover.

- **Gertrude G. Michelson.** Senior vice president, External Affairs, R.H. Macy & Co. Other boards/memberships: Chubb, Goodyear, Harper & Row, Irving Trust, Quaker Oats, Stanley Works; Columbia University, Federal Reserve Bank of New York; Markle Foundation, Helena Ruberstein Foundation, Rand Corp.

- **Barbara Scott Preiskel.** Attorney, New York. Other board/memberships: R.H. Macy & Co., Massachusetts Mutual, Textron, **Washington Post,** American Women's Economic Development, Ford Foundation, New York City Board of Ethics, Yale Univ.

- **Lewis T. Preston.** Chair, J.P. Morgan & Co./Morgan Guaranty Trust. Other boards/memberships: Business Roundtable, Council on Foreign Relations, Federal Reserve Bank of New York.

- **Frank H.T. Rhodes.** Geologist and President, Cornell Univ. Other boards/memberships: Carnegie Foundation for the Advancement of Teaching, Committee for Economic Development, Gannett Foundation, Mellon Foundation, Memorial-Sloan Kettering Cancer Center.

- **Andrew C. Sigler.** Chair and CEO, Champion International (paper and forest products). Other boards/memberships: AMF, Bristol-Meyers, Chemical Bank; Business Roundtable.

- **William French Smith.** Former Attorney General and partner, Gibson, Dunn & Crutcher. Former lawyer to Ronald Reagan. Other boards/memberships: American International Group, Fisher Scientific, H.F. Ahmanson, Earle M. Jorgenson Cos., Pacific Lighting, Pacific Telephone, Weintraub Entertainment; Center for Strategic and International Studies (Georgetown), Kennedy School of Government (Harvard), National Symphony, Ronald Reagan Presidential Library, University of California.

Capital Cities/ABC:
No. 2, and Trying Harder

In 1985, Capital Cities, a company with interests in TV, radio and publishing, spent $3.4 billion to take over the **American Broadcasting Co.**, a company four times its size. At the time, ABC employees feared their new parent's tight fists and sharp eyes. Cap Cities management has certainly lived up to its advance billing; the acquisition, which looked a little grandiose in 1985, effectively paid for itself in four years.

Cap Cities/**ABC** is a diversified media conglomerate with little debt and $1.1 billion in the bank. Just under 80 percent of 1989 sales (which totaled $4.96 billion), and 86 percent of profits (1989 total: $922 million), came from broadcasting, with the balance from publishing. Within broadcasting, however, lie several stories. The radio share of sales and profits is small—8 percent and 11 percent, respectively. (These are estimates by First Boston; Cap Cities/**ABC** doesn't provide a detailed breakdown.) The network, though responsible for 62 percent of Cap Cities' sales, produced only 20 percent of its broadcasting profits, and the profit margin (profits/sales) was an anemic 7 percent.

Radio, video and cable TV—the latter two considered broadcasting here—are far more lucrative, with margins around 30 percent. But the real money-spewers are the eight local TV stations the network owns, which reach just under the legal maximum of 25 percent of the U.S. population. Though they produce only 21 percent of sales, they contribute more than half of broadcasting profits, and their profit margin is 54 percent. This is the highest for the three networks; **NBC**'s owned-and-operated stations had a 42 percent margin; **CBS**'s, 36 percent.

Network profits are low, and local station profits high, because networks pay their affiliates to broadcast their programming, and split the ad revenue with them. (Obviously, if you own the station, you save the fees and keep all the ad revenue.) With the growth of cable, VCRs, and a fourth web, Rupert Murdoch's **Fox Network**, this old order is changing.

From EXTRA!, Mar-Apr, 1990. Reprinted with permission.

The networks' share of primetime audience eyeballs has fallen from 94 percent in 1978 to below 70 percent, and is likely to continue its downward slide, especially as Washington, Los Angeles, Chicago and outer boroughs of New York City are increasingly wired for cable. **NBC** president Robert Wright sees the mid-50 percent range as its likely resting place; ad people are about 10 percentage points more optimistic.

Even though 50 percent of the primetime audience is nothing to sneeze at, the networks are not entirely happy with the future of broadcast TV. In what may be a taste of things to come, **ABC** started charging a Florida affiliate to carry its programming in early 1989. Even if this doesn't become standard procedure, networks want to reduce payments to affiliates, since local stations would have to pay up for substitute product. And they're looking to milk the broadcast cow with more vigor.

THE BILL CASEY CONNECTION

Several Capital Cities founders and board members have had intelligence connections, but none more prominently than the late CIA director William Casey.

Casey, along with broadcaster Lowell Thomas, Republican leader Thomas Dewey and others, started Cap Cities in 1954. Serving as the company's chief counsel, Casey was also a board member until 1981, when he was appointed by Reagan to head the spy agency. When Casey was forced to put his stocks in a blind trust in 1983, he quietly kept control of his largest single holding: $7.5 million in Cap Cities stock.

Despite his close connections to a company in the news business, no one ever accused Casey of being a fanatical supporter of the First Amendment. In November 1984, in his official capacity as CIA director, he asked the Federal Communications Commission to revoke all of **ABC**'s TV and radio licenses, in retaliation for an **ABC News** report that suggested the CIA had attempted to assassinate a U.S. citizen (**ABC News**, 9/19/84, 9/20/84). In February 1985, the CIA asked the FCC to apply Fairness Doctrine penalties to the network. The following month, **ABC** was bought by Casey's Cap Cities.

(See "The Seizing of the American Broadcast Company," by Andy Boehm, L.A. Weekly, 2/20-26/87.

While it's hard to work up much sympathy for an industry that collectively made $610 million on sales of $7.8 billion in 1989, the three networks nonetheless feel terribly put upon. Consequently, they are practicing the classic techniques of a monopoly suddenly faced with competition: slashing staff and wages, outsourcing, diversifying and searching for new sources of revenue.

Like **NBC** and unlike **CBS**, the network is getting more deeply into cable and is beginning to move overseas. Cap Cities/**ABC** owns 80 percent of **ESPN**, 38 percent of **Arts & Entertainment**, and 33 percent of **Lifetime**, as well as 25-50 percent interests in several satellite and cable channels in Europe.

With all three networks now in the hands of hard-nosed operators (Laurence Tisch at **CBS**, and GE at **NBC**), the culture of network TV, once characterized by an almost royal indifference to costs, has now joined the business mainstream. And Cap Cities/**ABC** is a virtuoso at fattening its bottom line. Morgan Stanley estimates that corporate overhead has been reduced by $50 million a year under the new regime. In 1988, **ABC News** was the first network news division to make money in a presidential election year, usually a time of high costs and skimpy ad revenue. (According to Wall Street estimates, **CBS News** broke even, and **NBC News** lost $50 million in the same year.)

Some of the cost-cutting is hard to argue with—like having Peter Jennings cover the Iowa caucuses from inside the state capitol instead of building a $500,000 temporary studio.

But the favorite target of the cost-cutter is always labor, especially in an industry with relatively low capital costs. And this is an area where Cap Cities chair Thomas Murphy—who recently announced his partial retirement—shines. As a Newspaper Guild official said of Murphy shortly after the **ABC** takeover was announced, "If I ever get to hell, I know I'll meet him there."

Cap Cities had a long history of labor conflict, especially at its newspapers, an industry that has suffered from a squeeze not unlike that of today's broadcasting business. Unionists argue that the Cap Cities style is confrontational and penny-pinching, the kind of stuff that alienates people and sends morale into the tank. No one seems to have an accurate count of how many people have been laid off—the company refuses to give a count—but private estimates are around 1,500, which would put **ABC** at the head of the network class.

Wall Street, of course, loves to see a company on the labor offensive, one of several reasons it has long carried a torch for Cap Cities. Brokerage reports on the company typically gush with admiration for Murphy and the Cap Cities team.

The consensus is that **ABC**, currently the No. 2 network in the ratings and in profitability, is best positioned for the long haul. **NBC** and **CBS** are in the hands of financiers; the Cap Cities crowd has three decades' experience in the broadcasting business.

The eight TV stations it owns, more than the other two networks, are likely to remain money machines despite the encroachment of cable. And **ABC** has cable covered too—while **ESPN** is paying off nicely, **NBC** is new to the game, and **CBS** hasn't even tested the waters yet.

ABC has several new hit shows—including **Doogie Howser, M.D., thirtysomething, Roseanne** and **America's Funniest Home Videos**—while **NBC**'s fare, especially **The Cosby Show**, is getting a little long in the tooth. The news division, as viewers are frequently reminded, is the nation's No. 1 source of information (or whatever it is that Jennings and Koppel deliver).

Cap Cities' other lines of business, radio and publishing, are suffering from "softening" trends in national advertising, but TV is at the heart of the company's business. About the only negative is the rising cost of programming, especially big-time sports—like the $900 million **ABC** had to pay to keep the rights to **Monday Night Football**, or the $450 million **ESPN** paid for a Sunday night package.

It's sometimes said that there's only enough room for two-and-a-half networks; Cap Cities/**ABC** is unlikely to be the one bisected. In fact, should the global media universe condense into about ten giants, Cap Cities is almost certain to be in that pantheon.

BOARD OF DIRECTORS

Chair Thomas S. Murphy was a member of the group that started Capital Cities in 1957, when it was a rag-tag collection of small TV stations; among his colleagues was the late CIA director William Casey, Casey was on the board from 1976 until he became chief spook in 1981. Casey's failure to disclose his holdings in Cap Cities caused a mild furor when it was revealed by **Newsday** in 1985. Casey was, and Murphy and fellow board-member Thomas Macice are, members of the Knights of Malta, a secretive international club of right-wing ruling class Catholics with long-suspected intelligence links.

INSIDE (Cap Cities/ABC employees)

- Daniel B. Burke. President. Will become CEO in June 1990. Former head, Jell-O division, General Foods; brother of retired Johnson & Johnson chair and eminence grise James Burke. Other boards/memberships: Avon, Conrail, Rohm & Haas; American Film Institute, American Women's Economic Development Corp., National Urban League, N.Y. Botanical Garden, Ohio Wesleyan Univ., Conference Board, Council on Foreign Relations. 1988 salary: $969,286.

- Thomas S. Murphy. Chair and CEO. Will retire as CEO in June 1990 while retaining chair. Other boards/memberships: General Housewares, IBM, Johnson & Johnson, Texaco. Member of legendary class of '49, Harvard Business School. Member, Knights of Malta. 1988 salary: $1,030,501.

- John B. Sias. Executive vice president, ABC Television Network Group and veteran of Cap Cities' publishing division. Sias has a reputation as a cut-up—the kind of guy who wears a Captain Marvel T-shirt under his white business shirt. 1988 salary: $815,286.

OUTSIDE (non-employees)

- Robert P. Bauman. Chair, SmithKline Beecham. Harvard Business School classmate of Daniel Burke. Former General Foods exec and former vice chair of Avco and Textron. Other boards/memberships: Avco, McKesson Corp.

- Warren E. Buffett. Legendary billionaire investor based in Omaha, with major holdings in Cap Cities (16.6 percent), Saomon Bros., **Washington Post Co**. Close friend of **Post** publisher Katharine Graham and **CBS** head Laurence Tisch. Owner, **Buffalo News**, several insurance companies and retailers. Promoter of population control, nuclear nonproliferation, rhino preservation, and U.S.-Soviet friendship. Other boards/memberships (partial list): Berkshire-Hathaway (Buffett's investment vehicle), **Omaha World-Herald**, Salomon Bros.; Boys Clubs of Omaha, Grinnell college, Urban Inst.

- Frank T. Cary. Retired chair, IBM. Other boards/memberships: Hospital Corp. of America, J.P. Morgan, Merck, New York Stock Exchange (whose chair and vice-chair are members of the Knights of Malta), PepsiCo, Texaco; Business Council, MIT.

- Leonard H. Goldenson. Retired chair, **ABC.**

- Leon Hess. Chair, Amerada Hess; owner, New York Jets. Other boards/memberships: Mutual Benefit Life.

- George P. Jenkins. Consultant to W.R. Grace & Co; retired chair, Metropolitan Life. Other boards/memberships: Bethlehem Steel, Chicago Pacific, Trammel Crow.

- Frank S. Jones. Professor of urban studies, MIT.

- Ann Dibble Jordan. Social worker and consultant to University of Chicago Medical School and Stroh Co. Other boards/memberships: **Granite Broadcasting**, Johnson & Johnson, National Bank of Washington; National Symphony, National Foundation for Learning Disabilities, World Population Institute.

- Thomas M. Macioce. Partner, Shea & Gould (New York law firm); former chair, Allied Stores. Member, Knights of Malta. Other boards/memberships: Columbia Press, Grossman's, Manufacturers Hanover, the Vatican Bank.

CBS:
Tiffany Goes to K-Mart

*Poor CBS. Once known as the "Tiffany of networks," for its pretensions to high-mindedness, three years in the ratings basement have reduced it to doing a promotional deal with K-Mart. The network, which spent three decades on the top of the heap, is a prime-time disaster. And its news division, which once thought of itself as the **New York Times** of the air-meant as self-praise, of course—has lost both ratings leadership and Diane Sawyer to **ABC**.*

CBS, once led by the aristocratic William Paley, is now in the hands of a Wall Street operator, Laurence Tisch. Once an entertainment conglomerate, with interests in movies, records and publishing, the network is now a mere broadcaster, with sales of only $2.8 billion last year.

Paley didn't found **CBS**, but he might have. The son of a cigar manufacturer, Paley wanted to rub shoulders with the rich and famous. The tobacco business was no way to do that—but radio was. So, in 1928, the 27-year-old mogul-to-be bought a group of radio stations that were having a rough time against the almighty **NBC**. Among his first actions was to hire Edward L. Berneys, an early genius in the infant field of public relations. Bernays, a veteran of the World War I propaganda machine, thought the task of the media and the PR industry was the "engineering of consent" through the use of "scientific principles."

Though Paley is revered by those who lament the debasement of broadcasting by the bottom-line crowd, he didn't run **CBS** like a philanthropy. In early radio, it was crass to mention the price of a product in an ad, and toothpaste was considered too personal a product for public huckstering. Neither of these conventions inhibited Paley. In 1931, he urged Cremo cigars to mention the low price of 5 cents; by the mid-30s, **CBS** was running laxative ads.

Paley had no great interest in bold programming. In the early years, his strategy for building the radio network was to hire away **NBC**'s stars, rather than produce anything original. Appropriately enough, Paley's **CBS** was a pioneer in developing modern ratings and market research systems. For example, a randomly selected audience was asked to listen to a radio program under development and to express their reactions by pushing buttons installed in their chairs. Less than ten years after taking over **CBS**, Paley was celebrated as a hero in the

---

From EXTRA!, Oct-Nov, 1989. Reprinted with permission.

young **Fortune** magazine. While the rest of the economy was mired in depression, **CBS** boomed.

CBS also developed the practice of producing its own programs and selling air time to advertisers, rather than having the advertiser produce the show. Not that this would reduce the influence of advertisers on programming; in the late 1940s, Paley brought in a group from the Young & Rubicam ad agency to staff the programming department.

Almost from the beginning **CBS** was the leader in entertainment TV: Ed Sullivan, Jackie Gleason, and Lucy and Desi all worked on Paley's farm. Over the decades Paley made it quite clear that it was popularity, not prestige, that primarily concerned him. Despite being the network that brought the world **Green Acres** and **Mr. Ed**, the image of **CBS** as being a cut above endured.

Objectivity

Central to the Tiffany image was the news division and its stars—Edward R. Murrow, Douglas Edwards, Walter Cronkite, and the rest. Some of the reputation was earned; specials like "Hunger in America" and "The Selling of the Pentagon" as well as Murrow's attack on Joe McCarthy stood out of the crowd—even though Murrow and the network held back for years until well after McCarthy had done most of his damage. And blacklisting employees for their political views continued at **CBS**, not only after the broadcast but even after McCarthy's censure by the Senate.

Every brush with controversy seemed to make the network more timid the next time around. The result of all the controversy was to promote that dread ideal of U.S. journalism: objectivity. The cult of evenhandedness at **CBS** goes back to the 1930s. In 1931, the network cadged an appearance out of George Bernard Shaw, who praised Soviet Communism; the resulting outcry was predictable. And, in 1935, Alexander Woolcot devoted a commentary to a condemnation of Hitler; the resulting outcry seems shocking from this distance, but criticizing Nazism in the mid-30s was hardly a sure thing. Paley's response was a new "fairness" policy: "Broadcasting...must forever be...militantly non-partisan," he said in 1937.

Many of the **CBS** staff resisted this muzzling at first; news executives urged the rebels to place their opinions in the mouths of

CRONKITE FOR HIRE

Once labeled the "most trusted man in America," former CBS anchor and current boardmember Walter Cronkite has come under attack for accepting $25,000 from the extremist, industry-sponsored American Council on Science and Health (ACSH). For that fee, he narrated the pro-pesticide documentary, "Big Fears, Little Risks," which aired on **PBS** stations this summer. In the documentary, Cronkite pooh-poohs consumer fears of pesticides as "chemophobia." Without the pretense of balance, the film presents only the views of scientists who support ACSH's anti-environmentalist, anti-regulatory positions. Cronkite adds some ridicule: "Can we find ourselves placing a hazardous warning label on every salt shaker in America?"

As **Columbia Journalism Review** pointed out (Sep-Oct 89), the documentary was indirectly funded by pesticide makers Dow and Monsanto, pesticide promoters like the National Agricultural Chemicals Association, and right-wing financiers such as Joseph Coors and Richard Mellon Scaife.

others—"all you've got to do is say, 'a prominent authority declared,'" was the helpful advice of one executive. But when Walter Cronkite took up the torch from Murrow as the news division's chief symbol in 1962, mealymouthedness triumphed. As Lewis Paper puts it in his biography of Paley, "Cronkite was comfortable, safe. There were not going to be any more stomach aches."

Moments

The **CBS News** tradition was that professionals should decide what the public needed to know. Murrow advised wartime recruits in the 1940s: "Imagine yourself at a dinner table with a local editor, a banker, and a professor, talking over coffee. You try to tell what it was like [in Europe], while the maid's boyfriend, a truck driver, listens from the kitchen." The maid, one guesses, was too busy polishing the silver. This was not philosophy that could survive into the 1980s.

One of the first signs of the new order was Dan Rather's replacement of Cronkite in 1981. For a while, Rather floundered and ratings sank. **CBS** was distraught; they'd agreed to a 10-year, $22 million contract with the erratic "anchor monster" and they feared for their investment. (Rather described the contract as a "covenant of excellence.") **CBS** brought in Van Gordon Suter, a Hemingway-wannabe who'd turned around two network-owned TV stations, to transform Rather.

Together, Rather and Suter embraced "moments," the lump-in-the-throat approach to the news. A story on unemployment shouldn't explore the reasons behind joblessness, but should focus instead on the sad faces in the unemployment line. Given a choice between opening the newscast with the Falklands war or Princess Di's new baby, Rather went for the royal neonate on what he called the back fence principle: "You imagine two neighbor ladies leaning over a back fence at the end of the day and one is asking the other what happened today and you figure out which of your stories they'd most want to know about." The main similarity between this principle and Murrow's is that they insult the intelligence of women.

The aim was to turn news from a cost center to a profit center, which fit in nicely with the agenda of the political right. As Peter Boyer tells it in **Who Killed CBS?**, the Sauter regime thought stories about Reaganomics or El Salvador were "borrrrrr-ring," and would send viewers to the nearest game show. (Sauter himself is quite conservative, and Rather is given to misty displays of patriotism.)

According to Boyer, Sauter let Leslie Stahl do critical reports on the administration, but producers would often illustrate her words with pictures contradicting her message. A story examining the harmful effects of Reaganomics on the elderly would be accompanied by a picture of the president opening a new nursing home. Except for a minority of word junkies, the pictures would carry the day.

Suter is gone, but "moments" live on.

Tisched

No matter the evidence; **CBS** and Rather were "too liberal," bellowed the extreme right. In 1985, Senator Jesse Helms and his allies launched a campaign to take over the network. They failed, but they put **CBS** "into play." Among the sharks who sniffed blood was Ted Turner. The network responded by borrowing lots of money to fight off the Georgian, whom the WASPy chair Thomas Wyman demeaned as "not moral enough" to own **CBS**. (Wyman and the board

BOARD OF DIRECTORS

INSIDE (CBS employees)

- Walter Cronkite. Consultant to CBS.
- William S. Paley. Acting chairman; ran CBS from 1928-1983. 1/3 interest in International Herald Tribune. Worked with FBI in 1940s and 1950s. Allowed CIA to use CBS as cover for agents and to funnel contributions through his personal foundation. Other boards/memberships: Columbia Univ., Harriman Inst. (Soviet studies), Museum of Modern Art. 1988 compensation: $700,000.
- Laurence A. Tisch. President and CEO. Militant supporter of Israel. Once denounced Peter Jennings as pro-Arab. Other boards/memberships: ADP, Bulova, CNA, Loews, Petrie Stores, R.H. Macy, N.Y. Stock Exch.; Carnegie Corp., Council on Foreign Relations, Metropolitan Museum of Art, N.Y. Public Library, NYU. 1988 pay: $1.25 million.

OUTSIDE (not CBS employees)

- Michael C. Bergerac. Private investor. Former chair, Revlon former executive, ITT. Other boards/memberships: ICN Pharmaceuticals, Manufacturers Hanover, Topps; Cornell Medical Coll., N.Y. Zool. Society.
- Harold Brown. Consultant and chair, Foreign Policy Inst., Johns Hopkins. Secretary of Defense, 1977-81; Secy. of the Air Force, 1965-69. Pres., Cal Tech, 1969-77. Other boards/memberships: AMAX, Cummins Engine, IBM, Philip Morris, Synergen; Atlantic Council, Cal Tech, Council on Foreign Relations, Natl. Acad. of Sciences, Rand Corp., Rockefeller Fdn., Trilateral Commission.
- Roswell L. Gilpatric. Retired partner, Cravath, Swaine & Moore. Other boards/memberships: Corning Glass, Eastern Air Lines; Metropolitan Museum, N.Y. Public Library.

- James R. Houghton. Chair and CEO, Corning Class. Other boards/memberships: Dow Corning, Metropolitan Life, J.P. Morgan & Co.; Metropolitan Museum, Pierpont Morgan Library.
- Henry Kissinger. Former Sec. of State. (See box)
- Newton N. Minow. Chicago lawyer and former chair, FCC. Other boards/memberships: Aetna, Encyclopedia Britannica, Foote Cone & Belding, Sara Lee; Carnegie Corp., Carnegie Endowment, Northwestern Univ., Notre Dame, Rand Corp.
- Henry Schacht. Chair and CEO, Cummins Engine. Other boards/memberships: AT&T, Chase Manhattan; Brookings Inst., Business Council, Cmte. for Econ. Devel., Ford Fdn., Yale Univ.
- Edson W. Spencer. Chair, Ford Fdn. Retired chair, Honeywell. Other memberships/boards: Carnegie Endowment, Mayo Clinic. Franklin A. Thomas. President and CEO. Ford Fdn. Other boards/memberships: AT&T, Alcoa, Citibank, Cummins Engine.
- Preston R. Tisch. President and co-CEO of Loews Corp. Brother of Laurence. Postmaster General, 1986-88. Other boards/memberships: Bulova, CNA, Hasbro, Rite-Aid; NYU.
- Marietta Tree. Architect, consultant, socialite and city planner. Other boards/memberships: Pan Am, U.S. Trust; Citizens Cmte. for N.Y. City, Cooper-Hewitt, Winston Churchill Fdn.
- James D. Wolfesohn. Investment banker and business partner of Paul Volcker. Friend of Ted Kennedy and David Rockefeller. Other boards/memberships: Brookings Inst., Carnegie Hall, Institute for Advanced Study (Princeton), Joint Center for Political Studies, Metropolitan Opera, Rockefeller Univ.

had deposed Paley in 1982.) The debt crippled the network; morale plummeted and the stock price sagged. They needed a white knight to keep all those immoral hands at bay. Wyman thought he'd found one in Coca-Cola, but the **CBS** board had a different idea. They turned to their largest stockholder, Larry Tisch.

HENRY KISSINGER:
The Walking, Talking Conflict of Interest

On September 13th, the day Henry Kissinger ended his tenure as a paid analyst for ABC News, he became the newest member of CBS's board of directors. Kissinger's ties to the TV networks have always been close; no other "expert" is as ubiquitous on TV, commenting on what US policy should be toward countries from Eastern Europe to the Middle East to Latin America.

In recent months, Kissinger has used his high media profile in a spirited defense of China. In a **Washington Post/L.A. Times** column ("The Caricature of Deng as a Tyrant Is Unfair," 8/1/89), Kissinger argued against sanctions: "China remains too important for America's national security to risk the relationship on the emotions of the moment," He asserted: "No government in the world would have tolerated having the main square of its capital occupied for eight weeks by tens of thousands of demonstrators."

Kissinger's defense of China and other repressive governments has sometimes raised eyebrows. What it has not raised is tough questions from TV interviewers about Kissinger's business ties to these same governments. In a column alluding to FAIR's study which found Kissinger to be **Nightline**'s most frequent guest, the **Washington Post**'s Richard Cohen (8/29/89) sounded an urgent appeal: "Will someone please ask Henry Kissinger the 'C' question?" The "C" stands for conflict-of-interest.

When he's not pontificating in the media about foreign affairs, he's engaging in foreign financial affairs through his secretive consulting firm, Kissinger & Associates. The firm represents 30 international companies—including American Express, H. J. Heinz, ITT and Lockheed—earning profits by "opening doors" for investors in China, Latin America and elsewhere (NY Times, 4/30/89).

A **Wall Street Journal** article by John Flalka, "Mr. Kissinger Has Opinions On China—And Business Ties" (9/15/89), exposed that Kissinger also heads China Ventures, a company engaged in joint ventures with China's state bank. As its brochure explains, China Ventures invests only, in projects that "enjoy the unquestioned support of the Peoples Republic of China." The Journal article was unusual in exploring the private business interests behind US foreign policy, not a strong suit of the media—even when, as in Kissinger's case, they are rolled into one person.

In a letter to network TV news programs, FAIR urged that guest analysts be questioned about their financial links to the subjects they are discussing, and that such links be disclosed on the air: "Our society demands financial disclosure of politicians and government officials; shouldn't we expect the news media to disclose the financial interests of their guest experts when such interest are related to the issues under discussion?"

Tisch and his family owned the Loews hotel group, which they'd used as an investment vehicle to swallow up Lorillard Tobacco, CNA Financial, and Bulova Watches. The Tisches have made their name by buying up troubled companies cheaply and nursing them back to health. Larry Tisch certainly bought into **CBS** cheaply; instead of launching an expensive takeover, he quietly bought up shares on the open market as the Helms/Turner brou-haha faded, thereby saving himself a pile.

Like all victors, Tisch promised to leave the network in peace, but he started shaking things up almost as soon as he took command in 1986. He was amazed how high on the hog **CBS** execs were living; he couldn't understand how the news people could spend $300 million a year on little more than a 22-minute nightly newscast. He sold the publishing and record divisions, closed news bureaus, and laid off hundreds. Ironically, this is exactly what Turner proposed to do. Morale sank again and infighting took off.

Climbing Out

Unlike the other networks, **CBS** has no interest in cable; In fact, the properties Tisch sold are just the kind of things other media moguls are paying through the nose for. Consequently, pundits have nick-named him Wrong-Way Larry—but it's long been Tisch's style to go against the current. (Discontented **CBS** staffers have reportedly taken to Spy's nickname—"Dwarf Billionaire," adding the modifier "liver-spotted.") He is loudly on record as expecting an economic catastrophe in the near future, and he's chosen to plow the cash from the asset sales into tax-free municipal bonds and wait for the sky to fall. Last year, about 44% of **CBS**'s pretax profits came from interest on the $3 billion cash hoard.

Tisch now believes he was too chintzy in commissioning new programming, so his plan is to spend the network's way out of the basement. This is being tested this fall, as a bunch of new sitcoms have hit the airwaves, and the expensive Connie Chung has arrived. She presides over **Saturday Night with Connie Chung**, an infotainment show that uses simulations extensively—including skits about the toughest prisoner in New York, teen abortions, and the Pan Am jet crash in Lockerbie, Scotland. Tisch also paid big to land the rights to pro baseball. The entertainment strategy for the 1990s will be to stress "family-oriented values." Among the new shows will be "Normal Life," starring Frank Zappa's daughter Moon Unit and son Dweezil. Take that, Tipper Gore.

If the economy crashes down, or the grand synergy strategies of Time Warner and other media conglomerateurs fail, Tisch will end up looking like a genius. By sticking with the broadcast business, Tisch's CBS will be a perfect test of the wisdom of cross-media and cross-border combinations.

The Washington Post:
The Establishment's Paper

Don't get too far from the establishment.

—Walter Lippmann to Katharine Graham

In 1933, when Graham's father, Eugene Meyer took control of the bankrupt **Washington Post**, it enjoyed only physical closeness to power. The paper badly needed the wealth and connections that Meyer had in spades: Over the years, he'd been a Wall Street banker, director of President Wilson's War Finance Corporation, a governor of the Federal Reserve, and director of the Reconstruction Finance Corporation. And Meyer wanted a soapbox. "People like to be told what to think," he once said, happy to oblige.

After World War II, when Harry Truman named this lifelong Republican as first president of the World Bank, Meyer made his son-in-law, Philip L. Graham, publisher of the paper. Meyer stayed at the Bank for only six months and returned to the **Post** as its chairman. But with Phil Graham in charge, there was little for Meyer to do. He transferred ownership to Philip and Katharine Graham, and retired.

Phil Graham maintained Meyer's intimacy with power. Like many members of his class and generation, his postwar view was shaped by his work in wartime intelligence; a classic Cold War liberal, he was uncomfortable with McCarthy, but quite friendly with the personnel and policies of the CIA. He saw the role of the press as mobilizing public assent for policies made by his Washington neighbors; the public deserved to know only what the inner circle deemed proper. According to Howard Bray's *Pillars of the Post*, Graham and other top Posters knew details of several covert operations—including advance knowledge of the disastrous Bay of Pigs invasion—which they chose not to share with their readers.

When the manic-depressive Graham shot himself in 1963, the paper passed to his widow, Katharine. Though out of her depth at first, her instincts were safely establishmentarian. According to Deborah Davis' biography, *Katharine the Great*, Mrs. Graham was scandalized by the cultural and political revolutions of the 1960s, and wept when LBJ refused

"We live in a dirty and dangerous world. There are some things the general public does not need to know and shouldn't. I believe democracy flourishes when the government can take legitimate steps to keep its secrets and when the press can decide whether to print what it knows."

—Katharine Graham addressing senior CIA employees at Agency headquarters in November 1988 (**Regardie's** magazine, Jan. 90).

From EXTRA!, Jan-Feb, 1990. Reprinted with permission.

to run for reelection in 1968. (After Graham asserted that the book was "fantasy," Harcourt Brace Jovanovich pulled 20,000 copies of *Katharine the Great* in 1979. the book was re-issued by National Press in 1987.)

The **Post** was one of the last major papers to turn against the Vietnam War. Even today, it hews to a hard foreign policy line—usually to the right of **The New York Times**, a paper not known for having transcended the Cold War.

There was Watergate, of course, that—model of aggressive reporting led by the **Post**. But even here, Graham's **Post** was doing the establishment's work. As Graham herself said, the investigation couldn't have succeeded without the cooperation of people inside the government willing to talk to Bob Woodward and Carl Bernstein.

These talkers may well have included the CIA; it's widely suspected that Deep Throat was an Agency man (or men). Davis argues that **Post** editor Ben Bradlee knew Deep Throat, and may even have set him up with Woodward. She produces evidence that in the early 1950s, Bradlee crafted propaganda for the CIA on the Rosenberg case for European consumption. Bradlee denies working "for" the CIA, though he admits having worked for the U.S. Information Agency—perhaps a distinction without a difference.

In any case, it's clear that a major portion of the establishment wanted Nixon out. Having accomplished this, there was little taste for further crusading. Nixon had denounced the **Post** as "Communist" during the 1950s. Graham offered her support to Nixon upon his election in 1968, but he snubbed her, even directing his allies to challenge the Post Co.'s TV license in Florida a few years later. The Reagans were a different story—for one thing, Ron's crowd knew that seduction was a better way to get good press than hostility. According to Nancy Reagan's memoirs, Graham welcomed Ron and Nancy to her Georgetown house in 1981 with a kiss. During the darkest days of Iran-Contra, Graham and **Post** editorial page editor Meg Greenfield—lunch and phone companions to Nancy throughout the Reagan years—offered the First Lady frequent expressions of sympathy. Graham and the establishment never got far from the Gipper.

War on Labor

The president who smashed the air-traffic controllers union (PATCO) in 1981 took a page from Graham's book. (See "**Washington Post** Labor Struggles," **Extra!**, May/June 1989.) A **Post** reporter, Peter Perl, researching a story on union-busting consultants, was told by a practitioner that his paper was "a leader in the field." When he attended one of the anti-union classes, Perl found four **Post** execs as fellow students.

As Davis tells it, shortly after Graham took over the **Post**, Jack Patterson, a veteran newspaper executive, offered the following advice: Use rewards and punishment to pit workers against each other; take union officers into your confi-

The Post Company

The Post empire includes Cowles Media (**Minneapolis Star Tribune** and other outlets, 26% interest); **International Herald Tribune** (33.3% interest; circ. 190,000) **Newsweek** (circ. 3.8 million); **Washington Post** (circ. 800,000 daily, 1.1 million Sunday); **Washington Post National Weekly Edition** (circ. 70,000); **L.A. Times-Washington Post News Service** (50% interest; 600 clients); **Washington Post Writers Group**; **Post-Newsweek Cable TV** (in 15 states); **WDIV** (Detroit, **NBC**); **WPLG** (Miami, **ABC**; named for Philip L. Graham); **WFSB** (Hartford, **CBS**); **WJXT** (Jacksonville, **CBS**)

dence and give them a taste of privilege; automate, and bring in nonunion workers to operate the new machines; and treat journalists as professionals, thereby causing them to compete with each other, killing whatever interest they had in such odd blue-collar notions as solidarity. This latter idea dovetailed nicely with Bradlee's Hobbesian strategy for running the newsroom: "creative tension." Only the strong survive this war of each against all, a style called "hairy-chested journalism" by macho Posters.

Graham, who handed out garment workers' union literature in her college days, broke the press workers' union in 1975 by provoking a strike and putting out the paper with scab labor and out-of-town contractors. Other blue-collar unions, tamed by this example, have accepted job-eliminating automation quietly.

Fresh from this victory, the paper instituted a two-tier system, in which all news-room workers hired after 1977 are paid an average of $200 a week less than pre-1977 hires. According to the Newspaper Guild, this arrangement saves the **Post** about $1.5 million a year, about 1% of pretax profits, or enough to pay Kay Graham's salary for 15 months.

The Guild, which represents about 40% of the paper's 2,000 employees in news, circulation and advertising, had worked without a contract from July 1986 to August 1989, a tense interval that reporter and Guild activist Frank Swoboda called "one of the most bizarre labor relations environments I've ever seen, and I've covered labor for 35 years." Union sources speculate that the Post Co. management finally tired of warfare and decided to sign a five-year contract, which included a no-strike pledge, the first in the Guild's 51 years at the paper.

Even though Graham runs around the country preaching the need for day care, she still refuses to grant her employees this benefit. And the **Post** still refuses to pay reporters over-time—something most big papers do. The Guild has filed suit over the matter.

The contract did address a long-standing Guild complaint—the huge spread between low- and high-paid workers. But even after a disproportionate raise for the low-end employees, the **Post**'s minimum salary for reporters is still $250 per week below that of **The New York Times**. Unsurprisingly, the ranks of the low-paid are heavily female and nonwhite. According to the union, women reporters make $121 a week less than men, and black women make $172 a week less than white men. If circulation and advertising workers are included, the gaps are even wider, with black women making an average of $322 a week less than white men.

The **Post** says this is the result of its aggressive affirmative action policies—non white non-males are more recent hires than white men, so the salary differentials are just an artifact of relative tenure. The Guild says its figures are adjusted for experience. The matter will be adjudicated by the D.C. Office of Human Rights, where the Guild has filed a complaint against the **Post**.

Despite the normalization of labor relations, in late November the **Post** ceased to allow union representatives into the building on routine business, a privilege it grants to advertisers, and refuses to allow the union to hold meetings on the premises, a privilege it grants to virtual strangers.

Money Machine

Graham is reportedly fond of saying that "unions interfere with freedom of the press." A more likely explanation for her hostility to labor can be found in the Post Co.'s financial performance.

The Post Co. is consistently one of the most profitable publishers in the business. According to the Newspaper Guild, the **Post** earned a profit of $42,700 per employee in 1988, the highest of any newspaper, well ahead of the second-place **Dow Jones** ($25,200) and the #3 **New York Times** ($15,800), and four times the national average of $11,000.

The **Post**'s newspaper profits fell slightly from 1987 to 1988, the result mainly of higher newsprint prices (partly offset by the Post Co.'s interests in two paper mills) and severance payments to redundant typographers and mailers. Though advertising income has slowed for most papers, the **Post** has bucked the national trend—important to a company that earns 70% of its revenue from advertisers.

Over the years, the **Post**'s competitors have all died, leaving the paper as a virtual monopoly in a virtually recession-proof, newspaper-dependent city.

Corporate Profile: *The New York Times*

*The **New York Times** is not only the newspaper of record for the Fortune 500, it is also a member in good standing of that elite group of corporate giants. Though a number of press critics have dissected the ideological biases, deadly prose and institutional arrogance of the **Times**, its business operations are less frequently studied. Doug Henwood, editor of **Left Business Observer** [from which the following is adapted], reports that today's **Times** is dancing to a marketing beat.*

In 1878, Adolph Ochs bought a failing paper, the *Chattanooga Times*, for $5,570 in mostly borrowed money. Through a dedication to "objective" reporting, nepotism, upgraded typography, tight management and civic boosterism, he made his first *Times* profitable. Eighteen years later, with $75,000 of borrowed money and a letter of recommendation from President Grover Cleveland, Ochs repeated his trick with the *New York Times*.

PUFFING MERCK

An article in the **New York Times Magazine** (1-8-89) sang the praises of Merck, a major pharmaceutical firm, which recently gave away an anti-parasitical drug to some 400,000 people in West Africa to prevent river blindness. Merck had sold about a billion dollars worth of this drug, which had originally been developed for cattle, not Africans.

Investigating the origins of this piece, **New York Newsday** media columnist D.D. Guttenplan (1-18-89) discovered that the idea for the article originated at an editorial lunch when senior editors of the **Times** heard the president of Merck talk about his company's activities in West Africa. **Times Magazine**'s James Greenfield thought it was a great idea for a story. He later denied to Guttenplan that he knew Mary S. Heiskell (one of the Sulzbergers) is on the board of Merck. Heiskell told Guttenplan, "Oh, they all knew. I mentioned it myself if no one else had." This wasn't mentioned in the **Times**' puff piece on Merck.

From EXTRA!, Mar-Apr, 1989. Reprinted with permission.

Ochs made the *New York Times* a profitable operation, but, as legend goes, profit was never Job One; Wall Street analysts joke that the paper was run like a nonprofit enterprise for most of its life. That began to change in 1973, a year when only deft accounting allowed the company to report a profit. This brush with death converted the paper's management to the cult of Marketing. Zeal for the religion is now total: the title of the *Times' 1987 Annual Report* is "The Marketing of Excellence." In his introduction, *Times* executive editor Max Frankel boasted that "The News Department of the New York Times does not wince at the thought of 'marketing'…their many products."

True to the title's promise, the report is a homage to the fruitful marriage of advertising and editorial product. Frankel celebrates the new single-theme pages ("Keeping Fit," "Eating Well," "Consumer's World") and a new focus on "lifestyle patterns." The editorial environment of such pages is, of course, extremely attractive to specialized advertisers.

The report is especially proud of the new Sunday magazine product, "Good Health," a wonder of marketing. The paper sponsored health fairs around Manhattan where *Times* writers like Marian Burros and Jane Brody preached the same gospel of bodily vigilance they preach in the *Times*. This promotion of good health stimulated interest in "Good Health," to the cheer of advertisers. One of the happiest advertisers is Schering-Plough, manufacturers of Fibre Trim, who hadn't previously advertised in the *Times*. The nation's colons are deeply in debt to this miracle of synergy. As for the nation's hungry, well, they're bad news. And advertisers hate bad news.

But filling the pages is only half the marketing battle; you've also got to sell papers. And the *Times* is at the cutting edge here, too. As the *Report* says, "Making extensive use of demographic data, the Times targets its potential readers, sometimes by sites as specific as a single street—and then uses marketing tools to get people started on what can quickly become a life-long habit." This is a healthy habit, of course.

Communications Empire

The *New York Times* is the highly profitable flagship of a highly profitable media conglomerate, the New York Times Co. Besides the newspaper of record, the company publishes 26 daily and nine nondaily newspapers, mainly in the southeast and California. The company also owns five TV stations, two radio stations, and a number of consumer magazines (e.g., *Family Circle*, *Golf Digest*, and *Tennis*). The Times Co. has a joint venture with Time Inc. to distribute both companies' magazines. The firm also has a 33% interest in the *International Herald Tribune*, an 80% interest in a Maine paper mill, and a 49% interest in three Canadian paper mills—which sheds fresh light on the *Times* editors' enthusiasm for the US-Canada trade pact that eases the cost of doing business with Canada.

On January 9, the Times Co. announced the sale of its cable TV unit in southern New Jersey to a group of investors including two larger cable operators and a group of black investors. The black group is led by J. Bruce Llewellyn, chair of two Coca-Cola bottling companies and a Buffalo TV station. The two cable operators will each own 40% of the new company; the minority partners will own 20%. This 20% is enough to earn the Times Co. $55 million in tax breaks under a law designed to encourage minority ownership in the broadcasting business.

THE BOARD OF DIRECTORS

The Ochs-Sulzberger familial combine controls about 70% of the New York Times Co.'s voting shares. Thus the directors listed below as "Outside" don't have the same kind of authority commonly associated with their position in conventionally structured public companies; they are there for mutual prestige.

Boardmembers interlock with military contractors, such as General Dynamics, IBM and Ford, as well as other leading blue-chip firms (J.P. Morgan, American Express, Manville, New York Life, Merck, Phelps Dodge). IBM and Phelps Dodge are notoriously anti-union firms; Manville is famous for evading its asbestos liabilities by leaping into bankruptcy while in a state of rosy financial health. Also represented are various branches of the permanent government (Council on Foreign Relations, Business Roundtable, New York Federal Reserve). Charles H. Price, US Ambassador to Great Britain, was recently nominated to serve on the board of the **New York Times**, pending approval at the company's annual stockholders meeting in April.

OUTSIDE

- **John F. Akers.** Chair and chief executive officer (CEO) of IBM. Other boards: Business Roundtable (co-chair), California Institute of Technology, Metropolitan Museum of Art, United Way, Yale School of Management.
- **William R. Cross, Jr.** Retired executive, J.P. Morgan & Co. Other boards: AMAX.
- **Richard L. Gelb.** Chair and CEO, Bristol-Meyers. Other boards: New York Life; Federal Reserve Bank of New York, Lincoln Center, Phillips Academy, Memorial-Sloan Kettering Cancer Center, Council on Foreign Relations. Member: Business Roundtable, Conference Board.
- **Louis V. Gerstner Jr.** President and director, American Express. Other boards: Caterpillar, Melville Corp., Squibb; Joint Council on Economic Education, New York International Festival of the Arts, Statue of Liberty/Ellis Island Commission, Harvard University, Council on Foreign Relations, Business Committee for the Arts.
- **George B. Munroe.** Retired chair and CEO, Phelps Dodge. Other boards: Manufacturers Hanover, Manville Corp., New York Life, Santa Fe Southern Pacific, Southern Peru Copper Corp. Member: American Bar Association, Council on Foreign Relations, various metals industry organizations.
- **George L. Shinn.** Chair and director, First Boston (investment bank). Other boards: New York Life, Phelps Dodge. First Boston has underwritten a number of securities offerings for the Times Co. and advised the firm on the sale of its cable TV system.
- **Donald M. Stewart.** President, College Entrance Examination Board; former president, Spelman College. Other boards: Bankers Life of Iowa, National Bank of Georgia. Member, Council on Foreign Relations.
- **Cyrus R. Vance.** Partner, Simpson Thacher & Bartlett. Former positions: Secretary of State, Deputy Secretary of Defense, Secretary of the Army. Other boards: General Dynamics, Manufacturers Hanover; Federal Reserve Bank of New York (chair), Japan Society (chair).

Business Sags since the Crash

Though the Times Co. earned $160 million in profits on $1.7 billion in sales in 1987, up 927% and 246% respectively from 1978, things are slowing down; profits for late 1988 and early 1989 are anemic. The magazine business is hobbled by startup costs for *Child, Decorating Remodeling, Southern Travel, and Snow Country*—new magazines whose names reflect the company's *au courant* dedication to upscale niche marketing. The Times Co.'s TV stations are feeling the pinch of cable competition for ad spending. And the newspaper business is caught between the Scylla of high capital expenses and the Charybdis of stagnating ad revenue.

The business slowdown in newspapers is being led by the "crown jewel," the *New York Times*. (The Times Co. doesn't disclose the *Times* profits; it lumps them together with the regionals in financial reports. But Wall Street analysts estimate the flagship produces 55-60% of total corporate profits.) Scylla here is the $400 million, million-square-foot printing plant in Edison, N.J., which should be completed in early 1990. Some of the Sunday paper's ad-rich sections—the Book Review, Travel, Real Estate, Arts & Leisure—will be printed here, in living color. (Color, of course, commands higher ad rates.) New black and white presses will enable the *Times* to print far more copies with no more workers than today. This will be good news for the paper's bottom line—assuming there are buyers for all the new copies and advertisers ready to pay higher rates for fresh acres of publicity.

For the moment, though, advertising is "soft," because of trouble in three crucial areas—financial services, real estate, and retailing. Financial services linger in their post-crash torpor, the New York real estate market has been slowing since mid-1987, and retailing is suffering a quiet mini-recession. Macy's and Bloomingdale's, both major *Times* advertisers, have been cutting back on ad spending because of heavy takeover-induced debt loads.

The next few years at the Times Co. should be interesting. On the death of 95-year old Iphigene Ochs Sulzberger, the family trust controlling the paper will dissolve, its stock holdings to be distributed among surviving family members. Though it's theoretically impossible for the shares to be sold to outsiders, unsentimental heirs can hire creative lawyers to challenge anything. And *Times* publisher A.O. "Punch" Sulzberger is soon likely to turn his job over to A.O. "Pinch" Sulzberger Jr., while retaining the chair of the Times Co.

According to a *Manhattan, inc.* article (August 1988) by Ed Klein, former *Times Magazine* editor Pinch wants to turn the paper into even more of an "advertiser-driven medium." Klein also says that Times Co. president Walter Mattson wants to do away with the last vestiges of paternalism at the firm and turn it into a tightly managed operation. If advertising stays sluggish, the *Times* of the 1990s could evolve into a slicker and even more toothless product than today's.

24 | Free the Media
Mark Crispin Miller

The chart[s] in [this article] offer just a partial guide to our contracting media cosmos. It demonstrates the sway of the four giant corporations that control the major TV news divisions: NBC, ABC, CBS and—if the Feds allow it—CNN. Two of these four corporations are defense contractors (both involved in nuclear production), while the other two are mammoth manufacturers of fun 'n' games. Thus we are the subjects of a *national entertainment state*, in which the news and much of our amusement come to us directly from the two most powerful industries in the United States. Glance up from the bottom of each quarter of the chart, and see why, say, Tom Brokaw might find it difficult to introduce stories critical of nuclear power. Or why it is unlikely ABC News will ever again do an exposé of Disney's practices (as *Prime Time Live* did in 1990); or, indeed, why CNN—or any of the others—does not touch the biggest story of them all, i.e., the media monopoly itself.

Focused as it is on those colossi that control the TV news, this chart leaves out other giants: Rupert Murdoch's News Corporation, John Malone's Tele-Communications Inc. and Sumner Redstone's Viacom, none of which are (yet) telejournalistic powers. Likewise, the octopus that is S.I. Newhouse has not one tentacle appearing here, since he mainly glides within the world of print, darkening magazines and publishing concerns instead of newscasts. There are also foreign players, like Sony (Columbia, Tri Star), whose holdings are not charted here.

We therefore need further maps of this contracting universe: more big pictures—and also local maps, so that folks everywhere will know who owns their daily paper, TV and radio stations, cable franchise and city magazine. We need industry-specific maps, to show who owns each culture industry: the newspapers, the magazines, the book business and music business, cable, radio and the movie studios—as well as the major online services that help us get around the Internet.

> *The time has come to free the media. Let's create a new, broad-based movement dedicated to an all-important mission: antitrust.*

Such maps will point us toward the only possible escape from the impending blackout. They would suggest the true causes of those enormous ills that now dismay so many Americans: the universal sleaze and "dumbing down," the flood-tide of corporate propaganda, the terminal inanity of U.S. politics. These have arisen not from any grand decline in national character, nor

---

Reprinted with permission from the June 3, 1996 issue of *The Nation* magazine.

from the plotting of some Hebrew cabal but from the inevitable toxic influence of those few corporations that have monopolized our culture. The only way to solve the problem is to break their hold; and to that end the facts of media ownership must be made known to all. In short, we the people need a few good maps, because, as the man said, there must be some kind of way out of here.

Certainly the domination of our media by corporate profiteers is nothing new. Decades before Mr. Gingrich went to Washington, there were observers already decrying the censorious impact of mass advertising. The purveyors of "patent medicine"—mostly useless, often lethal—went unscathed by reporters through the twenties because that industry spent more than any other on print advertising (just like the tobacco industry a few years later). The electrical power industry attacked the concept of public ownership in an astonishing campaign of lies, half-truths and redbaiting that went on from 1919 to 1934. That propaganda drive entailed the outright purchase of newspapers (e.g., the Copley chain) and the establishment of trust-oriented stations for the NBC radio network.

Although the utilities' program was exposed, the corporate drive to eat the media was not halted by the New Deal. Indeed, as Robert McChesney tells us, the Communications Act of 1934 killed the soul of U.S. broadcasting, defining it forever as commercial. Thereafter, with ever fewer exceptions, radio and then TV were subject to the market-driven whims of the sponsor, who by the early sixties had on the whole made pap of both the news and entertainment sold through the electronic media. Some of the brightest talents spoke out memorably against the drift: Edward R. Murrow scored the trivialization of TV news, and Rod Serling, before his exile to *The Twilight Zone*, publicly condemned the fatal softening of TV drama by the like of U.S. Steel and BBD&O.

Bad as they often were, those earlier manipulations of the media were only a foretaste of what is happening now. Here no longer is a range of disparate industries, with only certain of them dangerously prey to corporate pressure, or to the warlike caprice of some Hearst, Luce or Northcliffe. What we have now, rather, is a culture gripped in every sector by an ever-tightening convergence of globe-trotting corporations, whose managers believe in nothing but "the market" *über alles*.

This new order started to get obvious in the spring of 1995, when the F.C.C. summarily let Rupert Murdoch off the hook for having fudged the actual foreign ownership of his concern (an Australian outfit, which Murdoch had not made clear to the busy regulators). The summer then saw ABC sucked into Disney, CBS sucked into Westinghouse, and Ted Turner's mini-empire slated for ingestion by Time Warner: a grand consolidation that the press, the White House, Congress and the F.C.C. have failed to question (although the F.T.C. is finally stirring).

With the mergers came some hints of how the new proprietors would henceforth use their journalists: Disney's ABC News apologizing to Philip Morris—a major TV advertiser, through Kraft Foods—for having told the truth, on a broadcast of *Day One*, about P.M.'s manipulation of nicotine levels in its cigarettes; and CBS's in-house counsel ordering the old newshounds at *60 Minutes* to bury an explosive interview with whistleblower Jeffrey Wingand about the addictive practice of Brown & Williamson.

Such moves portend the death of broadcast journalism, as does the radical cost-cutting now being dictated by the networks' owners. And yet some good seems also to have come out of this *annus horribilis* of big waivers, big mergers, a big layoffs and big lies. Suddenly, the risks of media monopoly are now apparent not just to the usual uptight minority of activists and scholars but, more and more, to everyone. People want to know what's going on, and what to do about it. The time has therefore come to free the media by creating a new, broad-based movement dedicated to this all-important mission: antitrust.

Although it will certainly go to court, this movement must start with a civic project far more arduous than any spate of major lawsuits. In fact, there can be no such legal recourse yet, because there is no organized mass movement that would endow such actions with the proper standing. Since the bully days of Teddy Roosevelt, the drive against monopoly has always been initiated not by solitary lawyers but by an angry public. "The antitrust laws are enforced in one period and not enforced in another, and the reason is pure politics," notes Charles Mueller, editor of the *Antitrust Law & Economics Review*. Such laws can take on the media trust, says Andrew Schwartzman of the Media Access Project, only when "the general public helps convince the prosecutors in the federal government that the future of democracy depends on freedom in the marketplace of ideas."

Thus this movement must start by getting out the word—and there's the rub. Our problem has no precedent, for what's monopolized today is no mere staple such as beef or oil but the very media whereby the problem could be solved. Indeed, the media trust suppresses information and debate on *all* monopolies. "You and I can't get the antitrust laws enforced," says Mueller, "and the reason we can't is that we don't have access to the media." To fight the trust directly, then, would be to resume the epic struggle that gave us our antitrust laws in the first place—one that the robber barons themselves soon halted by buying interest in the magazines that had been attacking them. With reformist monthlies like *McClure's* thus safely "Morganized," the muckrakers were quieted by 1912, as their vehicles were pulled into the same formation that now threatens to contain us all. Today's antitrust campaign will therefore have to be a thorough grass-roots effort—one that will work *around* the mainstream media so as to free them by and by.

The constitutional and sanely capitalistic way to fight mass sleaze is an infusion of diversity into the corporate monoculture.

This movement will depend on those idealists who still work within the media: those who would do a good job if they could, but who've been forced to compromise, and those working from the margins—the stalwarts of the alternative press and of groups like Fairness & Accuracy in Reporting. All should henceforth pay attention to developments within the different culture industries. The American Booksellers Association, for instance, filed an antitrust suit against Random House for illegally providing discounts to the national bookstore chains and retailers [see André Schiffrin, page 29]. Those in other industries should likewise make a fuss. With the help of independents in the film business, the Justice Department ought to take a look—again—at monopolistic practices in Hollywood. Creative Artists Agency, for instance, yearly packages a number of obscenely pricey movies for the studios, in each case demanding that the studio either use the agency's own stars, writer(s) *and* director—*and* pay them the salaries dictated by the agency—or take a hike. Since C.A.A. itself grabs the commissions on those salaries, its way of doing business represents a highly profitable conflict of interest.

The National Entertainment State

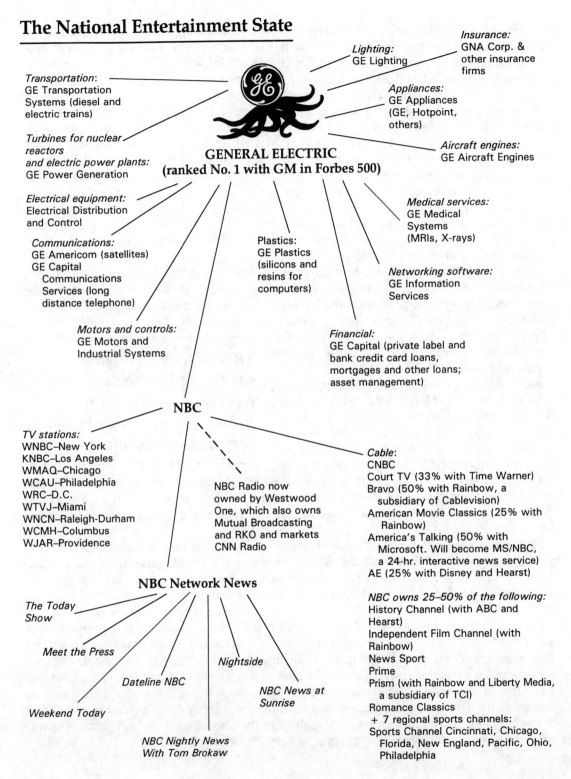

Lighting:
GE Lighting

Insurance:
GNA Corp. &
other insurance
firms

Transportation:
GE Transportation
Systems (diesel and
electric trains)

Appliances:
GE Appliances
(GE, Hotpoint,
others)

**Turbines for nuclear
reactors
and electric power plants:**
GE Power Generation

**GENERAL ELECTRIC
(ranked No. 1 with GM in Forbes 500)**

Aircraft engines:
GE Aircraft Engines

Electrical equipment:
Electrical Distribution
and Control

Medical services:
GE Medical
Systems
(MRIs, X-rays)

Communications:
GE Americom (satellites)
GE Capital
Communications
Services (long
distance telephone)

Plastics:
GE Plastics
(silicons and
resins for
computers)

Networking software:
GE Information
Services

Motors and controls:
GE Motors and
Industrial Systems

Financial:
GE Capital (private label and
bank credit card loans,
mortgages and other loans;
asset management)

NBC

TV stations:
WNBC–New York
KNBC–Los Angeles
WMAQ–Chicago
WCAU–Philadelphia
WRC–D.C.
WTVJ–Miami
WNCN–Raleigh-Durham
WCMH–Columbus
WJAR–Providence

NBC Radio now
owned by Westwood
One, which also owns
Mutual Broadcasting
and RKO and markets
CNN Radio

Cable:
CNBC
Court TV (33% with Time Warner)
Bravo (50% with Rainbow, a
subsidiary of Cablevision)
American Movie Classics (25% with
Rainbow)
America's Talking (50% with
Microsoft. Will become MS/NBC,
a 24-hr. interactive news service)
AE (25% with Disney and Hearst)

NBC Network News

The Today
Show

Meet the Press

Dateline NBC

Nightside

NBC News at
Sunrise

Weekend Today

NBC Nightly News
With Tom Brokaw

NBC owns 25–50% of the following:
History Channel (with ABC and
Hearst)
Independent Film Channel (with
Rainbow)
News Sport
Prime
Prism (with Rainbow and Liberty Media,
a subsidiary of TCI)
Romance Classics
+ 7 regional sports channels:
Sports Channel Cincinnati, Chicago,
Florida, New England, Pacific, Ohio,
Philadelphia

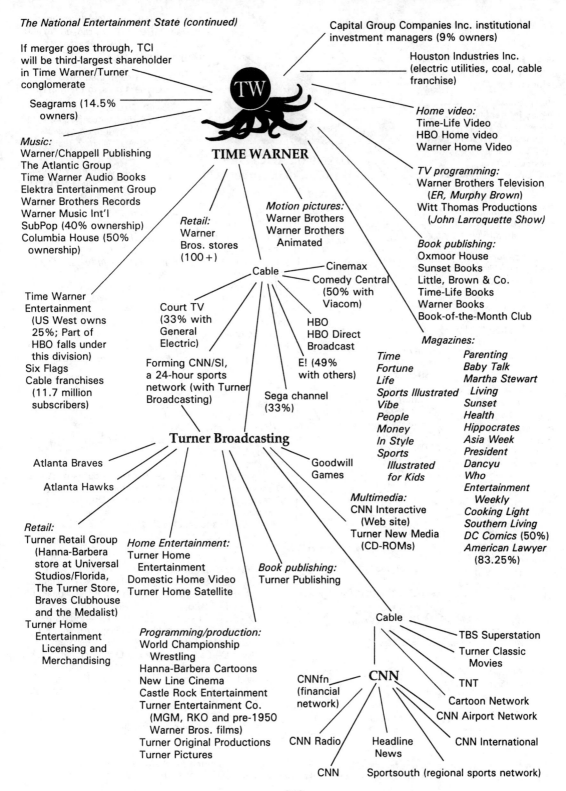

The National Entertainment State (continued)

Capital Group Companies Inc. institutional investment managers (9% owners)

If merger goes through, TCI will be third-largest shareholder in Time Warner/Turner conglomerate

Houston Industries Inc. (electric utilities, coal, cable franchise)

Seagrams (14.5% owners)

TW

TIME WARNER

Home video:
Time-Life Video
HBO Home video
Warner Home Video

Music:
Warner/Chappell Publishing
The Atlantic Group
Time Warner Audio Books
Elektra Entertainment Group
Warner Brothers Records
Warner Music Int'l
SubPop (40% ownership)
Columbia House (50% ownership)

Retail:
Warner Bros. stores (100+)

Motion pictures:
Warner Brothers
Warner Brothers Animated

TV programming:
Warner Brothers Television (ER, Murphy Brown)
Witt Thomas Productions (John Larroquette Show)

Book publishing:
Oxmoor House
Sunset Books
Little, Brown & Co.
Time-Life Books
Warner Books
Book-of-the-Month Club

Cable

Cinemax
Comedy Central (50% with Viacom)

Time Warner Entertainment (US West owns 25%; Part of HBO falls under this division)
Six Flags
Cable franchises (11.7 million subscribers)

Court TV (33% with General Electric)

Forming CNN/SI, a 24-hour sports network (with Turner Broadcasting)

HBO
HBO Direct Broadcast

E! (49% with others)

Sega channel (33%)

Magazines:
Time   Parenting
Fortune   Baby Talk
Life   Martha Stewart
Sports Illustrated   Living
Vibe   Sunset
People   Health
Money   Hippocrates
In Style   Asia Week
Sports   President
  Illustrated   Dancyu
  for Kids   Who
                    Entertainment
                      Weekly
Multimedia: Cooking Light
CNN Interactive   Southern Living
(Web site)   DC Comics (50%)
Turner New Media   American Lawyer
(CD-ROMs)   (83.25%)

Turner Broadcasting

Atlanta Braves

Atlanta Hawks

Goodwill Games

Retail:
Turner Retail Group (Hanna-Barbera store at Universal Studios/Florida, The Turner Store, Braves Clubhouse and the Medalist)
Turner Home Entertainment Licensing and Merchandising

Home Entertainment:
Turner Home Entertainment
Domestic Home Video
Turner Home Satellite

Book publishing:
Turner Publishing

Cable

TBS Superstation
Turner Classic Movies

Programming/production:
World Championship Wrestling
Hanna-Barbera Cartoons
New Line Cinema
Castle Rock Entertainment
Turner Entertainment Co. (MGM, RKO and pre-1950 Warner Bros. films)
Turner Original Productions
Turner Pictures

CNNfn (financial network)

CNN

TNT

Cartoon Network
CNN Airport Network

CNN Radio

Headline News

CNN International

CNN

Sportsouth (regional sports network)

279

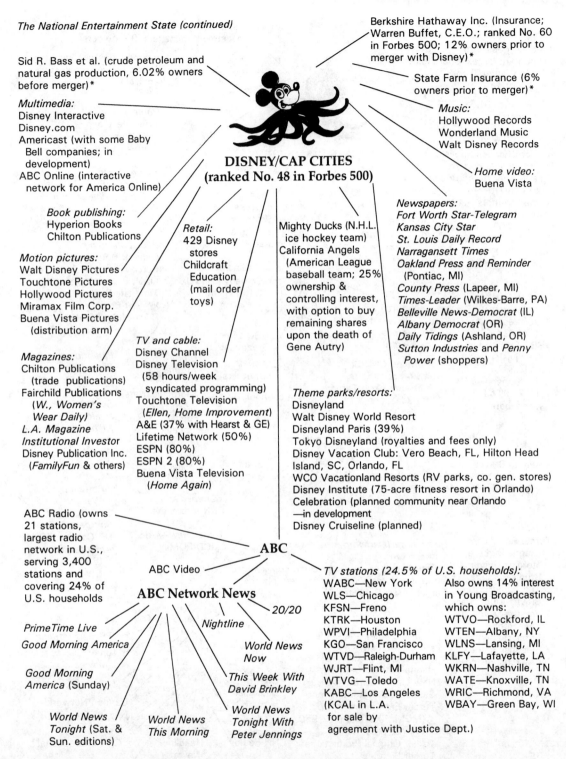

Berkshire Hathaway Inc. (Insurance; Warren Buffet, C.E.O.; ranked No. 60 in Forbes 500; 12% owners prior to merger with Disney)*

Sid R. Bass et al. (crude petroleum and natural gas production, 6.02% owners before merger)*

State Farm Insurance (6% owners prior to merger)*

Multimedia:
Disney Interactive
Disney.com
Americast (with some Baby Bell companies; in development)
ABC Online (interactive network for America Online)

Music:
Hollywood Records
Wonderland Music
Walt Disney Records

Home video:
Buena Vista

DISNEY/CAP CITIES
(ranked No. 48 in Forbes 500)

Book publishing:
Hyperion Books
Chilton Publications

Retail:
429 Disney stores
Childcraft Education (mail order toys)

Mighty Ducks (N.H.L. ice hockey team)
California Angels (American League baseball team; 25% ownership & controlling interest, with option to buy remaining shares upon the death of Gene Autry)

Newspapers:
Fort Worth Star-Telegram
Kansas City Star
St. Louis Daily Record
Narragansett Times
Oakland Press and Reminder (Pontiac, MI)
County Press (Lapeer, MI)
Times-Leader (Wilkes-Barre, PA)
Belleville News-Democrat (IL)
Albany Democrat (OR)
Daily Tidings (Ashland, OR)
Sutton Industries and Penny Power (shoppers)

Motion pictures:
Walt Disney Pictures
Touchtone Pictures
Hollywood Pictures
Miramax Film Corp.
Buena Vista Pictures (distribution arm)

Magazines:
Chilton Publications (trade publications)
Fairchild Publications (W., Women's Wear Daily)
L.A. Magazine
Institutional Investor
Disney Publication Inc. (FamilyFun & others)

TV and cable:
Disney Channel
Disney Television (58 hours/week syndicated programming)
Touchtone Television (Ellen, Home Improvement)
A&E (37% with Hearst & GE)
Lifetime Network (50%)
ESPN (80%)
ESPN 2 (80%)
Buena Vista Television (Home Again)

Theme parks/resorts:
Disneyland
Walt Disney World Resort
Disneyland Paris (39%)
Tokyo Disneyland (royalties and fees only)
Disney Vacation Club: Vero Beach, FL, Hilton Head Island, SC, Orlando, FL
WCO Vacationland Resorts (RV parks, co. gen. stores)
Disney Institute (75-acre fitness resort in Orlando)
Celebration (planned community near Orlando —in development
Disney Cruiseline (planned)

ABC Radio (owns 21 stations, largest radio network in U.S., serving 3,400 stations and covering 24% of U.S. households

ABC

ABC Video

ABC Network News

20/20

Nightline

PrimeTime Live
Good Morning America

World News Now

Good Morning America (Sunday)

This Week With David Brinkley

World News Tonight With Peter Jennings

World News Tonight (Sat. & Sun. editions)

World News This Morning

TV stations (24.5% of U.S. households):
WABC—New York
WLS—Chicago
KFSN—Freno
KTRK—Houston
WPVI—Philadelphia
KGO—San Francisco
WTVD—Raleigh-Durham
WJRT—Flint, MI
WTVG—Toledo
KABC—Los Angeles (KCAL in L.A. for sale by agreement with Justice Dept.)

Also owns 14% interest in Young Broadcasting, which owns:
WTVO—Rockford, IL
WTEN—Albany, NY
WLNS—Lansing, MI
KLFY—Lafayette, LA
WKRN—Nashville, TN
WATE—Knoxville, TN
WRIC—Richmond, VA
WBAY—Green Bay, WI

*Ownership percentages are not finalized. Because 82% of stockholders opted for shares and not cash, Disney is still working out with shareholders whether they will be paid in fractional shares or with partial cash payments.

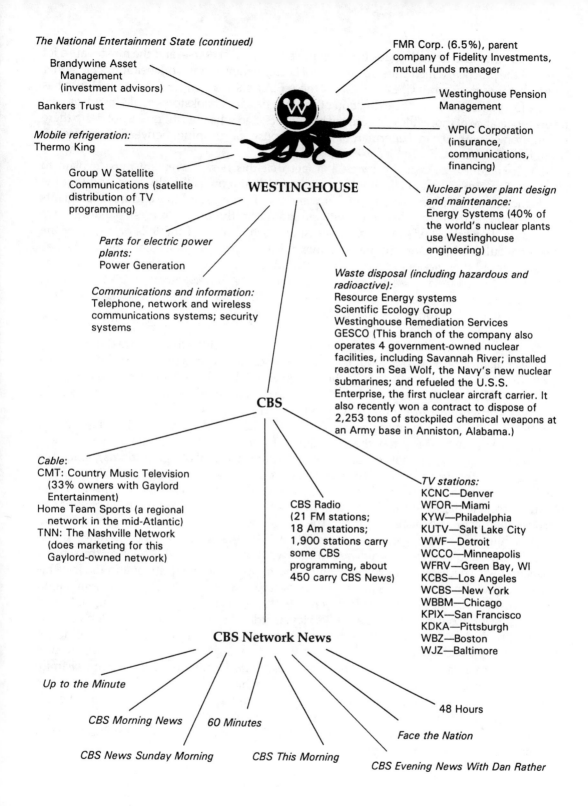

The National Entertainment State (continued)

FMR Corp. (6.5%), parent company of Fidelity Investments, mutual funds manager

Brandywine Asset Management (investment advisors)

Bankers Trust

Westinghouse Pension Management

Mobile refrigeration:
Thermo King

WPIC Corporation (insurance, communications, financing)

Group W Satellite Communications (satellite distribution of TV programming)

WESTINGHOUSE

Nuclear power plant design and maintenance:
Energy Systems (40% of the world's nuclear plants use Westinghouse engineering)

Parts for electric power plants:
Power Generation

Communications and information:
Telephone, network and wireless communications systems; security systems

Waste disposal (including hazardous and radioactive):
Resource Energy systems
Scientific Ecology Group
Westinghouse Remediation Services
GESCO (This branch of the company also operates 4 government-owned nuclear facilities, including Savannah River; installed reactors in Sea Wolf, the Navy's new nuclear submarines; and refueled the U.S.S. Enterprise, the first nuclear aircraft carrier. It also recently won a contract to dispose of 2,253 tons of stockpiled chemical weapons at an Army base in Anniston, Alabama.)

CBS

Cable:
CMT: Country Music Television (33% owners with Gaylord Entertainment)
Home Team Sports (a regional network in the mid-Atlantic)
TNN: The Nashville Network (does marketing for this Gaylord-owned network)

CBS Radio
(21 FM stations; 18 Am stations; 1,900 stations carry some CBS programming, about 450 carry CBS News)

TV stations:
KCNC—Denver
WFOR—Miami
KYW—Philadelphia
KUTV—Salt Lake City
WWF—Detroit
WCCO—Minneapolis
WFRV—Green Bay, WI
KCBS—Los Angeles
WCBS—New York
WBBM—Chicago
KPIX—San Francisco
KDKA—Pittsburgh
WBZ—Boston
WJZ—Baltimore

CBS Network News

Up to the Minute

CBS Morning News

60 Minutes

CBS News Sunday Morning

CBS This Morning

48 Hours

Face the Nation

CBS Evening News With Dan Rather

That scam has also helped to jack up ticket prices for the rest of us—and the movies are a lot worse for the practice, which pairs up talents not because they might work beautifully together but just because they profit C.A.A. Likewise, the A.B.A's showdown with Random House has far broader implications, for the extinction of the independent bookstores could insure as well the disappearance of those titles that are not best sellers, and whose authors will not be up there trading ironies with David Letterman of Westinghouse, or grinning, between commercials, through a segment of GE's *Today Show*.

That the media trust costs everyone is a fact that this new movement must explain to everyone. The public, first of all, should be reminded that it owns the airwaves, and that the trust is therefore ripping everybody off—now more than ever, since those triumphant giants don't even pretend to compensate us with programs "in the public interest." Likewise, we should start discussing taxes on mass advertising. Such a tax, and the tolls on usage of the airwaves, would yield enough annual revenues at least to pay for public broadcasting, whose managers would then no longer have to try to soothe the breasts of savage Congressmen, or sell out for the dubious largesse of Mobil, Texaco and other "underwriters." In 1994, according to *Advertising Age*, corporations spent a staggering $150 billion on national advertising. That year, it cost just $1.8 billion to pay the full tab for PBS *and* NPR.

And yet, to most Americans, the economic arguments against the trust may matter less than its offenses against taste. Grossed out by what they see and hear, a great majority have had their unease exploited by the likes of Pat Buchanan and Bob Dole, and ignored, or mocked, by many on the left. This is a mistake. The antitrust movement should acknowledge and explain the *cultural* consequences of monopoly. While the right keeps scapegoating "Hollywood" (*a k a* "the Jews"), this movement must stick to the facts, and point out that the media's trashiness is a predictable result of the dominion of those few huge corporate owners.

Thus our aim is certainly not censorship, which is the tacit goal of rightist demagogues like Ralph Reed and the Rev. Donald Wildmon. The purpose, rather, is a solution wholly constitutional—and, for that matter, sanely capitalistic. We would reintroduce a pleasurable diversity into the corporate monoculture. Some crap there always is, and always ought to be: It is the overwhelming volume of such stuff that is the danger here inside the magic kingdom. Where just a few huge entities compete, ever more intently, for the same vast blocs of viewers, and where the smaller players are not allowed to vary what we're offered, the items on the screens and shelves will, necessarily, have been concocted to appeal to what is worst in us. It is this process, and not some mysterious upsurge of mass barbarism, that will explain the domination of the mainstream by the likes of Murdoch, Jenny Jones, Rush Limbaugh, Judith Reagan, Arnold Schwarzenegger, Howard Stern, Charles Barkley, Gordon Liddy, Butt-head and Bob Grant.

Although, thus far, the right alone has decried the media's nastiness, when it comes to antitrust, those pseudo-populists would never walk the walk, since they themselves are part of the behemoth: Limbaugh's TV show belongs to Gannett/Multimedia, Pat Robertson's Family Channel is partly owned by TCI, and Bob Dole—despite his mock attack on Time Warner—has done his best to give the giants all they want. Those on the right would not dismantle the monopoly, which they would like to run themselves (and which to some extent they do already). It is therefore the left's responsibility to guide this movement, since on this issue it is actually much closer to the people.

Such an effort will require that the left stop being too hip for its own good, and start to honor the concerns of the appalled majority. "Two-thirds of the public thinks TV shows have a negative impact on the country," notes *U.S. News & World Report* in a major poll released in April, "and huge majorities believe TV contributes to social problems like violence, divorce, teen pregnancy and the decline of family values." This is no hick prejudice but a sound mass response to the routine experience of all-pervasive titillation. "The greatest anxieties are expressed by women and by those who are religious, but," the pollsters found, "the anger is 'overwhelming and across the board.'"

Of course, there are some deep antipathies between the left and those uneasy "huge majorities"—some out there don't want to be disturbed by *anything*, and the general audience may never go for feminism, and may forever cheer for shows like Desert Storm. Nevertheless, we have the obligation to make common cause with the offended—for what offends both them *and* us has all alike been worsened by the downward pressure of the trust. The ubiquitous soft porn, the gangsta manners, the shock jocks and the now-obligatory shouting of the F-word are all products of the same commercial oligopoly that is also whiting out the news, exploiting women, celebrating gross consumption, glorifying guns and demonizing all the wretched of the earth.

There are pertinent movements under way. In early March, there was an important and well-attended Media & Democracy Congress in San Francisco, organized by the Institute for Alternative Journalism, whose purpose was to unify the forces of the progressive media to fight the trust before it can rigidify beyond democracy. Soon after, in St. Louis, the first convention of the Cultural Environment Movement was held; founded by George Gerbner, the C.E.M. is committed to the broadest, toughest possible campaign for media reform.

The arousal of mass interest would raise possibilities for major legal action. The F.C.C. could be served with a class-action suit for its neglect of the antitrust laws—as could President Clinton for his failure "to see that [those] laws are faithfully executed." It might be feasible to sue them on First Amendment grounds. Although the giants themselves cannot be nailed for censorship, the movement could, says antitrust attorney Michael Meyerson, sue the U.S. government for collusion in the corporate move against our First Amendment rights.

While such distant possibilities await broader public support, some current cases show what could be done. Time Warner's acquisition of the Turner Broadcasting System has not yet won the blessing of the F.T.C., and there have been some strong petitions to deny the agency's approval. [For other steps, see Jeffrey A. Chester and Anthony Wright, page 21.] Looking further ahead, we must begin undoing what the media trust itself accomplished through the Telecommunications Act of 1996, which was devised to rush us in the wrong direction (and which the media—both mainstream and alternative—largely failed to examine). For a start, we might consider Chester's notion of an eventual move to force the four colossi to divest themselves of their beleaguered news divisions. For P.R. purposes, GE (say) could still boast its affiliation with NBC News—a most impressive civic contribution—but the annual budget for the news would come primarily from the same sort of trust fund, based on corporate taxes, that would pay for PBS.

Right now, however, what we need to do is tell the people who owns what. This campaign of public information must involve the whole alternative press, as well as unions, churches, schools and advocacy groups—and progressives on the Internet, which is still a medium of democratic promise, although that promise is also at risk. Indeed, the same gigantic players that control the elder media are planning shortly to absorb the Internet, which could be transformed from a thriving common wilderness into a immeasurable de facto cyberpark for corporate interests, with all the dissident voices exiled to sites known only to the activists and other cranks (such renovation is, in fact, one major purpose of the recent telecommunications bill). Therefore, to expect the new technology to free us from the trust is to succumb to a utopian delusion [see Andrew L. Shapiro, "Street Corners in Cyberspace," July 3, 1995].

Which is another way of saying that there is no substitute for actual democracy—which cannot work unless the people know what's going on. And so, before we raise the proper legal questions and debate the legislative possibilities, we need simply to teach everyone, ourselves included, that this whole failing culture is an oversold dead end, and that there might be a way out of it.

25 | Giveaway of the Century
Sam Husseini

By 1933, Lee De Forest was angry. The radio pioneer was not happy with how his labor was being used. In the previous decade, educational institutions and hobbyists had been forced off the air or onto secondary stations by government agencies acting largely as proxies for the commercial broadcasters. De Forest told one audience, "To be known as the 'Father of Broadcasting' was once an honor of which I was proud, but I'm disgusted and ashamed of my pet child." He called commercial broadcasting in the United States "a vulgar, cheapjack show designed solely to coax dollars out of the pockets of the public."

> *Broadcasters are making a silent grab for the new spectrum allotted for digital TV on the public airwaves.*

That year, a media-reform movement proposed the Wagner-Hatfield bill, which would have set aside a quarter of all radio stations for a variety of non-commercial uses. That bill was defeated in the Senate by a vote of 42–23 after intense lobbying by the broadcasters. Instead, President Franklin Roosevelt signed the Communications Act of 1934, which allowed the commercial broadcasters, like RCA, to dominate the airwaves. That law made control of a broadcast license dependent on serving "the public interest"—something that has never been seriously defined or enforced. As Robert W. McChesney, author of *Telecommunications, Mass Media, and Democracy*, notes, the debate over how to use a mass medium "has been decidedly 'off-limits' in public discourse" since then.

Earlier this year, President Clinton signed the Telecommunications Act of 1996. Its proponents claimed that the law, which deregulated phone and cable services, would increase competition and result in lower phone and cable rates. In fact, since no real competition exists in most local markets, the law has simply consolidated the power of the corporate giants. By increasing the number of TV and radio stations that one company can own, the law has already resulted in greater media concentration. It greased the wheels for recent media mergers such as Disney-ABC and Westinghouse-CBS-Infinity. Still, one major media issue remains on the table: digital TV.

In the late 1980s, there was a lot of talk about "high-definition TV" (HDTV) that would provide crystal-clear TV pictures. The owners of TV stations—which are mostly the big television networks, other major media corporations, or local rich guys—argued that they should get a new piece of the broadcast spectrum on which to broadcast HDTV. While content would remain the same, people who bought the new digital-compatible TV sets would have a picture of greatly superior quality, akin to the transition from black-and-white to color. The conversion to the new spectrum is likely to begin two years from now, and it will take from 10 to 20 years to complete. Once the TV-watching public had all purchased the new TV sets, the broadcasters would return the current spectrum, which could then be used for other purposes. At that point, current TV sets would become obsolete.

Technological advances—and the prospect of big money—have made a straightforward transition to HDTV unlikely. Digital technology (based on ones and zeros rather than the current analog system) makes it possible to broadcast four to six different regular-quality TV programs on the width of spectrum that one HDTV channel would have used. A portion of the new spectrum could even be used for other purposes, like paging and wireless data transmission.

This presents a number of urgent questions: Who should control the new spectrum? How should it be used? The broadcasters are demanding what is euphemistically called "spectrum flexibility." That scheme would mean that the broadcasters get the new spectrum for free. In return, all they would have to do is provide one standard-definition digital channel to the public. They would be free to use the remainder of the new spectrum for whatever services they wish—free, that is, to make as much money as they want from the publicly owned airwaves.

Gigi Sohn, deputy director of the Media Access Project, says that the broadcasters "determined that it would be far more lucrative to provide non-HDTV pay TV, paging and data services over the new spectrum." The broadcaster would probably switch to HDTV only for special events like the Super Bowl. The new digital TV sets would be capable of receiving either the several regular-quality channels or the HDTV channel.

"It's corporate welfare at its worst," says Anthony Wright from the Center for Media Education about the prospect of just giving the new spectrum to the broadcasters. Basically, three alternatives exist: 1) an auction, which would give the spectrum to the highest bidders; 2) a comparative hearing, which would award space on the spectrum to those who demonstrated that they could best serve the public interest; or 3) giving the spectrum to the broadcasters, but placing genuine public-interest requirements on them.

The digital TV issue was sidestepped in the telecommunications legislation after Bob Dole denounced the prospect of handing over the new spectrum to the incumbent broadcasters as "the biggest giveaway of the century." Dole said he would rather auction of the new spectrum, which could raise anywhere from $11 billion to $100 billion. The Federal Communications Commission (FCC) has already auctioned off the cellular phone spectrum and other much smaller slivers of spectrum for more than $10 billion. While an auction would not give space to new non-commercial voices, the money earned from an auction could be used to establish a trust fund to finance independent, non-commercial media.

Nolan Bowie, a lecturer on public policy at Harvard University, questions the wisdom and possibly the constitutionality of an outright auction of the broadcast spectrum. "An auction may mean transferring actual ownership [of the airwaves]," he says. "The public would have to compensate the broadcasters if it wanted the spectrum back." Bowie proposes a user fee instead.

According to the law, the new spectrum licenses should be given to those who can best serve the public interest. Given their record, it is doubtful that most of the current broadcasters qualify. The Media Access Project's Sohn says legal precedent would seem to require that the FCC hold comparative hearings to determine who merits the new licenses. Such a scenario would allow church, educational and civic groups to directly challenge the dominance of the commercial broadcasters.

Saul Shapiro of the FCC Mass Media Bureau says that from an administrative point of view, comparative hearings would be extremely difficult to conduct. He says, however, that it would be "quite simple" to have stringent requirements that a certain percentage of broadcasts be public-interest programming.

Such requirements have a sound legal foundation. The Supreme Court has ruled that "There is nothing in the First Amendment which prevents the Government from requiring a licensee to share his frequency with others...[since] it is the right of the broadcasters, which is paramount."

A variety of non-commercial voices—labor, educational, environmental, consumer, feminist, political, ethnic minority, religious, and other independent producers—could be given a significant portion of the new spectrum, which would be administered by the current broadcasters. This sort of programming would add real diversity to what is shown on TV and would have a profound impact on our culture. If the broadcasters ran pay TV on one or more of the digital channels—or if the political will existed to tax advertising on the new spectrum—a share of the monies could go toward funding this independent public media.

In January, Newt Gingrich and the new Senate majority leader, Trent Lott, promised to "conduct open hearings and move legislation" on the digital-spectrum issue. On June 19, however, with Dole out of the way, they sent a letter to FCC Chair Reed Hundt telling the commission to give the spectrum to the current broadcasters "as expeditiously as possible." As Rep. Barney Frank quipped, "I did not realize that I would miss Sen. Dole so quickly."

"Lott and Gingrich seem to think that free-market theory is good enough for everyone but wealthy broadcasters," says Sohn. For its part, the Clinton administration seems content with making sure that the broadcasters give back the current spectrum in about 15 years, after most people have bought new digital TVs.

Hundt, who has called the upcoming changes a "true watershed," seems to presume that the new licenses will simply be turned over to the current analog license holders. In return, the FCC chair is urging the broadcasters to devote 5 percent of the broadcast time on some of their new channels to public-interest programming, by which he means mostly children's TV and time for political candidates. With his talk about "voluntary ethical behavior," Hundt is meekly trying to nudge the broadcasters to be more "responsible." "I probably should be embarrassed for asking so little in return for the public's property," he recently confessed.

Early this year in a meeting with Clinton, the network heads promised to be more responsible about TV violence. Around the same time, Fox's Rupert Murdoch proposed giving Clinton and Dole TV time just before the election. Says Anthony Wright from the Center for Media Education, "Part of the reason the broadcasters have been responsive to pressure on TV violence, time for political candidates, and even, to a point, children's TV time is because they're mindful of how important this spectrum is. That's how central it is to them."

Good behavior at birth seems to be a habit with new corporate media. Wright notes that cable, when it was in its infancy, made all kinds of promises about giving time to community voices. Now, says Wright, "you have public access in only 15 percent of the country. Instead of diversity, much of cable consists of reruns of programs that are owned by the cable companies."

The four major broadcast networks are already gearing up to fill the new digital TV slots that they hope to control. After it announced its takeover of ABC last summer, Disney outlined a plan for four "program services" (sports, news, children's and soap opera) that Disney noted, may not be "for distribution on cable." In other words, Disney will presumably use digital TV to broadcast them. Disney backed away from plans to launch a new all-news network on cable to compete with CNN. That about-face suggests that the company may be planning to launch a news network on the new spectrum.

It's not clear how digital broadcasting will affect the cable industry. For example, will cable operators, which are mandated to carry the one signal now aired by each broadcaster, be compelled to carry several channels? Curiously, the cable industry has not vigorously challenged the broadcasters for control over the new spectrum. "Picking a fight with them [the broadcasters] on advanced [digital] television spectrum was probably not worth the risk of stirring them up on [cable price] dereg," a cable lobbyist told Multichannel News. The comment suggests that once again the powers collude and the people get screwed.

Despite the importance of digital broadcasting, discussion of the issue has been largely confined to trade magazines and the business section of newspapers. The broadcasters, of course, have hardly raised the subject on their news programs. "They don't want folks to know they're being unjustly enriched," says Harvard University's Nolan Bowie.

The future of digital TV will likely be decided in the coming months either by Congress, or if it does not act, by the FCC. This is literally a once-in-a-lifetime opportunity for reformers to question who controls the public airwaves. If the broadcasters' attempt to silently grab the new spectrum succeeds, the public may be treated to entire channels of infomercials, Rush Limbaugh clones and pay TV. If that happens, television will expand but still remain a vast wasteland.

The Invisible Public Resource:
Highlights of how the electromagnetic spectrum is used.

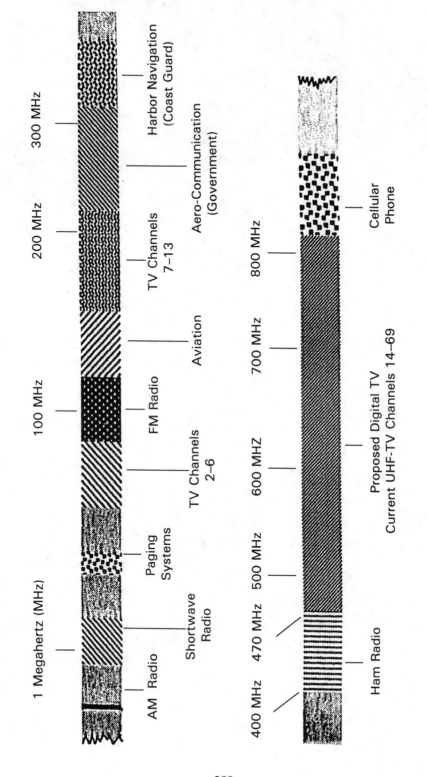

1 Megahertz (MHz)

100 MHz

200 MHz

300 MHz

AM Radio

Shortwave Radio

Paging Systems

TV Channels 2–6

FM Radio

Aviation

TV Channels 7–13

Aero-Communication (Government)

Harbor Navigation (Coast Guard)

400 MHz   470 MHz   500 MHz   600 MHz   700 MHz   800 MHz

Ham Radio

Proposed Digital TV
Current UHF-TV Channels 14–69

Cellular Phone

Diagram is not to scale

289

26 | Info-Bandits

Jim Naureckas

There's a Latin phrase that people use—*cui bono*—which translates as "for whose good?" It means that you can figure out who is responsible for a situation by looking at who benefits from it. Sometimes, though, it's easier to figure out who benefits by looking at who is responsible.

This rule greatly simplifies the task of comprehending the sweeping Telecommunications Act recently passed by Congress and signed into law by President Bill Clinton. Supporters widely praised the bill as beneficial to the public at large. It would lower prices and improve service, they claimed, by allowing the giant conglomerates of the telecommunications industry to compete with one another. Vice President Al Gore went so far as to call it an "early Christmas present for the consumer."

But the law was not created with consumers in mind. In effect, the bill was bought and paid for by the very telecommunications conglomerates it is supposed to bring under the discipline of the market.

Far from mandating competition among telecommunications companies, the act encourages already-mammoth corporations to pursue further mergers and allows businesses to form alliances with their supposed rivals in other sectors, greatly reducing the risk that new technologies will provide consumers with meaningful choice.

Media conglomerates hijacked telecommunications policy with millions in PAC contributions.

"This was conceived as: How do you get all the industries on board? You give everyone what they want legislatively," says Anthony Wright of the Center for Media Education, an advocacy group that tried to blunt the bill's worst excesses. "You just give as many carrots as you can. Unfortunately, the consumers weren't invited to that feast."

This kind of special-interest lawmaking has often been the norm in Washington, but the congressional class of 1994 seems to have scaled new heights in eliminating the awkwardness of public discussion from the legislative process.

"A lot of the public-interest sector felt totally shut out," says Kevin Taglang, who monitored the process for the Benton Foundation, which promotes public-interest media. "No one saw the final draft of the bill before it was passed. The industry found a Congress it could work with; a Congress that doesn't allow the public into the debate was a perfect setting for getting the bill through."

"The telecom bill was to the 104th Congress what health care was to the 103rd, in terms of attracting a lot of big money contributors," says Nancy Watzman of the Center for Responsive Politics (CRP) in Washington. "It flowed in from all different sectors." The center, one of the prime sources of information about money and politics, documented political action committee (PAC) contributions from the telecommunications industry to members of Congress in the first half of 1995. The numbers are striking: Altogether, the industry contributed more than $2 million in that six-month period, nearly three-quarters of which went to the newly ascendant Republicans. A full $640,000 went to the 45 representatives and senators on the joint conference committee that hammered out the final version of the bill in the late fall of 1995. By contrast, Watzman points out, "Consumer groups contributed little, if anything."

It should be noted that these figures do not include individual contributions given by telecommunications industry executives or investors, which may amount to as much or more than the institutional PAC money. And powerful legislators sent clear messages that their votes were for sale. David Samuels of *Harper's* magazine captured the spirit in which this money changed hands in an excerpt from a speech in which Sen. Robert Dole (R-KS) shook down Republican contributors in Massachusetts. Dole cut to the chase with admirable tact:

> *I want to thank Senator Pressler for coming in. I want to say just one word about Senator Pressler. He's running for re-election in '96—he takes money. He takes checks. It's legal in South Dakota to take money out of Massachusetts. Well, let me tell you something about Senator Pressler. There are probably a lot of people here interested in the Telecommunications Bill—it's the best thing that we've done all year as far as the future's concerned in technology and jobs. And the chairman of that committee, and the one leading the effort right now on a day-to-day basis, has been Senator Larry Pressler from South Dakota. Larry, thank you very much.*

Dole's pitch apparently paid off. Pressler, chair of the Senate Commerce, Science and Transportation Committee, took in more than $103,000 in telecom PAC contributions alone in the first half of 1995. Rep. Jack Fields (R-TX), chair of the House Telecommunications and Finance Subcommittee, followed close behind with almost $98,000. Rep. Thomas Bliley (R-VA), who chairs the committee that oversees Fields' subcommittee, received $31,000. Members were rewarded in proportion to their power over the bill, and to their enthusiasm for advancing industry goals. "It was an investment," says the Center for Media Education's Wright. "For most of the companies, it paid off quite well."

In addition to the money that went directly into legislators' campaign chests, industry coffers paid for expensive lobbying campaigns. "Every trade association and every corporation in every industry had representatives in Washington," Wright says. These lobbyists-for-hire were selected for their connections: Ex-members of Congress and former staffers of key officials were in high demand.

As is often the case in contemporary Washington, the lobbyists' involvement went beyond persuading, cajoling or even doling out money to members. To a great extent, the lobbyists took over the act of writing legislation itself. "If you want to be a serious player, you're asked to submit language," said Jamie Love of the Center for Study of Responsive Law, a Naderite consumer group.

Looking at industry's campaign contributions, lobbying efforts and bill-writing is the only way to explain much of the Telecommunications Act. The law is filled with provisions that make no sense from a public-interest point of view but make perfect sense for the industries involved. Consider the deregulation of broadcasting. In the name of "competition," limits on TV station ownership are being raised so much that networks like ABC and NBC will be able to buy twice as many stations. (CBS, whose new owner, Westinghouse, already had stations of its own, needed the limit raised just to avoid having to sell off stations.)

In radio, all national limits on stations ownership are eliminated under the bill; on the local level, one company may own as many as eight stations in a large market. In smaller markets, two companies will be allowed to own all the stations between them.

The bill also guarantees that when the Federal Communications Commission (FCC) assigns new space on the broadcast spectrum for digital television, the only entities that will get a chance to be assigned such space will be those that already have TV stations.

Furthermore, because of a new technology known as data compression, the new broadcast frequencies being given for digital TV will be much wider than needed to duplicate traditional analog TV programming. Under a provision of the bill known as "spectrum flexibility," broadcasters will be able to use this technology to put out four or five different channels in the space formerly occupied by one. Or they can use the excess spectrum to sell something completely different—cellular phone service, say, or paging systems. They can use it for whatever they want: It's "flexible."

For decades, the FCC has regulated ownership of stations, saying that it was necessary to prevent concentrated ownership from monopolizing scarce spectrum space. One might expect regulators to regard new technologies like data compression as an opportunity to bring new voices into the broadcast discussion that have previously been shut out. But the Telecommunications Act looks at the spectrum not as a public resource to be shared, but as a private preserve whose investment value must be protected. Granting multitudes of new licenses would deplete the value of those already on the market.

The merits of the broadcasters' case no doubt became clearer to legislators thanks to the PAC money the National Association of Broadcasters showered on Congress ($142,000 in the first half of 1995). On top of that came big money from other companies with interests in broadcasting, such as General Electric, Time Warner and Viacom. The network point of view also got a boost from lobbyists like Fox's Peggy Binzel, who was formerly legislative director for Rep. Fields of the Telecommunications Subcommittee. On the Democratic side, the networks enlisted the help of Martin Franks, a senior vice president at CBS and the former head of the Democratic Congressional Campaign Committee.

With this kind of money and talent, the networks were able to roll over Dole when at the last minute he objected to the spectrum flexibility plan as "corporate welfare." Some observers believe Dole demurred out of loyalty to other telecommunications companies that had paid good money to the FCC for rights to use spectrum space for cell phone services and the like; they didn't want to be competing with networks that had gotten such space for free. Others suggest that Dole just hasn't liked broadcasters lately. "The networks had been giving him lousy reporting on the shutdown of the government," one analyst noted.

Whatever his motives, Dole was unable to delay a bill that offered goodies not only to the broadcasters but to the entire range of telecommunications sectors. In the end, Dole had to settle for an assurance that the FCC would not go ahead with the spectrum giveaway before Congress had a chance to re-examine the issue. But few expect Dole to make any legislative headway before the networks are happily camped out on their new spectrum.

If the broadcast provisions of the Telecommunication Act aim to preserve and expand the dominant positions of TV and radio networks, the sections of the bill that deal with cable have an even more perverse purpose: They allow cable companies to take full advantage of their local monopolies, and encourage them to make financial alliances with potential competitors from other telecommunications sectors.

Local and regional telephone companies will not be allowed to compete with cable companies to provide video service; cable companies, in turn, are authorized to provide phone service. But cable companies and regional phone companies are both local monopolies—and make the kind of profits that only monopolies can. There is little incentive for either to lay out the massive investment necessary to go into the business of the other, only to reap the greatly reduced profits available in a competitive environment. It would be like a newspaper chain trying to launch a new daily in a city where another chain already had a local monopoly. It just doesn't happen.

Instead of competing, these industries are likely to collude, and the Telecommunications Act does much to encourage them to do so. In areas with fewer than 35,000 people, for example, the local phone company can completely buy out the local cable company (or vice versa, though telephone companies generally have more cash to play with). Elsewhere, telephone and cable companies may buy a 10 percent stake in each other—which is enough to ensure that the two industries see no economic sense in going after each other.

The chimera of cable-telephone competition was used to justify granting the cable industry its heart's desire: total deregulation of cable prices, starting in 1999. (Smaller systems, as well as those where the phone company is providing virtually anything that can be labeled competition, will be deregulated immediately.)

As the Center for Media Education's Wright points out, "A deregulated monopoly is the worst of both worlds." *Consumer Reports* estimated last year that deregulation of cable rates (under a less sweeping proposal) would result in a 50 percent hike in the average monthly cable bill. Not a bad return on the cable lobbyists' investment—$264,000 in the first six months of 1995 alone. TCI, the largest cable company, by itself gave $200,000 in soft money to the Republican party days before the '94 election.

The bill's most contentious dispute—and the most expensive, in terms of influence-peddling—pitted regional Bell telephone companies against long-distance carriers. The Baby Bells—cash-rich companies such as Nynex, Ameritech and Bell South—wanted access to the long-distance market. The long-distance companies—mainly AT&T, MCI and Sprint, though there are many others—wanted to keep the Baby Bells out of their business, unless the Baby Bells gave up a significant share of the local market.

The long-distance companies have good reason to fear competition with the regional Bells. Though both AT&T, still the leading long-distance provider, and the Baby Bells sprang from the break-up of the old Bell Telephone monopoly, they've since evolved into quite different businesses. While AT&T has been dogged by genuine competition with the other long-distance companies, as their constant struggle to snatch customers from each other demonstrates, the Baby Bells have grown quite rich from their local monopolies.

Owning the phone wires leading to individual homes had given local phone companies a great deal of power over consumers. Up to now, they've switched customers from one long-distance service to another with a minimum of bother. But once they've entered the long-distance market themselves, they may not act so obligingly when customers seek to switch to their competitors. "There are all sorts of things cable and phone companies can do to prevent competition," says the Center for Media Education's Wright.

With untold billions at stake in this battle, both sides brought out the big guns. The long-distance companies' lobbyists were particularly impressive: AT&T hired political heavy-weights such as Republicans Charles Black and Vin Weber as well as Democrat Robert Strauss, not to mention the law firm of Reagan Chief of Staff Howard baker. MCI, for its part, retained the ubiquitous lawyer-lobbyist Tommy Boggs.

The long-distance companies had more famous names, but the Baby Bells outspent them: The local and regional telephone companies gave more than $847,000 in PAC money to Congress in the first half of 1995—heavily targeted at Republicans and members of the key committees—while long-distance companies gave $371,000.

And the Baby Bells' lobbyists, while less recognizable to the average C-Span junkie, were more strategically connected: BellSouth's Daniel Mattoon, for example, is not only a former Republican House staffer, but, as *Legal Times'* T.R. Goldman pointed out, "also chairs the National Republican Congressional Committee's PAC Advisory Committee, the influential group that hands out money to candidates around the country." That's not a person Republican lawmakers want to be on the bad side of.

BellSouth's vice president for government affairs, Ward White, who hails from Robert Dole's hometown of Russell, Kan., spent two years working on the senator's staff. The BellSouth team was so well-connected, in fact, that BellSouth's R.L. "Mickey" McGuire was said to have written much of the law's language. "Mickey's fingerprints are all over this bill," one observer told *Legal Times*.

Not surprisingly, the final draft of the act favored the Baby Bells over long-distance carriers. AT&T and its allies were hoping to make regional companies' entry into the long-distance market contingent on certification by the Justice Department. Instead, the Justice Department will merely play an advisory role as the FCC unleashes the Baby Bells.

If the public-interest point of view was lost in the debate over the Telecommunications Act, it was because the bill's primary beneficiaries included media corporations—the same institutions that, in theory, are supposed to inform the public about what its elected representatives are up to.

"The broadcasters made no effort whatsoever to cover the huge giveaways they were getting under the legislation," notes Andy Schwartzman of the Media Access Project, which advocates for public-interest communications reform. According to the *Tyndall Report*, a newsletter that tracks the amount of time nightly network newscasts devote to various issues, neither the passage nor the signing of the most sweeping telecommunications legislation in 60 years made the top 10 stories in their respective weeks.

What coverage there was focused on the probably unconstitutional restrictions on Internet indecency and on the V-chip. Rhetorical attacks on "immoral" speech, a routine many Republicans can probably now perform in their sleep, served to distract attention from the bill's procorporate economic agenda.

Print media covered the story little better—in large part because nearly every major newspaper group owns a stake in broadcast media, cable or both. When the *New York Times* editorialized that "after four years of legislative struggle, there was one clear winner—the consumer," it overlooked another clear winner: the New York Times Co., whose five TV stations and two radio stations will vastly appreciate as a result of deregulation.

27 | The Crushing Power of Big Publishing
Mark Crispin Miller

Gentle reader, here is what the world of letters looks like toward the end of the millennium: It's a small world after all. It might look vast inside a Borders or a Barnes & Noble, and the big numbers do seem to reinforce the sense of matchless cultural bounty: more than $20 billion in U.S. book sales (the most ever!) for 1996, with trade books at an unprecedented $5.7 billion!

And yet that world is small. First off, it's tiny at the top, as our map shows. Aside from Norton and Houghton Mifflin (the last two major independents), some university presses and a good number of embattled minors, America's trade publishers today belong to eight huge media conglomerates. In only one of them—Holtzbrinck—does management seem to care (for now) what people read. As to the rest, books are, literally, the least of their concerns. For Hearst, Time Warner, Rupert Murdoch's News Corporation, the British giant Pearson, the German giant Bertelsmann, Sumner Redstone's Viacom and S.I. Newhouse's Advance, books count much less than the traffic of the newsstands, TV, the multiplex: industries that were always dominated by a few, whereas book publishing was, once upon a time, a different story.

The trade has also shrunk in other ways. Yes, it's easy to idealize the past, but it's even easier to shrug it off entirely: "There were bad books then, and we have good books now, so what's the difference?" The difference is immense. Where once the trade was based on love of books, today it's based on something else—as these brief histories may remind us.

§ Little, Brown (est. 1837) was one of two great Boston houses that survived the trade's gradual removal to New York. (Houghton Mifflin was the other.) After a staid half-century of local sure things (John Quincy Adams, Francis Parkman) and solid reference works, L.B. flowered—with Emily Dickinson and Louisa May Alcott, Balzac and Dumas (and Fannie Farmer's cookbook). Later came Marquand, Evelyn Waugh, James Hilton and C.S. Forester, all of whom Alfred McIntyre, L.B.'s beloved director, supported well before the market justified it.

As part of Time Warner (Time Inc. bought it in 1968), L.B. now mainly sells Time Warner and its peers. In L.B.'s latest list we find *Joan Lunden's Healthy Cooking* (ABC/Disney), a bio of La Streisand (Sony), a "tribute" to Kurt Cobain (Universal), *McCall's Best One-Dish Meals* (Bertelsmann), *Star Wars: The Death Star* (Fox) and Alan Grant's *Batman and Robin*, timed for the next T.W. bat-boom in the multiplexes.

Reprinted with permission from the March 17, 1997 issue of *The Nation* magazine.

In these turbid shallows are some books that aren't just marketing: John Fowles's essays, Martin Lee on neo-Nazism. But they get pennies for promotion, whereas, say, for *Dr. Bob Arnot's Program for Perfect Weight Control*, T.W. will shoot the works (eleven-city tour, big ads, TV), since Dr. Bob is famous for his health-bites on the *CBS Evening News*. Celebrity is all at Little, Brown, which—despite the quaint old logo—*is* Time Warner. Thus could the house whose credo after 1930 was "Fewer and Better Books" now be the house that does *I Want to Tell You* "by" O.J. Simpson, for whose warm musings ("I'm a loving guy") Time Warner paid enough—$1.4 million—to cover his defense.

§ Random House (est. 1927) soon led the upstart New York houses that awoke the business after World War I. Into what had always been a WASP profession, such ardent Jewish book lovers as Alfred Knopf, Ben Huebsch and the Boni brothers introduced a spirit of cultural adventure. Thus did the trade take on the glamour of a bold and elegant modernity, as those innovators broke ideological taboos and otherwise took risks—and none took more or better ones than Horace Liveright, Random's accidental father.

For conglomerate publishers, books count far less than the traffic of newsstands, TV, the multiplex—industries always dominated by a few.

As head of Boni and Liveright ("Good Books"), then briefly on his own, that charming and tormented gambler brought American readers every sort of modern classic, lavishly. It was Liveright who first published Faulkner, Hemingway, Hart Crane, cummings, Dorothy Parker, Duna Barnes and Lewis Mumford; who published Dreiser, Anderson, O'Neill and Pound, *The Waste Land* and Anita Loos, Freud's first U.S. title and several books by Bertrand Russell. (Liveright often braved the censors, twice in court.)

His cash cow was The Modern Library, which he sold to Bennett Cerf in 1925. On that rich basis Cerf and Donald Klopfer started Random House, so named because, while fussing over Liveright's baby, they wanted just "to publish a few books on the side at random." A far sharper businessman than Liveright, Cerf nonetheless did share with him a lifelong passion for the objects of their trade. Random did *Ulysses* in 1934 (having fought for it in court), and Proust in Scott Moncrieff's translation; soon added over 300 titles to The Modern Library and created the Modern Library Giants; and ended up as home to an unprecedented range of authors—hard Modernists like Auden, Faulkner and Gertrude Stein, traditional craftsmen like John Cheever and Robert Penn Warren, sure winners like John O'Hara and James Michener, as well as Ayn Rand (and *Masters of Deceit* "by" J. Edgar Hoover).

Cerf wanted to get big. In 1960, with Random taken public, he and his associates kicked off the Age of Mergers by acquiring Knopf (and Vintage Paperbacks), Beginner Books and textbook firm I.W. Singer, then Pantheon. RCA bought it all in 1966, and in 1980 sold it to S.I. and Donald Newhouse, who by now also own *The New Yorker, Vanity Fair, Parade, GQ, Gourmet* and *Vogue* (among other glossies), the nation's fourth-largest newspaper chain and a cable operation—and Times Books, Fawcett, Crown, Villard, Ballantine et al.

This "Random House" is something else. Where Liveright courted T.S. Eliot to get *The Waste Land* (because Pound had recommended it), and where Cerf went to Paris to ask James Joyce for *Ulysses* (because Morris Ernst had pledged to fight the ban in court), Newhouse made his bones as publisher by getting Donald Trump to do *The Art of the Deal* (because Trump's puss had sent sales of *GQ* through the roof).

§ Bantam Books (est. 1946) was the second U.S. house to offer paperbacks—a momentous trend begun by Pocket Books in 1939. Ian Ballantine's first list included (at 25c apiece!) *Life on the Mississippi, The Great Gatsby, The Grapes of Wrath, What Makes Sammy Run?*, Booth Tarkington's *Seventeen*, Sally Benson's *Meet Me in St. Louis* and Saint-Exupéry's *Wind, Sand and Stars*, as well as several mysteries, Rafael Sabatini and Zane Grey.

Today, as part of Bertelsmann (since 1980), Bantam Books does *Acupressure for Lovers, Diet 911, David Letterman's Second Book of Top Ten Lists* and *Strong Women Stay Young*, among many others, some hardbound (*The Rocky and Bullwinkle Book*, $50), most in paper (*The Corporate Mystic*, $13.95). Bantam also has a cool new series out for (male) preteens: "Barf-O-Rama" offers them *The Great Puke-Off, The Legend of Bigfart* and *Dog Doo Afternoon*. These tales of "buttwurst" and "scab pie" are quite a stretch from Bantam's *Flavors of the Riviera*—a range that shows how broad the vision is at Bertelsmann.

Critiques like this one tend to jar, because they threaten the big myth that we have more and better "choices" today than our poor parents did with their three channels and two colas. Surely any hard look back at what folks really used to read will show that most of it was lousy—just like now. "'Twas ever thus: anyone who imagines that a hundred years ago Americans were rushing out to buy the new Henry James is kidding himself," writes Anthony Lane in *The New Yorker*.

Of course, the common run of literature has always been just that. Revisit any seeming "golden age" and read it all, and you'll find mostly dreck. Here, it was mostly dreck in Liveright's day—as in England, even back when Dickens and George Eliot were writing. And earlier, throughout the first great "golden age" of English fiction—Richardson, Fielding, Sterne—dreck ruled.

So there's been no golden age—yet books are worse, despite the gems. Today's worst, first of all, is much worse than the trash of yesteryear. Low intellectually—and morally, as William Bennett might care to observe (although his publisher is also Butt-head's)—books are even poor materially, because of editorial neglect. Where the houses prized the subtle labor of their editors, the giants want their staff not poring over prose but signing big names over lunch. Hence countless books are incoherent and obese—as reviewers often note, decrying flaws that ought to have been caught already by an editor. So Andrew Young "accords the same detail to his devouring slabs of ribs and bowls of gumbo as he does to the tear-gassing of black marchers in Slema in 1965" in *An Easy Burden* (HarperCollins), Michael Mandel's *The High-Risk Society* (Times Books) clunks with "annoying repetition" and Richard Schickel's *Clint Eastwood* (Knopf) is swollen with "bland talk and gassy moralizing"—to quote some recent shots in *The New York Times Book Review*.

The text today is often slighted too by proofreaders: not out of indolence but because they've been replaced by less-experienced freelancers; and the giants often further "save" by skipping galleys, so that manuscripts go straight to page proofs. Typos abound: in Erick Hobsbawm's *The Age of Extremes*, a noble holdover from Pantheon ("industralization," "Western countries"); in Richard Gid Power's *Not Without Honor: The History of American Anticommunism*, a dog from the Free Press ("blacks members," "propandistic"); and in Tom Dardis's *Firebrand*, a fine biography of Horace Liveright, published not too carefully by Random House ("distain,"

"Ogonquit"). to see how Random prizes Liveright's legacy, consult the Modern Library edition (1993) of *The Wings of the Dove*, in which "Densher hoped for visit," "he" appears as "she," and "'It will be capital to find you to find you there.'" (There's even a typo on the dust jacket.)

Such goofs would not have been permitted by the houses' prior owners—for whom the product *was* the payoff. This is the all-important difference between then and now: As book lovers and businessmen, they did the high-yield trash so as to subsidize the books they loved (although those books might also sell). No longer meant to help some finer things to grow, the crap today is not a means but (as it were) the end.

That shift started in the sixties, and grew out of several factors. The ruinous overvaluation of best sellers was first an economic consequence of the great boom in subsidiary rights: book-club and, especially, paperback rights. As the paperback houses were, throughout the go-go years, paying hardcover publishers ever-higher prices to reprint the hottest titles, the value of subrights exploded—until the publishers were making more on those once-secondary deals than on their own hardcover sales. Soon dependent on such income (in 1979, $3 million to reprint *Princess Daisy*), the publishers became less interested in "good books" than in this or that potential monster. (Now that the giants also do paperbacks, such competition has waned.)

Meanwhile, the sway of hype had been expanded hugely by TV, in whose national sales-arena modest readerships seemed ever less worthwhile. It started early: In 1957 Prentice-Hall did Art Linkletter's *Kids Say the Darndest Things*, and the book—flogged weekly by the author on his show—was a best seller for more than a year; and Simon & Schuster got two big winners out of Alexander King, a witty regular on Jack Paar's *Tonight Show*. TV was soon a grim necessity, with the houses jockeying to get their authors on *Today*, *Tomorrow*, Johnny, Merv and Donahue. Now that TV's grip is tighter still, the giants are that much deeper into it, staying close to shows like *60 Minutes*, *20/20* and—above all—*Oprah* (whose "Book Club" can increase sales by more than 1,000 percent). The books thus plugged are few, and will rarely blow your mind, since TV likes friendly monosyllables and authors with great hair, thereby abetting the survival of the cutest.

Lite books have been encouraged also by the overconcentration at the sales end of the business: a field long shadowed by bookstore chains but whose seizure by a few has reached the crisis point. By 1980, the two leading chains—B. Dalton and Waldenbooks—had reduced the independents' market share to less than 40 percent. Today that scrap looks ample, now that countless independents have been broken by those two hip predators, Borders (which owns Waldenbooks) and Barnes & Noble. Whereas prior chains stayed mainly in suburbia, the Big Two take over city blocks, often near each other, going head to head to wipe each other out.

While it offers benefits to local shoppers—kids' programs, folk music, good espresso—that corporate feud is, in the long run, only further narrowing the culture. The gross demand of those commercial fortresses requires the giants to provide them with the dumbest titles in fantastic quantities: enough to fill each fortress with proud towers of, say, *Airframe*—an in-store boost for which the giants pay the superstores (who also sell window placement). The independent stores get no such subsidy; and that collusion also hurts the smaller houses, who lack the cash to have their books heaped up so awesomely.

Then there's the practice of returns. The superstores have generally ordered tons more books than they could ever sell—and then paid for those they've sold by sending back the ones they haven't. This titanic rip-off has distorted the whole trade. While the Big Two do, in fact, stock more small-press titles than the independent bookstores can, they also "pay" the smaller houses with returns; and those houses can't afford it, while the giants—with their bad dailies, cable TV, talk-radio, etc.—have sufficient capital to take the hit. But the giants too are losing; and so they spend still more to push their crudest items, and that much less (if anything) to find the smaller market for their mid-list titles. (Those items sit not only in the superstores but in airports, supermarkets, Wal-Marts—venues that now sell more books than bookstores do.)

While the Big Two get lots of press, the trade is lessened also by another—and invisible—duopoly. Book distribution is now dominated by two national companies: Ingram and Baker & Taylor. Those two, in fact, have gone beyond mere distribution to the active marketing of books to B&N and Borders, a service only the giants can afford. The distribution can also hurt the little guy in other ways, their size enabling them to pay their bills when they feel like it—a casualness inimical to modest houses. "Small publishers are not being paid [quickly] enough to keep them in business," Lyle Stuart, owner of Barricade Books, said of his tiff with Ingram. "They feel you can't do business without them. But we can't stay in business if we keep dealing *with* them."

Finally, the giants' drift toward dreck has been accelerated also by the mad increase, since the sixties, in the sums they pay up front to V.I.P.s. Now that all the imprints are unstable, with editors forever leaving, writers go from house to house searching not for a home but for the sweetest deal. As elsewhere in the culture of TV, epidemic self-promotion has made stars of some agents, who have lately jacked advances up to drug-lord levels: $2.5 million for Dick Morris (Newhouse), more than $5 million for Gen. Norman Schwarzkopf (Bertelsmann), $6.5 million for Gen. Colin Powell (Newhouse), $3.5 million for former O.J. pal Paula Barbieri (Time Warner), etc. The editors seem heedless as to whether this or that big book will ever make the money back. Nor do they mind the gross inequity of those advances—because of which so many other authors just scrape by, or simply don't get published.

Although the giants did not create this system, they are themselves the biggest problem with it, for it is they—and not the TV-addled masses, or the bursting superstores or greedy agents—who have done the most to wreck the trade. From their book units, they expect profits way too steep for publishing, which never yielded high returns. For decades, notes New Press publisher André Schiffrin, the trade thrived on an after-tax profit rate of roughly 4 percent, most of it re-invested. By contrast, the giants want their houses to show profits of from 12 to 15 percent—comparable to what they make from movies, dailies and TV, but absurd for publishing.

Before the giants came, publishing was, for book lovers, a great way to make a living, albeit low-paying (and at the top, of course, all-white and mostly male). Today, fiduciary pressure is incessant and direct. With the houses now absorbed into the media trust, its top dogs tend to relegate the trade to others like themselves—not readers, or even lucid speakers of the language. This is true not only of the Hollywood imprints like Disney's Hyperion and Viacom's MTV Books. Avon has a three-year, thirty-title deal with Brandon Tartikoff, onetime programming whiz at NBC. "I think when you hear a star is interested in a film project, it could lend itself to a book property," Tartikoff told *Publishers Weekly*. "Some things can be baked into the literary work."

Likewise, Michael Lynton, C.E.O. and chairman of Pearson's Penguin Group, was formerly a suit at Disney, where he ran Hollywood Pictures—helping to produce, among other winners,

The Media Nation: Publishing

HEARST

Privately held; George Hearst Jr., chairman

HEARST BOOKS
1995 combined revenues: $160 million (est.)

AVON BOOKS
WILLIAM MORROW & CO.
Hearst Books
Hearst Books International
Hearst Marine Books
Quill Trade

NEWSPAPERS
Albany (NY) Times Union, Beaumont (TX) Enterprise, Edwardsville (IL) Intelligencer, Houston Chronicle, Huron (MI) Daily Tribune, Laredo (TX) Morning Times, Midland (MI) Daily News, Midland (TX) Reporter-Telegram, Plainview (TX) Daily Herald, San Antonio Express-News, San Francisco Examiner, Seattle Post-Intelligencer; 7 weeklies

MAGAZINES
Esquire, Good Housekeeping, Colonial Homes, Cosmopolitan, Country Living, Country Living Gardener, ESPN, House Beautiful, Marie Claire (with Marie Claire Album), Motor Boating & Sailing, Popular Mechanics, Redbook, SmartMoney (with Dow Jones), Sports Afield, Town & Country, Victoria and Harper's Bazaar. Also, 9 magazines in the U.K. and 81 international editions.

CABLE
Part owner of Lifetime (50% with Disney); A&E and History Channel (37.5% with Disney and NBC); ESPN; ESPN2; and ESPNEWS (20% with Disney); one foreign channel (partially owned)

STATIONS
7 TV stations; 6 radio stations

TV PRODUCTION
24-hour news channel in New England; entertainment programming (Flash Gordon)

MULTIMEDIA
Kidsoft (kid's software, 29.4%); Netscape (1.5%); Books That Work (how-to software, 17.5%); I/Pro (Internet provider; minority interest)

COMICS
King Features Syndicate (Blondie, Beetle Bailey) and others

OTHER
Timber, ranching and real estate in California

1995 revenues: $2.3 billion

NEWS CORPORATION

C.E.O. Rupert Murdoch controls about 30% of stock

HARPERCOLLINS
1995 revenues: $550 million (est.)

HARPERCOLLINS
Harper Reference	Harper Perennial
Harper Business	Basic Books
Harper Prism	Regan Books
Harper San Francisco	Westview Press

NEWSPAPERS
New York Post; The (London) Times, The Sun and others, together accounting for 30% of newspaper sales in the U.K.; more than 200 wholly and partially owned papers in Australia and New Zealand; papers in Fiji and in Papua New Guinea (partially owned); inserts for 622 U.S. papers

MAGAZINES
Pacific Islands Monthly, Premiere (50%), TV Guide, The Weekly Standard; 40% of 18 weekly and monthly magazines in Australia, New Zealand and Europe

TELEVISION
Fox Network; Twentieth Century Fox Television (The X-Files; Chicago Hope)

CABLE & SATELLITE TELEVISION
In the U.S.: fxM: Movies from Fox; in partnership with TCI-owned Liberty Media (50%) for: Fox Sports Net, Fox Sports International and fX; Fox Kids Worldwide (50%), Fox News Channel; in partnership with MCI (50%) to develop ASkyB, satellite TV in the U.S.; STAR TV, satellite TV that reaches all of Japan, China, India, Southeast Asia and into Africa; BSkyB (40%), satellite TV in the U.K., which holds 49% interest (with Kirk Gruppe) in Germany's DF1; developing JSkyB in Japan (50% with Softbank); FOXTEL (50%) cable operator and two sports networks (50%) in Australia; Canal FOX, cable TV in Latin America

TELEVISION STATIONS
22, including 1 in each of the top 4 markets (N.Y., L.A., Chicago, Phila.)

MOTION PICTURES
Twentieth Century Fox, Fox 2000, Fox Searchlight Pictures, Fox Family Films, Fox Studios Australia

MULTIMEDIA
CD publishing; about 20 Web sites (including iGuide)

OTHER
Sheep farming; paper production (46.2% of Australia's only newsprint plant); an Australian airline (50%)

1995 revenues: $9 billion

This chart does not include university presses or genre, large print or electronic imprints. Trade publishers' revenue figures come from the July 1996 "Book Publishing Report" or from the publishers themselves. They include adult and children's U.S. trade books only.

PEARSON PLC

THE PENGUIN GROUP
Combined 1995 revenues: $617 million (est.)

VIKING PENGUIN	PUTNAM BERKLEY
Studio	G.P. Putnam's Sons
DUTTON/SIGNET/PLUME	Grosset/Putnam
Dutton	Boulevard
Donald I. Fine	Price Stern Sloan
Signet	Jeremy P. Tarcher
Onyx	Berkley Books
Topaz	Jove
Plume	Ace
Meridian	Perigee
Mentor	HP Books
	RIVERHEAD BOOKS

NEWSPAPERS
The Financial Times; newspapers and magazines in Spain and France; financial newspaper in South Africa

MAGAZINES
The Economist (50%)

TELEVISION PRODUCTION
Thames Television (The Bill); Grundy Worldwide (Neighbors); Financial Times Television (all in U.K.); ACI in L.A.; BSkyB (4%); Hong Kong's TVB (10%); U.K.'s Channel 5 (24% with others)

SATELLITE TELEVISION
BBC Prime; BBC World (6% with BBC)

MOTION PICTURES
Phoenix Pictures (20%)

MULTIMEDIA
Mindscape

FINANCIAL
Lazard Frères & Co. (9% profit interest); Lazard Brothers (in U.K.) 50%

THEME PARKS/AMUSEMENTS
Port Aventura theme park in Spain (40%); Madam Tussaud's wax museum, the London Planetarium, Rock Circus, Alton Towers, Warwick Castle, Chessington World of Adventures (all in U.K.); Madam Tussaud's Scenerama (in Amsterdam); Madam Tussaud's 42nd St. (coming to N.Y.C.)

1995 (est.) revenues: $2.8 billion

VIACOM

C.E.O. Summer Redstone controls 61% of voting stock

SIMON & SCHUSTER
1995 reveues: $832.7 million (est)

SIMON & SCHUSTER	POCKET BOOKS
Lisa Drew Books	Star Trek
Scribner	Minstrel Books
Touchtone	Archway
Fireside	Folger Shakespeare
Aguilar	Library
Libros en Español	Washington Square
THE FREE PRESS	Press
Lexington Books	MTV Books
Martin Kessler Books	Pocket Star Books

*Also, largest educational publisher in U.S.
(1995 sales over $1 billion)*

MOTION PICTURES: Paramount Pictures

MOVIE THEATERS
Famous Players in Canada; UCI (50% with MCA) and Films Paramount in Europe; Cinamerica (50% with Time Warner) in western U.S.

CABLE
MTV; M2: Music Television; VH1; Nickelodeon; Nick at Nite's TV Land; Showtime; FLIX; Sci-Fi Channel (50% with Seagrams); Comedy Central (50% with Time Warner); The Movie Channel; Sundance Channel (45% with PolyGram & Robert Redford); USA Network (50% with Seagrams); Paramount Channel (in U.K. with BSkyB)

TELEVISION
UPN Network (50% with Chris Craft) includes 152 affiliates, reaching 92% of U.S. TV homes; Spelling Entertainment (Melrose Place, Beverly Hills, 90210), 75%; Paramount Television syndication (Cheers, I Love Lucy) and production (Frasier, Entertainment Tonight)

TV STATIONS: 11

RADIO STATIONS: 10

HOME VIDEO
Blockbuster stores; Paramount Home Video

OTHER ENTERTAINMENT
Theme parks (Kings Dominion, Kings Island, Great America, Carowinds, Canada's Wonderland)

1995 revenues: $11.3 billion

OTHER HOUSES OF NOTE — A Few High-Volume Niches

UNIVERSAL PRESS SYNDICATE
Third-largest newspaper syndicate of columns (William F. Buckley, Mary McGrory) & comics (Doonesbury, Calvin and Hobbes)

ANDREWS AND McMEEL
1995 revenues: $92.4 mil. (est.) 10th-largest trade publisher

DISNEY
The second-largest media company (1995 revenues about $12 billion), the company's book division had estimated 1995 adult trade revenues of $75 million

HYPERION
Miramax Books
As yet unnamed ESPN imprint

THOMAS NELSON PUBLISHERS
1995 revenues; $145.7 million (est.) 9th-largest trade publisher, specializing in religious books

READER'S DIGEST
1995 revenues: $2.1 billion. Second-largest overall publisher in U.S. specializing in direct mail and condensed books

ADVANCE PUBLICATIONS

Privately held by Newhouse family

RANDOM HOUSE

1995 revenues: $1.26 billion (est)

RANDOM HOUSE	Vintage
The Modern Library	FODOR'S
Times Books	CROWN
Times Business	Crown Trade Paperbacks
Princeton Review	Harmony Books
ALFRED A. KNOPF	Clarkson N. Potter
Everyman's Library	Bell Tower
Pantheon	BALLANTINE
Villard	Del Rey
Schocken	Fawcett

NEWSPAPERS

Birmingham (AL) News and Post-Herald, Mobile (AL) Press, Huntsville (AL) Times, Mobile (AL) Press Register, New Orleans Times, Picayune, Springfield (MA) Union News & Sunday Republican, Ann Arbor (MI) News, Flint (MI) Journal, Grand Rapids (MI) Press, Kalamazoo (MI) Gazette, Bay City (MI) Times, Muskegon (MI) Chronicle, Saginaw (MI) News, Jackson (MI) Citizen Patriot, (Pascagoula) Mississippi Press, St. Louis Post-Dispatch Jersey Journal (Jersey City), (Newark) Star-Ledger, Staten Island (NY) Advance, The Times of Trenton (NJ), Syracuse Herald-Journal and Post-Standard, Cleveland Plain Dealer, The Oregonian (Portland), Harrisburg Patriot-News; business weeklies in 35 cities

MAGAZINES

Condé Nast publications:
Allure, Architectural Digest,
Bon Appetit, Bride's, Condé Nast House and Garden,
Condé Nast Traveler, Details, Glamour, Gourmet, GQ,
Mademoiselle, Self, Vanity Fair, Vogue; also
NASCAR Winston Cup Illustrated,
NASCAR Winston Cup Scene,
The New Yorker,
On Track, Parade

CABLE

Discovery Channel, Animal Planet and
The Learning Channel (24.6% with TCI, Cox
Communications and John Hendricks)

CABLE FRANCHISES

4.5 million households
(33% with Time Warner)

OTHER

The Nature Company, Scientific Revolution and
Discovery Channel stores (24.6%); Cartoon Bank

1995 (est.) revenues: $5.3 billion

BERTELSMANN AG

Privately held; controlled by Reinhard Mohn

BANTAM DOUBLEDAY DELL

1995 revenues: $670 million (est)

BANTAM BOOKS	DELL
DOUBLEDAY	Delacorte Press
Anchor Books	The DIAL Press
Currency Books	Delta
Nan A. Talese Books	Island Books
Image Books	Laurel
	BROADWAY BOOKS

One of Germany's largest trade publishers. Also, 2.5 million book club members worldwide in the Literary Guild and other book clubs in the U.S., most of Western Europe, Canada, Australia, New Zealand and, beginning this year, in China (70% with state-run company)

MAGAZINES

Family Circle, McCall's, Parents, Child, Fitness,
American Homestyle and Garden, Ser Padres
Network, YM; 34 magazines in Germany, including
Stern and Der Spiegel (part owner); magazines in
France, Spain, England, Italy and Poland.
About 40 professional magazines

NEWSPAPERS

Six dailies in Germany; part-ownership of papers
in Hungary and Slovakia

TELEVISION

CLT-UFA (50%); largest European broadcaster, with
television and radio stations and television
programming branches

MUSIC

Arista, RCA, others (14% of music sold worldwide);
music publishing

MULTIMEDIA

Includes partnership with American Online in Europe;
publishes reference CDs

OTHER

Printing; CDs for data storage

1995 revenues: $14 billion

EDUCATIONAL PUBLISHERS

(Firms that no longer concentrate on trade publishing

HARCOURT GENERAL

Publishes some trade books under both Harcourt
Brace and the Harvest imprint. Publishes extensively
in education (8.6% of U.S. market in 1995) and
professional areas

McGRAW-HILL

Publishes some trade, and extensively in education
(11% of U.S. market in 1995) and professional areas

TIME WARNER

Ted Turner holds 10% of stock, TCI chairman John Malone and Seagrams each control 9%, and L.A. investment firm The Capital Group has 7.5%

TIME WARNER PUBLISHING
1995 revenues: $325 million (est)

WARNER BOOKS	LITTLE BROWN
Warner Treasurers	Bullfinch
Warner Vision	Back Bay
Aspect	

MAIL-ORDER BOOKS
Time-Life Books	Book-of-the-Month Club
Oxmoor House	Sunset Books

MOTION PICTURES
Warner Bros. (75%), Castle Rock Entertainment, New Line Cinema, library of MGM, RKO and pre-1950 Warner Bros. films

CABLE & SATELLITE TV
CNN, Headline News, CNNfn, CNN Airport Network, CNN Interactive, CNN/SI, CNN Newsource, TBS Superstation, Cinemax, Comedy Central (50%), Court TV (33.3%), Sega Channel (33%), Turner Classic Movies, TNT, Cartoon Network, HBO (75%); Primestar (31% with others) satellite TV in U.S.

CABLE FRANCHISES
12.1 million subscribers
(about 20% of U.S. TV homes)

TV PROGRAMMING
Warner Bros. Television (Friends and ER); WB Television Network with (Chicago) Tribune Broadcasting (84% of U.S. TV homes); Warner Bros. Television Animation (75%), Warner Bros. International Television (75%), Telepictures Production, Hanna-Barbera Cartoons (The Flintstones, The Jetsons), World Championship Wrestling, Turner Original Productions, Turner Sports, Turner Learning (noncommercial daily newscasts for schools)

MUSIC
Atlantic, Elektra, Warner labels (22% of U.S. music sales)

RADIO: CNNRadio

MAGAZINES
Asiaweek, Baby Talk, Coastal Living, Cooking Light, Dancyu, DC Comics, Entertainment Weekly, Fortune, Health, Hippocrates, In Style, Life, Money, Parenting, People, People en Español, President, Progressive Farmer, Southern Living, Southern Accents, Sports Illustrated, Sports Illustrated for Kids, Sunset, This Old House, Time, Time for Kids, Weight Watchers, Who
THEME PARKS: Six Flags (49%)
SPORTS: Atlanta Braves, Atlanta Hawks, Goodwill Games

OTHER
Home video and satellite, CD-ROM production, some retail stores

1995 revenues: $8.1 billion

HOLTZBRINK

Privately held by Dieter von Holtzbrinck, president

FARRAR, STRAUS & GIROUX
Hill & Wang	Noonday Press
North Point Press	

ST. MARTIN'S PRESS
Robert Wyatt Books	Thomas Dunne Books

HENRY HOLT & CO.
Metropolitan Books
1995 combined revenues $267 million (est.)

Major trade publisher in Germany and the U.K.

NEWSPAPERS
Dailies and weeklies in Germany, including Die Zeit and Tagesspiegel

MAGAZINES
Scientific American

MULTIMEDIA
Part-owner of N.Y. firm Voyager

TELEVISION
part owner of #2 rated channel in Germany

1995 (est.) revenues: $2 billion

SOME INDEPENDENTS

An incomplete and arbitrary list of houses that, either because of size or contribution to the field, warrant mention

HOUGHTON MIFFLIN
Franklin Mutual Advisers owns 5.3% of stock
1995 revenues: $87.2 million

Clarion Books
Also publishes in education (5.2% of U.S. market)

W.W. NORTON
Employee-owned — 1995 revenues: not disclosed

Norton Professional
COUNTRYMAN PRESS	LIVERIGHT PUBLISHING

GROVE/ATLANTIC INC.
1995 revenues: $13.5 million
Grove Press	Atlantic Monthly Press

BEACON PRESS
Non-profit; publishing arm of the Unitarian-Universalist Association — 1995 revenues: $4.5 million

WORKMAN PUBLISHING
Peter Workman, president & publisher
1995 revenues: not disclosed
Trade imprints:
Algonquin of Chapel Hill, Artisan Publishing

NEW LEFT BOOKS
Privately held; largest shareholder is the nonprofit New Left Trust — 1995 revenues: $3.5 million
Verso

THE NEW PRESS
Nonprofit; associated with the Fund for Independent Publishing
1995 revenues: $3.5 million

THE LIBRARY OF AMERICA
Nonprofit — 1995 revenues: $2 million (est.)

Demi Moore's *The Scarlet Letter*, with its happy ending and her excellent jugs. HarperCollins C.E.O. Anthea Disney's previous work for Rupert Murdoch included running Fox TV's *A Current Affair*, then overseeing *TV Guide*—and goosing up its numbers with a *People*-style "INSIDER" and, on every other cover, hunks flexing or babes pouting. Disney had no background in book publishing when Murdoch (who also has none) appointed her.

Under those who cut their teeth in TV, or at *TV Guide*, books themselves become TV—and not only in content. While B&N is jammed with weightless items "by" such telestars as Seinfeld, Leno, Oprah and Ellen, books are also getting televisual in *form*. Thus, while the text may be a mess, the cover cost some money—since, in this universe, that's what counts most. And nonfiction is being stripped of its least viewer-friendly features. Notes, for instance, are in trouble even at the academic presses. "Our marketing department tells us that footnotes scare off people," says an editor at Harvard—so perhaps it shouldn't be surprising that there are no notes in, say, John Keegan's *Fields of Battle* (Knopf) or Richard Meryman's life of Andrew Wyeth (HarperCollins) or Edvard Radzinsky's *Stalin* (Doubleday). On the other hand, it's strange to see nonfiction books with no index, as if that elementary guide might also "scare off" readers: Walter Cronkite's and David Brinkley's memoirs (Knopf) are index-free, as in Jane Kramer's book on modern Germany, *The Politics of Memory* (Random House).

When book publishing was still a cottage industry, it was "the freest form of expression we have," Curtice Hitchcock wrote in 1937. "The large circulation magazine, the newspaper, the motion picture, or the radio program, since they are intended for a mass audience, must perforce avoid taboos held sacred by an substantial portion of that audience, or they fail. A book can, and to a considerable extent does, find its own level of taste, appreciation and intelligence." Gradually, it might make people think and see. "If the book is important, however unpalatable it may be to large groups of people, the author can feel with some measure of truth that despite a small sale his ideas have been started in circulation and may seep (as ideas have a way of doing) beyond the range of the actual cash customers."

A long shot at the best of times, such dissemination is less likely than ever. The slow course of an idea or vision through some subculture of thoughtful readers (as opposed to the endless wildfire on the Internet) is hardly possible when those who own the trade want only big returns right now. Thus have the giants shrunk the culture automatically, through that objective "market censorship" whereby, say, Pantheon went from doing Hans Magnus Enzensberger, Marguerite Duras and Martin Walker to overdoing *Water Gardening* and *Decorating Magic*.

Defenders of the system like to charge its critics with elitism, a pseudo-populist stance quite belied by the history of publishing.

However, the giants have also shrunk the culture actively—by dumping, or red-lighting, any book that offers revelations irksome to themselves. Such titles quickly end up on the same unspoken *index librorum prohibitorum* that lists important books on U.S. foreign policy by authors like Christopher Simpson, Burton Hersh, Noam Chomsky, Gerard Colby, Frank Kofsky. Although solid and eye-opening, such works usually induce an eerie quiet in the mainstream press—and not always by accident, as John Loftus learned from someone at the C.I.A. A former assistant to the Attorney General (in the

Nazi War Crimes unit), Loftus must let Langley vet his work, and did so with *The Secret War Against the Jews* (St. Martin's), his and Mark Aarons's dark history of the C.I.A.'s relations with big oil. The manuscript would be O.K.'d, he heard from an agency source—"but you'll never get a review in America."

This being the national entertainment state, books are also whacked in New York or Hollywood without a word from Langley. Full of creepy news about its subject (F.B.I. fink, anti-Semite), Marc Eliot's *Walt Disney: Hollywood's Dark Prince* was aborted suddenly by Bantam in 1991, because, his editor said, it was "not of publishable quality" (although he'd only sent some notes). Eliot then learned of Bantam's "Disney Library" series for sale in supermarkets—a deal worth far more than his book would have been. (It later came out from Birch Lane Press.) In 1993 Robert Sam Anson's book-in-progress on the Disney company was dropped by Simon & Schuster, apparently because Martin Davis, head of Paramount (S&S then-owner) and a player in Disney's history, didn't want the press [see Jon Wiener, "Murdered Ink," May 31, 1993].

While killing books distasteful to its bosses, the media trust can also flood the world with its own sunny counterstory. Starting in December 1979, all copies of *Katharine the Great*, Deborah Davis's life of *The Washington Post*'s Katharine Graham, were pulped by Harcourt Brace Jovanovich, despite the house's late enthusiasm for the work. H.B.J. had been spooked (so to speak) by a threatening letter from Ben Bradlee alleging factual errors. Davis believes that Bradlee was angered mainly by her claims that he and Graham had C.I.A. connections. Whereas Davis's bio vanished (it came out from National Press Books), Graham's own big *Personal History* has gotten quite a push from her machine: cover story in the *Post*'s Sunday mag, a rave in that day's *Book World*, then excerpts in the *Post*'s style section and in *Newsweek*, etc.

The bigger the mogul, the deader any book that might offend him—a truth confirmed by the Orwellian experience of Thomas Maier, author of a 1994 book on our pre-eminent Stealth Mogul. *Newhouse* tells the whole absorbing story of S.I.'s rise to dominance: the newspaper monopolies set up in city after city; the commercialist aesthetic of the magazines, whose articles are meant to look like ads; one of the biggest tax-evasion trials in U.S. history—a contest fumbled by the I.R.S.; Newhouse's life-long friendship with Roy Cohn, through whom the family helped Joe McCarthy, Jackie Presser and the Chicago mob; and all those brusque beheadings at Random, Condé Nast and *The New Yorker*. Thorough and low-key, *Newhouse* is a sobering "parable on American media power," as Maier puts it—but what befell it is, on that subject, almost as edifying as the book itself.

At the start, no one would touch it—not even in London, where the Bloomsbury Press responded typically: "'We love it, but we're sorry, we do business with S.I. Newhouse,'" as Meier recalls it.* St. Martin's finally took the book—and had a hard time selling it: *Vanity Fair* refused an ad, and Lix Smith's item was, that day, oddly missing from her column in the Newhouse newspapers. The book was not reviewed or even mentioned in New York—where Maier also found *himself* blacklisted. Although Dr. Benjamin Spock had granted him permission—and full access—for a first-ever biography, Maier found he had "become persona non

---

* In Britain, Newhouse owns Chatto & Windus, Jonathan Cape, the Bodley Head, Century, Hutchinson, Arrow Books, Ebury Press, etc., and will soon buy Heinemann, Secker & Warburg, Methuen, Sinclair Stevenson, Mandarin and Minerva.

grata with about 40 percent of the book-publishing world." *Newhouse* would have sunk without a trace had not Johnson Books (in Boulder, Colorado) brought it out in paperback.

And so B&N's offering is not as comprehensive as it looks; for all the books that do shine there, important others can't. A title's initial shelf life, furthermore, is often now its whole life—and that span grows ever less. While we lack hard numbers on it, those who know say that most new books have—at most—as long to live as most new TV shows. First of all, the giants keep tiny backlists, since the I.R.S. decreed, in 1979, that publishers may not write off the costs of warehouse inventory. With shelf-space tight inside the superstores, moreover, a book often has a mere few months—or less—before it gets returned. And so the giants' mid-list books, deprived from birth, now have the life expectancy of houseflies.

And what of the alternative—the independents and the university presses? Many independents are worrying that they may not make it through the year, as libraries cut back on orders and returns keep pouring in. Meanwhile, the academic houses are now pressed by cost-conscious university administrators to make it on their own, without institutional subsidies. Thus those houses too are giving in to market pressure, dumping recondite monographs in favor of trendier academic fare or, better yet, whatever sells at Borders—which, presumably, means few footnotes. Those publishers are so hard pressed there's talk in the academy of changing tenure rules, because it's next to impossible to get an arcane study published—a dark development indeed.

Defenders of the system like to charge its critics with elitism. That pseudo-populist stance is quite belied by the history of publishing, which at its best had always sought mass readership. "He was a genius at devising ways to put books into the hands of the unbookish," Edna Ferber said of Nelson Doubleday. "A publisher who can do that is as important—or nearly—as Gutenberg." If today's giants are so good at selling to the people, why is the trade in trouble? Like the culture trust's big movies and CDs, its books are mostly duds: Last summer was the worst season in five years, with returns as high as, or exceeding, 40 percent of gross sales.

Inside a B&N or Borders, such failure is not obvious—nor is the actual sameness underlying all that seeming multiplicity. Look closer, and you'll see how many of those new books from Hyperion are merely ads for Disney—including Oprah's aptly titled *Make the Connection* (she and Disney have a multi-picture deal). You'll see that Pantheon has done four volumes of *The Flavors of Bon Appetit* (and *Bon Appetit 30-Minute Main Courses*) because Newhouse also owns *Bon Appetit*. Find *The New Yorker* on the magazine rack, and chances are that the issue's fiction, or nonfiction, came from one of S.I. Newhouse's houses. (Last year more than half the magazine's twenty-six excerpts came from Random titles.) Look too at Random's books on *other* giants, and note how uncritical they are—Kay Graham's memoir (Knopf) and Steven Cuozzo's *It's Alive* (Times Books), a paean to Rupert Murdoch.

Then think ahead, imagining the day when either B&N or Borders wins their war—and try to picture what that seeming multiplicity will look like. When there's just one chain left, its superstores will not be ordering those offbeat books from the remaining small houses, which will then fold. For those who like to read, the prospect is a frightening one, but not as frightening as the fact that people won't know what they're missing. Before that happens, we should ask some serious questions about culture and democracy—and antitrust—before there's nothing left to help us answer them.

28 | Survival of the Biggest

Mandy Stadtmiller

It's Saturday night in New York and another independent bookseller is closing down on the Upper West Side. You can tell from the "Marauding Megastore" commentary posted in the window alongside the bright pink signs reading "Inventory Clearance," "All Sales Final," and "Bookcases for Sale." Only Tiger, the gray tabby nestled inside the empty children's classics box, seems unmoved by the half-empty shelves and flea-market chaos. After a decade and a half of business in the literary-minded heart of Manhattan, Shakespeare & Co. is closing its doors.

But not to worry. Within 10 minutes' easy walk, there's not one but two new Barnes & Noble superstores. To the south, the 11-month-old Lincoln Center store sprawls out over six levels and 60,000 floral-patterned square feet, making it one of the five largest Barnes & Nobles in the country. Up north, the 82nd Street store is only half the size, but still dwarfs its neighbors. The omnipresent "Since 1873" logo is off by about 120 years; the store opened in April 1993—a fact easily discerned from the trail of collapsed independents in its wake. First, Eeyore's Books for Children at Broadway and 79th Street closed down. Then last summer, Endicott Booksellers at Columbus Avenue and 81st Street announced it was going out of business. Meanwhile, across town on the Upper East Side, the Burlington Book Shop on Madison Avenue went under, overwhelmed by its own next-door superstore.

Since 1992, Barnes & Noble has opened a total of seven superstores in New York City. Over the same period, seven major independents have closed their doors. You needn't be a conspiracy theorist to see a connection. This will be the pattern as long as huge chain stores continue to muscle their way into neighborhoods whose small bookstores do not have the same leverage with publishers nor the financial wherewithal to indulge people's God-given right to plush chairs and high-powered air conditioners.

In a New York Times article on the Endicott and Burlington closings last July, Lisa Herling, vice president of corporate communications for Barnes & Noble, danced around charges that the chain deliberately surrounds independents—especially venerable ones like Shakespeare—in order to squeeze them out. "Our goal is to keep focused on the needs of customers," she said. "They decide every day where they want to shop." Today she sticks to the same line: "Judging from the success of the store, we think we read neighborhoods pretty well."

Shakespeare & Co. co-owner Bill Kurland reluctantly agrees. "In many ways, we are a bellwether store," he says. "We're the first to go. If at the center of publishing you can't survive,

---

you wonder what will happen around the country. A lot of the independents are under siege right now."

According to the American Booksellers Association (ABA), chains such as Barnes & Noble, Borders and Crown expanded their market share by almost a quarter between 1991 and 1995, from 22.1 percent to 26.2 percent. Over the same four-year period, independents watched their market share slip from 32.5 percent to 19.5 percent. (Mail-order houses and mass market outlets account for most of the rest.)

"Everybody understands it to the extent that they've seen it happen before. They've seen it happen with the family farm and with the family grocery store. They've seen it happen with the dynamic of the community and neighborhood economics," says Richard Howorth, vice president of the ABA and owner of Square Books in Oxford, Miss., for 17 years. "If books go the way of everything else, then there is nothing left to hope for."

But the space that Barnes & Noble occupies—both physically and in the public mind—is so comfortable that it's hard for most people to take such warnings seriously. As Barnes & Noble's Herling says, they want to make bookstores "exciting, inviting and fun" for a demographic that doesn't respond to fluorescent lighting and an "if you paid full price. . ." sales pitch. So Leonard Riggio, the chain's founder and a very good businessman, has always been willing to experiment with departures from the standard book-selling formula—shopping carts, books by the pound—to find out exactly what the public wants in a bookstore.

Then he struck gold. *We don't want a department store that makes us feel like proletarians at McDonald's for a value meal. We're intellectuals: We want something upscale, with just a hint of personality and a touch of funk and subversion.*

We want culture.

Just ask author and *Nation* editor Victor Navasky. His op-ed piece in the *New York Times* three months ago opened with a confession: "[W]hile giving lip service to the idea of independent shops like Shakespeare & Company...I have been buying most of my books from Barnes & Noble, whose two new superstores have come down on my old neighborhood shop like the Assyrians who came down like the wolf on the fold." He liked the superstores not for their "yuppie trappings," he assured the skeptics, but because they encouraged taking private space into the public sphere.

Independent booksellers openly expressed their disgust. In a letter to Navasky, Andy Ross of Cody's in Berkeley wrote: "Retail bookselling in America is the primary engine for the distribution of ideas in our culture....Many of America's great writers were discovered and promoted by independent stores and ignored by chains until their reputations developed. Without early support by independents, such writers as Barbara Kingsolver, Allen Ginsberg, Carlos Castañeda, Tom Robbins, Russell Banks, Erica Jong, Alice Walker, Wallace Stevens, Richard Ford, Noam Chomsky, Toni Morrison, Alexander Cockburn—yes, and Victor Navasky—would never have found their audience."

The real threat to independents, though, comes not from the Navaskys of the world but from the stacks of best-sellers heaped in the front of every superstore. While publishers are willing to pay any bookstore for favorable placement, in practice the money goes overwhelmingly to chains. Each book in prominently positioned dump-bins can net a chain $120,000 a year, according to a *New York Times* article earlier this year. In Barnes & Noble's case, publishers can shell out another $150,000 for inclusion in the "Discover Great New Writers" series, which includes front-window placement in all superstores for two or three months and a review of the book in the chain's in-house journal. The program purports to offer an introduction to the "best books being published [sic] this summer" and "some of the finest writers on today's literary [sic] scene." I particularly like the review of *Derby Dugan's Depression Funnies*, where the narrator "roams the city in the company of a cartoonish assortment of mobsters, communists, writers and other eccentrics."

But if you're not in the mood for whatever "writers and other eccentrics" are producing these days, there's always music, software and gourmet coffee. Enjoy a $4 frappuccino at 66th Street under a mural of 31 authors painted all whites and creams, with an ashen Langston Hughes thrown in for good measure. Shakespeare & Co.'s Kurland demurs: "I'm not sure that a better bookstore should be a cafe. It just seems like this huge concession to American consumerism. People are buying the sizzle." It seems oddly appropriate that the site where Chelsea's Verso Books once stood is now occupied by a Starbucks.

In the end, though, the most serious objection to chains is not the atmosphere, but the danger that as decisions about bookselling are concentrated in fewer and fewer hands, authors deemed inappropriate or outside the mainstream will find themselves excluded from bookstores. This happens more literally in some cases than in others.

When Thom Jones, the author of *The Pugilist at Rest* and *Cold Snap*, traveled to Cedar Rapids, Iowa, in July to do a reading at Barnes & Noble, he was greeted by rude employees who, unfamiliar with his work, told him to go to the children's section for the reading even after he explained that the story contained profanity. Sure enough, after the first "motherfucker," two men who weren't in the audience—one of them, he later learned, a state trooper—started talking louder. One of them snapped at him, "Why don't you just shut up, mister?" "If you've got a story about a hot golf game or a big fish," Jones asked them nicely, "why don't you come over here and tell everybody about it?"

When the men continued their conversation and the Barnes & Noble staff made no move to quiet them, Jones resorted to violence: He threw a book at them. Then he threw another. With one paragraph to go, a clerk—"this fellow in a little vest. He could have been working anywhere," says Jones—came up and announced that he was placing him under citizen's arrest. When Jones refused to leave, the clerk said, "Somebody call the police."

As they say, the customer is always right.

Exercises

NAME _____

Research the political economy of a university or community radio station, newspaper, or magazine. Complete the worksheet below with as much detail as possible.

Media outlet _____

Ownership _____

Revenue Sources _____

Decision-making structure (manager, publisher, producer, editor, etc.):

Decision-making process, participants and their positions, frequency, purview:

Production practices, norms, standards:

Programming or publishing format:

Social relations among administrators, journalists, technicians, communities, "audiences":

How does the above political economy of communication compare to what you know of the political economy of the mass media?

Communication Technology and Democracy

Cheaper by the Dozen, a popular 1950s-era movie series starring Clifton Webb and Myrna Loy, recounts the life story of a turn-of-the-century family. Although the film is appreciated mostly for its portrayal of traditional family life and the work ethic, it also inadvertently reveals how much modern technology has changed social life. Most of the socio-cultural practices shown in these movies are long gone. Group sing-a-longs? Gone. Parlor games? Gone. Soda fountains? Gone. Corner stores? Gone. Doctor's home visits? Gone. Rotary phones, record players? Gone. Thanks to technology, we have created a different set of practices. We now have home stereos, video games, bottled soft drinks, national chainstores, medical specialists.

Past change is nothing compared to the changes ahead—at least according to news reports from industry and government. It seems we have entered a communication revolution, triggered by telecommunications technology. *Chicago Tribune* columnist Bob Greene has related a simple illustration of the impact communication technology may have on everyday life. Greene was watching a ball game on television (an experience impossible even a few decades ago) and noticed a kid in the stands who appeared to be listening to the game on his radio. As it turned out, the kid was talking on a cellular phone—obviously to someone watching television, because whenever the kid appeared on screen he would wave at the camera. Broadcast over a cable "superstation," television images were bounced off a satellite to a cable receiver and then transmitted to viewer's sets; the kid's voice on the cellular phone was being bounced off a satellite to a receiver and then over the lines to someone's phone. Greene noted wryly that someone was probably videotaping the broadcast so the kid could watch the whole affair later. For all we know, the kid was also wearing a beeper, in case someone else wanted to call. Greene concluded that the kid playing with all this communication technology "is not good or bad: It just is. It's here now—something new. It replaces something old, something that is on its way out—the assumption that there are places we can't be reached."

Like *Cheaper by the Dozen*, Greene's nostalgia-laden essay includes striking images of social change. Telecommunications technology not only allows us to witness more events more quickly—as the kid at the ballpark indicates, it also breaks down barriers between home and work, public life and private. Such technology changes the way we experience the world and relate to each other. It changes the speed, tempo, and place of life. Because we can be everywhere, we often find ourselves nowhere at all. Indeed, the emerging "global village" of communication is less about creating interactive communities of citizens than organizing individuals into discrete demographic consumer markets. Thus, news and advertisements relating the benefits of the information superhighway are driven as much by wishful thinking as they are by product sales goals. Can Greene's requiem for the erosion of private space—away from commercials, sales pitches, and work demands—be revised? Might existing technology have other social consequences such as increased social interaction, non-commercial information exchange, and democratic community building?

This section only intimates some answers for future reflection and discussion. The readings here consider only a few of the connections between communication technology and possible democratic practices. Of course, the readings in this text have already underscored how much social, political, and cultural impulses drive dominant communication practices, including practices dependent on technology.

In describing the relationships between technology, culture, and politics, John Street opens by writing that "what we conceive of as human or natural is more often than not the creation of our technology. The way we see and experience the world, the way we come to define our place within it...is achieved by and through technology...at same time, the technology we employ and the ends it is intended to serve, are themselves shaped by political processes" (179). In short, technology and the social change it incites or inspires depend on the political and social processes of its development and use.

Street prefers a "cultural approach" integrating politics with technology to better understand the processes of technological innovation. He urges us to consider the political or social needs that develop certain technologies and the social needs those technologies serve. He argues that we are neither creatures nor controllers of technology, but caught up in technology—"simultaneously directing and coping with its influence" (182). Although Street is not explicitly concerned with communication, his case study of media technology illustrates the usefulness of his approach for understanding technology and communication practice. Street's reference to the need for participation and evaluation of technology use singles out dialogue as a necessary practice. In other words, interactive, democratic communication links social values with technological use.

Media activists often speak of the democratic potential of popular videomaking and the Internet. Yet, if one accepts the thrust of most of the readings in this text, any particular communication practice is already imbedded in larger cultural practices and power arrangements. No one medium or communication practice—especially one marginalized by dominant cultural practices—can resolve the lack of public access to media production. Indeed, in most communities, "community access cable" has already been devoured by cable industry giants, like TCI and Viacom. Community media projects like videomaking can only be one small part of a larger communication strategy for opening public discourse to the public in all of its diversity.

For proponents of democratic communication, the rise of the Internet holds great hope. In a short article included here, Frank Beacham warns us that such hope is being challenged by commercial interests which would undermine the democratic potential of the Net. According to Beacham, an Internet filtered through AT&T and other commercial providers replaces a participatory interactive medium with a "crass commercialism" as users are reduced to consumers. He argues that such an outcome is not pre-determined, but depends on a pending political battle of "remarkable proportions" over the Net's common carrier status.

Finally, as a contemporary counterpart to Dewey's early 20th century insight, the closing essay "bookends" this text. Dianne Rucinksi presents reciprocal communication as a theoretical model for measuring and organizing democratic communication. Applicable to any communication practice, mutual and reciprocal access and participation has a particular urgency for contemporary issues. The concept of reciprocal communication should be interjected into current debates about the mass media, international telecommunications, and democratic life. Modern technology—purposefully deployed—could significantly increase reciprocity in mass society. If media technology can link studio audiences with diverse communities around the nation in face-to-face conversations about funny home videos, why can't that same technology link communities in interactive discussions about important social and political issues? If media technology can interview participants in social struggles on the other side of the globe, why can't that same technology transmit questions and responses from people on the other side of the barricades or on this side of the globe?

If we follow Street, Garnham, Rucinski, and others cited in previous chapters, the answer lies in widespread democratic access to prevalent communication practices and their technology. To paraphrase John Dewey, individual self-realization can only be accomplished through a democratic community which can be constructed only through the process of participatory communication. However technology changes our perceptions of the world and each other, its application depends largely on the decision-making process. Technology available to and directed by a diversity of public, community, and cultural groups would enhance citizen participation in communication practices.

REFERENCES

Greene, Bob. "At the Ball Park: A Measure of How the World's Changed." *Chicago Tribune* 13 May 1997: C1.

29 | Democracy and Technology
John Street

Democracy

Any account of democracy works with a number of central ideas in its attempt to give shape to "rule by the people." It seeks to establish means by which "the people" can articulate their values, wishes or desires. These have then to be registered within the political system and converted into a set of policies or procedures, which in turn have to be implemented and assessed. For such a process to work, certain conditions and mechanisms have to exist. The ability to articulate views, for example, depends upon some version of freedom of speech; the expression of these views also requires the presence of political organisations (trade unions, pressure groups, movements, political parties) which can mediate between popular opinion and the political system. In turn, the political system has to be capable of representing or responding to the demands put upon it. There has to be some means by which its authority can be legitimated. All these activities need to be contained within a political culture which nurtures and maintains the values of democratic practice. And finally, there must be some means by which political authority can be checked whilst remaining sufficiently resilient to resist rival illegitimate claims to its power. There is nothing very controversial about this simple model of democracy (although there are many variants upon it), But in all its aspects it is profoundly affected by communications technology; this is especially true of freedom of speech.

Freedom of Speech

There is no doubting the importance of freedom of speech to theories of liberal democracy. John Stuart Mill writes in *On Liberty*, the principles of which underpin his account of representative government, that "if all mankind minus one were of one opinion, and only one person were of the contrary opinion, mankind would be no more justified in silencing that one person, than he, if he had the power, would be justified in silencing mankind" (Mill, 1972, p. 79). Joseph Schumpeter (1976, p. 295), despite his desire to revise "classical" accounts of democracy, also insists that for his new democracy to work there must be "a large measure of tolerance for

From *Politics and Technology*, pp. 184–192 by John Street. Reprinted by permission of Guilford Publications, Inc.

difference of opinion." Today, such principles are enshrined in documents such as the Universal Declaration of Human Rights: "Everyone has the right to freedom of opinion and expression; this right includes freedom to hold opinions without interference and to seek, receive and impart information and ideas through any media and regardless of frontiers" (Article 19). The general sentiments of such claims are widely shared, and are an organising principle of groups like Amnesty International and Charter 88.

What is most frustrating about such pronouncements is that virtually nothing is said about the means by which the various goals are to be achieved. Writing about the mass media and democracy, John Keane comments that "almost nobody asks basic questions about the relationship between democratic ideals and institutions and the contemporary media" (Keane, 1991, p. x). What exactly is meant by "freedom of speech" in a world in which the means of communication are owned by media conglomerates and in which access to these means is very restricted? "Whereas the media have changed dramatically over the last two centuries," writes Simon Lee (1990, p. 2 1), "the same old arguments over free speech seem to carry on regardless." Part of the explanation may lie in liberalism's predominant concern with restraining the powers of government. As John Thompson argues: "By placing so much emphasis on the dangers of state power, the early liberal theorists did not take sufficient account of a threat stemming from a different source: from the unhindered growth of media industries qua commercial concerns" (Thompson, 1990, p. 18). This is a serious omission because, as Lee observes (1990, p. 24), "Those who can buy a newspaper or a television station have far greater access to the socalled free marketplace of ideas than have ordinary citizens." In short there are two gaps in the link between democracy and the technology of mass communication. The first is the *meaning* of "freedom of speech" in the context of mass communications, the second is its *operation*.

There is a history to this predicament. As Ithiel de Sola Pool (1983) argued, despite the US Constitution's commitment to protect freedom of speech through the First Amendment, it has found no direct expression in the actual organisation of broadcasting. Instead, the allocation of radio frequencies has been determined by the demands made by radio stations and by the relative weakness of the Federal Communications Commission, the regulatory body. A weakly regulated market cannot guarantee freedom of speech.

In Britain, by contrast, the failure to integrate the principle into practice can also be traced to the origins of broadcasting. Unlike in the US, in Britain the allocation of radio frequencies was carried out very cautiously and protectively. But this caution did not arise from a concern for the principle of free speech; it derived from the military security considerations which accompanied the development of radio technology in Britain (see Chapter 3). Broadcasting was (and still continues to be) treated as an aspect of the state's interests, rather than the people's.

But to observe the origins of this divide between political principles and technical systems is not to reunite them. For that, there needs to be further analysis of the features and functions of the technology. Few attempts have been made. Pool (1983) and Enzensberger (1976) are notable exceptions.

In his *Technologies of Freedom*, Pool sees communications technology as bringing about the conditions of freedom. "Electronic media... allow for more knowledge, easier access, and freer speech than were ever enjoyed before" (1983, p. 251). The only threats to this process are interfering politicians and their bureaucratic routines. The answer lies with the free rein of market forces, albeit framed by the commitment to freedom of speech enshrined in the First Amendment. By contrast, Enzensberger sees electronic media as contributing to freedom only when they are organised in a more deliberative way. The possibility of an "emancipatory use of media" depends on a number of conditions being fulfilled. These are illustrated by the comparison he draws with the current, "repressive" mode:

Repressive	Emancipatory
Centrally controlled	Decentralized control
One transmitter, many receivers	Every receiver a potential transmitter
Immobilisation of isolated individuals	Mobilization of the masses
Passive consumer behaviour	Interaction of those involved, feedback
Depoliticization	A political learning process
Production by specialists	Collective production
Control by property owners	Social control by self-organization

Source: Enzensberger, 1976, p. 38.

Enzensberger offered these alternatives in the 1960s, but the underlying theme still echoes. Keane, for instance, presents the "public service media" as an important challenge to the rival claims of "technocratic solutions": "Democratic public service media are reflexive means of controlling the exercise of power. They are unsurpassed methods of checking the unending arrogance and foolishness of those who wield it" (Keane, 1991, pp. 179–81). At the same time, he advocates the use of new technology—"interactive television, digital copiers, camcorders and music synthesizers"—to facilitate communication among citizens (ibid., p. 159). My immediate concern is not with the particular solutions offered by Pool, Enzensberger and Keane, but with the general categories contained within them. First, there is the *design* of the technology and its potential applications—as receiver and transmitter; secondly, there is the *organisation* of the use of the technology—who has access and control; and finally, there is the *content* which it carries—political education. The general implication of the argument is that the three elements must be included in any account of the politics involved. What follows is an attempt to see what might fall under these headings if democracy-as-freedom-of-speech and mass communications are to be combined.

Organisation

If the principle of freedom of speech is to be applied to mass communications technology, what might this mean? Tannsjo (1985) provides one answer by asking whether mass communications can serve democracy where the right to "freedom of expression" operates. "Freedom of expression" is realised in the private right to own the means of mass communication. Tannsjo asks whether this right is compatible with what he describes as "sound" mass communications. By this he means a situation in which mass communications:

1. "contribute effectively to the *growth of knowledge* in society";
2. "allow for *a pluralism of ideas*";

3. provide *"equal opportunity* for various social and cultural groups and strata in society to acquire access to media" (Tannsjo, 1985, pp. 553–4, his emphasis).

Tannsjo argues that none of these conditions can apply under a system of mass communications in which the "freedom of expression" is also recognised. He argues that the market in mass communications has led to "a concentration of capital and centralization of ownership." Although concentration of ownership in a few hands is the key defining feature of the political economy of mass communications, it is also marked by both its transnational reach and the integration of media forms. The major media interests are not concerned with only one form of communication. The days of the press baron are over. TimeWarner, for instance, have interests in film, television, music and magazines. Rupert Murdoch has substantial interests in film, TV (cable and network), books and newspapers and magazines. This does not just represent a broad portfolio but an enclosed network of interests. TimeWarner sell films through the soundtracks they market, and vice versa. Murdoch's newspapers are used to promote the demand for satellite channels, and vice versa.

The new communications order represents an immense concentration of power. The effect of this can be to restrict access to the means of communication *within* conglomerates or to prevent competition *between* them. In such circumstances, Tannsjo concludes (pp. 557-9), "sound" mass communications can only exist where freedom of expression is *curbed.* Individuals must be prevented from purchasing their own television stations.

What is to replace the old, commercial order? Tannsjo argues, rather weakly, for "democratic political control," by which he does not mean state censorship but does mean "strong political interference with the flow of information." The feebleness of this conclusion is a result of the lack of any real attempt to address the other side of the argument: the content of "sound" mass communications, the second of Enzensberger's general categories. "Democratic political control" means nothing unless we also know what must be controlled and what provides control.

Content

In the argument about how democracy can be linked to mass communication, a key assumption is that the mass media—newspapers, radio, TV—are responsible for furnishing us with the political information that shapes our view of the world and of ourselves. As Angus and Jhally (1989, p. 2) write: "In contemporary culture the media have become central to the constitution of social identity." Today virtually no one, if the surveys are to be believed, depends upon conversation with their neighbours for political information (Negrine, 1989). It is true that there are variations in the sources upon which people draw. For example, readers of the tabloid press regard television as the most reliable source of political information; whereas readers of the broadsheet press regard their papers as the best source of information. Whatever the variations in people's perception, the standard claim is that mass media furnish us with information about the world.

A second assumption is that this information affects the way we behave, that citizens' political behaviour is powerfully shaped by the information they receive. The collapse of communism in Eastern Europe in 1989–90 was attributed to a wide range of factors, but one in particular stood out. It was the idea that the popular uprising against state socialism had been initiated by Western media coverage. The Deputy Editor of the British *Channel 4 News*, Garron Baines, wrote:

> It was a fitting climax to revolution in Eastern Europe that it was played out live to a worldwide television audience from the Romanian TV station that was itself a battleground....Western television has become a catalyst of revolution. Demonstrations and protests, subsequently broadcast by national television inside those countries undergoing change, has accelerated events at a rate only achieved by unfettered and direct communications.

Sir Geoffrey Cox, an ex-editor of the British Independent Television News, was equally convinced of television's revolutionary powers: "The revolution sweeping Europe is a television revolution. The television cameras have played the part of the trumpets of a modern Jericho." These extravagant claims for the power of television have to be treated with considerable caution. Television rarely, if ever, has such a dramatic effect, but this should not cause us to discount its influence completely. The question is whether the impact is determined by the content of the broadcast or the context in which it is received, or possibly in the way the original activities are designed to attract coverage?

Television has certainly made available new kinds of political actions. As Thompson observes:

> The very existence of the medium of television gives rise to a category or categories of action which is carried out with the aim of being televisable, that is, capable of being regarded as worthy of transmission via television to a spatially distant and potentially vast audience. Today part of the purpose of actions such as mass demonstrations and hijackings, summit meetings and state visits, is to generate televisable events which will enable individuals or groups to communicate with remote and extended audiences (Thompson, 1990, p. 231).

Television, in this sense, has become part of the practice of politics, and therefore has to be incorporated into the principles attached to politics. What access is granted, what is filmed and how, must be incorporated into an analysis of the media's role in a democracy and its impact on political behaviour.

Television does not just provoke actions, it also expresses political ideas. The issue is what such expression involves. The "speech" within "freedom of speech" cannot refer simply to the words that are spoken; it must also include images and sounds. Furthermore, it cannot be confined to those areas of the mass media which are formally designated as "political"—the news, current affairs, and so on. This broad definition of "speech" is implicitly recognised in current practice. One of the strangest features of the early days of the Gulf war was the way programme controllers in Britain became overwhelmed by a desire to "pull" shows that were deemed unsuitable for "a nation at war." Out went "Allo Allo," a situation comedy set in wartime France, and "The Clothes Show" dropped its item on current army fashions. Reports appeared in the papers that BBC Radio 1, the pop station, had issued a list of records that were deemed unsuitable. Out was to go Phil Collins' "In the Air Tonight," Elton John's "Saturday Night's All Right for Fighting" and Lulu's "Boom BangaBang." Sadly, these reports were denied by the BBC. But whether or not they were true, they were entirely plausible. There is never any shortage of people who will claim that pop music is the source of moral degradation or of political emancipation (Street, 1986). They are rarely right, but in their excess of enthusiasm for the power of popular culture, they have latched onto an important insight. What the programme controllers implicitly recognised in their agonising over suitable programmes is that "information" is only important when it is used, when it becomes "knowledge," when it is given a form and purpose which produces some action or reaction.

This is important to our attempt to link democracy and technology. The technical means employed in imparting knowledge actually changes the character of that knowledge. The form of the technology can alter the *kind of* news that is reported. This is not simply measured by the speed at which a report reaches its destination or by the quality of the broadcast sound and pictures. The introduction, for instance, of electronic news-gathering techniques means that it is possible to broadcast "as things happen." That, at least, is the rhetoric. The potential of the technology—to be carried easily, to be edited quickly and so on—becomes part of the business of covering the news. The technology is held to present a "truer" account of events. In fact, the technology introduces a new version of "events," which may be no more or no less true. Wallis and Baran describe, fo[...] ENG technology has changed the definition [...]

The engineer with th[...] [...]mes the first person
at an event, not the co[...] [...]t's happened. With
constant feeds from r[...] [...]sumes top priority,
sometimes even over[...] [...]eir emphasis).

Or as they remark els[...] [...]ency" (ibid., p. 220).
Meanwhile in the stud[...] [...]rovides new ways of
packaging and represe[...]

In reducing the cost [...] [...]sion, direct broadcast
satellites have also led t[...] [...]ase of access to global
TV actually allows for [...] [...]stant supply of news
provided by channels l[...] [...]g committed to local
news coverage (ibid., p. [...] a limited and narrow
horizon.

If the technology do[...] [...]ge it represents, then it is once more implicated in any attempt to analyse the democratic form of mass communications. It becomes necessary to ask how and in what way the technology changes the content of the knowledge being conveyed.

Design

Implicit in the answer to such questions is the role of design in democratic accounting. Technologies can be more or less capable of control by users, more or less drastic in the effects they create. Although design may not be the final determinant of such things, it plays a crucial part. Adorno and Horkheimer implied as much in the language they use to describe technological change:

[Handwritten marginal note: P. 324 NR+S 2 — "The introduction, for instance, of electronic news gathering techniques means that it is possible to broadcast "as things happen." That, at least, is the rhetoric. The potential of the technology - to be carried easily, to be edited quickly and so on - becomes part of the business of covering the news. The technology is held to present a "truer" account of events."]

The step from the telephone to the radio has clearly distinguished the roles. The former still allowed the subscriber to play the role of subject, and was liberal. The latter is democratic: it turns all participants into listeners and authoritatively subjects them to broadcast programs which are all exactly the same (Adorno and Horkheimer, 1979, pp. 121–2).

In a similar spirit, Rudolph Bahro specifies particular conditions which should be incorporated into a system of mass communications in order for it to meet the conditions of democracy. Included among these is the duty "to prevent the broadband cable network and computerized data gathering as instruments of increasing isolation, control and intimidation of the citizen" (Bahro, 1986, p. 41). Ivan Illich's (1975) notion of "convivial technology"—technology that is user friendly—conveys a parallel idea. In short, the design of the technology, the systems determining access to it, and the use made of it, have to be subjected to political analysis to establish the principles and values incorporated in it.

This case study of mass communications and democracy has examined three aspects of the technology: the way it is organized, how it shapes content, and what is incorporated in its design. Each affects the way it works and what, therefore, must be considered in introducing any form of democratic control. There are, of course, other ways in which the same technology could have been analysed, but the point has been to show what sort of technical questions have to be incorporated into an attempt to link politics and technology. The aim of this case study has been to provide an *approach*, rather than a set of answers. It suggests what ought to be considered in establishing freedom of speech within a system of mass communications; it has said little about the conclusions of any such examination. In the final pages of this book, I want to draw out the implications of this approach for the study and practice of politics.

REFERENCES

Adorno, T. and M. Horkheimer (1979) *Dialectic of Enlightenment* (London: Verso).

Angus, I. and S. Jhally (1989) *Cultural Politics in Contemporary America* (London: Routledge).

Bahro, R. (1986) *Building the Green Movement* (London: Heretic).

Enzensberger, H.M. (1976) *Raids and Reconstructions: Essays in Politics, Crime and Culture* (London: Pluto Press).

Illich, I. (1975) *Tools for Conviviality* (London: Fontana).

Keane, G. (1991) *The Media and Democracy* (Cambridge: Polity).

Lee, S. (1990) *Freedom of Speech* (London: Faber & Faber).

Mill, J.S. (1972) *On Liberty and Considerations on Representative Government*, Everyman edition (London: Dent).

Negrine, R. (1989) *Politics and the Mass Media in Britain* (London: Routledge).

Pool, I. (1983) *Technologies of Freedom* (Cambridge, Mass: Harvard University Press).

Pool, I. (1990) *Technologies without Boundaries* (Cambridge, Mass: Harvard University Press).

Schumpeter, J. (1976) *Capitalism, Socialism and Democracy* (London: Allen & Unwin).

Street, J. (1986) *Rebel Rock: the politics of popular music* (Oxford: Basil Blackwell).

Tannsjo, T. (1985) "Against Freedom of Expression," *Political Studies*, vol. 33, number 4, pp. 547–59.

Thompson, J. (1990) *Ideology and Modern Culture* (Cambridge: Polity).

Wallis, R. And S. Baran (1990) *The Known World of Broadcast News* (London: Routledge).

30 | Net Loss:
Corporate Moves Could Doom the
Internet's Participatory Culture
Frank Beacham

The change is subtle, and misleading by design, but the Internet is in full transition from a participatory interactive communications network to a broadcast medium dominated by electronic commerce.

The transition is occurring under the guise of making the technically daunting Internet cheaper and easier to use. At first glance, this new promise by corporate America to liberate cyberspace from its high-tech mantle appears to be a victory for ordinary people. However, as with most new technology, there's a hidden agenda that obscures the true cost of the deal.

AT&T, MCI and other phone companies are in a race to make Internet access as simple and cheap as standard phone service. Computer and consumer electronics companies like Oracle, Apple/Bandai and Sega Enterprises want to create cheap "network computers" that allow Internet access without the high cost of a fully-equipped personal computer. Both goals are being widely celebrated as needed breakthroughs to make the Internet accessible to a wider spectrum of the population.

However, if one combines the effects of the two developments, a subtle change occurs: The Internet shifts from being a participatory medium that serves the interest of the public to being a broadcast medium where corporations deliver consumer-oriented information. Interactivity would be reduced to little more than sales transactions and e-mail.

AT&T recently announced that as many as 80 million of its long distance customers can now get five hours of Net access for "free" over the next year. The telecom giant also claimed that it will make it easier to go online and eliminate the annoying technical glitches that currently plague the Internet experience.

> *The Internet shifts from being a participatory medium that serves the interest of the public to being a broadcast medium where corporations deliver consumer-oriented information. Interactivity would be reduced to little more than sales transactions and e-mail.*

But what does AT&T get in return for holding our hand and leading us into the chaotic and often anarchic world of the Internet?

Our loyalty and our trust, it hopes, followed by our money. Since most of AT&T's new customers are novices to the Internet, they will also be highly susceptible to the company's "suggestions" as to what makes up the Internet experience.

"The Internet can be a daunting place for people who suddenly arrive there," said Tom Evslin, vice president of AT&T WorldNet Service. "To just dump new users on the Internet is about as friendly as taking them out of town and dropping them into Times Square and asking them to find their way around."

For this reason, AT&T said, it is moving beyond providing just technical services to offering "edited navigation, directories and customer care to make it easy to use the Internet." This includes a directory of more than 80,000 Internet sites, including descriptions, ratings and reviews. It also includes an Internet "Exploration Station" that provides a series of theme areas for family entertainment and education.

Of course, AT&T's corporate guidance is not motivated by the public interest, and it would be naive to assume the corporate giant will direct any Internet user to a location that might criticize or reflect negatively on its corporate interests. One should not expect to find a critical analysis of long-distance phone service or AT&T's labor policies featured in an AT&T directory.

"Advertising revenue streams are part of our business plan," said Evslin, acknowledging AT&T's commercial mindset. "If you think of us as being the front door to the Internet, then there's the opportunity for advertisers. It's not very glamorous, but think of us as a billboard in a subway station."

The other side of this coin is a new stripped-down Internet access appliance that's been dubbed the "network computer." Since it's essentially a dumb terminal with little memory and no hard disk drive, this device depends on the Internet for its operating software.

Priced at under $500 and jokingly called "WebBoy," the network computer does little more than allow its user to browse the Internet and do simple transactions, such as playing games, using e-mail or shopping online.

Add AT&T's advertising approach together with the cheap WebBoy appliance, and what do you get? How about the functional equivalent of interactive commercial television. Good old advertising-based, consumer-oriented mass media just like we have today, plain and simple.

Under the AT&T/WebBoy scenario, the vision of a truly democratic, participatory interactive media gives way to crass commercialism. Internet users are reduced to "consumers" whose reason for existence is to continue a relentless cycle of buying and consuming goods and services.

This trend toward a broadcast model for the Internet is expected to accelerate even more as higher bandwidth delivery systems become available to the home. The cable television industry, seeing its future in interactivity, is racing to build high-speed, high-capacity systems that will handle full-motion video as well as audio, graphics and text information.

@Home, a new service of Telecommunications, Inc. (TCI), the nation's largest cable systems operator, and LineRunner, a new service of the No. 2 operator, Time Warner, are expected to deliver data to the home at speeds hundreds of times faster than conventional telephone lines. Both media giants are testing their services now, and hope to begin widespread deployment over the next couple of years.

These mega systems are not just high-speed connections to the Internet, but entirely new networks that actually circumvent the Net to offer more image-rich interactive multimedia productions.

"It would be very easy to sell just speed, but we see a lot of things we can do to add value to the product," said William Jasso, vice president of public affairs for Time Warner's Northeast Ohio division, in an interview with the trade newspaper **Inter@ctive Week** (2/26/96).

In addition to high-speed access to the Internet, the Time Warner service will offer the brand-name commercial online services, local content and Time Inc.'s national databases. @Home is currently courting partnerships with content providers with bandwidth-hungry, feature-rich applications that can make effective use of its super-high-capacity, 10-mega-bit-per-second network.

This race to create bigger data pipelines means the production values—and hence the cost to information providers—of interactive media will soon rise sharply. While all sites on the Internet's World Wide Web are limited today by the network's slow transmission capacity, that will not be true a few years from now. Those with big production budgets will be able to effectively exploit the added capacity, while those with lower budgets will have to be more creative in order to draw an audience.

The situation will be akin to the difference today between the high production value of network television versus the more modest production value of public access programming. Audiences are traditionally drawn to higher production value and tend to reject programs or information presented with lesser perceived value.

At the recent Media & Democracy Congress in San Francisco, Andy Sharpless, vice president of technology for Progressive Networks of Seattle, told a group of political activists and non-profit organizations that they have a window of no more than five years to compete on an even playing field with large corporate sites on the Internet.

"There will come a point when high bandwidth production values will make it hard to do what one can do now—that is, become a small Internet publisher with a small capital investment," Sharpless said. "There is a glorious moment and we are in it now. You can be in on the early days and be perceived by the audience to be as good as those big guys. But that day will change."

With the Internet clearly moving toward greater commercialism, some also worry that efforts will soon be made to squeeze out all messages that don't fit the mainstream corporate/government agenda—again, a progression toward a medium that looks more like today's commercial television.

As promising as the Internet is to the goal of media democracy, said Voyager Company founder Bob Stein, a political battle of "remarkable proportions" looms ahead over the Net's shaky common carrier status.

Stein, a leading electronic publisher also speaking at the Media & Democracy Congress, noted that the Internet has not yet been used by a powerful leader to organize people with a non-mainstream agenda. He predicts that in today's highly reactionary political environment, any serious challenge to those in power will be met with censorship.

"Does anybody here really believe that the powers that be would allow a situation where somebody like Malcolm X could have his own channel and talk to everybody every day?" he asked. "Seems to me impossible."

Against a backdrop of rapid technological change, clashing political agendas and a corporate gold rush mentality, the Internet—perhaps the first new mass communications medium in half a century—is now very much in play. The trend to commercialize the Net is overwhelmingly clear. Whether the medium can retain its early promise as a democratic forum of free expression remains an open question.

31 | The Centrality of Reciprocity to Communication and Democracy

Dianne Rucinski

Recent challenges to the received wisdom about electoral democracy within large nation-states have practical implications for much research and theory on political communication (Barber, 1984; Calhoun, 1988). Participatory theorists have focused their attention on developing approaches to collective decision-making (referenda, initiatives, etc.) and to the problem of fully integrating large nation-states. They have not sufficiently theorized the communication processes that must precede collective decision-making (Calhoun, 1988).

This paper focuses on the implications of participatory democratic theory, as compared to those of elite democratic theory,[1] for political communication theorists. In particular, the concept of *reciprocity* provides political communication researchers with a tool for gauging the successes (or failures) of various communication systems in enhancing participatory democracy. The paper suggests how mass-mediated communications might contribute to the achievement of reciprocity.

The Challenge of Participatory Democratic Theory

The central problem for students of electoral democracies is to reconcile the classic definition of "democracy" (self-rule) with the supposedly representative forms of government and social process (most citizens are far removed from effective debate and resolution of the political, economic, and social issues that daily touch their lives). To resolve that paradox, elite democratic theorists have redefined democracy as a procedure for electing leaders: A political system is considered democratic if there is competition among leaders (Bachrach, 1967; Dahl & Lindblom, 1953).

Interest in establishing alternatives to elite democratic theory has ebbed and flourished, with the latest wave beginning in the 1960s (Burnheim, 1985; Graham, 1986). Of particular concern here is the dissatisfaction with the theory's minimal integration of the citizen and the system.

Participatory democratic theorists argue that elite theory too narrowly constrains citizen participation to casting votes, communicating with those in decision-making positions, and aligning with groups that have the power to influence elected officials.[2] Participation thus is restricted to a few, minimal acts, and political discussion is limited to a narrow set of issues

---

From *Critical Studies in Mass Communication*, 8 (1991), pp. 184–194. Used by permission of the Speech Communication Association.

considered "political." In such a system, rule of the people by the people arguably becomes a meaningless slogan, divorced from concrete experience.

Another unsatisfactory feature of elite democratic theory is its rationale for rule by elites (Dahl & Tufte, 1973). The argument, as described by Berelson, Lazarsfeld & McPhee (1954), is that low levels of political knowledge and high levels of citizen apathy prevent meaningful, widespread citizen participation; thus, the business of government must fall on the shoulders of elites. Research employing participatory theory suggests that the causal mechanism may be the reverse: When individuals are in decision-making positions, their interest in participation increases (Blumberg, 1968).

For example, Couch & Weiland (1986) found greater involvement in group procedures and negotiation sessions when subjects were uncertain of their leadership position. Their study suggests that low levels of traditional forms of participation may result from, rather than lead to, the concentration of decision-making power in the hands of elites. Such findings, participatory theorists have argued, may offer insight into how participation may be increased in other domains and on a wider scale.

Differences between Elite and Participatory Theory

Elite democratic theory offers two competing conceptions of individuals and their relations—abstract individualism and pluralism (Gould, 1988; Graham, 1985). Abstract individualism sees the individual, guided by rationality and self-interest, as the primary entity determining the course of social action. Individuals are thought to be related externally, meaning that their basic nature is unchanged by social interaction. The primacy granted to all individuals and the normative value of political equality are transformed into the concrete practice of "one person, one vote," and democracy is defined as the additive aggregation of individual interests and actions. Political macro-structure is formed through the periodic selection of representatives by individual actors; democracy is achieved when majority will is expressed through representative selection.

Pluralism treats individuals as the primary entities of social life as well, but it sees groups as the effective operative units in the political sphere. Individuals are defined by and exercise influence through their group affiliations, which are determined by individual interests (Gould, 1988). Societies therefore consist of the aggregation of groups, and the process of democracy becomes the mediation of group conflicts by elites.

Participatory democratic theorists argue that both of these conceptions ignore the social relations that make up daily life (Gould, 1988; Macpherson, 1977; Pateman, 1970, 1979) because they both suggest a model of society in which individuals are barely connected. If we accept that much, if not all, of human thought and behavior is formed through interactions with others, then understanding democratic processes requires us to focus on the social contexts of individuals as they interact, negotiate, and coordinate their activities. Specifically, we must understand, first, how shared and divergent interests are formed and altered through communication; and, second, how conciliatory processes allow collective action. Just as groups and group behavior are more than the mere aggregation of individuals and individual action, the participatory theorist argues, political processes must be examined through the interactive, dynamic social relationships that form and transform individuals and social units.

The nature of democratic relations from this perspective has been articulated best, perhaps, by Gould (1988). Without surrendering the dimensions of individuality and autonomy, Gould proposes that the fundamental entities comprising democratic systems be conceptualized as *individuals-in-relations*. In this perspective, primacy is granted neither to social structures nor to individuals alone. Individuals gain their identity through social interaction. Macro-social factors, rather than rigidly determining individual thought and behavior, *influence* thought and behavior by providing contexts for micro-social interactions.

Participatory democratic theorists view individual action not as an outcome of atomized self-interest and egoism but as the product of social relations and voluntaristic behavior based upon common or shared goals and activities. Activities such as economic production, education, religion, child-rearing, and so on are considered to be the result of individual actions stemming from common purposes. These patterns of interaction occurring across time and place define the macro-social structure emerging from micro-social interaction. In contrast to merely aggregated individual activities (e.g., voting) that may be coincidentally coordinated, common activity can be described only with regard to shared aims and motives within a social system.

This leads to another contrast with traditional theory. Elite democratic theory conceptualizes democracy as "an institutional arrangement for arriving at political decisions in which individuals acquire the power to decide by means of a competitive struggle for the people's vote" (Schumpeter, 1943, p. 269) and thus concerns the *consequences* of individual thought and interest. In contrast, participatory democratic theory conceptualizes democracy as the *process* of interactive decision-making. This focus makes communication an essential component of participatory democratic theory.

Democratic decision-making requires that goals and aims of common activities be recognized and understood by the interactants. Yet, these goals and aims are often disputed and are constantly being renegotiated. Thus, participatory democracy is conceptualized as a set of continuous communicative processes that takes its concrete form in political discussion and debate. This conceptualization takes seriously Dewey's argument that "democracy is more than a form of government; it is primarily a mode of associated living, of conjoint *communicated experience*" (1916/1966; p. 87, italics added). Discourse and negotiation are the primary forms of citizen participation. Participation, then, includes the *negotiation* of whether or not political and social issues are or should be amenable to political solutions, and a determination of the range of alternative actions. Without an understanding of micro-social interactions in small-scale social units, the potential for theorizing (and developing) intermediate linkages in nationstates is seriously compromised (Collins, 1988). The initial task of researchers, then, is to describe the conciliatory processes that characterize ongoing collective endeavors. These descriptions must specify the individual, the micro-social, and the macro-social conditions that inhibit or advance the achievement of shared goals.

Defining communicative acts as important elements of citizen participation, and expanding the public sphere to economic, social, and conventionally defined political domains, affects the meaning of "political" in political discussion and debate. Whereas the "political" is often narrowly restricted by elite theory to the actions of elected representatives and formal political organizations, participatory theory suggests that political topics actually include any concern of citizens that involves the allocation of resources. Talk of wages, the availability of affordable housing and child care, the costs of health care and insurance, the division of labor in the home, the safety of products, and decision-making on the job are all "political" concerns in that they involve issues of autonomy, power, and the negotiation of the rights of individuals and the rights of the system.

Obviously, political participation does not end with talk. The process of conciliation, collective decision-making, and the enactment of shared goals are the mainstays of fully participatory democratic systems.

Reciprocity

The emphasis on shared activity and interdependence in participatory democratic theory, combined with an emphasis on discussion as the most common form of political participation, points to the centrality of the concept of *reciprocity*, defined as the shared knowledge of the perspectives of others and the interests underlying those perspectives. In ideal circumstances, such reciprocity is symmetrical. Obviously, many cases of collective action are characterized by asymmetry; but in any decision about collective action that does not rely on force, some minimal degree of symmetrical reciprocity among interactants must be achieved. For reciprocity to be achieved at the social level, individual citizens must possess some political knowledge, defined here as cognition that facilitates, and hence is linked with, social interaction. It is through communicative acts that reciprocity is achieved.

Reciprocity and Social Political Knowledge

The concept of reciprocity is described in anthropological and sociological literature as a fundamental condition of human association (Homans, 1961; Malinowski, 1961; Schutz, 1970; Shibutani, 1955; Sinunel, 1950). More central to a communication context, Habermas (1979, 1984) argues that, far from being solely a contingent moral norm, reciprocity serves as the basis for the "ideal speech situation," without which the conciliatory discourse necessary for the coordination of common activities is impossible. The process of conciliation and the achievement of compromise require that the parties in conflict know the position(s) of others.

A disposition to reciprocity is a normative attribute of democratic citizens.[3] Yet, reciprocity need not be thought of only as an ideal moral standard, attainable only in the abstract.

Two dimensions of reciprocity—shared knowledge of the perspectives of others within a social system, and shared knowledge of the interests underlying differences in perspectives— help explain the process of conciliation and how decisions over common goals and activities are made.[4]

The intrapersonal analog of the system concept of reciprocity is *socialpolitical knowledge*. Like reciprocity, social political knowledge has two dimensions: knowledge of the perspectives of others, and knowledge of the interests underlying those perspectives. Unlike reciprocity, however, social political knowledge is an intrapersonal, cognitive concept, referring only to the perceptions an individual has about the perspectives of others and the interests underlying them.

Reciprocity and social political knowledge are both variable concepts. There may be degrees of reciprocity at the system level, and degrees of social political knowledge at the intrapersonal level. Full, or symmetric, reciprocity occurs when all members of a collectivity know and understand the breadth of perspectives and their underlying interests existing in that social system. Partial reciprocity occurs in two primary ways: when all perspectives and underlying interests regarding a social/political issue are not known by all members of a collectivity; or when the perspectives are known, but the interests are not. Obviously, in less pluralistic social systems, smaller social systems (e.g., dyads, small groups, families), and systems whose communication channels reflect the diversity of perspectives, full reciprocity is more likely to be achieved.[5] At the intrapersonal level, it is possible for a social actor to understand the perspectives of others but not know their principles or interests. It is also possible for a social actor to understand the interests of others but be unaware of their perspectives or of how their interests and perspectives are related.

Increases in an individual's level of social political knowledge do not necessarily lead to higher levels of system reciprocity; full system reciprocity is possible only when knowledge is *shared*. Conversely, the existence of greater degrees of reciprocity does not necessarily imply that all members of a collectivity have achieved higher levels of social political knowledge.

Conventional measures of political knowledge have been criticized for emphasizing facts over explanations (see Clarke & Kline, 1974; Gaziano, 1983; Graber, 1988; Gurevitch & Levy, 1986). The possession of social political knowledge, in contrast, means that one is capable of providing an account for or explanation of differences between social actors' positions and why those differences exist. This type of knowledge is essential, at least theoretically so, to the process of conciliation necessary for collective action.

Traditional measures of knowledge also have been criticized for being researcher defined rather than respondent-defined (Clarke & Kline, 1974; Dervin, 1980; Gitlin, 1978; Gurevitch & Levy, 1986). But the conceptual definition of social political knowledge locates the objective referent of knowledge both in the respondent and in the collectivity of which the respondent is a member. The role of the researcher becomes one of revealing what is relevant to members of a collectivity.

A researcher can accomplish this by encouraging individuals to discuss issues that are relevant to them in terms of their perceptions of underlying causes of the problems(s), possible solutions, perspectives of others, and principles or reasons for differences in perspectives. To determine an individual's level of social political knowledge, a researcher would compare that individual's responses to the responses given by all other members of a sample representing the collectivity of which the respondent is a member.

The level of reciprocity within a system can be assessed by examining the direction and degree of association between the range of perspectives and the corresponding underlying interests within a collectivity and the extent to which members jointly understand the viewpoints of others and the interests underlying those perspectives. Operationally, then, reciprocity is the ratio of *perspectives and underlying interests known* to the *perspectives and underlying interests available* across members of a collectivity. A collectivity with no reciprocity (that is, total asymmetry) would be one whose members can not articulate any perspective other than their own. Negative reciprocity would exist when members of a collectivity express perspectives that they believe to be held by others but, according to other members, are actually held by no one. Positive reciprocity would exist when some members of a collectivity are capable of accurately and fully describing the perspectives and interests of others. The substantive content of both the intrapersonal (social political knowledge) and the systemic (reciprocity) concepts are defined by members of the collectivity and interpreted by the researcher. [6]

To summarize, social political knowledge, an intrapersonal concept, reflects the potential for reciprocity and is partially defined as knowing the perspectives of others and interests underlying those perspectives. The breadth of perspectives and the extent to which the perspectives are known and understood (with respect to underlying principles and interests) jointly determine the degree of social political knowledge among members of a social system. The level of reciprocity is determined by the degree to which the perspectives of members of the system are represented in the social political knowledge of members of the system.

Communication and Reciprocity

Regardless of the size of a collectivity, some level of reciprocity is necessary for participatory decision-making about continuing collective actions and maintaining conciliatory discourse. The process of conciliation is defined as communication between two or more individuals (or groups) whose perspectives differ or who are discussing perspectives held by members not represented by either party. Conciliatory discourse continues until some agreement is achieved, making collective action possible, or until one or more members terminate contact. Collective action continues until a change in the environment leads to conflict, at which point the process of conciliation must resume. Coser (1956) notes that, through conflict, perspectives and interests are highlighted, questioned, and evaluated. Conflict may also enhance an individual's understanding of his or her own perspective(s), interest(s), and role in fostering a solution to a social/political issue.

In the development of social political knowledge and reciprocity and during the process of conciliation, the contributions of communication depend on the context, size, and nature of the collectivity, as well as the structural properties of the media organizations serving the collectivity. For example, in small communities whose members have similar world views, interests, and experiences, individuals will likely learn the perspectives and interests of others through informal, face-to-face communication. In such communities, the incidence of public conflict tends to be minimal,[7] and because of the decisions of media gatekeepers, full descriptions of the nature of the conflicts are unlikely to reach the public agenda through the local mass media, (Tichenor, Donohue, & Olien, 1980). However, external media, or the dominant media serving a region, may provide some individuals with information about other perspectives. In this manner, face-to-face and indirect communications might complement each other in providing members of a collectivity with information that would increase social political knowledge and reciprocity.

In social systems characterized by a high degree of variance in world views, interests, and life experiences, such as the modern city or large nation-state, mass media systems must provide the linkages between the small-local units and the intermediary and larger ones (i.e., regions and nation-states). Without these technological tools, democratic processes would rely on management by elites or specialists, pushing democratic practices away from the goal of citizen participation.

The assumption that face-to-face interaction is necessary for the functioning of participatory democratic systems has led some theorists and activists to conclude that participatory democracy will never exist in systems too large to permit face-to-face communication. Others, more optimistically, believe that such communication technologies as computers, satellite systems, and cable systems will provide the *interactive* communication necessary for conciliatory discourse and collective decision-making. This train of thought is exemplified by Naisbitt (1982), who views computers as suitable mechanisms for linking individuals, and by Thompson (1990), who believes that the extensive diffusion of cable and satellite systems will transform media systems from systems of scarcity to systems of multiplicity.

But Naisbitt, Thompson, and others who share the redemptive vision of new technologies forget that in most cases access to communication technologies is hopelessly skewed in favor of the already privileged (Golding, 1990). As Gamham (1990) notes, widespread use of video by nonprofessionals in no way guarantees that citizens' work will be disseminated. Witness *America's Funniest Home Videos* for an example of the type of "citizen" video attractive to corporate sponsors.

If the newer technologies have brought only old wine in new bottles, then they cannot contribute to the creation and maintenance of participatory democratic systems. Indeed, older technologies have been described as making even less of a contribution to public discourse. Calhoun (1988) contends that television, radio, newspapers, and magazines, especially in postindustrial societies, are unlikely to provide channels for supra-community collective decision making. The wide reach of network television makes it perhaps the only medium capable of providing the common forum, but the unidirectionality of message flow precludes interactive dialogue. Even if television *could* provide a forum for collective discussion via newer technologies (e.g., the interactive potential of systems such as QUBE), the possible creation of a public sphere continues to be compromised by the marketing and advertising research that serves to create markets rather than publics, connecting people through their purchasing behavior rather than through common goals and activities.

Despite this dismal picture, there is some hope for the notion that mass media can enhance participatory democracies. First, in order for participatory democracies to flourish, changes in political structure and media systems must occur simultaneously; political change cannot facilitate participatory systems without the creation of a public informed through political discussion and debate.

Second, the social, political, and economic upheavals throughout the world, even the comparatively minor fluctuations in the United States, may provide moments of "rupture" (Mattelart, 1979) necessary for structural change. During these moments of rupture, changes in media systems are more likely and may even be necessary. These changes may be as minor as the reconstitution of older technologies for use in participatory systems. In Nicaragua, for example, citizen access to the airwaves was strictly denied under the Somoza dictatorships. Soon after the Sandinistas took power, the Corporacion de Radiodifusion del Pueblo (CO-RADEP), a radio network developed by and for the people of Nicaragua, trained "community correspondents" in basic news writing skills. Open discussions of topics such as cultural imperialism and criticisms of government initiatives were often aired—events unthinkable under the Somoza dictatorships. Although critics are more likely to denounce the censorship of *La Prensa* as a discouraging outcome of sociopolitical change in Nicaragua, the widespread use of radio in Nicaragua (especially in comparison to the limited reach of *La Prensa*) lends credence to the position that the Sandinista government was interested in promoting a media system for and of the people.[8]

Whether radio led to greater reciprocity in Nicaragua under the Sandinistas is unclear. We should be aware, however, that airing perspectives alone is insufficient for the achievement of reciprocity among members of a collectivity. For media to provide knowledge of the perspectives of others and knowledge of the interests underlying those perspectives requires diversity in the perspectives represented and an analysis of the rationales underlying those perspectives.

It is not enough for citizens to have access to mass media, and to create and disseminate their own messages. Multiplicity can lead to further fragmentation of collectivities, as magazine and radio audience segmentation demonstrates. Nor is it sufficient to present many perspectives by increasing the number of sources journalists select. For mass media to contribute to the achievement of reciprocity, the definition and production of news must change. In participatory democratic systems, news must place greater emphasis on telling us "why" rather than telling us "who" (Carey, 1986).

Conclusion

To specify the communicative conditions that would enhance…a democracy, a theory of communication and democracy must specify the type of democracy to be achieved.

This paper discussed the distinctions between elite and participatory democratic theories in terms of the implications of each to the practice of communication studies. The strength of democracy in elite theory relies on the strength of individual decision and vote choice; the strength of democracy in participatory systems depends on the development and achievement of reciprocity. Struggles over the meaning, salience, and causes of and solutions to social and political problems are continuous (Edelman, 1964, 1988; Hilgartner & Bosk, 1988; Cobb & Elder, 1983) and are fundamental to determining which shared and common activities will be pursued in a democracy and for what purposes.

If participatory democratic systems are to exist in large collectivities, where face-to-face communication is impossible, mass-mediated communication must link members and enable them to develop reciprocity. At present, the ability of mass media to serve this function is severely hampered by the news production procedures commercial systems have fostered.

NOTES

[1] Graham (1986, p. 126) notes that elite democratic theory is often misleadingly called "empirical democratic theory" or "empirical theory," which suggests that no normative claims or expectations are evoked. Adhering to Graham's distinctions, I use "elite democratic theory" throughout this article to refer to democratic theories focusing on the selection of representatives or on the influence of interest groups on those representatives.

[2] In a recent literature review, Bennett and Bennett (1986) noted that, while there was some variety in definitions of political participation, "most involve some notion of actions undertaken by ordinary citizens that are intended directly or indirectly to influence the selection of government personnel and/or the policy decisions they make" (p. 160).

[3] Gould (1988) describes several varieties of the disposition to reciprocity, differentiated primarily by the degree to which they are ritualistic (customary), the result of legal contracts (formal), based on self-interest (instrumental), and based on mutual respect and recognition of needs (social).

[4] These two dimensions are related to the notion of intersubjectivity in interpersonal communication research (Hewes & Planalp, 1987) and accuracy in coorientation literature (McLeod & Chaffee, 1973) but are derived from different theories. For instance, McLeod and Chaffee based the coorientation measurement model on cognitive balance theories.

[5] This might be expected based on Tichenor, Donohue, and Olien's (1980) research on degrees of community pluralism structure and the magnitude of the knowledge gap.

[6] As in all investigations of social phenomena, there are problems associated with observation and interpretation. These issues have been discussed in philosophy of social science (see Bernstein, 1978) and critical studies literatures (see Carragee, 1990).

[7] Even in highly homogenous systems, it is unlikely that all members agree completely on all issues that affect collective decisions.

[8] Artz (1989, 1991) provides an excellent discussion of the dramatic changes in production and content during and after the Somoza dictatorships.

REFERENCES

Artz, L. (Summer/Fall, 1989). Public access and censorship. *Nicaraguan Perspectives, pp.* 29–32.

Artz, L. (1991). *Mass media, public media: Community radio in Nicaragua 1979–1989.* Unpublished manuscript, University of Iowa, Department of Communication Studies, Iowa City.

Bachrach, P. (1967). *The theory of democratic elitism.* Boston: Little, Brown.

Barber, B. (1984). *Strong democracy.* Berkeley, CA: University of California Press.

Bennett, S., & Bennett, L. L. M. (1986). Political participation. In S. Long (Ed.), *Annual Review of political Science* (Vol. 1, pp. 157–198). Norwood, NJ: Ablex.

Berelson, B., Lazarsfeld, P.F., & McPhee, W.N. (1954). *Voting: A study of opinion formation in a presidential campaign.* Chicago: University of Chicago Press.

Bernstein, R. (1978). *The restructuring of social and political theory.* Philadelphia: University of Pennsylvania Press.

Blumberg, P. (1968). *Industrial democracy.* New York: Schocken Books.

Burnheim, J. (1983). *Is democracy possible?* Berkeley, CA: University of California Press.

Calhoun, C. (1988). Populist politics, communications media and large scale societal integration. *Sociological Theory, 6,* 219–241.

Carey, J. W. (1986). The dark continent of American journalism. In R.K. Manoff & M. Schudson (Eds.), *Reading the news* (pp. 146–196). New York: Pantheon.

Carragee, K. M. (1990). Interpretive media and interpretive social science. *Critical Studies in Mass Communication, 7,* 81–96.

Clarke, P., & Kline, F. G. (1974). Media effects reconsidered. *Communication Research, 1,* 224–240.

Cobb, R. W., & Elder, C. D. (1983). *Participation in American politics. The dynamics of agenda-building* (2nd ed.). Baltimore: Johns Hopkins University Press.

Collins, R. (1988). The micro contribution to macrosociology. *Sociological Theory, 6,* p. 242–253.

Coser, L. (1956). *The functions of social conflict.* Glencoe, IL: FreePress.

Couch, C.J., & Weiland, M. W. (1986). A study of the representative-constituent relationship. In C. J. Couch, S. L. Saxton, & M. A. Katovich (Eds.), *Studies in symbolic interaction, supplement 2: The Iowa School* (part B). Greenwich, CT: JAI Press.

Dahl, R., & Lindblom, C. (1953). *Politics, economics, and welfare.* New York: Harper and Row.

Dahl, R., & Tufte, E. (1973). *Size and democracy.* Stanford, CA: Stanford University Press.

Dervin, B. (1980). Communication gaps and inequities: Moving toward a reconceptualization. In B. Dervin & M. J. Voigt (Eds.), *Progress in communication sciences* (Vol. 2, pp. 73–112). Norwood, NJ: Ablex.

Dewey, J. (1966). *Democracy and education.* New York: Free Press. (Original work published 1916).

Edelman, M. (1964). *The symbolic uses of politics.* Urbana, IL: University of Illinois Press.

Edelman, M. (1988). *Constructing the political spectacle.* Chicago: University of Chicago Press.

Gamham, N. (1990). The myths of video: A disciplinary reminder. In *Capitalism and communication: Global culture and the economics of information.* London: Sage.

Gaziano, C. (1983). The knowledge gap: An analytical review of media effects. *Communication Research, 10,* 447–486.

Gitlin, T. (1978). Media sociology: The dominant paradigm. *Theory and Society, 6,* 205–253.

Golding, P. (1990). Political communication and citizenship: The media and democracy in an egalitarian social order. In M. Ferguson (Ed.) *Public communication: The new imperatives* (pp. 84–100). London: Sage.

Gould, C.C. (1988). *Rethinking democracy. Freedom and social cooperation in politics, economy and society.* Cambridge, MA: Cambridge University Press.

Graber, D. (1988). *Processing the news: How people tame the information tide* (2nd ed.). White Plains, NY: Longman.

Graham, K. (1986). *The battle of democracy.* Brighton, England: Wheatsheaf Books.

Gurevitch, M., & Levy, M. R. (1986). Information and meaning: Audience explanations of social issues. In J. R. Robinson & M. R. Levy (Eds.), *The main source. Learning from television news* (pp. 159–179). Beverly Hills, CA: Sage.

Habermas, J. (1979). Moral development and ego identity. In *Communication and the evolution of society* (T. McCarthy, Trans.). Boston: Beacon Press.

Habermas, J. (1984). *The Theory of communicative action* (Vol. 1) (T. McCarthy, Trans.). Boston: Beacon Press.

Hewes, D., & Planalp, S. (1987). The individual's place in communication science. In C. R. Berger & S. H. Chaffee (Eds.), *Handbook of communication science* (pp. 146–186). Newbury Park, CA: Sage.

Hilgartner, S., & Bosk, C. (1988). The rise and fall of social problems: A public arenas model. *American Journal of Sociology, 94,* 53–78.

Homans, G. C. (1961). *Social behavior: Its elementary form.* New York: Harcourt, Brace and World.

Macpherson, C. B. (1977). *The lives and times of liberal democracy.* Oxford: Oxford University Press.

Malinowski, B. (1961). *Crime and custom in savage society.* London: Routledge and Kegan Paul.

Mattelart, A. (1979). Introduction: For class analysis of communication. In A. Mattelart *(Ed.), Communication and class struggle, Vol. 1: Capitalism, imperialism* (pp. 23–70). New York: International General.

McLeod, J. M., & Chaffee, S. H. (1973). Interpersonal approaches to communication research. *American Behavioral Scientist, 16,* 469–499.

Naisbitt, J. (1982). *Megatrends.* New York: Warner.

Pateman, C. (1970). *Participation and democratic theory.* Cambridge: Cambridge University Press.

Pateman, C. (1979). *The problem of political obligation.* Chichester, England: John Wiley.

Schumpeter, J. A. (1943). *Capitalism, socialism and democracy.* London: Allen and Unwin.

Schutz, A. (1970). *On phenomenology and social relations* (H.R. Wagner, Ed.) Chicago: University of Chicago Press.

Shibutani, T. (1955). Reference groups as perspectives. *American Journal of Sociology, 60,* 562–569.

Simmel, G. (1950). Superordination and subordination. In *The sociology of Georg Simmel* (K. Wolff, Ed.). Glencoe, IL: Free Press.

Thompson, J. B. (1990). *Ideology and modern culture: Critical social theory in the era of mass communication.* Stanford, CA: Stanford University Press.

Tichenor, P. J., Donohue, G. A., & Olien, C.N. (1980). *Community conflict and the press.* Beverly Hills, CA: Sage.

PART IX | Exercises

NAME _____

Refer to the lists of characteristics of oral and literate communication practices which appear in the introductions to Part Three and Part Four. Compile comparable lists of the characteristics of communication by fax, e-mail, and Internet Web sites.

FAX   E-Mail   Internet

How do the above characteristics potentially alter our knowledge and understanding of the world?

What is the democratic potential of these contemporary communication technologies?

What asymmetrical communication practices can these technologies support?